The Audit of War

Correlli Barnett is the author of such distinguished books as *The Desert Generals, The Swordbearers, Britain and Her Army* (Royal Society of Literature's Heinemann Award 1970), *The Collapse of British Power* (the first book in his *The Pride and the Fall* series on British Power in the twentieth century), *Marlborough, Bonaparte* and *Engage the Enemy More Closely: the Royal Navy in the Second World War* (Yorkshire Post Book of the Year Award 1991). His challenging study of Britain's poor performance as an industrial country during the Second World War, *The Audit of War: the Illusion and Reality of Britain as a Great Nation* (1986), has had major impact in the fields of industry, education, Westminster and Whitehall. The third book in his *The Pride and the Fall* series, *The Lost Victory: British Dreams, British Realities 1945–1950*, was published in July 1995 to tremendous critical acclaim, and has now appeared in a Pan paperback edition.

From 1977 until March 1995 he was Keeper of the Churchill Archives Centre, Cambridge, and still continues to be a Fellow of Churchill College. From 1973 to 1985 he was also a Member of Council of the Royal United Services Institution for Defence Studies, and in 1991 was awarded the Institute's Chesney Gold Medal for his contribution to military history. In 1993 he was awarded the Degree of Doctor of Science (Honoris Causa) by Cranfield University. He is a Fellow of the Royal Society of Literature, the Royal Historical Society and the Royal Society of Arts.

THE AUDIT OF WAR

The Illusion and Reality of Britain as a Great Nation

CORRELLI BARNETT

PAN BOOKS

First published in 1986 by Macmillan

First published in 2001 by Pan Books
an imprint of Pan Macmillan Ltd
Pan Macmillan, 20 New Wharf Road, London N1 9RR
Basingstoke and Oxford
Associated companies throughout the world
www.panmacmillan.com

ISBN 0 330 34790 X

3 5 7 9 8 6 4

A CIP catalogue record for this book is available from the British Library.

Printed and bound in Great Britain by
Mackays of Chatham plc, Chatham, Kent

For my first three grandchildren
Alexander, Julia and Philippa

in the hope that England may yet prove
stronger than the storms

Contents

Acknowledgements

Once again I must first and foremost thank my wife Ruth for patiently and accurately typing a fair copy of a much edited working script, and for acutely pointing out lapses in clarity or style; and for fulfilling as always the role of a highly professional one-woman general staff.

Secondly, I would like to thank those who were kind enough to read the typescript in whole or in part: Professor Sir Hermann Bondi, Professor Sir William Hawthorne, Professor Roy Acheson, Dr Wijtold Tulasiewicz, Dr Richard Overy, Dr Derek Morris, Mr Aubrey Jones and Mr Keith Williams. Their wise criticisms and specialised knowledge saved me from many errors of fact or interpretation, but not, I fear, from those that remain. I am especially grateful to my editor, Mr Peter James, for his meticulously detailed scrutiny of the text and sources.

I wish to express my gratitude to Mr Michael Alcock, my publisher, for his support, understanding and forbearance during the long gestation of this book; and to Mr John Bright-Holmes, who encouraged me to pursue the original idea. I would also like to take this opportunity of thanking my agent, Mr Bruce Hunter, for all his valued counsel and help over the years.

My particular thanks are due to the Economic and Social Research Council, without whose financial backing it would not have been possible to carry out the necessary researches. I must also thank the National Economic Development Office, the Ready Mixed Concrete Company and BOC plc for their supplementary support.

I wish to express my indebtedness to the professional knowledge, courtesy and willing help of the Search Room staff at the Public Record Office, Kew, where so much of the research for the book was carried out; to my colleagues in the Churchill Archives Centre, Cambridge, and to the staffs of the following institutions: the University of East Anglia Library; the London Library; the Library of the Royal United Services Institute for Defence Studies; the Churchill College Library, Cambridge; the Statistisches Bundesamt in Bonn; and the US Army Military History Institute.

The author also wishes to thank all those numerous readers who wrote to me appreciatively about the first edition of *The Audit of War*, sometimes furnishing from their own experience in wartime industry fresh evidence in support of my analysis, and sometimes pointing out incidental errors of fact. These I have sought to correct in the present edition.

*

The author is indebted to the following for permission to quote from works in their copyright:

Dr E. G. Bowen: the Bowen Papers in the Churchill Archives Centre, Cambridge. The British Library: the Chuter Ede Diary. Croom Helm: *Mining and Social Change: Durham County in the Twentieth Century* edited by M. Bulmer. Chatto & Windus: *The Uses of Literacy: Aspects of Working-Class Life, With Special Reference to Publications and Entertainments* by R. Hoggart. The Lord Wilson of Rievaulx: *New Deal for Coal* by H. Wilson. George Allen & Unwin: *The Pillars of Security and Other War-Time Essays and Addresses* and *Full Employment in a Free Society* by Sir W. H. Beveridge. Basil Blackwell: *History of the British Steel Industry* by J. C. Carr and W. Taplin. Harvard University Press: *The British Shipbuilding Industry 1870–1914* by S. Pollard and P. Robertson. Oxford University Press: *William Temple Archbishop of Canterbury: His Life and Letters* by F. A. Iremonger. Victor Gollancz: *The Making of the English Working Class* by E. P. Thompson. Routledge & Kegan Paul: *The Social Background of a Plan: A Study of Middlesbrough* edited by R. Glass. Trustees of the United Kingdom Carnegie Trust: *Disinherited Youth: A Report on the 18-plus Age Group; Enquiry Prepared for the Trustees of the United Kingdom Carnegie Trust.*

The author also wishes to thank the following newspapers for permission to quote from their columns: the *Daily Mail*, the *Daily Mirror*, the *Daily Telegraph*, the (Manchester) *Guardian*, the *Sunday Times* and *The Times*.

Extracts from Crown Copyright material are reproduced with the permission of the Controller of Her Majesty's Stationery Office.

Author's Preface

This book is an operational study; its purpose is to uncover the causes of Britain's protracted decline as an industrial country since the Second World War. For industrial strength supplies the fundamental factor in total strategy, the essential basis of a nation's power and its material well-being alike. The book locates the causes of the British eclipse not in the events and policies of the postwar era, but in the British record during the war itself – for total war submits nations to a ruthless audit of resources, talents and failings: human, social, cultural, political and technological no less than military. In the cases of France, Germany and Japan this audit was bluntly manifested in the fact, impossible to ignore, of outright defeat and occupation. In the case of Britain the audit of war remained hidden by the outward façade of victory, the propaganda about the scale of the national effort, and the deceptive inflow of American aid under Lend-Lease; it lay buried in the secret files of wartime production ministries and Cabinet committees. As a consequence, the British people never had to face the reality about themselves and their future place in the world, let alone come to terms with it and adapt to it accordingly.

It is therefore more than time for the audit of war on Britain to be rendered. But in rendering it this book explores much more than technological performance in the narrow sense. It ranges across the education and training of the nation; the human quality of the workforce; the capability of management; the cultural values and attitudes of the governing class and intelligentsia; even the influence of religion. For all these factors inter-reacted to determine the level of British operational efficiency as an industrial society.

The book also examines wartime national aspirations and government planning for the postwar era, and analyses the conflict of priority between reconstructing the industrial machine and building a new social order. It searches back for the historical roots of wartime problems; it looks forward to the consequences in the postwar period of wartime failures to tackle those problems. The underlying themes of the book lie in the contrast between national pretensions and desires, and national resources; in the clash in the British mind between realism and romanticism, reason and emotion; above all, in the powerful resistance throughout society to the changes essential for the achievement of maximum success as an industrial nation – resistance maintained even under the spur of a war for survival itself.

Correlli Barnett
East Carleton, Norfolk
and
Churchill College, Cambridge
September 1985

Prologue

In the last days of April and the first days of May the light of peace began to glow strangely on the familiar Britain of sirens and tin-hats, battledress and sandbags, stirrup-pumps and air-raid shelters. It transmuted at a touch all such apparatus of recent survival into historical relics, at one with the medieval battlements of England's castles and the pikes and halberds in the Tower Armoury. Henceforward the British people would need tools of a different kind in order to hold their place among the nations; skills and spirit of a different kind too. Meanwhile they could listen to the final news reports of the fading war on 'the Nine O'Clock' with pride as well as thankfulness.

On 2 May 1945 the German forces south of the Alps, nearly a million strong, surrendered to a British field marshal, Sir Harold Alexander, the Supreme Allied Commander Mediterranean. Three days later, all the German armed forces by land, sea and air in north-west Germany, the Netherlands and Denmark surrendered to another British field marshal, Sir Bernard Montgomery, commanding the allied 21st Army Group. It was the greatest single German capitulation in the field during the Second World War, signed in classic military form in a tent pitched on a heath under a Union Flag whipping in the breeze. It presaged the unconditional surrender of the Third Reich to the allies which followed on 8 May 1945. Neither Marlborough after Blenheim, nor Wellington after Waterloo, nor Haig after his victorious offensives in 1918 had enjoyed more signal moments of triumph over the sovereign's enemies than these. Far off, in that other war to defend the British Empire against Japan, the fall of Rangoon on 2 May consummated Lieutenant-General Sir William Slim's epic reconquest of the British colony of Burma.

For the British people the 'official' VE-Day ('Victory in Europe Day') on 9 May therefore marked the occasion of proud remembrance of their long struggle from early defeat through to this ultimate victory – the only allied nation to fight Nazi Germany from first to last. Once again in their history they had won, as they had always assumed they would. The very ritual of the victory thanksgivings proclaimed the continuity of British life and British institutions while foreign tyrants came, briefly puffed themselves up into a menace, and went. On 8 May Germany's unconditional surrender was formally announced by the Prime Minister to a House of Commons which had continued in free debate throughout the war. The

Commons then walked in procession from the St Stephen's Porch of the Palace of Westminster to their service of thanksgiving at St Margaret's Church – Winston Churchill following the Speaker and the Serjeant-at-Arms with the Mace as the bells pealed out above, while their Noble Lordships of the Other House were led by Black Rod and the Clerk of the Parliaments to their own service in Westminster Abbey. Away in the City, beneath the unscathed dome of St Paul's Cathedral, the Lord Mayor of London and the Lady Mayoress were also thanking God for the victory. Outside Buckingham Palace citizens came together in a great swarm under a pale May sun to cheer their sovereign, and to shout, 'We want the King!' When George VI, in the uniform of an admiral of the fleet, appeared on the balcony with the Queen and the two princesses, his subjects responded by roaring out 'For he's a jolly good fellow'. Then, at about 5.30 p.m., Winston Churchill joined the Royal Family in a fresh appearance on the balcony. The crowds roared again; and the film cameras recorded it all for the nation at large to see on the newsreels – the first minister of the Crown, who had brought the realm safely through the greatest peril in its history, standing in comradeship with a Royal Family bonded even more closely to the British people by reason of their courage, humour and simplicity through the shared dangers and discomforts of war; and all of them together personifying a constitutional monarchy that had survived unshaken, had indeed never been more firmly rooted.

On Sunday 14 May the King and Queen rode out in an open horse-drawn landau to St Paul's for the national service of thanksgiving, just as Queen Anne had ridden out to St Paul's to give thanks for Marlborough's great victories two and a half centuries earlier. At Temple Bar, gateway to the City, they were greeted in traditional ceremony by the Lord Mayor of London in a black and gold robe over court dress, and flanked by the Aldermen in gowns of scarlet silk. When the royal carriage stopped at the foot of the steps that sweep up to the cathedral entrance, trumpeters of the Household Cavalry in gold lace and scarlet sounded a fanfare; a scene evocative of so many royal and national celebrations in the past. In the cathedral, where Wellington and Nelson lay in the crypt, the Archbishop of Canterbury preached the sermon; the anthem reverberated up into Sir Christopher Wren's majestic vaults; the King and Queen and the dignitaries and the crowds went home; and it was really all over at last after five and a half years.

It was no wonder that at such a time and in such a mood the British took it for granted that Great Britain was, and would always remain, a first-class world power. She alone of pre-war European great nations had never been reduced to impotence during the war by defeat and occupation. Her formidable armed forces ranked her with Soviet Russia and the United States in the 'Big Three' that had waged and won the war against Nazi Germany: a navy that kept every sea and ocean from home waters to the Pacific; armies numbering nearly 3 million soldiers standing in Germany, Italy, the Middle East and Burma at the end of arduous marches to victory; an air force that had inflicted Germany's first and decisive defeat in the Battle of Britain, had pounded German cities into rubble, and acted as a vital partner in all the army's and navy's successes. Moreover Britain, in the shape of Winston Churchill's bulldog personality, had sat in all the wartime summit conferences as an equal partner with America and Soviet Russia, most recently at Yalta in February 1945. She was currently engaged, again as an equal partner, in discussions at the world security conference in San Francisco on the structure of the new international order. Her Prime Minister would attend a forthcoming tripartite summit, probably in Germany, to decide the future of Europe – the role played by Wellington and Castlereagh at the Congress of Vienna in 1814–15 and by Lloyd George at the Paris Peace Conference in 1919.

Yet, as the British saw it, Britain's world role did not rest on the strength of the United Kingdom alone; it rested also on that of the British Empire and Commonwealth. The war had witnessed a heart-warming revival of imperial loyalties, as the British press reminded its readers in the hour of victory. In the words of the Conservative and middle-class *Daily Telegraph* on 8 May, 'the whole Empire has played a valorous and ungrudging part. . . . It is the Empire's "finest hour", too.' Next day the mass-circulation left-wing *Daily Mirror* struck a no less imperial note in a leading article entitled 'We Remember', which recalled:

> the grand Canadians who, when our peril was greatest, came to nourish and sustain our resistance . . . the Australians and New Zealanders who bore the brunt of the battle in Egypt and Greece . . . the South Africans who tore from Mussolini's grasp the first fruits of his treachery . . . the loyal Indians and sons of Colonies who won new battle honours in Egypt and Italy.[1]

For all its loyalty, however, the empire had produced only one-tenth of the munitions of war supplied to Britain and the empire together, whereas the United Kingdom itself had produced seven-tenths.[2] The British people were well aware that Britain's place in the ranks of world powers in war and in peace was sustained first and foremost by her own industrial machine – on the enterprise, energy and skill of her managers and workforces; on the inventiveness of her scientists and technologists. And this too provided a major theme in the celebrations of Britain's victory. The War Premier himself in the course of his victory broadcast over the wireless praised the 'marvellous devices' which British ingenuity had conceived and constructed in order to make the Normandy landings possible. He reminded his listeners: 'and, mark you, our scientists are not surpassed by any nation in the world, especially when their effort is applied to naval matters. . . .'[3]

During the next three weeks, fresh disclosures of wartime secrets bore out his words. There was the 'Pluto' pipeline unrolled across the bed of the English Channel like an enormous garden hose to supply the invasion armies with petroleum; the 'Fido' device for clearing fog from operational airfields by means of powerful petrol flares along both sides of the runway. *The Times* asserted on 24 May in regard to 'Pluto' that 'success in this novel and daring project could not have been achieved if there had not been available in the country's need British engineers, modern Elizabethans, who had gained unique experience in pioneering enterprises in all parts of the world'. Next day the same newspaper concluded a leading article entitled 'Science at War' (which also referred to 'Pluto') by saying that 'The lessons for peacetime progress of this combination of scientific imagination, technical skill, and efficient workmanship are manifest.' The *Daily Telegraph*, for its part, reckoned that 'Pluto' had been 'as brilliant in execution as in conception':

> This achievement is not only a triumph for British brains but British private enterprise. . . . altogether 33 private firms share the credit for furnishing the Allied armies with these lifelines. It was they who had organised the resources in equipment, brains and skill, and who put them energetically at the disposal of the State.[4]

The *Daily Mirror* blew the trumpet for the national genius in general:

> As the secrets of the war are revealed British achievements take on a new glamour. Great things have been done by our engineers and scientists. The 'Pluto' pipeline laid across the Channel is the latest example. This feat stands as a magnificent tribute to British brains, British energy and British foresight.

On 8 June the news broke, via a leak in the United States, of perhaps the most amazing of all British technological triumphs in the war – radar. The *Daily Mail* sounded a fanfare across its front page:

> RAF'S RADAR SECRETS REVEALED BY AMERICAN AVIATION JOURNAL
>
> Thus once again America has been privileged by inconsistencies of censorship to reveal to the world a British discovery developed by British scientists and engineers into the biggest single war-winning factor produced for many years.

Next day *The Times* discreetly thundered:

> NIGHT BOMBING OF BRITAIN
>
> GERMANS BAFFLED BY BRITISH DEVICES
>
> TRIUMPH FOR SCIENCE

It went on to carry a report 'from our special correspondent, Cambridge' about the 'great regret' voiced the previous day by the managing director of Pye, the electronics manufacturers, that 'the British people cannot yet be told by the British Press the full story of our scientific and technical achievements in all forms of radio location.' Pye's managing director nonetheless proceeded to give details of General Control Interception radar and Airborne Interception radar, modestly pointing out Pye's role in these developments.

But he was not the only company spokesman to vaunt his firm's technological prowess at this time. Chairmen of boards addressing their annual general meetings supplied the background woodwind in the national victory anthem. On 25 May 1945 it was the turn of Lord McGowan of ICI to boom away. But then he had already said it all in a speech the year before:

> When the history of this war can be written I am sure we shall find that every new manifestation of enemy research, whether at sea, on land or in the air, has been matched, and more than matched, by counter-discovery in this country, to say nothing of the lead we have given to the Allies in all sorts of directions connected not only with attack and defence, but with the health of the people. I need only cite the Jet-propelled aircraft on the one hand and Penicillin on the other – both of them British.

After outlining ICI's postwar development plans, McGowan asserted: 'The point I make is that private enterprise has been and is capable of showing that spirit of adventure and courage on which the Empire has been built.'[5]

On 3 June 1945, the chairman of John Summers and Sons, the steel makers who owned Shotton steel works in Wales, was reported as telling his shareholders:

> Too little credit has, I think, been given to the steel trade for the part it has played in winning the war. I believe that when the full story of the steel trade's contribution to winning the war is made known, it will be a clear vindication of private enterprise, and the policy of improvement and modernisation which was carried out in the national interest just prior to the war.[6]

In a very different branch of technology the chairman of The British Photographic Industries proudly described how his firm's cameras and camera film had helped the war effort, especially advanced models for aerial reconnaissance using a new ultra-high-speed lens shutter. He buoyantly predicted that in the postwar era his company would develop a range of cameras, film projectors and scientific instruments 'which will be as good as the German products previously paramount'.[7] And at the annual general meeting of Leyland Motors, the truck manufacturers, as reported in the *Daily Telegraph* on 21 June, the chairman sounded off on behalf of British engineering: 'as American propaganda had been widespread and censorship here very strict no clear conception of the immense re-organisation, re-equipment and achievement of the British engineering industry had as yet been possible. . . .'[8]

In fact, the British people hardly needed all these reminders of the scale, ingenuity and success of their productive effort. Ever since 1940 it had supplied a major topic of the Ministry of Information's home propaganda, of BBC wireless reporting and of such documentary films as *Tyneside Story* and *Clydebuilt*, which showed how British shipyards and their workpeople had arisen from the rusting death of pre-war slump to wartime prodigies of productivity.[9] The magazine *Picture Post*, the pioneer in British photojournalism and the most widely seen and therefore most potent visual medium in the absence of television, had also carried many features on the industrial war effort. Indeed that effort had been part of the nation's daily consciousness, thanks to wireless programmes like *Music While You Work* and concerts and variety shows broadcast from factory canteens. Jolly women machine-tool operators in overalls and with headscarves knotted on top of the head, cloth-capped stalwarts in heavy industry, and assembly-lines of tanks and bombers were as much a part of the national image of the war as men in uniform fighting battles.

In any case, the government had published a White Paper in November 1944 on *Statistics Relating to the War Effort of the United Kingdom*[10] with the very intention of telling the British people themselves and Britain's allies (especially America) how great was the national achievement.[11] The grand totals, widely summarised in the press, had a blast effect on the British mind akin to one of Dr Barnes Wallis's bombs on a German tenement block. Between June 1939 and June 1944 the number of men and women in the armed forces or industry had risen by 3½ million, or nearly a fifth. Nearly half the total number of women of working age were either in the women's services, in full-time civil defence or in war industry; a far higher proportion than in either Germany or America, although the White Paper did not say so. By June 1944 the British armed forces had reached a total of 4½ million men and women. All this, pointed out the White Paper, represented a greater degree of national mobilisation than that achieved even in the Great War.

But it was the figures for war production which bore the convincing witness to Britain's technological strength. Between September 1939 and June 1944 her shipyards had produced over 700 major war vessels, over 5000 smaller naval craft and 4½ million tons of merchant shipping. Her aircraft industry had turned out by June 1944 over 100,000 aircraft, of which over 10,000 were heavy bombers. From the production lines of the motor industry, engineering industry and Royal Ordnance Factories had come 135,000 artillery equipments (field, medium and heavy) and over 21,000 anti-aircraft gun equipments, over 25,000 tanks, over 900,000 wheeled vehicles and getting on for 4 million machine-guns. Steel production had risen by nearly 2 million tons between 1939 and 1943. And British agriculture had raised its output in terms of calories and vitamins by 70 per cent over pre-war, while land under the plough had grown from under 13 million acres in 1939 to over 19 million in 1943. Moreover there was a special factor which added a brighter lustre to the British productive achievement, as the White Paper pointed out:

> it should be remembered that the vast re-organisation of the British economy which the figures show has been carried through in particularly difficult living and working conditions. For five years men and women have lived and worked under complete black-out. . . . Production has been made more difficult by the dispersal of factories to frustrate the air attacks of the enemy and by the need for training new labour to unaccustomed tasks.

According to the weekly Home Intelligence Report to the Ministry of Information, the British people 'enthusiastically approved' the publication of the White Paper, considering that it was 'high time we told the world and blew our own trumpet'.[12]

The war had also acted as a veritable spur to technological progress, as the War Premier had reminded the nation in a broadcast on 21 March 1943 in which he had looked forward to the postwar era:

> We have learned much about production under the stress of war. Our methods have vastly improved. The layout of our factories presents an entirely new and more modern picture to the eye. Mass-production methods have been forced upon us. . . . There are some significant new industries to give scope to the inventiveness and vigour which made this country great.
>
> When the fetters of wartime are struck off and we turn free hands to the industrial tasks of peace, we may be astonished at the progress and efficiency we shall suddenly see displayed.[13]

Yet it was generally accepted that Britain's war production had not just been a matter of new factories and machines and methods. The prime mover of the whole industrial machine lay in a new-found sense of national community and team effort, obliterating the old peacetime antagonisms of social class and sectional interest. Everyone had 'gone to it' in the common cause. This was what had really released the latent energies and genius of the British people.

The national mood on VE-Day was well caught by the *Daily Mirror* in a leading article of 11 May 1945 entitled 'Forward with the People', when it wrote: 'We may, therefore, perhaps, regard today as the gateway through which we are stepping into a new era.' In the general election that followed on the victory celebrations almost without a pause, there proved to be remarkable agreement between the political parties about Britain's future place in the world. She would, they concurred, continue to be a global and imperial power, one of the 'Big Three' with Russia and America jointly settling the great international issues through the new United Nations Organisation. And British technology, rendered even more inventive and resourceful by suitable government policies, would switch from its war-production triumphs to a no less successful conquest of overseas markets, in order to amass the wealth that would support Britain's role of first-rank power abroad and sustain her standard of life at home among the highest in the world. Of course, the politicians acknowledged, it would be hard going for a few years. But in the continuing mood of victory politicians and people shared, in Churchill's words, an 'invincible confidence in the genius of Britain'. They assumed that they would indeed, as Churchill lushly put it in his final election broadcast, march in the vanguard of the United Nations in majestic enjoyment of their fame and power.[14]

It was certainly in no man's mind and certainly no man's intention that the next forty years should see Britain diminished to fourteenth place in the non-communist world in terms of Gross National Product per head,[15] with a balance-of-payments deficit in goods other than North Sea oil of over £11 billion and a deficit in manufactured goods of £3.6 billion;[16] with little more than a third of West Germany's manufacturing output per head and a half that of the United States;[17] with mass unemployment standing at over 13 per cent of the insured population, a rate one-third worse than in West Germany and four times worse than in Japan;[18] and with the wasting short-term asset of North Sea oil alone standing between her and economic catastrophe. It was an astonishing decline for a victor of the Second World War, the more so by contrast with the resurgence of Germany and Japan from abject defeat to the status of economic world powers. Its root causes do not lie in the postwar era, as some have argued.[19] Nor did it derive from an unfair fate which, according to later popular myth, penalised the victor and favoured the vanquished.[20] Britain's postwar decline began in wartime British dreams, illusions and realities. The British people had brought it on themselves even before the bunting was hung across the streets in rejoicing and hope on VE-Day.

Part I

Dreams and Illusions

The people will have won both struggles. . . . They deserve and must be assured a happier future than faced so many of them after the last war.

(*Labour Party manifesto, 1945*)

I am almost frightened by the vitality these Germans show after what they've undergone. I believe, once they've been given the word GO, they'll have a bridge over the Rhine in three months, and that in a short time their output of steel will be huge.

(*British colonel, the Ruhr, 2 May 1945*)

Chapter One

The Dream of New Jerusalem

While in 1940–1 Winston Churchill and the nation at large were fighting for sheer survival in the face of Nazi Germany's then victorious power, members of the British cultural élite had begun to busy themselves with design studies for a 'New Jerusalem' to be built in Britain after the war was won. Selfish greed, the moral legacy of Victorian capitalism, would give way to Christian community, motivating men to work hard for the good of all. In this community the citizen would be cushioned against the stab of poverty by full employment, welfare grants and pensions – all provided by a beneficent state – from infancy to the end of earthly life. Universal free health care in elegant modern hospitals and in health centres on the Swedish model would replace grim and run-down Victorian infirmaries and the ragged safety-netting of existing free medical services. The physical as well as the moral legacy of Victorian capitalism would be removed by slum clearance on the grand scale, and by transferring population from overcrowded conurbations to apartments standing in wide green spaces. Here was a vision of a garden-city society filled with happy, healthy children, smiling mothers, bustling workers, serene elderly souls in a golden twilight of state pensions; all living in houses furnished in Gordon Russell's simple good taste, and, having been equally well educated in a reformed education system, all busy in cultural pursuits other than dog racing or going to the pictures.

Ironically this vision emanated from the same kind of people, indeed in some cases the very same people, whose earlier utopian vision of a world saved from conflict through disarmament and the League of Nations had done so much to bring about Britain's desperate plight in 1940–1, by persuading British governments in the 1920s unilaterally to disarm, so rendering Britain helpless in the face of aggression in the 1930s, and by even then delaying her eventual rearmament by their passionate opposition.[1] For New Jerusalemers and pre-war 'moralising internationalists' alike were drawn from the Labour and Liberal parties, from the small-'l' liberal intelligentsia and, garlic in the salad flavouring the whole, from the religious with a social mission – what may be collectively termed the 'enlightened' Establishment. And New Jerusalemism and moralising internationalism were alternative expressions of the same belief that the evils besetting man could be banished by the creation of an ideal society founded on justice, virtue and good feelings. Whereas the 'enlightened' Establishment had evangelised this belief in the form of moralising internationalism so successfully before the war as to determine the broad aims, and cramp the choices, of British total strategy, it now proceeded no less successfully to render a similar service, in the form of New Jerusalemism, with regard to the purposes and priorities of British domestic policy after the war.

The 'enlightened' Establishment had been a hundred years and more in the making, its ancestry beginning with (to put it in stud-book form) romanticism out of emotion by idealism. The early-nineteenth-century romantic movement had reacted against Georgian materialism and cold rationality; it turned away in disgust from the ugly visage of industrialising Britain and the coarseness of living humanity; and it found refuge in beautiful other worlds of the imagination.[2] Where Wordsworth and Sir Walter Scott showed the way, Pugin, Morris and the Pre-Raphaelites followed with their stained-glass visions of the middle ages, and, after them, Royal Academy painters like Lord Leighton and Sir Edwin Poynter with their immaculate ancient Rome inhabited by noble asexuals. Round the turn of the twentieth century, men of letters, artists and architects had persuasively reinterpreted the earlier romantic conceptions of an ideal world, laying a new emphasis on the moral and physical beauty of an imagined rural life compared with the squalor and greed of urban Britain. Voysey's sweeping gables and Lutyens's dreaming manor houses evoked a gentle past that never was; E. M. Forster sentimentally portrayed the supposed rural virtues in his novel *Howard's End*; and Ebenezer Howard succeeded in realising his dream of a 'garden city' at Letchworth, where cottages for clerks nestled amid leafy roads that might almost be country lanes. The intelligentsia of the first three decades of the twentieth century retreated to their own rural Camelots: the Bells at their cottage at Charleston in Sussex; the Woolfs at Asham and Rodmell; Lady Ottoline Morrell's circle at Garsington Manor; Harold Nicolson and Vita Sackville-West at Sissinghurst. The yearning for other worlds more beautiful than the here and now of modern Britain, the rural nostalgia, was also hauntingly expressed in music by composers such as Delius, Elgar and Vaughan Williams.

All these strands of romantic imagination wove together to make the texture of the 'enlightened' Establishment's sensibility, explaining the aesthetic vision of New Jerusalem as a sun-lit garden-city society inhabited by a race at once comely and happy. Yet from the time of Pugin and Morris perfect worlds of the imagination had been perceived in terms of moral as well as physical beauty. Camelot not only made prettier pictures than Coketown, but also inspired a Victorian ideal of knightly conduct. Such manifestations as the Eglinton Tournament in 1839, when gentlemen in side whiskers and full armour and ladies in medieval crinolines played at being at the court of Edward III, and high-minded novels about knightly heroes like Kenelm Digby's bestseller *The Broad Stone of Honour* (published 1828–9, republished 1844–8 and 1877) were far from being mere costume entertainments: they were aspects of a cult of chivalry that was profoundly to shape the mind of the upper classes. Kenelm Digby, for example, expressed the true spirit of the romantic movement when he attacked 'that principle, the curse of modern times, which leads men to idolise the reason and understanding, and to neglect and even despise the virtues of the heart.'[3] Propagated in novels as influential as *The Broad Stone of Honour*, in the verse of Tennyson and Newbolt, in the art of the Pre-Raphaelites, translated later into an imperial setting where Sir Galahad in a topee carried the white man's burden, the cult of chivalry had produced by the end of the nineteenth century the uniquely British stereotype of the 'gentleman':

> He was always ready to give up his own time to come to the help of others, especially those less fortunate than himself. He was an honourable opponent and a good loser; he played games for the pleasure of playing, not to win. He never boasted. He was not interested in money. . . .[4]

The stereotype of the 'gentleman' supplied a key element in the character of the twentieth-century British Establishment as a whole; and, in the form of upper-middle-class politicians and intelligentsia motivated by a wish to come to the help of those less fortunate than themselves, it was especially strong in the 'enlightened' wing of that Establishment.

Unlike its Georgian predecessor, whose claim to rule had rested on rank and property, the claim of the new chivalric élite to rule reposed on its devotion to moral principles.[5] In turn the chivalric élite's moral principles were consciously Christian – but Christian in the particular interpretation given to Christianity by the religious revival of the early nineteenth century.

And here, in this religious revival, is found the most powerful of all the influences that went to form the character of the British Establishment a hundred years later, and to inspire its progressive members with their faith that justice and love must prevail in human affairs. For the romantic movement expressed itself in Britain above all through religious emotion: a scorching flame of sin, guilt, salvation and righteousness that forged a mentality which saw the problems of society in moral terms and looked to their solution in the application of Christian principle. Religious emotion inspired the cult of chivalry as well as the artistic vision of medievalists like Pugin and Morris; religious faith coupled with intense moral purpose led Charles Kingsley, Frederick Maurice and later Robert Blatchford to conceive of 'merrie Englands' to be brought about through 'Christian Socialism' – and Dr Arnold to educate 'Christian gentlemen':

> rather than have it [science] the principal thing in my son's mind, I would gladly have him think that the sun went round the earth, and that the stars were so many spangles set in the bright blue firmament. Surely the one thing needed for a Christian and an Englishman to study is a Christian and moral and political philosophy. . . .[6]

The Victorian and Edwardian public school, as developed from Dr Arnold's prototype at Rugby in the 1830s, was to serve as the principal transmitter of romantic idealism in a Christian garb to generations of governing-class Britons, including those in high places during the Second World War. It averted its gaze from the muddy topics of the contemporary world and real human nature, and neglected science in favour of the moral precepts, the chivalric code and the ideal humanity enshrined in religion and the classics. Victorian Oxbridge, too, followed the example of the public school, believing with John Ruskin that the purpose of a university was to provide a liberal education, and the purpose of a liberal education, to quote Ruskin himself, was to train young men to 'the perfect exercise and knightly continence of their bodies and souls'.[7] In pursuit of this ideal the ancient universities successfully preserved the overwhelming predominance of the liberal arts over science and modern studies, let alone such subjects as engineering, until long after the Great War. Meanwhile the nonconformist chapel was serving a purpose similar to that of the public school and Oxbridge in indoctrinating the 'respectable' lower classes with religious emotion and high moral purpose, with similarly far-reaching effects on the future climate of British feeling and opinion.

After 1870 the narrow torrent of religious passion broadened out into new and secular causes:

> Humanism and Humanitarianism, Liberalism and Internationalism [wrote Sir Herbert Butterfield] . . . emerge as a result of the tendency to translate into secular terms certain movements and aspirations which had characterised a Christian civilisation. . . . humanitarianism, for example, is an anaemic substitute for the doctrine of New Testament love.[8]

First of all Gladstone's Liberal Party and later the nascent Labour Party were inspired by a crusading idealism, not least because nonconformists were prevalent in both parties. A socialist could write, for example, of Labour Party work in the early 1900s in such terms as these: 'A veritable crusade was led throughout Scotland in those years with all the fervour and fanaticism of a new holy religion. . . .'[9] In the 1890s there was even a Socialist Sunday School movement with heartfelt socialist songs instead of hymns, and a declaration of socialist precepts based on 'Justice and Love' and modelled on the Ten Commandments:

> We desire [proclaimed one of these precepts] to be just and loving to all fellow men and women, to work together as brothers and sisters, to be kind to every living creature and so help to form a New Society with Justice as its foundation and Love as its law.[10]

Or as Clement Attlee, Leader of the Labour Party, wrote in 1935: 'Socialism . . . is something more than a political creed or an economic system. It is a philosophy of society. . . .'[11]

After the Great War even the much less doctrinaire Conservative Party also fell victim to a spirit of secularised religious idealism, for Baldwin and

Chamberlain and their closest colleagues were true Victorian moralists seeking to do good at home and abroad by the exercise of the Christian virtues, not least by forgiving those who trespassed against them, such as Adolf Hitler. In several cases too their backgrounds showed a former personal or family connection with Liberalism and/or nonconformism (cf. Baldwin, Chamberlain, Simon and Hoare). The younger generation of Conservative reformers in the 1930s and 1940s, men such as Quintin Hogg and R. A. Butler, represented the chivalric and Christian tradition of concern for the underdog first established in the party by Lord Shaftesbury, an outstanding Victorian exponent of the application of the Christian conscience to social questions.

Thus a century of cross-breeding between the aesthetic and moral strains in romanticism had made the 'enlightened' British Establishment of the 1940s what it was: tender-hearted and highminded, in that order; latter-day White Knights riding out in wartime Britain to combat evil with the flashing sword of moral indignation, and questing in simple faith for the grail of human harmony and happiness.

The churches and the religious were, not surprisingly, as prominent in the muster rolls of the crusade to win a New Jerusalem as they had been in pre-war support of the League of Nations and disarmament.[12] Common Wealth, the new political party founded during the war which won three by-elections against official coalition government candidates, was a straight revival of mid-Victorian Christian Socialism; its leader, Sir Richard Acland, a recent evangelical convert who believed that what was morally wrong could never be politically right,[13] and that the choice of social, industrial, economic and financial apparatus depended on which one was 'morally the most righteous'.[14] Among Methodists, the Reverend Donald Soper, later a nuclear disarmer, was also holding forth on the new society founded on Christian love that must be built after the war. The Society of Friends agonised over a restatement of their 1918 'Eight Foundations of the Social Order'. The Reverend Mervyn Stockwood, a future Bishop of Southwark, announced that he would vote Labour at the next election because 'As a Christian it is my duty to work for a Britain which will be characterised by justice, fair dealing, peace and prosperity.'[15]

Most conspicuous of all churchmen in promoting the vision of a New Jerusalem, however, was William Temple, Archbishop of Canterbury from 1942 until his death in 1944; and his upbringing and education make him a perfect exemplar of the descent of New Jerusalemism from the original religious expression of the romantic movement. Born in 1881, already a young man therefore when Edward VII succeeded Queen Victoria, he was in essence a late Victorian, his outlook formed when the tide of Victorian optimism and moral idealism was still running high. His father, a fellow of Balliol and later headmaster of Rugby, had also been Archbishop of Canterbury. Temple was to recall fifty years later the lasting influence of the daily prayers of his childhood:

> in making natural and spontaneous that whole outlook upon life which the Bible expresses. Whereas one of our great troubles now is

> that the predominant outlook upon life is formed by scientific and not by religious categories. Causation is much more prominent in men's thoughts than purpose and judgement.[16]

In 1894 Temple went to Rugby, the school that Dr Arnold had remodelled in the 1830s in order to produce Christian gentlemen; and through him Dr Arnold was to speak to the Britain of the 1940s, for Temple acknowledged Arnold's intellectual influence on his early life. At Rugby Temple naturally studied classics, leavening them with love of English poetry and wide reading in ancient and modern philosophy; at Balliol he read classics too. Here was an absolutely typical élite Victorian education, leaving out anything to do with understanding the modern world or Britain's place in it. As he himself wrote: 'I regret to say that it is perfectly possible to obtain a Double First in Oxford without a sympathetic understanding of what a trade union is: and that seems to me, *so far as it goes* [author's italics], a flaw in the system.'[17] In a presidential address to the Workers' Educational Association in 1912 he acknowledged that traditional British education needed 'greater energy and efficiency' and 'greater and more living contact with the world of today', nevertheless characteristically adding: 'but I shall regret the day when we become efficient at the cost of our spirit.'[18]

Temple's own career hardly put him into closer contact with 'the world of today': first a fellow of the Queen's College, Oxford, lecturing on Plato; then headmaster of Repton, teaching divinity and classics to the sixth form; and thereafter Bishop of Manchester. In the opinion of a colleague, he was 'entirely unspotted of this world'.[19] Thus equipped, Temple was asking as early as 1906 for 'the application of Christian principles to everyday life, whereby the Housing Problem etc will solve themselves. . . .'[20] This wish eventually impelled him in 1918 to join the Labour Party on the grounds that the Labour programme both for home and foreign policy was 'based on moral ideals',[21] and was 'essentially an effort to organise society on the basis of freedom and fellowship. As such it has a right to claim the sympathy of the Church. . . .'[22] In the 1930s Temple – again representative of his generation and upbringing – was calling for a foreign policy based on moral principles rather than Machiavellian statecraft. He did in fact preach the opening sermon at the foredoomed World Disarmament Conference in 1932, perhaps a manifestation of what his biographer describes as his 'unworldly innocence and his determination to see the best in every man'.[23]

It was therefore entirely appropriate that Temple should convene a conference at Malvern early in 1941 to consider, in his own words, 'how Christian thought can be shaped to play a leading part in the reconstruction after the war' – one of the first and most effective gambits in launching the New Jerusalem movement.[24] The conference was attended by some 400 clergy and 15 bishops, and the speakers included such notables of the intelligentsia and the good as John Middleton Murry (classicist, pre-war disarmer and founder of a 'community' in Suffolk), T. S. Eliot, Dorothy Sayers and Sir Richard Acland. It achieved wide coverage in the British and American press. This early venture by Temple into postwar reconstruction was followed in 1942 by his Penguin Special *Christianity and the Social Order*, which sold nearly 140,000 copies. Interestingly enough, the economist J. M. Keynes (Eton and King's; intimate friend of E. M. Forster) himself commented (on the book's proofs) on the importance of ethical considerations in English notions of economic thought.[25] Temple, now dubbed 'the people's Archbishop', continued until his death in 1944 to preach influentially on the Christian Socialist Britain to be created after the war, telling the Bank Officers' Guild, for example, in a speech at the Albert Hall in 1943 about 'the Christian view of the right relationship between Finance, Production and Consumption'.[26]

Clement Attlee, wartime Deputy Prime Minister, despite being temperamentally far from a romantic personified another element in nineteenth-century romanticism – the 'gentleman' as created by the public school and the cult of chivalry. Like Temple, Attlee was a member of the late-Victorian governing class, born in 1883, educated at Haileybury and University College, Oxford (where he read history), his socialism inspired by his experience of East End slums while secretary of the Toynbee Hall mission before the Great War. As a 'gentleman' who led by virtue of moral qualities and who accepted the duty to help those less fortunate than himself, he followed the example of earlier Haileyburians who had devoted their lives to improving the lot of the poverty-stricken natives of India, and devoted his life to performing the same service for the natives of Britain. Matter-of-fact a man as he was, he could nevertheless pursue a vision of a new human order, 'a philosophy of society'. Although muzzled in public until 1945 by membership of the coalition War Cabinet he was quietly influential within government in encouraging plans for 'reconstruction'

Harold Laski, one of the Labour movement's more notorious intellectuals, was certainly untypical in being Jewish rather than evangelical Christian, but otherwise the pedigree was characteristic enough, with his father a prominent Liberal and philanthropist in Manchester, himself a favourite pupil of a High Master of Manchester Grammar School, completing his education at New College, Oxford (where he switched from science to history). As a young man, his biographer tells us, he 'was for the underdog'. Although Laski represented the intellectual side of romantic moralism rather than the religious, the end-product was much the same: 'Politics never destroyed Laski's confidence in progress and the essential goodness of man. He was a product of the French Revolution and spoke with the voice of Condorcet.'[27] In fact Laski's wartime bestseller *Where Do We Go From Here?* reads like a moralising tract, Victorian in its affection for words like 'good' and 'evil', and perceiving the problems of society not as technical and practical but as moral and ideological:

> nothing less than a revolution in the spirit of man is necessary if we are to enter the Kingdom of Peace as our rightful inheritance: and a revolution in the spirit of man, as all history goes to show, must follow, and cannot precede, a revolution in the relationships of that material world by the exploitation of which he must live.[28]

So, for Laski, 'our choice is between the dark age of privilege, and the dawn of an equal fellowship between men.'[29] Laski's biographer himself, Kingsley Martin, editor of the highly influential journal the *New Statesman*, while no less a moralist and visionary, even better exemplified the ancestry of New Jerusalemism, having a nonconformist minister and Radical for a father, having started life as a Liberal before becoming a socialist, and having been an evangelist for disarmament and the League of Nations before the war.

Only Stafford Cripps broke this pattern by being both a Christian moralist and a realist, who in 1945 warned the Labour Party conference against promising that there was 'some easy Utopia'.

Among numerous intellectual mandarins pressing forward to lay a brick of the better Britain after the war, the historian E. H. Carr (Merchant Taylors' and Trinity, Cambridge) had the ear of the governing class through his assistant editorship of *The Times* from 1941 onwards. As early as 1 July 1940 Carr had persuaded the editor, Robert Barrington-Ward (Westminster and Balliol College, Oxford), to publish a leading article written by himself on 'The New Europe':

> If we speak of democracy we do not mean a democracy which maintains the right to vote but forgets the right to work and the right to live. If we speak of freedom, we do not mean a rugged individualism which excludes social organizations and economic planning. If we speak of equality we do not mean a political equality nullified by social and economic privilege. If we speak of economic reconstruction, we think less of maximum production (*though this too will be required* [author's italics]) than of equitable distribution.[30]

Behind such prophets of New Jerusalemism marched a devoted array of activists who were likewise the same kind of people who had crusaded in the 1930s for the League of Nations Union or the Peace Ballot, and who by their numbers and passionate idealism gave New Jerusalemism its popular momentum. For one of the most significant end-products of romanticism lay in the phenomenon of the activist, emotionally dependent on the adrenalin generated by the excitement of a campaign for some highminded cause or other.

Thus in the midst of a twentieth-century total war the spirit of the early-nineteenth-century romantic movement blazed up again in Britain, and in its rays a renewed moral fervour brightly glowed like the gospel in stained glass.

Yet the cultural descent of the 'enlightened' Establishment implied negative common factors of hardly less importance than the positive. In the first place not one of the leading New Jerusalemers was an engineer, an industrialist or a trade unionist; not one of them had ever had experience of running any kind of operation in the real world in which Britain competed commercially in peacetime and fought for very life in wartime, unless running a political party or a church or editing a newspaper be counted as such. Products of the closed loop of British élite education and culture, not so much men of straw as men of paper, the members of the 'enlightened' Establishment were no better equipped to design a working

New Jerusalem for this real world than Adolf Hitler, another kind of romantic fantasist, was equipped to run a real war. And in the second place it followed from this that they were almost all middle-class, even in the Labour Party. New Jerusalem was their own vision, not the spontaneous effusion of the nation at large;[31] it was their highminded gift which they proceeded successfully to press on the British people between 1940 and 1945, with far-reaching effects on Britain's postwar chances as an industrial power struggling for survival and prosperity.

The marketing of New Jerusalem took place in parallel inside Whitehall and outside in pulpits and print. There existed, moreover, a constant osmosis between Whitehall and the wider intellectual élite on the topic, thanks to shared membership of clubs, committees and dinner tables, just as there had been in the 1920s and 1930s with regard to international affairs. The state of the war itself served as a stimulus and a justification for the progress of the marketing operation. In fact, New Jerusalem as a wartime project owed its very inception to the military catastrophe of May and June 1940 when France collapsed, its promoters arguing that it was essential to hold out a vision of a better Britain in order to sustain the nation's spirit through dark times. In any case they genuinely believed even in the circumstances of 1940 that it was not a sufficient war aim merely to survive or eventually to restore the European balance of power; just as in the Great War, the highminded wished to transform the struggle into a crusade for a nobler world, and succeeded.

On 4 June 1940, only three days after the end of the Dunkirk evacuation had marked the final destruction of the entire allied northern army group on the Western Front, the Home Morale Committee of the Ministry of Information (MOI) was recommending a 'statement on peace principles'.[32] On 18 June, four days before France signed an armistice with Nazi Germany, the director-general of the MOI raised the question at the ministry's Policy Committee 'whether opportunity should be taken of an all-Party Government to make some promises as to social reforms after the war'. In his opinion, 'Our aim should be to redress grievances and inequalities and create new opportunities.'[33] The task of drafting a memorandum on the subject was given to the minister's Parliamentary Secretary, Harold Nicolson, National Labour MP for West Leicester. Nicolson, educated at Wellington and Trinity, Cambridge, was a former diplomat, a man of letters and, in the judgement of his son, a man of 'emotionalism and clemency' who possessed 'a sentimental side to his nature' and 'could be moved to tears by a film or play in which virtue was triumphant or innocence abused. . .'.[34] He drafted his recommendations with the avowed purpose of combating war weariness and answering the question 'why are we fighting?'; and in so doing fingered out the motto theme that was to swell over the next five years into an Ode to Joy with full orchestra and double choir:

> We should proclaim that we intend to make a better world at home in which the abuses of the past shall not be allowed to reappear.

> Unemployment, education, housing and the abolition of privilege should form the main planks of such a platform.[35]

On 26 July 1940, when the Luftwaffe was attacking shipping in the English Channel in the preliminaries of the Battle of Britain, the War Cabinet discussed Nicolson's paper (now the MOI's paper), and instructed the Minister of Information, Duff Cooper, to set up a body to look into the whole question of war aims. New Jerusalemism in official circles was now off the slipway. On 23 August, a day of lull in the Battle of Britain owing to poor weather, the War Cabinet decided to create its own 'War Aims Committee'; it did so at the instigation of Lord Halifax, the Foreign Secretary, in order, as he put it, to prevent the topic getting into the hands of 'professors and propagandists'.[36] The new committee was asked not only to sketch a future world political system, but also 'to consider means of perpetuating the national unity achieved in this country during the war through a social and economic structure designed to secure equality of opportunity and service among all classes of the community.'[37]

These words were to be exactly repeated as the terms of reference given in January 1941 to the new Cabinet Committee on Reconstruction Problems (see below, p. 22), which in turn was to spawn other committees that between them produced in 1943–5 the official blueprints of New Jerusalem. However, the new War Aims Committee did little until December 1940, when some members of the governing élite, including Nicolson, feared that national morale would crumble in the long nights of air attack in the Blitz unless the government issued some uplifting public statement of war aims.[38] This time the War Aims Committee had the advantage of a paper written by Professor Arnold Toynbee, one of the country's most distinguished sages, and equally a representative figure of British élite culture, being educated at Winchester and Balliol College, Oxford, a fellow of Balliol, an expert on Greek civilisation, and now director of the Foreign Research and Press Service of the Royal Institute for International Affairs. Toynbee's paper, outlining the promised land in the highflown language of a Victorian prophet, called for new social-security and education systems, the rebuilding of cities and government action to prevent unemployment.[39]

The memorandum that was actually placed before the War Cabinet blended Toynbee's draft with another by Lord Halifax, himself the very embodiment of high Victorian moral idealism, and was based, so said its preamble, on Christianity and other religions.[40] While this draft statement on war aims concerned itself mostly with an ideal world society rather than with Britain's own ideal society, it did assert that 'we can no longer tolerate the existence of abject poverty and unemployment';

> Already the war has broken down many old barriers and prejudices. The social conscience of the whole people has been aroused. These testing days are bringing to the front numbers of energetic and daring men and women drawn from all classes and sections of the community, determined that this great opportunity shall not be

> missed. . . . We must use the qualities of youth as well as the experience of war-time administration to overhaul our economic, social and educational practice, in order to secure for all a reasonable standard of Life.[41]

This sermon did not impress the War Cabinet, least of all Winston Churchill; and on 20 January 1941 they decided not to make any such statement, as being the more likely to lead to dissension than to impress the public. And there, so far as the War Cabinet were concerned, rested for the time being the question of New Jerusalem's official presentation to the nation.

Its promoters, however, were already seeking other outlets. In October 1940 Kenneth Clark, the eminent aesthete, art historian and Wykehamist employed (like so many other members of the intelligentsia) in the Ministry of Information, convinced the proprietor of the magazine *Picture Post*, Edward Hulton (Harrow and Brasenose College, Oxford), that he should run a special issue on postwar Britain. Hulton agreed; and his editor, Tom Hopkinson, set to with an enthusiasm all the greater because he himself was a classic product of the post-romantic British élite – son of an archdeacon, educated at St Edward's School and Pembroke College, Oxford, a former assistant editor of the *Clarion*, and a passionate and lifelong chivalric champion of underdogs and idealistic causes.

Forty pages long, the special issue of *Picture Post* appeared on 4 January 1941, the first of the year, and achieved immense popular impact, as was demonstrated by the 2000 letters received from readers afterwards. The cover bore the title 'A Plan for Britain' across the top of a photograph of six happy naked children on a playground slide; and the entire issue similarly milked the reader's emotions with a skilled journalistic hand. Pre-war pictures of the unemployed slouching on street corners and of idle industrial works, labelled 'The Tragic Tale', provided the object lesson as to what must never happen again. In presenting the sun-lit Britain of the future, grim old institutional schools were contrasted with cheerful new ones; an aerial view of an existing town with its streets of little terrace houses on one page faced on the next an architect's vision of tomorrow's city of glass and concrete geometrically laid out in wide grassy spaces. The related article by Maxwell Fry, the distinguished modern architect, proclaimed that 'the new Britain must be PLANNED.' An Oxford economist, Thomas Balogh, explained how management of the economy by the state could secure 'Work for All'; A. D. Lindsay, the master of Balliol, another much respected humanist mandarin of the time, sketched 'A Plan for Education'; Julian Huxley, the scientist and broadcaster, showed how to achieve 'Health for All'; and J. B. Priestley, novelist, broadcaster, Yorkshireman and 'a moralist of a very English kind' with 'a temperament innately romantic',[42] painted the rich life of culture and recreation in the new Britain 'When Work is Over'.

But it was *Picture Post*'s editorial foreword which caught the essence of New Jerusalemism; its emotion, its romantic vision. It recalled that, after the Great War, 'We got no new Britain, and we got no new Europe' because peace came so suddenly in the end that it took the nation by surprise, and there was lacking 'imagination, planning, an idea of the country we wanted to make, and a passionate – actually passionate – determination to make it'.

> This time we can be better prepared if we think now. This is not the time for putting off thinking 'till we see how things are'. . . . More than that, our plan for a new Britain is not something outside the war, or something *after* the war. It is an essential part of our war aims. It is, indeed, our most positive war aim. The new Britain is the country we are fighting for.

Whether Churchill and the War Cabinet liked it or not, the topic of a better Britain after the war had now been turned into a national talking-point. From now on the Cabinet would come under ever increasing public pressure to commit itself to a blueprint for this better Britain, however much the War Premier might try to stonewall. Moreover, Churchill was under pressure too from Labour members of his own government. While there is no evidence of a direct connection, it is a fact that the new Cabinet Committee on Reconstruction Problems was set up within six weeks of *Picture Post*'s 'A Plan for Britain'.

Meanwhile New Jerusalem promoters were also busying themselves within the BBC. On 3 January 1941 a memorandum by the BBC's Director of Talks, Sir Richard Maconachie (Tonbridge and University College, Oxford; formerly in the Indian Civil Service), on 'reconstruction' defined the word as meaning not only physical rebuilding but also in the widest sense 'building Jerusalem in England's Green and Pleasant Land'; and noted that, with the approval of the Ministry of Information, the BBC was discussing a possible radio series under the title *Reconstruction: What Does It Mean?*[43] Toynbee was looking to the BBC as well as the Cabinet for a vehicle for his vision of the postwar world; and on 11 January his colleague in the Royal Institute of International Affairs Foreign Research and Press Service, Professor Charles Webster, wrote in from their wartime field headquarters in Balliol to suggest to the BBC that it should put on a weekly 'Radio Forum' called *Democracy Thinking Aloud* at the peak hour after the news on Sunday nights, the talks to be reprinted in the *Listener*. Webster, a history man educated at King's College, Cambridge, was 'transparently a man of goodwill' who had been confirmed by his experience as a researcher with the British delegation at the 1919 Paris Peace Conference in 'a belief in progress and in Great Britain as a progressive force'.[44] He and his proposal were to be shunted to and fro inside the BBC and the MOI and in between them for the next six months. Arthur Greenwood, the Minister without Portfolio and chairman of the new Cabinet Committee on Reconstruction Problems, was consulted; Attlee, the Lord President of the Council and Deputy Prime Minister, expressed approval of the project. Gradually the project died. The BBC would not open up broadcast discussion on future public policy without certain government backing,[45] and the War Premier, in this spring of the Greek disaster and Rommel's first counter-stroke in the

Western Desert, refused to give such backing, even though Greenwood himself thought Webster's suggested talks 'highly desirable'. As Greenwood put it in a letter to Duff Cooper on 1 July 1941, 'The difficulty has been the objections entertained by the Prime Minister.'[46] On 22 July 1941 the BBC executive board agreed that the idea of a talks series in the autumn 'on the whole Brave New World business' is 'dead'; there would only be programmes on physical reconstruction.[47]

Greenwood, however, had not given up. Working-class by origin, a one-time lecturer in economics at Leeds University, an early Fabian, a protégé of Arthur Henderson (who as Foreign Secretary had unsuccessfully tried to apply Methodist principles to grand strategy), Greenwood counted as one of the Labour Party's intellectuals. He now took advantage of the publication of the so-called Atlantic Charter after the War Premier's meeting with President Roosevelt on two battleships moored in Placentia Bay, Newfoundland, in August 1941. Though Churchill took a major hand in the drafting of this document, the lofty initiative came from Roosevelt; and the Charter is the Second World War equivalent of President Wilson's Fourteen Points of 1918 in terms of sentimental rhetoric applied to the future of international relations. Greenwood for his part thought that public interest should now be focused on the home aspects of the postwar order, and that in order to achieve this focus the Ministry of Information should deliberately launch a national debate:

> I feel that nothing but good could come if it were possible to arrange to have questions such as Unemployment, Education, Housing, Nutrition, the future of Trade Unions, the position of women, etc, discussed over the wireless and elsewhere by competent persons.[48]

It was taken within the MOI and the BBC that this meant a relaxation of the previous ban on such a debate.[49] In any case the BBC was already running its approved autumn series of twelve talks on physical reconstruction under the title *Making Plans*, with further talks in mind for January to March 1942, while yet another series was due to start that November with the condescending title *The Working Man Looks at Reconstruction* and dealing with bread-and-marge issues like production, trade unions and communal feeding. On 17 December 1941, ten days after the Japanese air strike on Pearl Harbor brought America into the war and so transformed Britain's own situation, Greenwood himself gave a broadcast talk called *No New World Without Victory*, which, though largely a cautionary tale about the vileness of the enemies to be defeated, also commented on the postwar task 'to begin to build, on the foundations of the freedom we have retained, an edifice worthy of our grim struggle and our great sacrifice'. Part of that edifice, according to Greenwood, would be 'social security'.[50]

The year 1942 marked the turning-point for the New Jerusalem movement just as it did for the course of the Second World War. In February Temple became Archbishop of Canterbury and later published his bestselling paperback *Christianity and the Social Order*. Laski's tract *Where*

Do We Go From Here? also appeared in paperback. In May Priestley's '1941 Committee' brought out a Nine-Point Declaration, the ninth point of which demanded preliminary plans for providing full and free education, together with employment and a civilised standard of living for everyone.[51] The 1941 Committee was a typical 'enlightened' Establishment pressure group, including in its membership Sir Richard Acland, Tom Hopkinson (the editor of *Picture Post*), David Astor of the *Observer*, Gerald Barry (editor of the Liberal *News Chronicle*), Kingsley Martin of the *New Statesman*, Victor Gollancz (the publisher of the Left Book Club), the Right Reverend A. W. Blunt (the socialist Bishop of Bradford), Douglas Jay and Christopher Mayhew (both of them journalists, Labour politicians and wartime civil servants), and Lady Hinchingbrooke and Peter Thorneycroft, later co-founders of the Tory Reform Committee.[52] On 25 June the progressive journalist Tom Driberg won a sensational victory over the official coalition government candidate in a by-election at Maldon in Essex on the platform of the Nine-Point Declaration, a result owing in unknown proportions to the public's growing appetite for New Jerusalem or its diminishing respect for Churchill's leadership following the fall of Tobruk on 21 June. The 1941 Committee thereafter merged with another pressure group, Forward March, to form Common Wealth, soon to be led by Sir Richard Acland, the born-again Christian and all-purpose revivalist.

In the meantime the Army Bureau of Current Affairs (founded in autumn 1941, under the direction of W. E. Williams, a pre-war Director of the Workers' Educational Association) was encouraging the rank and file of the army to start talking about postwar questions in the course of their weekly compulsory ABCA briefing sessions. In an ABCA *Current Affairs* booklet in September 1942 the architect Ralph Tubbs repeated Maxwell Fry's passionate plea in the *Picture Post* special issue for new cities on the grand scale. Wrote Tubbs: 'a very large building programme is certain after the war. The quality of this building will be one of the means whereby future generations will judge our civilisation. Are we going to fail again?' Tubbs's article, like Fry's, was embellished by a line drawing showing the glass-and-concrete city of the future standing immaculate in its parkland.[53] The 10 October 1942 issue of *Current Affairs* was devoted to the question 'What Price Victory?', and it was posed and answered by ABCA's Director, W. E. Williams, himself, in the tone of romantic excitement and idealistic uplift common to all New Jerusalem preaching. 'We are fighting,' he wrote, 'not only for the Britain we know, but for the better Britain it could become':

> The vision of victory is in fact indivisible from the immediate war effort. We are fighting not to win, but to win *something*: and the more we clear our minds here and now about the world we want after the war, the more likely we are to attain it.[54]

The broad and rising tide of New Jerusalemism during 1942 was already beginning to scour round the foundations of the wartime coalition government, widening the concealed fissures that still divided its

Conservative from its Labour members on issues other than mere prosecution of the war. To paraphrase W. E. Williams, while Churchill still thought that it was enough to be fighting to *win*, the Labour ministers who dominated home-front policy believed that the country was fighting to win *something*. They therefore wished the government to catch the popular tide. On 5 June 1942, the chairman of the Committee on Reconstruction Problems in succession to Greenwood, William Jowitt, wrote to Brendan Bracken (who himself had succeeded Duff Cooper as Minister of Information):

> As you know I am watching very carefully the growing public interest in matters of reconstruction, having specially in mind the time when I might properly begin to make more specific reference to them in my speeches and the general lines on which publicity might be planned.[55]

Jowitt in himself perfectly demonstrated the lineage of the 'enlightened' Establishment: born in 1885 the only son of the rector of Stevenage, educated at Marlborough and New College (a First in jurisprudence), a Liberal MP until invited by Ramsay MacDonald to become Attorney-General in the first Labour government in 1929, a National Labour MP in 1931 and then back to the Labour Party proper in 1936. With his agreement, Bracken ordered a Home Intelligence Survey to be carried out in order to gauge as accurately as possible the state of national feeling about 'reconstruction'. The resulting report ('Public Feeling on Post-War Reconstruction')[56] in November 1942 was not based on the statistically representative sampling method used by public-opinion polls today, but on material collected over two months by thirteen intelligence officers on the staff of regional information officers in the civil defence regions, or derived from the Postal Censorship Department and the BBC's Listener Research Department. It indicated that there was broad popular agreement across the country on the topic of reconstruction, and that top priority in people's minds was 'guaranteed jobs for all'. In the report's own words, 'In all classes of the community unemployment is thought to be the outstanding postwar problem. It is, indeed, more than a problem; it is a personal and individual fear. . . .' Second in priority came the replacement of private profit by service to the community, followed by financial security for those unable to work, decent houses for everyone, and the same education for all in order to ensure equality of chances.

This report indicates how successful New Jerusalem evangelism had by now been in crystallising the British people's postwar aspirations. Not surprisingly it delighted Labour members of the government. As Jowitt wrote to Bracken on 20 November 1942, 'This is an extraordinarily valuable document and I am deeply obliged to your Ministry for preparing it. . . .'[57] Hugh Dalton, President of the Board of Trade (son of a canon of Windsor, educated at Eton and King's College, Cambridge, 'a somewhat romantic socialist through his strong adolescent dislike of privilege'),[58] told Jowitt: 'This is a most interesting and encouraging document, which should stimulate us all, Ministers and officials alike, to quicken our steps and to leap over the obstacles placed in our path by timid, short-sighted, or sinister persons.'[59] Dalton wanted the report circulated to all of Whitehall concerned with reconstruction – 'This document is too good to keep within a narrow circle' – and even published as a White Paper, a proposal scotched by Bracken.[60] Jowitt and Dalton were the more gleeful because the report on 'Public Feeling on Post-War Reconstruction' coincided with the advent of the report of the Beveridge Committee on Social Insurance and Allied Services (the Beveridge Report) which was circulated to ministers as a draft White Paper in November 1942.

It was the Beveridge Report that provided the battlefield on which the decisive struggle to win a national commitment to New Jerusalem was waged and won. The committee had been sixteen months at work taking evidence and framing its proposals[61] for a comprehensive national insurance scheme, including children's allowances, that would shield the citizen from poverty caused by sickness and unemployment, or in infancy and old age. Their plan for a welfare state also assumed a National Health Service. The committee's chairman, Sir William Beveridge, may be considered the most influential of all the prophets of the 'enlightened' Establishment who strove in wartime for the vision of a New Jerusalem. Another high Victorian, born in 1879, he was the son of a judge in the Indian Civil Service, and a grandson of a Congregationalist bookseller; his maternal grandfather was a self-made businessman Liberal in politics and Unitarian in religion. At Charterhouse he studied classics and Hebrew; classics again at Balliol, where he was, according to his daughter and biographer, 'deeply influenced' by the then master who 'preached lay sermons to the Balliol men about the Christian ethic'.[62] As sub-warden of the Toynbee Hall mission he was, like Attlee, much affected by direct contact with the misery of the unemployed, and thereafter pursued a career as a civil servant concerned with this question and also that of social insurance. 'I really do think', he wrote at the age of nineteen, 'that no man can really do progressive work who had not one idea carried to excess. . . . The man must have one great ideal to aim at, to a certain extent excluding all else and his convictions must be very strong.'[63] After service during the Great War in the Ministry of Reconstruction dealing with his one idea carried to excess – to wit, social insurance and employment – he became director of the London School of Economics in 1922, there to remain until appointed master of University College, Oxford, in 1937. As appropriate for a prophet and a brilliant Oxford intellect, Beveridge thought a lot of himself, so that righteousness went hand in hand with authoritarian arrogance and skill at manipulating the press to make him the Field Marshal Montgomery of social welfare.

From the very beginning Beveridge used his chairmanship of the Interdepartmental Committee on Social Insurance and Allied Services to turn it into a vehicle for his own preconceptions, so that it was no mere piece of convenient nomenclature to dub the resulting White Paper the 'Beveridge Report', but an all too accurate description. As he briefed his committee at their very first meeting: 'The central interest of the Committee was security: security against misfortune and loss of earning power resulting from the accidents that befall individuals.'[64] It was Beveridge who in December 1941 laid before the committee a memorandum on the 'Basic Problems of Social Security with Heads of a Scheme', which constituted the preliminary sketch of the final plan; Beveridge whose later draft proposals supplied the focus of internal Whitehall argument in the spring and summer of 1942 about financing the welfare state.[65] It was Beveridge again who was mainly responsible for the first draft of the final report in July 1942,[66] which was circulated under a covering note signed by Sir William himself saying that 'The draft sets out a full Plan for Social Security as an objective. . . .[67] Moreover it was Beveridge who personally conducted a further argument with the Treasury and the Government Actuary over costings that ran from August into October. And finally it was Beveridge who in masterly style leaked news of the sweeter chocolates in his welfare assortment to the press, in order to whet public appetite and so bring pressure on the Cabinet.

Beveridge likewise meant to make the very most of the resulting publicity once the report was published, as Brendan Bracken for one divined, writing to Churchill on 27 October about the press leaks to say: 'I have good reason to believe that some of Beveridge's friends are playing politics and that when the report appears there will be an immense amount of ballyhoo about the importance of implementing the recommendations without delay.'[68] The Chancellor of the Exchequer, Sir Kingsley Wood, Beveridge's principal opponent (see below p. 47), further believed that some of the politics were being played by Beveridge himself. All this was reinforced by a memorandum to the War Cabinet from Bracken as Minister of Information on 16 November seeking guidance as to whether to grant Beveridge's request for facilities to hold a press conference on his report and for permission personally to brief lobby correspondents before publication. 'It appears', said Bracken's memorandum, 'that he intended to disclose not only the recommendations in the Report, but his own views on these recommendations; and there were indications that he was working up a political campaign on the question.'[69]

On 16 November the War Cabinet at Bracken's request discussed the fraught question of whether or not to publish the Beveridge Report as a White Paper at this time – the start of ten days of agonised correspondence between ministers. Kingsley Wood as Chancellor fired in a personal note to Churchill the day after this Cabinet meeting to urge in language almost of desperation that Beveridge's scheme 'is ambitious and involves an impracticable financial commitment', and that therefore publication ought to be postponed:

> Whether the report is valuable will be the subject of much argument. But it is certainly premature. . . . Many in this country have persuaded themselves that the cessation of hostilities will mark the opening of the Golden Age (many were so persuaded last time also). However this may be, the time for declaring a dividend on the profits of the Golden Age is the time when those profits have been realised in fact, not merely in the imagination.[70]

Nothing could of course have been more out of key with the spirit of New Jerusalemism or of romanticism in general than such sordid accountancy. When Churchill sent Wood's note on to his personal assistant Lord Cherwell for comment, Cherwell agreed with Wood's financial analysis, but went on to point out the quandary into which the cunning Beveridge had now manoeuvred the Cabinet:

> On the other hand there has unfortunately been so much carefully engineered advanced publicity that the Government's hand may be forced. In my view a scheme on some such lines might be welcomed as an ultimate objective. But as things have turned out we seem to be faced, – owing to the improper leaks and reports which have been sedulously circulated, – with the alternatives of possible unhappy repercussions in America [for awarding ourselves social security more lavish than America's while existing on American hand-outs] if we accept it and of political difficulty here if we don't.[71]

Although Cherwell did not mention it, also relevant was the general rising tide of New Jerusalem aspirations in the country, as documented by the recent MOI Home Intelligence Report and in any case manifest in Driberg's by-election victory at Maldon and in the preachings of an archbishop, a bishop and other leaders of the 'enlightened' Establishment to enthusiastic congregations.

This tide, with Beveridge now the frothing crest, swamped the barriers erected by such unfashionable arguments as Kingsley Wood's. On 26 November the Cabinet came to the decision to publish the Beveridge Report White Paper[72] on 2 December. In answer to a query by Jowitt on 23 November as to whether Beveridge himself should be restrained 'from expounding his report or advocating the adoption of his recommendations', Churchill minuted in his own hand on Jowitt's letter: 'Once it is out he can bark to his heart's content.'[73] And this Beveridge proceeded with gusto to do, barking to the press and on the wireless with such effect that he and his report together henceforth became, as 'Beveridge' or the 'Beveridge Plan', at once short-hand for, and a touchstone of, postwar reconstruction. The final paragraph of the report (which sold over 800,000 copies) brilliantly played on public emotion, being a masterpiece of uplift that also perfectly expressed the spirit of New Jerusalemism and of the 'enlightened' Establishment that gave it birth:

> Freedom from want cannot be forced on a democracy or given to a democracy. It must be won by them. Winning it needs courage and faith and a sense of national unity; courage to face facts and difficulties and overcome them; faith in our future and in the ideals of fair play and freedom for which century after century our forefathers were prepared to die; a sense of national unity overriding the interest of any class or section. The Plan for Social Security in this Report is submitted by one [*sic*] who believes that in this supreme crisis the British people will not be found wanting in courage and faith and national unity, in material and spiritual power to play their part in

> achieving both social security and the victory of justice among nations upon which security depends.[74]

During his promotional tour he widened his subject-matter to include a vision of New Jerusalem as a whole. On 6 December, for instance, he spoke at Oxford on the topic of 'New Britain':

> I believe those two words are as good and short a motto as one can find for all that one wants to do in post-war reconstruction. Most people want something new after the war. . . . New Britain should be free, as free as humanly possible, of the five giant evils, of Want, [of] Disease, of Ignorance, of Squalor and of Idleness. . . .[75]

There could be no question about the colossal impact of the Beveridge Report, which so exactly caught the national mood as prepared by warm-up men like Temple. The MOI Home Intelligence reported that the plan had been 'welcomed with almost universal approval by people of all shades of opinion and by all sections of the community', and that it was seen as the first step towards postwar reconstruction and as 'the first real attempt to put into practice the talk about the new world'. According to this Home Intelligence report, the public was determined that the plan must go through, even though some expressed anxieties over the cost.[76] A British Institute of Public Opinion Report based on a sample taken in the fortnight after publication of the White Paper found that 95 per cent of the public had heard about it; that there was 'great interest in it', most markedly 'among poorer people'. The greatest criticism, the BIPO found, was that the proposed old-age pensions were not high enough. 'There was overwhelming agreement that the plan should be put into effect.'[77] The press gave vent to similar rapture on publication day, 2 December 1942. *The Times* pronounced the report 'a momentous document which should and must exercise a profound and immediate influence on the direction of social change in Britain'. The *Daily Telegraph* called it the consummation of the revolution begun by Lloyd George in 1911. The *Manchester Guardian* found it 'a big and fine thing'. The Archbishop of Canterbury said of it that it was 'the first time anyone had set out to embody the whole spirit of the Christian ethic in an Act of Parliament [*sic*]'.[78]

This tremendous popular acclaim for the Beveridge Report presented the Cabinet with an even trickier problem of political handling than the decision whether or not to publish. On 3 December Churchill minuted Jowitt, the Minister for Reconstruction Problems, on the need to go slow in approving postwar plans until Britain had negotiated a financial deal with the United States.[79] Even before publication the Cabinet had warily agreed that in the House of Commons Jowitt should express a cautious appreciation of the report, to the effect that the questions dealt with in it 'were of great interest and the Report itself was a notable contribution to their study. Time, however, would be required for detailed examination of the recommendations.' Moreover, the House should be reminded that the practicality of the proposals must also be examined.[80]

The prospect of a full-scale debate on the Beveridge Report, scheduled for February 1943 when Parliament reassembled after the Christmas recess, deepened the Cabinet's dilemma – not least because its Conservative and Labour members were split over the issue. The Cabinet therefore set up a new committee, chaired by Sir John Anderson, the Lord President of the Council, on 14 January 1943 to consider the Beveridge Plan and other 'substantial claims to financial assistance'.[81] When it met on 22 January in order to evolve the government's line for the coming Commons debate, it had before it a memorandum by Herbert Morrison, the Labour Home Secretary and Minister for Home Security, in which he disputed Kingsley Wood's financial pessimism, argued that the country could afford the Beveridge Plan and urged that therefore the government should accept it. He also remarked on the political implications of following Wood's advice:

> I need not point out to my colleagues that the great majority of the public is looking forward expectantly to the adoption of something substantially like the Beveridge Plan. It will be grievously disappointed if this cannot be done and will ask a number of searching questions to which the Government will have to find convincing answers.[82]

Despite this shrewd political diagnosis the committee's report to the Cabinet accepted Kingsley Wood's freshly reiterated financial warnings, and recommended that in the debate the government should merely accept 'the three basic Beveridge principles' of children's allowances, a 'Comprehensive Health Service' and 'the Maintenance of Employment', while making the proviso that 'no firm commitments can be entered into at the present time.'[83]

In following this recommended strategy when opening the debate on 16 February, the government got much the same response as a parent telling a child that Father Christmas would have to consider very carefully, in the light of this and that, when and whether and in what circumstances eventually to bring him his keenly expected bicycle. Labour backbenchers were moved to morally indignant tumult; they wanted their bicycle 'now'. The Conservative wing of the 'enlightened' Establishment, in the form of forty-five MPs of the Tory Reform Committee, demanded the immediate setting up of a Ministry of Social Security. In the division at the end of the debate ninety-seven Labour members, one Communist, three members of the Independent Labour Party, nine Liberals and eleven Independents voted against the government – an unprecedented rebellion which demonstrated how strongly the tide of New Jerusalemism was now running in the aftermath of Beveridge's brilliant promotion of his own launching, and how important a touchstone his Plan had become.[84]

The government's inept attempt at back-paddling against this tide also caused keen disappointment, not to say cynicism, in the country at large. According to MOI Home Intelligence reports, the people had been looking forward to the debate with 'intense eagerness', being 'impatient' to hear the government's intentions, for they had believed the debate would show 'if the Government really intends to give us a better world'.[85] After the debate there was 'a large disappointed majority' especially among the working-class, Labour and Liberal supporters and the Left, who thought that the government was trying to kill or whittle down the Beveridge Plan; 'an approving minority', however, believed that the government was right to postpone a decision until postwar financial conditions could be known.[86] A poll by the British Institute of Public Opinion found 29 per cent satisfied with the government's attitude, 47 per cent dissatisfied and 24 per cent 'don't knows'. Among social groups, 52 per cent of the 'upper' were satisfied, but only 34 per cent of the 'middles' were satisfied as against 45 per cent dissatisfied, and only 25 per cent of the 'lowers' were satisfied as against 49 per cent dissatisfied.[87]

The message that it was no longer politically possible openly to try to block or stall New Jerusalem was thrust down Conservative throats by the results of six by-elections held that February, all in Conservative-held seats. Except in one constituency where the Conservative vote actually rose by 10 per cent and another where it held steady, the party's support dropped by an average of 8 per cent.[88]

The decisive nature of the victory that had now been won by the 'enlightened' Establishment is shown by the government's decision to put the War Premier on the wireless on 21 March 1943 to palliate in his inimitable fashion the nation's disappointment over Beveridge and its suspicions of government good faith over the whole question of 'reconstruction'. At the beginning of March a meeting of home-front ministers had discussed 'the extent to which, in matters of postwar reconstruction, the field of public discussion has been left open to extremists',[89] as Sir John Anderson reported to Brendan Bracken. 'It was pointed out', Anderson went on, 'that on various postwar topics extreme views seemed to be catching the public imagination; and it was thought to be high time that the balance should be redressed by gaining a hearing for more moderate and realist views.'

In his broadcast, entitled 'After the War', Churchill for the first time switched his rich diction and richer rhetoric from the grandeur of wartime events to the perhaps less suitable topic of future domestic policy, and sought to achieve as best he might the proper blend of colourful optimism overall with touches of grey realism here and there. He warned his listeners to beware of imposing 'great new expenditure on the State without any relation to the circumstances which might prevail at the time. . . .'

> The difficulties which will confront us will take all our highest qualities to overcome. Let me, however, say straight away that my faith in the vigour, ingenuity and resilience of the British race is invincible. . . . the day of Hitler's downfall will be a bright one for our country and all mankind. The bells will clash their peals of victory and hope, and we will march forward together encouraged, invigorated, and still, I trust, generally united upon our further journey. . . .[90]

When Churchill came to 'peer through the mists of the future', he offered the prospect of 'a four-year plan' of reconstruction 'to cover five or six large measures of a practical character', this to be put to the electorate after the war and carried out by a new government. The measures included 'national compulsory insurance for all classes for all purposes from the cradle to the grave', the abolition of unemployment on the grounds that 'we cannot have a band of drones in our midst, whether they come from the ancient aristocracy or the modern plutocracy or the ordinary type of pub-crawler.' Unemployment would be prevented – and here spoke the voice of Keynes – by government action to 'exercise a balancing influence upon development which can be turned on or off as circumstances require'. Churchill even accepted that there was 'a broadening field for State ownership and enterprise'. His version of the New Jerusalem prospectus further comprised a housing drive, major reforms in education, and, finally, much improved health and welfare services, because, in his somewhat arch phrasing, there was 'no finer investment for any community than putting milk into babies'.

Thus in a fateful development did Churchill and the wartime coalition government commit themselves publicly to the principles of New Jerusalem, even if only an economy version, and even if final decisions about it were supposed to be left until after the war. Labour ministers, however, continued to press for more immediate action. On 26 June 1943 Attlee, Ernest Bevin (Minister of Labour) and Morrison submitted a memorandum to the Cabinet on 'The Need for Decisions', arguing that the Cabinet should guess the postwar financial situation as best it could and then decide on that basis as to what plans, on full employment, the future of industry, health, housing and so on, should be carried into law before the end of the war rather than face hasty pressures and decisions at the war's end. 'It seems wiser', they wrote, 'to accept the risks of acting upon our convictions and to bid for the advantages which normally accrue to the man or nation who faces the future with mind made up on fundamentals.'[91] This provoked Kingsley Wood's final (he died in September 1943) and for a time successful rearguard action, in which he argued that what the signatories were proposing was 'inconsistent' with the warning in the War Premier's broadcast against now committing future governments to 'great new expenditure'.[92] In October 1943, however, the War Premier himself sent a memorandum to his colleagues about the need to prepare for urgent tasks after the war, noting that there was a wide measure of inter-party agreement over education, social insurance and the rebuilding of cities, and suggesting that therefore plans ought to be brought to a 'high degree of preparation' during the war.[93]

Within Whitehall the ponderous and ever larger machinery of official and ministerial committees concerned with reconstruction, already in motion since 1941, ground away from 1943 to 1945, milling reports, studies and memoranda on such topics as the redistribution of the urban population, on town and country planning and redevelopment, on full employment, on the social services, on a national health service, on housing needs, on a reformed education system, into convenient rations of meal suitable for Cabinet digestion and decision. A Ministry of Town and Country Planning came into being in February 1943; a White Paper on education[94] appeared in July 1943, and led eventually to the Education Act of August 1944 (see below Chapter Fourteen); in February 1944 appeared a White Paper on a national health service; in May a White Paper on employment policy[95] which was commended to the House of Commons by Ernest Bevin and warmly welcomed by Henry Brooke, the Conservative backbench spokesman on industry, and by the Tory Reform Committee – a demonstration of how the 1940–1 vision of New Jerusalem was fast becoming the new political consensus. In September 1944 there followed a White Paper[96] setting out the government's scheme for national insurance, a somewhat watered down Beveridge Plan. The government's commitment to build 100,000–120,000 houses in the first year after the ending of the German war and 180,000–200,000 in the second year[97] was embodied in the housing White Paper of March 1945.[98]

For all Churchill's continued personal misgivings about saddling a postwar government with vast commitments, his only recourse in these last two years of the war lay in trying to slow up the Whitehall machinery by judiciously shoving wedges into the cogs, in the form of referring schemes agreed by the Labour-dominated home-front ministries and committees to Lord Beaverbrook (the Lord Privy Seal) and Brendan Bracken (Minister of Information). This gambit earned him a six-page letter personally typed by Attlee in January 1945 bitterly complaining about needless delays in deciding reconstruction policy, to which a choleric War Premier with his self-control strained to splitting point replied in a single sentence: 'You may be sure that I shall always endeavour to profit from your counsels.'[99] Nonetheless, despite Churchill, the Whitehall machinery had continued to rotate – driven by the remorseless prime mover of public expectation. For the sway of the New Jerusalem movement outside as well as inside government in 1943–5 was growing all the time stronger, partly because its vision of 'fair shares for all' in welfare, health, housing and educational opportunity chimed with the public's approval of wartime 'fair shares' through rationing and national service, partly bcause victory and therefore the prospect of the postwar era came ever nearer into sight, and partly because of their own unceasing and successful propaganda.

The most hearkened-to of all the prophets of a better Britain, Sir William Beveridge, 'the people's William', continued to busy himself mightily in speeches, articles and books. In March 1943, for instance, he spoke on a Liberal Party platform at the Caxton Hall on the theme of 'a people's war for a people's peace'.[100] In the introduction to his 1943 edition of wartime essays and addresses, *The Pillars of Security*, he remarked that during the Great War people had looked forward to a return to 'the good old pre-war days':

> Today there is no such prospect of contentment in going back, because the times before the Second World War were not good. The British people have learned by experience that after this war they must go forward to something new, not back to the old.[101]

In March 1943 he announced that he was going to conduct his own enquiry as a private citizen into the question of full employment. Some familiar names in the 'enlightened' Establishment such as David Astor and Edward Hulton rallied round with the necessary funding. The news of Beveridge's new venture panicked the government – it is not too strong a word – into setting on foot its own study of the question, with the aim of publishing before Beveridge in order to avoid being rail-roaded by Sir William a second time;[102] a further demonstration of the effect of outside pressure on Whitehall. The publication of Beveridge's new report, *Full Employment in a Free Society*, in November 1944[103] nevertheless achieved far greater éclat than the government's own rather cautious White Paper published in May that year; and more than any other influence this fresh revelation from the people's William nailed postwar governments to full employment as the main determining factor of economic strategy. Beveridge himself remarked that while his first report had taken as its aim 'freedom from Want', the aim of the new one was 'freedom from Idleness'. He proceeded in true Victorian moralistic style to observe that 'Idleness is a positive . . . evil which men do not escape by having an income.'[104] Freedom from this moral evil could, he averred, be easily secured – Keynes again – by government adjusting the tap of demand as necessary: 'The first condition of full employment is that total outlay should always be high enough to set up a demand for products of industry which cannot be satisfied without using the whole man-power of the country. . . .'[105]

After all, he argued, the war had shown that 'unemployment disappears and all men have value when the State sets up unlimited demand for a compelling common purpose. By the spectacular achievement of its planned economy war shows also how great is the waste of unemployment.'[106] Moreover full employment would have other benefits. Trade-union restrictive practices 'born out of a spirit of self-defence' would 'become unnecessary defences under full employment in peace'.[107] Beveridge saw no reason why full employment should lead to slackness at work or excessive wage demands, for 'Workmen have no love of idlers,' while 'organised labour in Britain has sufficiently demonstrated its sense of citizenship and responsibility to justify the expectation that it will evolve, in its own manner, the machinery by which a better co-ordinated wage policy can be carried through.'[108]

In the meantime the broader New Jerusalem movement was also proselytising with quenchless fervour. Common Wealth and the Independent Labour Party (which were New Jerusalem's political outlets while the official Labour Party was inhibited by membership of the coalition government from standing against Conservatives) fought fourteen by-elections in Conservative-held seats between February 1943 and May 1945, and achieved an average swing in their favour of 8.14 per cent.[109] Moreover, Common Wealth succeeded in winning three safe Conservative seats in this period, and at Chelmsford in April 1945 overturned a Conservative 70 per cent share of the vote at the general election of 1935. That other potent organ of the 'enlightened' Establishment, the Army Bureau of Current Affairs, continued to encourage the soldiery to think about what sort of Britain they wanted after the war, working on the assumption that Britain itself 'must and will play in this proud hour of destiny, a historic and memorable part', in the words of ABCA's Director W. E. Williams in July 1943.[110] In Williams's diagnosis, 'Politics, industry and society have reached what scientists call a climacteric, and in shaping the new world, Britain, with its genius for bloodless revolutions, may need to take the leadership of the United Nations.'[111] In November 1943 ABCA ran an issue of *Current Affairs* on 'Building the Post-War Home', which discussed the government's announced programme of building 3–4 million houses in ten years, compared with the pre-war total of 4 million in twenty years.[112] In June 1944, hard on the heels of the White Paper on employment policy, Gertrude Williams, wife of ABCA's Director and a lecturer at the London School of Economics, explained Keynesian demand management for the benefit of the squaddie in an article entitled 'Work for All'.[113]

In August followed a report, 'After the Blitz is Over', on the new *Plan for London*, itself one of the key documents in New Jerusalemism and widely reported in the media at home as well as by ABCA, in which housing, industry, shops and offices were to be redeployed and rebuilt on the grandest scale, vast areas of new parkland created, and the road network comprehensively laid out afresh. The ABCA booklet quoted the inspirational Preface to the *Plan* by Lord Latham, chairman of the London County Council:

> just as we can move mountains when our liberties are threatened and we have to fight for our lives, so can we when the future of London is at stake. . . . But let there be no mistake. A new London cannot be built of mere wishing. No bold plan can be carried out unless Parliament clothes us with ample power and resources.

Latham did not, however, enter into the question of whether the expectation of such ample power and resources might also be 'mere wishing'. The capital of New Jerusalem, like the rest of it, was to be constructed by faith, as the final words of the London *Plan*, quoted in this ABCA *Current Affairs* issue, make plain:

> We have learnt the value of planning for war; peace demands planning and efficiency no less. The energies, sacrifices, and bold financial measures that the war has called forth will be more necessary in time of peace. With the united efforts of all, we can build the new England which has been the inspiration, and must be the reward, of the citizen-soldier.[114]

Later that August *Current Affairs* turned to 'Schools for Tomorrow', and in November to a discussion of 'A Weapon Against Want', the government's new White Paper on social insurance.[115] In April 1945 an issue on 'Getting Back Into Harness' explained the government plan for preparing for a return to civilian jobs and ended with yet another paean of the romantic optimism which buoyed up the whole New Jerusalem movement:

> During the war years, undaunted by danger, insensible to strain and

> fatigue, the British nation has given to the world an unsurpassed example of co-operation and the will to endure. It remains for us to show in the no less arduous and complicated process of returning to a peace footing, we can show the same resilience . . . and, above all, that same steadfastness of purpose that have brought us from Dunkirk to the very vitals of the German Reich.[116]

The cumulative wartime message to the British people from all the organs of the 'enlightened' Establishment was therefore clear: given only faith and will, the New Jerusalem was to be had for the asking. But there was a corollary. It depended on which political party the nation asked. And from the moment when the Conservative-dominated coalition government so tepidly greeted the Beveridge Plan at the beginning of 1943, the nation – not without some interested persuasion – had come more and more to the conclusion that what stood between it and the Better Britain of its dreams was 'them', 'the old gang', the political leadership of the 1930s which in its meanness over expenditure and its lack of bold imagination had done nothing about unemployment or poverty before the war, and which in any case served as the defender of privilege and monopoly. Mass-Observation, in its survey of public opinion in 1944, *The Journey Home*, summed up its findings: 'It is the *contrast* which becomes steadily stronger, between the post-war Britain they feel can be built, and the post-war Britain they think will be built.'[117] This interpretation of the public mood is borne out by a MOI Home Intelligence Report in November 1944, which found that memories of the last postwar period were causing 'deep and widespread uneasiness on the part of all sections of the public about the future', especially over unemployment, and that the public was hoping that Beveridge would 'keep the Government up to the mark' over social insurance.[118] These troubled undercurrents of mistrust of 'the old gang' and of hope for a Better Britain, which had already welled up into the open in the by-elections of 1942–5, finally erupted in a mighty upsurge in the general election of July 1945, burying the pre-war political landscape and creating a new one.

For a vote for Labour was at once a vote for New Jerusalem and a vote for the party which the electors believed could be trusted – unlike the Conservatives – to deliver it. The Labour Party had, after all, been committed to New Jerusalem ever since the Labour movement was born in the late nineteenth century out of secularised religious emotion and idealism. Now at long last the party's dreams and the public mood had conjoined. The Labour election campaign itself constituted the climactic episode of all the wartime evangelising of an ideal Britain after the war.[119] Its essence was graphically expressed in a cartoon by Zec in the mass-circulation *Daily Mirror*, which shows outraged citizens standing in the 'Tory Peace Stores (Very Limited)' saying to the shopkeeper:'What do you mean – you're out of stock? I've paid twice for these goods, once in 1914 and once in 1939.' Under the counter are packages labelled 'Decent Schools', 'Good Homes', 'Jobs', 'Proper Medical Attention', all of them under a sign reading 'The Fruits of Victory. Reserved for the Privileged'.[120]

The Labour manifesto struck a similar note when referring to the victory already achieved over Germany and the national determination to defeat Japan: 'The people will have won both struggles. . . . They deserve and must be assured a happier future than faced so many of them after the last war.'[121] That the Conservatives too offered a version of New Jerusalem, based on the coalition government's 'four-year-plan', demonstrated that New Jerusalem had indeed become the political consensus.

The interest of the election in terms of Britain's future as a first-rank industrial power lies, however, less in political promises and rhetoric than in the order of priority in regard to national tasks and expenditure selected by the parties and the electorate. Housing came first, mentioned in 97 per cent of Labour candidates' election addresses and 94 per cent of Conservative, prominently discussed in both party manifestos, and chosen by 41 per cent of the electorate as the most important issue, according to a Gallup Poll early in the campaign.[122] Next came social security and full employment, topics mentioned in more than 70 per cent of both parties' election addresses, and rated by the electorate (according to Gallup) as second only to housing.[123] In contrast, although both manifestos acknowledged the need for industrial efficiency and successful exports, the Labour manifesto allotted to exports merely the fifth sub-section of a chapter entitled 'Industry in the Service of the Nation', while in individual candidates' addresses exports rated usually no more than a brief sentence, and then only in 35 per cent of Conservative addresses and 17 per cent of Labour.[124] The Conservative manifesto laid unfashionable emphasis on 'sound finance', while a Conservative pamphlet sought to explain that the money which the state spent had first to be earned by profitable economic activity, otherwise it would have to borrow, and borrowing would lead to inflation. The Labour manifesto, moral in tone throughout, accused the Conservatives in best New Jerusalem style of making finance 'the Master of the State' instead of its servant.

As foreshadowed by earlier by-elections, the electors put their trust in Labour rather than in those running the 'Tory Peace Stores (Very Limited)' on those issues which they took to be the most vital facing the country, such as housing.[125] To them victory in the war merited a rich reward, and they meant to have it: for the highminded a reward in the shape of an ideal society, and for the humbler in the shape of free welfare and a secure job.

So it came to pass that a romantic vision a century and a half in the making had at last found incarnation in the committed programme of a British government with a crushing majority in Parliament. Yet the cost of realising this programme was to fall not on the richest country in the world, not on that Victorian and Edwardian Britain in which the vision first had gleamed and which had made the New Jerusalemers what they were, but on a country with a ruined export trade, heavily in debt to its bankers (the Sterling Area Commonwealth countries and the United States), and with huge and inescapable continuing burdens with regard to the war with Japan. Yet the wartime promoters of New Jerusalem had pursued their vision in the face of economic realities perfectly well known to them – on the best romantic principle that sense must bend to feeling, and facts to faith.

Chapter Two

The Illusion of Limitless Possibility

That Britain's immediate postwar economic situation would be precarious to the last degree had been recognised outside Whitehall as well as inside during those wartime years which witnessed the rise of the New Jerusalem movement. There was the well-advertised fact of American aid under Lend–Lease from April 1941 onwards, when Britain ceased to pay for – ceased to be able to pay for – the immense shopping list of military and industrial equipment ordered from the United States; and this US aid became more and more directly manifest to the ordinary citizen because of the American groceries like Spam and dried egg that came to figure in British rations. Moreover, the extent to which Britain had sold off overseas assets and curtailed exports for the sake of the war effort became a matter of proud comment in the media, and as early as March 1942 ABCA circulated to every army unit a *Current Affairs* booklet, 'Paying for the War', devoted to this very topic.[1] The War Premier in his broadcast 'After the War' in March 1943 uttered his own warning about the economic difficulties that would then confront the country.[2] In July 1943 W. E. Williams, the Director of ABCA, in a *Current Affairs* article entitled 'When the Lights Go On' called attention to the postwar need to rebuild the lost export trade.[3] In November 1944 the journalist Macdonald Hastings informed the soldiery in another *Current Affairs* article, 'What Has Happened at Home?', that:

> the problem you'll hear most about is the economic one. To pay for the war Britain has had to sell out all her foreign securities (and foreign securities are a nation's bank balance). To fight the war we have had to give up all production except armaments production, which means that we've had to give up all our foreign trade (and foreign trade is a nation's income). . . . so that the most essential economic need now is to turn over to peace-time production, and to restore our foreign trade as rapidly as possible.[4]

That same month the White Paper on the war effort of the United Kingdom also made this point, although in far greater detail by way of fact, figure and graph. In May 1945 *The Economist* published a similar analysis of the British war effort and of the demolition of Britain's international trading role that this had entailed. It described how in 1944 alone Britain had had to sell overseas assets or borrow overseas to a total of £655 million, as against £70 million in 1938;[5] and in June 1945, during the general election campaign, *Current Affairs* used *The Economist* article as a basis for its own explanatory text.[6]

Within government the extent of Britain's progressive ruin as the war went on not only provided the routine subject-matter of current financial policy, but also prompted voluminous setpiece Treasury examinations of the question; examinations that were fully discussed by Cabinet committees on postwar reconstruction. In March 1942, the year when the New Jerusalem movement began to boom, the Treasury submitted a 'Very Secret' memorandum, complete with detailed appendices, on 'External Monetary and Economic Policy', arising out of a new mutual-aid agreement with the United States.[7] In this paper the Treasury attempted to predict Britain's immediate postwar economic position, on the premise that the war were to end by 31 December 1943. It foresaw 'unexampled economic difficulty in the external sphere':

> We shall start the period of peace with great liabilities and small resources both of exchange and of resources that could be turned into exchange. The Economic Section [of the War Cabinet Secretariat] have made estimates which suggest that in the absence of corrective measures our adverse balance of payments over the first five years taken as a whole may be in the region of £1000 millions.

In an explanatory note the Treasury became even glummer:

> Our British problem of gaining enough receipts overseas to balance our import requirements is so acute that we can scarcely hope to solve it except by . . . a strong expansionist stimulus throughout the world [which] provides willing markets for a largely expanded volume of our exports. . . .

The Treasury predicted a balance-of-payments deficit in the first year after the war of £250 million and £215 million in the second year. Even with imports reduced to rock bottom – and that implied so low a level of economic activity as to entail 3 million unemployed – the deficit in the first year would be £100 million, though there would be a balance in the second year. The Treasury would not count on American aid continuing into peacetime (a piece of foresight that was to be only too well justified), writing: 'We may doubtfully hope to receive for a time a limited measure of continued assistance from the United States under the guise of Lease–Lend.' It even questioned whether the Sterling Area countries of the Commonwealth would continue to sell Britain goods for sterling. It therefore reckoned that total imports over two years that Britain herself could pay for would amount to £1835 million, which:

> might suffice to keep the population fed and to provide raw materials at about the present rate of use per head, but it is not clear whether it could suffice to provide the volume of raw materials required to meet the minimum peace-time requirements with full employment. . . .

One expedient – or, more likely, act of *force majeure* – for closing the estimated import–export gap of some £150 million (give or take £105 million) would lie in a drastic fall in the United Kingdom standard of living:

> if all other methods of adjustment fail, we shall, in the extremity, suffer such a fall in the exchange value of sterling and in the levels of employment and expenditure in this country as to force our consumption of imports within the straitjacket of our financial capacity to pay for them. But, even if such a reduction could be achieved without a total collapse of sterling, it is an eventuality which we would wish, if at all possible, to avoid.

The Treasury could only therefore place its hopes in a huge rise in exports, a solution, 'if it is feasible', that was 'obviously to be preferred to any alternative'.

Such was the basic text on Britain's economic prospects that was to lie on the table throughout the Whitehall grinding out of reconstruction plans in the years 1942–5 and throughout the period of the cumulative government public commitment to building New Jerusalem. It was supplemented in January and July 1943 by far-from-encouraging guesstimates of the postwar national income by the Chancellor of the Exchequer, Sir Kingsley Wood,[8] while in June 1944 the President of the Board of Trade concluded a memorandum on 'Post-War Exports' by observing: 'The prospects thus revealed look pretty bleak. It is clear that vigorous and varied action must be taken, if we are to realise our post-war hope and make good our promises.'[9]

By 1944 Britain's visible exports could not, in fact, finance one-seventh of her overseas requirements; it was now foreseen that after the end of the German war British foreign debts would exceed British reserves by nearly fifteen times; and that the adverse balance on current account over the first three postwar years could hardly be less than £1000 million.[10] All in all, it is hard in retrospect not to applaud the Treasury comment in 1944 that 'the time and energy and thought which we are all giving to the Brave New World is wildly disproportionate to what is being given to the Cruel Real World'.[11]

How, then, did the promoters of the Brave New World inside and outside government reconcile in their own minds this wild disproportion? In the first place, they did so by hiving off Brave New World and Cruel Real World into hermetically sealed intellectual compartments. This enabled them to keep pushing the one while acknowledging the existence of the other. Clement Attlee, for example, a man at the centre of home-front affairs throughout the war, and in particular of reconstruction planning, entertained a belief that, despite the immediate postwar prospects, this was an age of abundance. Utilisation of abundance, according to Attlee in 1944:

> is the basis of our conversations with the Dominions and our Allies. It colours all our discussions on home policy. There follows from this the doctrine of full employment. The acceptance of this again colours our whole conception of the postwar set-up in this country. . . .[12]

This comforting assumption about abundance waiting to be utilised no doubt enabled Attlee, as Leader of the Labour Party, to give his blessing to an election manifesto in 1945 the basic message of which was that the people 'deserved and must be assured a happier future', and which therefore laid its emphasis on creating a welfare state and the building of no fewer than 4 million houses; and did so to the relative neglect of discussion of investment in industry and infrastructure.[13] Yet in stark contrast Attlee could tell Laski in 1944: 'I am sure you are under no illusion as to the press of problems which will face us at the end of the war or as to the difficult economic position of the country.'[14] He was similarly realistic in addressing his own constituents during the 1945 general election:

> I do not seek to conceal from you that the postwar years will not be easy. They will require from the nation in peace the same resolute spirit as shown in war, but I believe that within a few years we can, if we will, attain to a higher standard of life than ever before and a more just social system.[15]

Hugh Dalton could urge in November 1942 that the coalition government should catch the public tide now running in favour of New Jerusalem, but then, in 1944 and writing in his departmental capacity as President of the Board of Trade, he could report that the postwar prospects for British exports looked 'pretty bleak'.[16] Herbert Morrison could table a memorandum to the Reconstruction Priorities Committee during the wrangle over the government's treatment of the Beveridge Report in which, in his own words, 'I have simply sought to show that this boon of social security, which has good claims to an absolute priority among all other claims of home policy, represents a financial burden which we should be able to bear, except on a number of very gloomy assumptions';[17] and yet in September 1944 tell his colleagues, according to the minutes of the Reconstruction Committee, that he was 'profoundly disturbed about the future of our economic prosperity. We had made much progress in the preparation of our plans for reconstruction in the field of social reform, but it was essential that this should be firmly based upon a healthy industrial foundation.'[18] And Beveridge himself could pursue his one-man crusade for a welfare state to cost the economy in its first year £86 million at his own reckoning, and nevertheless at the same time state publicly that it was right to dispel:

> the popular idea that when the fighting stops and we turn from making means of destruction to making useful things we shall at once be able to afford almost anything. We are not paying for the war today either out of our own income or out of current income [*sic*]. There

> will be heavy burdens which can only be met by the Central Government in the immediate aftermath of war.[19]

Similarly in his report on *Full Employment* in 1944 Beveridge urged an unquantified outlay of government funds in order to stimulate enough demand to bring about full employment, while admitting that such a policy in 1938 would have caused a balance-of-payments deficit of £130 million. His remarks read in hindsight as a complete give-away of the whole New Jerusalem case:

> Britain with her output capacity of 1938 would not have found it easy to do, at one and the same time, all the things that were undeniably desirable for her: that is to say, she would not have found it easy simultaneously to balance her payments abroad, in place of living on overseas capital; to consume as freely as before; and to destroy the social evils of Want, Disease, Squalor, Ignorance and Malnutrition. The standard of living in Britain before the war was high but it was by no means equal to needs or desires of the people, and it was being maintained in 1939 in part by living on the savings that had been made by earlier generations.[20]

Beveridge's answer to the conundrum lay in re-equipping industry and expanding output and exports, yet he offered no detailed analysis, no pondered advice, as to how these desirable objects were to be achieved; no costings of the investment needed and how it was to be funded; and he certainly failed to consider what effect the burden of the welfare state and the cost of maintaining full employment might have on such industrial investment. In any case he placed the need to modernise British industry and raise its productivity only third in priority in his 'chosen route of planned national outlay'.[21]

The official and ministerial committees concerned with various aspects of reconstruction display a similar intellectual compartmentalisation. It was the role of the Cabinet Committee on Reconstruction Problems and the Cabinet Committee on Reconstruction Priorities (and after November 1943 of the Reconstruction Committee of the new Ministry of Reconstruction which superseded them) to weld all the specialist studies, reports and recommendations filtering upwards from such other committees as those on social insurance policy, or on post-war employment, or on internal economic problems, into a coherent corporate strategy. In fact no coherent corporate strategy was ever so welded, nor did either of the main reconstruction committees or the War Cabinet (the ultimate policy-making body) ever themselves sit down and design such a strategy in order that specialist committees could be given briefs defining their scope and budgets within the strategy. The nearest approach to a corporate strategy is found in the report of the Reconstruction Priorities Committee (itself a hastily convened *ad hoc* body) to the War Cabinet on the Beveridge proposals on 11 February 1943, which certainly laid down some admirable broad national priorities:

> At this stage, therefore, we can say no more as regards the new claims than that we are satisfied that the expenditure necessary to ensure international security must have first place, and that, second only to this, we would put the expenditure necessary to establish trade and industry on a healthy footing, to maintain employment at the highest attainable level and to foster our export trade.[22]

As regards all other claims on public funds, such as agriculture, education, the colonies, the social services, the committee averred that it was 'impossible at this stage to establish any order of priority or to enter into definite commitments'.[23]

Yet this report merely led to the short-term result of determining the government's tactics in the forthcoming Commons debate on Beveridge, and its wider message was soon lost in the thickets of Whitehall detail; it certainly did not form the basis of a fully worked-out corporate strategy,[24] nor did it serve as an acknowledged guide to priorities in the future work of committees concerned with different aspects of 'reconstruction'. These continued to follow their own bent, and the main reconstruction committees tried as best they could to fit the results together piecemeal afterwards. Since these results or recommendations came before them as numbered items on an agenda to be taken one at a time, there was no positive reason why a decision on a certain project should be related to a decision on another; certainly no reason why projects should be jointly weighed and decided. This was equally true of one meeting and another, not just one item and another. Departmental representatives on a committee might argue with each other over competing projects, or some major question like the Beveridge Report might be referred for special discussion and report, but otherwise Treasury memoranda and debate thereon had to provide the substitute for consideration of corporate strategy across the board. Thus on 22 January 1943 the Chancellor of the Exchequer at the first meeting of the new Reconstruction Priorities Committee opposed government endorsement of the Beveridge Report on the ground of Britain's uncertain postwar prospects; and a week later in the same committee likewise opposed publication of a White Paper setting down housing targets, also on the ground of the likely limits on future national income, and because a building programme of the size proposed could only be at the expense of industrial investment.[25] In June 1944 the Department of Overseas Trade also argued that the housing programme was too large and too rapid, in view of the fact that 'We shall have many calls upon our available resources. . . .'[26] Often interdepartmental disputes within a committee were resolved by postponing a decision, or, just as bad, bargaining a compromise. Whitehall was like a general with pebble-lenses rather than a telescope. Thus it happened that the cumulative weight of attention, in terms of agenda items or memoranda, given by the principal reconstruction committees turned out to lie on social objectives rather than economic needs.[27]

This mole-like pursuit of desirable objectives along separate tunnels finally accumulated that pile of commitments which evoked the Treasury *cri de cœur* about the disproportion between work on the Brave New World and consideration of the Cruel Real World. But of course such Whitehall compartmentalisation and ad-hockery were simply basic characteristics of the British governmental machine, and had been no less evident in the shambles of pre-war grand strategy, defence policy and foreign policy. There was, moreover, no equivalent in wartime social and economic plannin~ for the postwar era to the Defence Requirement Committees and their major grand-strategic reports in 1934–6.

To New Jerusalemers themselves, intellectual compartmentalisation served as only one of the no doubt unwitting psychological tricks by which they evaded the Cruel Real World. True to their romantic ancestry they 'solved' the problems of this world by effortlessly leaping over them into the Brave New World of their imagination, although not without challenge from critics lacking their gift of faith. At the extreme, in the form of the reborn Christian Socialists of Common Wealth and socialist prelates like Temple, New Jerusalem was simply a matter of applying the Ten Commandments to a twentieth-century industrial society and choosing, in Acland's phrase, the most morally righteous system. But the broader 'enlightened' Establishment also preferred to talk about the ends rather than the means. The *Picture Post* issue in January 1941 offering 'A Plan for Britain' attempted no costings of its grandiose schemes for new cities, health services, welfare, education and leisure, no suggestion as to how they might be financed, no discussion of whether the postwar British economy could support them; only a glib article by Thomas Balogh asserting that state management of the economy could assure 'Work for All'. ABCA *Current Affairs*, the voice of the 'enlightened' Establishment in the armed forces, devoted ten issues to New Jerusalem topics and nine to the damage done by the war to the British economy and the consequent need for caution over postwar prospects: an apparently not unbalanced coverage. Yet the inspirational language of the New Jerusalem articles, coupled with omissions of vital matters from those on the economy, in fact swing the balance strongly in favour of the vision of 'the world we want after the war'.[28] In his article in October 1942 entitled 'What Price Victory?', for example, the director of ABCA very properly briefs army discussion-group leaders on the need to point out that:

> peace will not be found on top of the beanstalk on Armistice Day, but will be a slow and complicated process of adjustment and reconstruction. It is better that we should fight for the genuine vision of a new and different world, however hard it will be to build and consolidate, rather than that we should think of peace as the mere climax of a Cup Final.

Yet the same article makes no mention of the likely balance-of-payments difficulties, no mention of industrial investment. Its order of priorities is quite otherwise:

> We shall want to resume and multiply production not only for our own needs, but also for the needs of the scorched and denuded

Continent. At home, moreover, we shall need to rebuild our cities, improve our transport system, continue to reclaim our agricultural land.[29]

Similarly ABCA briefings on the original Beveridge Report in 1943 and what it called the government's 'Social Security Plan' in November 1944 omit any discussion of how the resources for the welfare state were to be found out of a war-ruined economy.[30] Again, Ralph Tubbs's vision of new cities in *Current Affairs* in September 1942 steers clear of what they would cost and whether the resources could be found; so does an issue in November 1943 on 'Building the Post-War Home', which discusses construction priorities in terms of cottages before cinemas and skating rinks, and makes no mention of infrastructure or industrial plant.[31] Other articles in *Current Affairs*[32] certainly note the rundown of British overseas trade and investment, and give further warnings against over-optimism and about 'the need to cut our coat according to our cloth',[33] but they too fail to tackle the crucial question of the British industrial base and the paramount importance of investment. Curiously enough, in the entire series of 100 ABCA *Current Affairs* booklets the most pointed comments on Britain as an industrial power come backhandedly in articles mainly devoted to American, German or Japanese industry.[34] The reader was told, for instance, that by comparison with the Ruhr 'our own "Black Country" looks like a brick kiln on a slag heap,'[35] and that Japan was a country 'in some ways more efficient than Britain. The Japanese railway system, for instance, is more up-to-date than ours. . . .'[36]

However, as perhaps might be expected, it was Sir William Beveridge, the most important single influence on public opinion with regard to the postwar era, New Jerusalem incarnate, who levitated most successfully above any practical factor that stood in the way of his full-employment welfare state. This was the case with both his chairmanship of the Interdepartmental Committee on Social Insurance and Allied Services and his later public evangelising. In the first place, out of a total of forty-four meetings of his committee and 248 memoranda the basic question of national resources for the scheme only came up in three meetings and eight memoranda,[37] and even then three of the memoranda were critiques originating outside the committee from the Government Actuary and the Economic Section of the War Cabinet Secretariat.[38] At its second meeting on 24 September 1941 the Beveridge Committee agreed to defer consideration of the whole question of finance to a later meeting. It certainly did consider that question at its next two meetings on 15 and 29 October 1941, but only in terms of different ways of designing the internal financial arrangements of the scheme; not at all in terms of overall costs in relation to what the economy could afford.[39] In December 1941 Beveridge submitted a memorandum to his committee on the 'Basic Problems of Social Security with Heads of a Scheme' which actually included a section on 'Costs of a Scheme'. In it he notes the 'heavy new costs' on the Exchequer resulting from his suggestions of children's allowances, higher old-age pensions and a national health service, and asks: 'Is there any way other than a means test of keeping down such needless expenditure [as giving benefits to those who did not need them] and so preserving limited resources for real needs?' The question never received an answer: and even this paper never got down to the fundamental question of whether or how the economy could afford much more lavish social services.[40]

A second paper by Beveridge in the same month goes through the shopping-list of welfare items in order to suggest 'some statistical short cuts on Finance of Social Security', but it too fails to tackle overall costings.[41] In the minutes of the committee's second meeting of 1942 there is an airy reference in discussion to the possibility of the state having 'to float off any deficiency . . . in the early period of a scheme'.[42] Even when tabling a first draft of his report in July 1942, Beveridge could write: 'It is neither possible nor necessary at the present moment finally to determine rates of benefit or contributions, since the future level of prices and the economic condition of the country when the scheme will begin are uncertain.'[43] Indeed, Beveridge's personal covering note to this draft offers a remarkable demonstration that, for him, designing a scheme came first and considering the burden on the economy a long way second:

> The draft sets out a full Plan for Social Security as an objective. The next and urgent task is to consider the financial implications of the plan, that is to say the scope of the Security Budget. The principal points for discussion are: What should be included in the social security contributions and budget? . . . Whether and how the plan can be reduced in cost, if it presents excessive financial difficulties?[44]

Given this first-things-last approach, it is not surprising that an appendix to the final draft was able to compare the Beveridge Plan with the social insurance schemes of eleven other countries, including Germany, the United States and New Zealand (the acknowledged leaders in the field), and find that it was the equal or superior to each of the others in its overall generosity of provision.[45]

It was left to the Government Actuary and the Economic Section of the War Cabinet Secretariat to explore, at a time when Beveridge's report was already in draft, those questions of cost and affordability which ought, it might be said, to have been tackled by Beveridge's committee right at the beginning of its work. Moreover, the Economic Section, in contrast to the visionary Sir William, predicted with admirable foresight the ill consequences of the new welfare state in the forty years that followed the war. On the basis of the Government Actuary's figures[46] it asked whether the extra cost of £300 million would not 'involve a heavy or insupportable burden on the country's resources'.[47] It further asked: 'will the transfer through the national Exchequer of an additional £300 million from taxpayers to beneficiaries cause rates of taxation to be raised to unduly high levels?' It drew attention to other and competing postwar demands on the Exchequer. It thought that sickness and unemployment benefits 'may reduce the incentive to work'. But even the Government Actuary had swallowed the notion that the £300 million was just 'an internal transfer' and did not constitute a loss of resources to the country as a whole, thereby ignoring the opportunity costs of foregoing expenditure of £300 million on other projects, or the effect on national investment of transferring such a sum from potential investors to certain spenders. The Economic Section concluded that there was 'no easy answer' to the question whether Beveridge's scheme would prove too heavy a burden. The Government Actuary in further memoranda on Beveridge's draft proposals calculated that their extra cost to the Exchequer over existing welfare provisions (excluding a national health service) would be £160 million in 1945; and that the total cost to the Exchequer of the complete Beveridge package, including a health service, would be £367 million in 1945 but £541 million in 1965.[48]

How blithely Beveridge had neglected the fundamental question of resources, not only with regard to the moment when the scheme first came into operation, but also far into the future, was exposed by the Chancellor of the Exchequer, Kingsley Wood, in blistering papers to the Cabinet and War Premier. In fact the Chancellor's criticisms amount to a percipient prophecy of the crisis that would eventually overtake the welfare state and its financing in the 1980s. Basic to Kingsley Wood's analysis was the incalculable and open-ended nature of Beveridge's vision. As he put it in a personal note to the War Premier on 17 November 1942: 'The scheme is presented as contributory but like the existing system depends on a deficiency grant, which will grow in the course of time to immense proportions, from the general taxpayer.'[49] A more detailed memorandum, prepared in the Treasury and sent to Churchill on 6 January 1943 marked in Kingsley Wood's own hand 'Secret PM Only', drove the point home: 'Acceptance of the complete plan involves a contract with many millions of beneficiaries, the continued fulfilment of which would properly have to be, in good or bad times alike, a prior charge upon the national resources. . . .'[50] The memorandum justly wrote of Beveridge's drafting:

> The broad impression left by the report on the ordinary reader is that in the author's view the general finance of the scheme can be carried without undue difficulty. There are, however, lying in the future, so far as it can be discerned, doubts and uncertainties suggesting that large financial commitments cannot be undertaken without misgivings.

It again made the point that 'any excess or short-fall of cost of the plan as a whole falls on the taxpayer. . . .' The projected increase in employers' insurance contributions at 2 per cent on present wages would be for 'very competitive exports . . . a dispiriting increase in the cost of production. . .'. Furthermore, the scheme would compete with other charges on the public purse. As Wood had put it graphically in his personal note to Churchill: 'Is this the time to assume that the general taxpayer has a bottomless purse?'

Unfortunately for Kingsley Wood, his strictures came far too late: the Beveridge Report was already a *fait accompli*, and its triumph over public opinion was ineluctably to follow.[51] Beveridge himself continued grandly to place ethics and ideals before resources, certain that, because he had willed the end, the means would be there. To the question 'Can we afford it?' at a public meeting in December 1942, he replied:

> Can we not afford it? Re-distribution of income does not abolish Want, unless there is enough in total. There was ample in total before the war, in spite of the last war and its destructive aftermath. There will be ample in total after this war if we can use our productive resources in productive employment.[52]

Cunningly he did not follow his Whitehall critics in discussing the future and its unlimited commitment, but emphasised what he considered to be the digestible cost (£86 million a year in his estimate) of the scheme at its inception: 'I can't believe that that won't be within our means when the war ends.'[53]

In his second blueprint *Full Employment in a Free Society* in 1944 Beveridge followed a similar pattern of placing his ethical ideal first and the practical considerations second, and then as meriting only brief mentions. In twenty opening pages on the moral and social desirability of full employment, and how it will lead to a happy spirit of co-operation among workpeople, he manages eleven lines on the key topic of adaptation to technical change. He wraps up the question of free collective bargaining under conditions of full employment by asserting that it 'must be responsible, looking not to the snatching of short term sectional advantages, but to the permanent good of the community. . .'.[54] This might be achieved by a TUC wages policy or, if necessary, by arbitration. His analysis of the reasons for pre-war mass unemployment (want of sufficient general demand) leaves out entirely the question of the market competitiveness of British technology, and the distinction between over-full employment in advanced technology and mass unemployment in old industries and among the unskilled. He reckons that a postwar programme of national outlay (or in other words corporate strategy) should be based on social rather than industrial priorities:

> On the view taken in this Report, the most urgent tasks in Britain, once war is over, are, on the one hand, the making of a common attack on the giant social evils of Want, Disease, Ignorance and Squalor, and on the other, the re-equipping of British industry, whether in private or public hands, with new and better machinery to ensure a steady increase in the standard of life. . . .[55]

To this latter and fundamental question he then devotes three lines, returning to it later with five more lines, and later again with a one-sentence reference to the need to re-equip to American standards.[56] To the topic of structural unemployment caused by technical change he devotes a paragraph, assuring his readers that control over location of industry and over the entry of youth into industry, coupled with training facilities for the older persons, will ensure that 'the resulting unemployment can be reduced to a point at which it represents no evil and is a small price to pay for progress.'[57] To 'Britain's Need of Exports' – another matter fundamental to British survival, prosperity and indeed full employment – Beveridge allots a thoughtful four and a half pages out of a 274-page main text, and comfortably concludes: 'On any alternative, the quantity of exports required is well within the capacity of the British industrial system.'[58] The maintenance of overseas trade in general, another not unimportant question in regard to full employment, merits five lines of discussion, including such penetrating analysis as that here was 'a vital objective of national policy. This is partly a general question of industrial efficiency, of regaining for Britain by technical research some of the leadership in invention which came to her historically at the beginning of the Industrial Revolution.'[59]

Full Employment in a Free Society is really a sermonising tract, gloriously sweeping over difficulties human and technological to the promised land beyond. And, in the last resort, Sir William justified the practicality of his vision by simple analogy with the achievements of the wartime British economy:

> The significance of war in relation to employment is that the scope of State outlay is increased immensely and indefinitely and that the State formally and openly gives up any attempt to balance its budget or limit its outlay by considerations of money.[60]

Similarly with regard to his plan for a welfare state, we are told by his daughter and biographer: 'To the critics who inquired "Can we pay for it?" the impatient reply was given, "We can always pay for wars, this one costs £15 million a day. We will just *have* to afford the Beveridge Plan.'[61]

Here, then, was the New Jerusalemers' most effective argument in persuading themselves and public opinion that New Jerusalem was a perfectly reasonable proposition. The seductive analogy between what could be done in war and therefore what could be done in peace was well expressed by Lord Halifax as early as July 1940, in reporting to Duff Cooper, the Minister of Information, about a Whitehall discussion on war aims:

> We were all conscious as the talk proceeded of the contrast between the readiness of the Nation, and particularly the Treasury, to spend £9,000,000 a day in war to protect a certain way of life and the unwillingness of the administrative authorities in peace to put up, shall we say, £10,000,000 to assist in the reconditioning of Durham unless they could see the project earning a reasonable percentage.[62]

War liberated public opinion not only from the dismal pre-war sense of financial limits, but also from any sense of limits on material resources. In the words of a 'progressive' soldier to a reporter in autumn 1944:

> We've shown in this war that we British don't always muddle through; we've shown we can organise superbly – look at these

> invasions of the Continent which have gone like clockwork; look at the harbours we've built on the beaches. No excuse any more for unemployment and slums and underfeeding. Using even half the vision and energy and invention and pulling together as we've done in this war, what is there we cannot do? We've virtually exploded the arguments of old fogies and Better-Notters who said we can't afford this and mustn't do that.[63]

During the general election campaign of 1945 the *Daily Mirror* expressed much the same buoyant sense that all things were now possible:

> We have in this country three fundamental raw materials. The first is the skill of British hands and British brains. The second is the coal which enriches our earth. The third is the steel we make on which many other industries depend. Upon these factors rests our prosperity. Upon that prosperity depend all our dreams of the future. As these riches are present in abundance, what is it that prevents such use of them as will bring the prosperity we desire?[64]

The *Mirror* had its answer: the only impediments lay in 'private "rings"' and 'Tory policy'. On 14 June 1945 the same newspaper cheered its mass readership with a classic statement of the now widely accepted analogy between production for war and production for peace:

> Housing will have to be tackled like a problem of war. We can make, as if by a miracle, tanks, aircraft, battleships, pipelines, harbours! Are we, then, incapable of building houses? No. But to get those precious products of peace we must show the same energy, the same brain power, the same spirit by means of which we made the fearful engines of war.

The analogy supplied a leading theme in official Labour Party propaganda before and during the general election. Attlee in a speech at Nottingham in March 1945 had claimed that 'great undertakings such as the artificial harbours in Normandy were signal examples of how men working for the community had shown unexampled enterprise, boldness and inventiveness'.[65] During the election campaign itself Ernest Bevin asserted that Labour would build 4–5 million houses, and when challenged by a Conservative as to how long this would take with the scarce available labour force, he answered:

> I have urged over and over again that they should make up their total demands for housing whether I could supply the labour or not, then I would have a target to work to in order to fulfil the obligation in just the same way as I did in 1940–1 when I had to man the factories of this country for shell production.[66]

Yet belief that the achievements of British war production augured well for British prosperity in peacetime, indeed that war and victory had vindicated British technology, went far wider than the New Jerusalem movement. The right wing of opinion – politicians and company chairmen alike – believed it too. As *The Times* put it on 25 May 1945 in the concluding words of its leading article on 'Science at War', and with reference to the 'Pluto' pipeline and ICI's contributions to the war effort, 'The lessons for peacetime progress of this combination of scientific imagination, technical skill, and efficient workmanship are manifest.'

Unfortunately, however, the British people's self-congratulation over their industrial record in 1939–45 rested on two basic fallacies. In the first place, the impressive total figures of war production had only been possible because Lend–Lease and Sterling Area credit had relieved Britain of the need to earn her own way through exports. This had enabled her to concentrate a far higher proportion of her economy on the war than either Germany or America. But in peacetime she would no longer enjoy the advantage of continuing to exist on an American life-support machine, and instead would have to survive by herself. In fact, President Truman was abruptly to end Lend–Lease on 17 August 1945, so presenting Britain, according to the Treasury, with 'an economic Dunkirk' that left her 'virtually bankrupt and the economic basis for the hopes of the public non-existent' unless fresh financial aid from the US could be cadged.[67]

The second fallacy related to the British industrial and technological record itself. For the burdens of the New Jerusalem were not being wished on a first-class modern industrial system well able to bear the weight, but on one which even in the crisis of total war had manifested the classic symptoms of what was later to be dubbed the 'British disease'.

Part II

Reality – The Industrial Machine

Our only chance of national prosperity lies in the timely remodelling of our system, so as to put it as nearly as possible upon an equality with the improved management of the Americans.

(*Richard Cobden, 1835*)

We had a case recently where a 1,000 tons of coal was lost and the reason for the strike was that the men wanted the dismissal of the lady in charge of the canteen.

(*Gwilym Lloyd George, Minister of Fuel and Power, in the House of Commons, July 1944*)

Chapter Three

'The Prospect Is Bleak': 1943–45

In the spring of 1944, while southern England was filling with troops, vehicles and weapons for the coming Normandy invasion, Whitehall embarked on thorough investigations of Britain's future export prospects once Nazi Germany was down. The investigations continued throughout the year and on into the spring of 1945, a hidden counterpoint to the triumphant allied liberation of Europe and the publication of plans for New Jerusalem. The work was delegated by the Ministry of Reconstruction to an Official Sub-Committee on Industrial Problems and a Ministerial Sub-Committee on Industrial Problems (Export Questions), which derived their information partly from working parties on particular industries but largely from Board of Trade (BOT) memoranda based on exhaustive enquiries within industry. Together these sources constitute an anatomy of British industrial competitiveness on the eve of the postwar era. It was, by and large, the anatomy of a geriatric of nervous disposition. Industry's export hopes were, in the already cited words of the President of the Board of Trade, 'pretty bleak' unless British exports could simply float up on a global expansion of international trade without the need to fight ferocious competition for limited markets. As the opening paragraph of a 27-page report by the Board of Trade in June 1944 expressed it:

> One of our dangers, perhaps the main danger, is that this country will fail to see clearly and early enough the grave difficulties that lie ahead of British industry after the transition from war to peace. There is prevalent a hazily optimistic assumption that this country will secure a substantial increase of export trade: an average increase of 50% is being authoritatively mentioned. But for many industries the prospect of securing an expansion of exports is doubtful, unless there is an increase in their competitive power, together with an increased prosperity in overseas markets and a decrease in the barriers hampering international trade.[1]

On the assumption that British industry failed to improve its competitive efficiency, and that international trading conditions remained as in the 1930s, the Board of Trade reckoned from the 1937 figures of imports and exports of various goods that 'we cannot expect any appreciable long term improvement of the import/export position for at least two-thirds of British manufacturing industry, and there may be some worsening to offset the improvement from the remaining third.' Some British industries had been beaten on design and cost; others because of the growth of new industrial countries. In any case the pull of the home market, the report feared, might well damage postwar exports. The evidence from various industries received over the previous year showed that 'Few seem to be contemplating any considerable increase of production or export trade, and many are apprehensive about foreign competition.' This even applied to engineering, one of Britain's better hopes. In consumer goods the main concern of industries was to obtain government protection, while few firms intended to expand their production capacity, or to change their methods of production or their selling methods, or to develop new products.

Said the BOT report:

> If, without improved efficiency, the general prospects of our traditional industries are so dismal, are those of the new industries brighter? Can we rely on the newer industries started before the war or during the war (wireless, television, rayon, nylon and plastics) to redress the balance?

The Board of Trade thought not. Once we had been a leading exporter of rayon, but now our share of world production was 10 per cent, barely enough for the home market, while since 1930 Japan, starting from scratch, had developed in five years an export trade in rayon five times larger than Britain's. As for television, 'our development before the war was based on American patents; our export rights are doubtful' – so much for the British popular myth about the achievement of that hopeless amateur and crank, John Logie Baird. The report considered that while the British electric-cable industry was 'well organised' and 'powerful' and could hold its own, the wireless industry was a 'weak element', with a heavy pre-war predominance of imports over exports. Though Britain was strong in heavy engineering like turbines and boilers, she lagged behind, according to the BOT, in production methods and technical development in such fields as automatic and special machine tools, accounting machines and synthetic fibre plant. Except for linen, natural textiles like wool, cotton and silk were on their way down, if not out. In the case of nylon, America held the patents and was already ahead of Britain. Britain imported almost all her clocks and watches, much of her photographic film and most of her scientific instruments. The carpet trade was 'disappointing', and would 'tend to lose quality trade on design and the cheaper trade on efficiency'. The BOT doubted whether the hosiery industry, even if largely re-equipped, could equal the German industry which had supplied much of the pre-war British market, while the future for footwear appeared far from watertight owing to the 'superior design' and the 'low price' of the foreign competition. With regard to iron and steel, a basic industry, the

BOT thought that the prospect of 'any considerable increase of exports or decline of imports are not good'; and in a footnote it remarked that 'The morale of this industry seems unduly low.'

Perhaps even more defeatist is an annex to this report summarising the views of individual British industries across the board, from the motor industry to clothing and photographic equipment, on likely postwar foreign competition. Almost all pleaded for government protection; almost all feared American competition and a revival of German and Japanese competition; many referred glumly to the growth of new industries making their products in the Commonwealth; many even doubted their ability to hold on to their own home markets. Of the fifty-three industries canvassed, only two, cosmetics and sewage-disposal plant, expressed unqualified optimism. It might have been a survey of French Army units in May 1940.

Later reports were to modify this depressing picture, but rarely in an encouraging way. In July 1944 the Reconstruction Committee discussed two memoranda on postwar prospects for the shipbuilding industry, and agreed that the omens were good for the first eight to ten years but beyond that period more doubtful:

> Although the short-term prospects . . . were favourable, it was important that during the early period of great activity steps should be taken to improve the long-term efficiency of the industry. Both on the employers' and the workers' side the industry tended to be conservative. . . .[2]

On 2 September 1944, the day the British Second Army entered Belgium in its pursuit from Normandy and when the imminent collapse of Nazi Germany seemed possible, Hugh Dalton, the President of the Board of Trade, reported that the cotton industry, once the spearhead of Britain's leadership in the first industrial revolution, was now in a worse state than before the war, with 'obsolescent machinery and an out-of-date form of industrial organisation'. Between 60 and 70 per cent of the buildings had been put up before 1900, and much of the machinery was older still. What was worse, the industry and even Lancashire members of Parliament 'showed no appreciation of the need for reorganisation and re-equipment'. Yet cotton before the war had still been one of Britain's largest export trades, with exports of a value a third higher than those of machinery and two and a half times higher than chemicals.[3]

In March 1945 Dalton rendered a fresh survey of 'Export Targets', which began with the cheering news that prospects for heavy electrical goods were bright, the industry hoping to double its pre-war exports; so too were prospects for steam locomotives, railway carriages and wagons, and chemical products, where ICI hoped to push up exports by 75 per cent. Rayon now offered the best chance of all, with a looked-for increase in exports of seven to eight times over 1938.[4] The drawback was that these industries with good prospects had accounted for only about £35 million out of £365 million of manufactured exports in 1938, whereas the prospect for traditional major export industries like iron and steel, coal and cotton (£129 million of exports in 1938), wrote Dalton, 'is bleak, and will remain so until they are thoroughly modernised and re-organised'.[5] Other reports presented evidence that Britain was so far showing a lamentable want of energy and enterprise in what had already become fast-developing markets (and which were in fact literally to boom in the postwar era) such as office machines and agricultural machinery. A BOT memorandum on 5 April 1945 noted that adding, calculating and tabulating machines constituted the 'most important section' of the office-machinery market, and yet:

> Almost all machines in this group were imported, mainly from the United States, though there is some Swedish and German production. During the war we have been entirely dependent on United States manufacturers for accounting machine supplies, and mainly so for adding and calculating machines. We have been importing about 7,000 machines p.a. [*sic*] from the US, mostly on Lend–Lease. . . .[6]

British manufacture in this field consisted of only three primitive adding or calculating machines, one produced at the rate of fifteen to thirty a week, and another, according to the Board of Trade, 'produced in very small quantities and often criticised for mechanical defects'. British production of typewriters just about equalled imports. And even though most domestic refrigerators for the British market were assembled in the United Kingdom, the compressors were imported.

A report by the Ministry of Agriculture and Fisheries three weeks after VE-Day foreshadowed the triumphant conquest of the British and world markets for agricultural machinery by American and European manufacturers, for the British industry:

> now consisted mainly of a large number of small firms, producing a multiplicity of different types and makes of implements, and was not expected to be able to meet the post-war home and overseas demand. . . . Improved and increased production by existing British firms did not at present seem likely to be on an important scale. . . .[7]

An expert witness confirmed that, given the structure, history, experience and personalities of the agricultural machinery industry, there was no prospect that it 'would rise to the occasion'.[8]

Yet more dismaying than this, more dismaying perhaps than any other single industrial survey, was a devastating indictment of the British car industry rendered two months earlier by the Official Sub-Committee on Post-War Resettlement of the Motor Industry.[9] The report argued that 'export prospects are gravely affected by the division of the industry into *too many, often small-scale units, each producing too many models.*' Its overseas marketing and service operations before the war 'generally were poor, and compared disadvantageously with those of the Americans. The lack of standardisation of components presents a difficulty in this field.' In any case 80 per cent of British pre-war car exports had gone to the

Commonwealth 'under specially favourable conditions'; the industry had really grown up as a supplier of a protected and easy home market with small low-powered cars of a kind foreign markets did not want; and, despite the postwar potential of 'a large and increasing export trade' for larger cars mass-produced in only a few models (so securing economy in production costs), the evidence was that the manufacturers had no intention of so exploiting this potential. Rather, according to the report, it did not seem that 'they propose to treat the export market as more than an accessory to their assured home market.'[10]

The 1944–5 dissections of Britain's postwar industrial future thus entirely bore out Dalton's comment in June 1944 that the prospects 'look pretty bleak'. The contrast between the gruesome anatomy uncovered by these dissections and the radiant picture of Britain's wonderful wartime production effort and brilliant technological invention painted by the wireless and newspapers and in politicians' celebratory speeches (and remembered ever after in national myth) is thus astounding and even sinister: an industrial Dorian Gray.

The paradox can be explained. In the first place, the British war economy existed in an entirely artificial environment subject to none of the harsh stresses of a peacetime climate of competition. Thanks to Lend–Lease and Sterling Area credit, the struggle for export markets had been abandoned. Nor was there any internal competition in the British home market, for all production and distribution was subject to a comprehensive array of government controls, allocations and rationing. Lend–Lease supplies constituted the only penetration into Britain by foreign products. British firms producing war supplies under government contract were working on the basis of 'cost-plus': that is, their actual production costs with a fixed profit rate added; so there was no spur to efficiency or cost-cutting. Similarly, over-full employment, with employers poaching skilled labour from each other, together with wage levels linked to the cost of living, meant that there was little incentive to the workforce to step up productivity; certainly no direct goad to match foreign levels of productivity. In any case, the fundamental operating principles of the wartime economy lay in maximum output of combat-effective products rather than cost-effective production of goods that could sell on design and price in an overseas market against competition. For instance, because the Spitfire certainly equalled the Messerschmitt BF 109 in overall performance as a fighter aircraft, it does not follow that Vickers-Supermarine could have sold it successfully overseas in commercial competition with the Messerschmitt. On the contrary, since the Spitfire took two-thirds more man-hours to build than the Messerschmitt, it would have been priced out of the market (see below p. 147). And finally, the entire British war economy was sustained, its artificiality made possible, by American aid.

Britain in wartime therefore presents a curious contradiction: beyond the ring fence of the armed forces and the sea lay the mortal threat posed by Nazi Germany, while within that ring fence the British nation had never enjoyed greater certainty and security of jobs, contracts, welfare, even nourishment.

Yet there is a further explanation for the sharp contrast between the war-production record on which the British at the time and ever after congratulated themselves and the dreary prognosis reached by Whitehall in 1944–5 over future export prospects. It lies in the real nature of that record.

The bald fact of Germany's defeat and Britain's victory has served to obscure from British minds the truth that German industry performed better overall during the war than British industry. In the first place, whereas between 1939 and 1946 (indices for the actual war years are not available) total manufacturing output in Britain rose by 4.6 per cent[11] it rose in Germany between 1939 and 1944 by 32.6 per cent.[12] In the metal-working industries British output rose by 24 per cent in 1939–46, whereas German output rose by 203.4 per cent in 1939–44 – a ten-times-greater increase.[13] According to one postwar British estimate, increase in productivity per head in the German munitions industries as a whole was probably twice as great as in the British.[14]

However, it is not only the comparison of percentage increases in wartime production and productivity that tell in Germany's favour, but also absolute comparisons of total figures of equipment inventories, of production and of manning. In the machine-tool industry British peak production (excluding small tools) at 95,788 units in 1942 compares with Germany's peak in 1940 of 199,940: 47 per cent of German production for a country with 58 per cent of the German population.[15] In terms of units produced annually per employee Britain trailed behind at 1.4 to Germany's 1.73.[16] The British metal-working industries as a whole possessed a peak wartime inventory of 740,000 machine tools as against the German total of 2,150,000: an average of 5.7 men per tool compared with the German 2.2 per cent, or more than twice the German ratio; or, to turn it round the other way, an average of 0.18 machine tools per British worker compared with 0.45 tools per German worker: figures indicative either of over-manning or of under-investment or of both.[17]

Although aircraft production was and remained a particular source of British pride, the figures again award the prize to German industry, with an output per day per worker in structure weight of 1.93 lb in the peak month compared to Britain's 1.28 lb.[18] Germany also led in production of armoured fighting vehicles (tanks, self-propelled guns and assault-guns), with a peak total of 19,000 in 1944 as against the British annual peak of 8600; and German productivity at 1.28 tons per worker in the peak year was one and a half times British productivity at 0.84 tons.[19]

Both British and German war industry depended on coal as virtually their sole energy source, whether directly burned for steam generation on the railways or in boiler-houses, or in power-stations to produce electricity. And here the British record also compares discreditably with the German. Total British coal output dropped by 12 per cent between 1938 and 1944, while German output rose by 7.2 per cent.[20] Even though nearly a third of German coal miners had been drafted into the forces by 1944 and replaced by foreign workers with barely more than half their productivity,

German production per wage-earner per annum at 298.7 metric tons remained significantly more impressive than the 1944 British figure of 252.2 tons. In the Ruhr, and despite allied bombing, total production dropped by only 1.18 per cent from 1938–9 to 1943–4.[21]

Of all the industries where figures are available to make comparisons possible, it was only in net-ton-miles moved by rail and in production of motor vehicles (at peak annual total of 160,522 to Germany's 119,725) that British performance clearly outstripped German.[22]

Moreover, in weighing Britain's and Germany's overall wartime industrial records, it must always be borne in mind that Germany's was achieved in the face of a strategic bombing campaign many times more destructive than the Blitz of 1940 on Britain; and stands as a tribute to the professional resourcefulness and steadfastness of German industrial 'troops' in expanding production under a bombardment that burned the roofs off their homes and brought the factories down on top of the machines. Again, in making comparisons it has to be recalled that Germany fought her war from first to last out of her own national resources or the resources of countries her army could occupy: the German machine-tool industry equipped German factories; German factories designed and manufactured the Wehrmacht's excellent equipment; and the Wehrmacht never ran short of munitions until the very end of the war. Britain, however, critically depended on the United States, not only as a basic economic lifeline, but also for huge supplies of equipment both for factories and for the armed forces. In the words of a report to the War Cabinet by the Minister of Production, Oliver Lyttelton, in April 1943:

> The magnitude and importance of the aid we are getting from the United States cannot be sufficiently stressed. A rough calculation suggests that the aid we hope to get during this year from the United States alone is equivalent to over 1,500,000 British workers. We have, that is, working for us in the United States the equivalent of another entire Ministry of Supply or Ministry of Aircraft Production.[23]

Nevertheless, historians have favourably compared the British war economy to the German in terms of overall planning and organisation. They have noted that German war production was a chaos of conflicting authorities, abruptly altered programmes and endlessly changed specifications, while in Britain the formulation of production targets, the harmonising of one production programme and another, and the establishment of priorities in allotting plant capacity, tools and labour were carried out with remarkable success.[24] There is a parallel here with the contrasting patterns of the military performance on both sides. The German higher direction of the war was a shambles of competing military authorities and fatally mistaken major strategic decisions, while the British and their allies successfully forged a sound joint strategy, making no calamitous key decisions. On the other hand, the actual German Army in the field was superior in professionalism and sheer *per capita* fighting effectiveness to all its opponents in the Second World War,[25] whereas allied armies in the field were too often clumsy and even lacklustre, winning their battles only by superior numbers. Yet all the fighting skills of the German soldier could not redeem Hitler's colossal strategic mistakes. It might be said that Germany possessed a military machine superbly engineered except in the steering mechanism, which was fatally defective, while the allies by good steering kept their inferior machine from running into the ditch, and so won the race.

And a similar contrast between the machine and the steering is also true of German and British war production. Here too the German strength lay in the 'field' itself, in industry where highly trained and motivated engineers, managers and workforces performed no less admirably than their army comrades in striving to redeem the fatal blunderings of Nazi leadership. In the case of British war production, however, it was in the 'field', beyond direct reach of bureaucratic planning and intervention, in the very factories and plants, that British performance proved inferior. Thus German shortcomings in production derived essentially from the nature of the Nazi regime and ceased with its demise; British shortcomings belonged to Britain's industrial system itself. As with an inferior army, the roots of those failings must be looked for in the age and design of equipment; in the organisation; in the command and control systems; in the standard of education and training at every level of rank; in the operational doctrine, indeed the underlying professional philosophy; and, related to all these factors but more important than any of them, in the quality of the leaders and led, and in the relations between them.

Chapter Four

An Industrial Worst Case: Coal

Field Marshal Lord Alanbrooke recorded after the war his impression of a visit in November 1939 to the French Ninth Army, commanded by General Corap, which was to collapse in instant rout six months later under the first German onslaught. Although the Ninth Army's artillery and much other equipment dated from the Great War, it was not so much this that remained so vivid a memory for Alanbrooke as the spectacle of Corap's guard of honour:

> I can still see those troops now. Seldom have I seen anything more slovenly and badly turned out. Men unshaven, horses ungroomed, clothes and saddlery that did not fit, vehicles dirty, and complete lack of pride in themselves or their units. What shook me most, however, was the look on the men's faces, disgruntled and insubordinate looks, and although ordered to give 'eyes left' hardly a man bothered to do so.[1]

The kind of leadership that had conduced to this spectacle was revealed when General Corap then took his visitor off for a colossal and extended lunch rather than on an inspection of anti-tank ditches.

Since industrial workforces are not similarly paraded for inspection by visiting top management, no eye-witness accounts of quite such pungency exist about British wartime heavy industry. Nevertheless, there are descriptions of material and moral dilapidation that certainly bear comparison, and especially with regard to coal mining:

> It is an unfortunate fact that the appearance of many colliery yards and offices often make an impression of dirt and disorder which must have contributed materially to the critical attitude of the general public towards the coal industry. The outside observer may be pardoned for drawing exaggerated conclusions as to the conditions within the mine, when there is often so much disorder and delapidation on the surface. Not only this: the appearance of the colliery premises can hardly fail to affect the psychology of all employed at the mine, and there can be no hope of creating among the workmen a pride in their place of employment unless

> managements make a serious attempt to create something of which to be proud.

Thus wrote the Technical Advisory Committee on Coal Mining chaired by Charles Reid, director of production at the Ministry of Fuel and Power, in the course of its thoroughgoing report in 1945.[2] As for a parallel to the 'disgruntled and insubordinate looks' which General Brooke (as he then was) had noted in Corap's soldiers, a visiting mission of American technical experts to British coal fields in 1944 felt compelled to point out that:

> the center of the problem [not enough production; not enough productivity] is the bad feeling and antagonism which pervade the industry and which manifests itself in low morale, non-cooperation and indifference. In almost every district we visited, miners' leaders and mine owners complained of men leaving the mines early, failure to clear the faces and voluntary absenteeism. . . .[3]

It is little wonder that the War Cabinet decided not to publish this American report, and to justify this decision to the House of Commons on the ground that the report was a secret document, whereas the true reason for not publishing lay in their fear that it would arouse anti-American feeling over American 'interference'.[4]

Just as Corap's troops, although a worst case, reflected shortcomings common to a greater or lesser extent to much of the French Army, so too did coal mining, Britain's worst industrial case, with regard to much of British heavy industry. Moreover, the deficiencies of the French Army and of British heavy industry alike sprang from a similar absurd coupling of complacency and incompetence, a similar predominance of tradition, habit and inertia; a similar underlying failure to adapt to major changes in the operating environment – the classic Darwinian recipe for ultimate extinction.

In the first months of 1942, while Malaya, Singapore, Java, Burma and the Philippines were falling to the Japanese and while Rommel was successfully counterattacking in the Western Desert, a sharpening energy crisis added itself to the anxieties of the British War Cabinet. For British war production was almost entirely based on coal-derived energy; and deep-mined coal output had dropped from 231,337,800 tons in 1939 to 224,298,000 in 1940 and 206,344,300 in 1941. By the second quarter of 1942 weekly production had fallen from the 1939 average of 4,647,000 tons to 4,023,000.[5] Although part of these falls could be attributed to a drop in the labour force from 773,083 in January–March 1939 to 706,722 in January–March 1942, the output per man employed had also fallen. By January–March 1942 it stood at only 90 per cent of the peak reached in April–June 1940.[6] At the same time the demand for coal, especially from the electricity-generation industry, had been rising as the war economy expanded. On 6 April 1942 the Lord President of the Council, Sir John Anderson, submitted a memorandum to the Cabinet pointing out that whereas to meet demands in the 1942–3 winter period a weekly production of 4,350,000 tons from now on through the summer was needed, actual production stood at only 4,100,000 tons, with a probable rise to no more than 4,150,000 in the summer. As a consequence there was likely to be a shortfall of some 10 million tons in the year ending 30 April 1943. The Lord President therefore invited the Cabinet to tackle the problem.[7] This marked the opening of the coal crisis that was to endure, with remissions and relapses, until the end of the German war – and after. Four days later the Cabinet, with the Lord President's paper before them, authorised the Minister of Labour to try to get 3000 miners back from the armed forces; it also set up a committee to work out 'detailed proposals for securing such practical control over the working of the mines as is necessary to increase the war-time efficiency of the industry and to put it in a position, at the end of hostilities, to compete for an early recovery of our export markets'.[8]

The new Committee on the Coal Mining Industry met under the Lord President on 20 April, took evidence from mine-owners, miners' leaders and technical experts for a month, and submitted its report on 28 May 1942, two days after Rommel had launched the offensive against the Eighth Army at Gazala that was to take him to Alamein. The technical evidence submitted to the committee was dispiriting enough. Whereas 63 per cent of output was mechanically cut and 61 per cent mechanically conveyed,[9] the coal thus cut was loaded on to the conveyers by men with shovels. A report by a mining engineer, T. E. B. Young, on the North Derbyshire and Nottinghamshire coal field therefore not only called for more mechanical cutters and conveyors but also recommended that 'the greatest possible use should be made of mechanical coal loading contrivances. Apparatus of this type is, as yet, in its infancy in this country but it is of the utmost urgency that no time should be lost in constructing a large number.'[10] Yet the same expert noted how the industry feared to adopt intensified methods of output, such as replacing trucks pulled by rope or pony with mechanical conveyers, in case older workers moved away to other collieries where the old and familiar systems were still in operation.[11] In any event, he pointed out, the quality of management direction and technical expertise were often poor: 'It is well known that for some years it has been found difficult to attract to the Industry a sufficient number of well educated young men likely to develop into first-class Mining Engineers.'[12]

As for the workforce, absenteeism, 'particularly among Coalface workers', was responsible, according to this witness, 'for a greater loss of output than any other single factor', amounting to 1½ million tons per annum in the North Derbyshire and Nottinghamshire coal field.[13] Percentage of shifts lost in one colliery through sickness had risen from 4.8 per cent in 1938 to 12.4 per cent in 1942, while with regard to accidents, 'It is well-known to Colliery Managers and Officials that there is a tendency among certain men to take a few days' rest on account of having sustained a very minor accident.'[14] However, another and more charitable expert witness, Dr H. S. Houldsworth, the Fuel and Power Controller for the

North-East Region, reckoned that much of the absenteeism was due to 'the poor physique of some of the older men'.[15]

More dismaying in terms of possible production benefits from re-equipment and redeployment was the evidence given to the committee about ingrained technical conservatism and entrenched local loyalties in the coal industry. The South Wales production technical adviser, for instance, noting how difficult older managers and men found it to adapt to mechanisation, counselled against forcing the pace of change, rather as if he might have been referrring to a pre-war cavalry regiment faced with the horror of re-equipment with tanks. The mine-owners' representatives remarked on the miners' wish to work in a colliery of their own choice, which cast doubt on the possibility of gains in productivity by shifting labour to the best seams or by closing pits.[16] The unions' representatives, for their part, pointed out the unwillingness of the miners to increase their effort or move to other pits if this 'resulted in an increase in owners' profits'.[17] The committee's own draft report to the Cabinet drew attention to a 'deep-seated reluctance on both sides of the industry to surrender any part of the independence of the individual districts', and also adverted to the need to go cautiously.[18]

However, as the evidence given to the Coal Mining Industry Committee indicated, the industry's shortcomings were not so much superficial or short-term as rooted deep in its very nature, human and technological. In the first place, its very anatomy told against efficiency, for it consisted of 1700 mines, of which 466 employed fewer than 20 men, so accounting for only 4059 persons out of the industry's total manpower of over 700,000. The ragged tail of 46 per cent of the total number of mines employed less than 3 per cent of the workers and produced only 2 per cent of the total output, whereas large-scale mines, 13 per cent of the total, employed 51 per cent of the workforce and produced 53 per cent of the output. Here was at once an astonishing contrast and a witness to the survival of primitive industrial forms in Britain.[19] The ownership of the industry evinced similar contrasts, for while in 1938 there had been as many as 950 separate colliery companies, 77 per cent of the output had been produced by just 129 undertakings and the final 10 per cent by 639 undertakings.[20]

There were no less striking discrepancies in productivity. In mines of fewer than 1000 workers, average production stood at 244 tons annually per man employed; in those of more than 1000 workers, at 296 tons. In much bigger mines productivity fell away again, to 290 tons per man per annum in mines of over 3000 employees.[21] But it was between the different coal-mining regions of the country that the most glaring contrasts of productivity were evident. For example, that of the Leicestershire coal field was two and a half times higher than that of Cumberland.[22] While the national average annual production per man employed was 275 tons, the South Wales regional district produced 220 tons, Lancashire and Cheshire 225, Durham 243 – as against North Derbyshire's 360 tons and Nottinghamshire's 373.[23] Output per man shift similarly varied, from 0.84 tons in South Wales and Monmouth, 0.85 tons in Lancashire and Cheshire, and 0.90 tons in Durham, to 1.48 tons in Nottinghamshire, 1.50 in South Derbyshire and 1.68 in Leicestershire.[24]

Unfortunately three-fifths of Britain's total output still came from low-productivity regions, and only two-fifths from the highly productive 'Midlands Amalgamated District' comprising Yorkshire, Nottinghamshire, Derbyshire and Leicestershire. It was this adverse balance that had pulled average British production per manshift in 1938 down to 1.17 tons, as against the Ruhr's figure of 1.55 tons.[25] The variations in productivity (partly caused by geological conditions) were reflected in operating costs, even though low-productivity areas paid lower wage rates. At the extremes, for example, Cumberland coal cost (1943 figures) 42*s* 6*d* per ton to produce as against Leicestershire's 20*s* 2*d*.[26] While such high costs might not matter in wartime, when maximum national production was what counted, they held grim long-term commercial implications.

The quality of management and the motivation of the workforce also presented deep-seated problems not readily solved by emergency measures in the middle of a world war. The shortage of able colliery managers and adequately trained engineers derived from a longstanding failure on the part of the industry to appreciate the need for such talent, and the complementary failure of the British education and training system to produce it. In 1927 – and little had changed since – there had been places for 200 students in mining engineering in Great Britain as against three times that number in Germany, and whereas the German courses were concentrated into four mining colleges, the smaller British provision was fragmented between fourteen institutions.[27] Similarly there was virtually no formal training of the new rank-and-file entrants into the mining workforce in Britain, whereas all entrants in Germany, including junior officials, received two years' part-time training in a training centre. In the judgement of the 1945 Technical Advisory Committee on Coal Mining, there was no doubt that this German training given to boys and junior officials 'has contributed to high efficiency and output'.[28]

Related to the scarcity of well-trained and high-quality management was the appalling industrial relations in the British coal industry. In spring 1942 the Lord President's committee on the industry faced what a Board of Trade memorandum to the committee described as 'the recent ugly turn in the coalfields and sudden flare-up of impatience and resentment'[29] – an ugly turn which was to raise the number of days lost through strikes in this turning-point year of the war to 833,000 compared with 500,000 in 1940.[30] The immediate cause of a stoppage might be some local grievance, as when in April 1942 the closing of a coal seam and the paying-off of twenty-seven men threatened to close the entire 8000-man-strong North Wales coalfield;[31] or it might be nationwide anger over wage rates and bonuses, especially when compared with those in other industries.[32] But ferocious industrial struggle was a long tradition of the industry. Between 1929 and 1938 an average of 2 million working days had been lost through strikes every year. With only 6 per cent of the insured working population of the country, coal had accounted for 64 per cent of the total number of disputes and 52 per cent of the total days lost by all industry in the four years before the war.[33] As Harold Wilson (now Lord Wilson of Rievaulx) remarks in his 1945 book *New Deal for Coal*, 'What statistics cannot record, however, is the persistent guerilla warfare which continues in the majority of pits between management and men.'[34]

This human bitterness and the technical and organisational weaknesses alike traced their origins deep down into the dark history of British coal mining from the start of the first industrial revolution. For the industry began as a late Georgian 'coal rush', in which profit-hungry and individualistic entrepreneurs sought to plunder local mineral rights as fast and as cheaply as possible in order to feed the roaring consumption of the steam engine, the furnace and the crucible.[35] In the absence of foreign competition during this period of British industrial pioneering, and with men, women and children (thrown off the land because of the concurrent agrarian revolution) desperate for work and bread, there was no need for sophisticated technical or managerial expertise, or for careful regard for good industrial relations; only a native aptitude for ruthless short-term exploitation of mineral and human resources. As Charles Reid's Technical Advisory Committee expressed it in 1945, the early employers and engineers were 'hard-working, adventurous and self-reliant', but their capital resources were 'often limited, and as soon as a mine was sunk, the cry was for output. Whatever planning was done was on a short-term basis,' and such an approach had left a legacy a hundred and more years later of 'mines not easy to reconstruct to fit the requirements of today. . . '[36]. The Reid Committee might have added that the early history of the industry had also bequeathed mentalities no more easy to reconstruct.

The fundamental problem with British coal mining was that it failed to evolve beyond the patterns set in this primitive stage of industrialisation before 1850. Coal provides a classic case-study of the survival in Britain of the 'practical man' whose horizon was bounded by the short-term gain; who learned on the job, whether in the boardroom or the manager's office, on the shop-floor or down the mine, by picking things up for himself or acquiring rules-of-thumb from his elders; worse perhaps, who learned from his elders traditional attitudes about how to deal with 'the men' or how to fight 'the Boss'. While other countries in the nineteenth century were evolving new coal industries sophisticated in technology, management, investment planning and marketing, there fossilised in Britain therefore the Klondike character of the original Georgian coal rush. In the expert diagnosis of the Reid Committee:

> The individualism of a large number of self-contained units was unlikely to encourage major developments in the science of mining. Managers were not sufficiently encouraged to widen their experience by visits to other countries, for example, and fresh ideas and different techniques spread but slowly. It was considered sufficient to keep ahead of your neighbours. . . . The numerous small undertakings did not employ a technical staff outside those engaged on day-to-day supervision of mining operations. . . . Concentration

> upon traditional practices, without analysis of the conditions which gave rise to them, was not conducive to the development of new techniques.[37]

The Victorian miner too shared this profound technical conservatism, so shackling the efforts of such innovating managements as existed, for he lived in isolated communities where he learned 'all the traditions and customs handed down from one generation to another'.[38] These, together with the nagging fear of unemployment:

> all combined to lead him to regard the introduction of machinery with misgivings, and sometimes with open hostility. He preferred to preserve his traditional methods of work and the customs with which he had grown up, unsuitable though they sometimes were, to the changing circumstances of the time. . . .[39]

Hence only a slow evolution of techniques and methods took place in British coal before the Great War.[40] But why should the colliery companies worry? As industrialisation spread rapidly through the entire Western world, the demand for coal rose insatiably, and British production and profits with it. Output soared from 170 million tons in 1888 to 287 million in 1913; employment more than doubled from 439,000 to 910,000; profits nearly trebled from about £11 million in 1890 to £28 million in 1913.[41] By 1913 Great Britain was producing half Europe's coal and a fifth of the world's; she was the world's leading exporter, at over 34 per cent of her total production.[42] If such prodigious success could be won by pick and shovel and brawn, managed by the 'practical man', why invest in costly new mechanical systems and proceed to expensive and uncomfortable reorganisations of pit layouts and methods? Here was the conundrum common to many British industries in the course of their transitions from market leadership to backwardness and decay: so long as order-books are full and profits good, there seems no good reason to innovate or invest; once demand has begun to decline and profits to fall, there is lacking both the available capital and the early prospective return, so that again it makes sense not to innovate and invest. In the case of coal before 1914, the United States had already emerged as the world's greatest producer, while British productivity in the almost complete absence of mechanisation had fallen from 403 tons per miner per annum in 1881 to 309 tons in 1911[43] – portents unheeded amidst the then current easy prosperity.

But if by 1914 owners and management had congealed in the mentality of the 1840s, so too had the workforce. A hundred years of ruthless exploitation, beginning in the camp villages of the new coal fields where half-naked women supplied the underground haulage power and children operated the safety trap-doors in the shafts, had gone to create the twentieth-century British mining community as a self-contained tribe apart from the rest of society, alienated in the classic Marxist sense, looking upon the owners and managers of their collieries as opponents in an inveterate and never ceasing combat, and themselves as heirs to their forefathers' sufferings and struggles; more than heirs, redeemers. An observer of life in a pit village at the end of the Second World War wrote:

> More than most men, too, the miners had a sense of the past. Their fathers and grandfathers had been miners, and had talked to them of their craft . . . and out of the long evenings of pit talk reaching back through generations had developed something like a tribal memory.[44]

The inwardness sprang from the physical isolation of the pit villages, gaunt rows of coal-stained cottages stranded in the midst of bleak uplands; it sprang too from a communal self-sufficiency:

> Nothing had come easily to this village. When it felt a need, it had tried to supply it for itself, and if anyone opposed the effort the village had fought. Every institution in the village, with the exception of the cinema, the post office and the church, the people had built for themselves or struggled for through the union. . . . Personal ambition was tamed to the Lodge office, the committee table, the pulpit and the craft of the pit. The customs of the community, both underground and on the surface, were old and honoured for their age; the double isolation of craft and geography had turned these people in upon themselves, so that they took their standards from their forbears instead of from the strangers in the city.[45]

Just as regiments of the British Army cherished their special traditions by parading their colours emblazoned with past battle honours, so for the miners their history lived again when they marched behind their bands and embroidered banners on such ceremonial occasions as the Durham Miners' Gala. As a miner-turned-novelist expressed it, 'the banner which was so beautiful, represented something very solid and substantial indeed' – the achievement that 'with the poorest of materials, in the poorest of circumstances, fighting a battle underground and fighting a battle against bad housing and bad sanitation on the surface and poor wages, people banded together and built in their villages little communities with quite something to live for.'[46]

Here was indeed communal effort and enterprise, but in no way enlisted in the cause of the higher productivity and progressive modernisation of the coal industry, or, as the miner himself would have put it, in the cause of higher profits for the owners. Rather these qualities lent their strength instead to the mining communities' mentality of self-contained tribe, or perhaps of waggon-circle against a hostile world; lent their strength to the negative fight against the employer, against technical change. Thus in 1914, when the British coal industry stood at the very peak of its world success, nearly 4 million man-days were lost because of labour disputes; even in 1915, with the country waging a total war, it was 1½ million, well over half the total for all industries.[47]

With such a workforce, with such management, with such an industrial structure and philosophy, this was an industry fit only to ride with little competitive effort on the crest of fast-swelling demand. Thanks to the Great War that demand continued to swell until 1920–1, then dropped during the immediate postwar slump in 1921–2, misleadingly swelled up again massively in 1923–4 when the Ruhr mines were st· pped by French military occupation and American mines by a strike, and finally shrank away in 1925. British coal exports fell from 113 million tons in 1923 to only 71 million in 1925.[48] However, British coal had not simply been left in the seam by an ineluctable fall of world demand. By 1929 world coal exports had actually recovered to a slightly higher figure than in 1913 – but the British share had fallen from 55 per cent in 1913 to 44 per cent.[49] Like an army rendered smug and unchanging by previous victory, the British coal industry, with its largely pick-and-shovel technology and its penny-packets structure and its 'practical man' leadership, had been routed by rivals reorganised and mechanised on a massive scale.

In the face of this sudden commercial disaster, the pre-1914 feckless shortsightedness gave way in 1925–39 to an obstinate reluctance to recognise that the industry's difficulties arose from its own backwardness; to a profound psychological distaste, historically understandable, on the part of the management and workforce alike for embarking on a thoroughgoing technological and organisational revolution. Change in British coal therefore came slowly; it came piecemeal. Between 1929 and 1938 the percentage of coal cut mechanically rose from 28 per cent to 59 per cent, and even by 1941 had only reached 63 per cent; a lower figure than the Ruhr's in 1927, and a third lower than the figure of 97 per cent achieved by the Ruhr in 1938.[50] The percentage of coal mechanically conveyed climbed from 17 per cent in 1929 to 54 per cent in 1938.[51] Yet increases in actual productivity were not even commensurate with these modest advances in mechanisation: output per manshift underground in Britain was no more than 30 per cent higher in 1939 than in 1927, as against an 86 per cent rise in the Ruhr.[52] In terms of absolute comparisons, the Ruhr coal fields in 1938 were a third more efficient than British, Upper Silesia 59 per cent more, the Netherlands 41 per cent more, and Poland 59 per cent,[53] while between 1933 and 1938 the British share in world exports of coal dropped from 46 per cent to only 37 per cent.[54]

The coal industry faced the onslaught of up-to-date foreign technology not merely with the methods of yesterday, but with the mentality of yesterday as well. How could men with attitudes and concepts appropriate to 1825 diagnose what needed to be done in 1925, and do it? Much more comfortable to see the foreign competition as temporary or 'unfair', or to believe that lower wages were the sole answer, or to take refuge in self-congratulating bluster. Thus a spokesman for the Council of the Institution of Mining Engineers told the Samuel Royal Commission on the Coal Industry of 1925 that his council resented public criticisms of an 'insufficiency of technical skill and scientific knowledge':

> The Council claim that the history of the British coal-mining industry shows that whatever defects are present in it, it is on the whole carried on by men who, whether they are manual workers, or

> engaged in the duties of supervision, management or financial control, are very strongly inspired by the ideals of good and loyal citizenship which have made the British Empire what it is.[55]

However, twenty years later the Reid Report, analysing the reasons for the sluggish pace of pre-war modernisation, contrasts the European coal industries' 'collective examination of their problems, and a scientific and analytical assessment of future prospects' to the British persistence of 'the long individualistic tradition', which had led to 'strong opposition to the principle of amalgamation' of colliery companies and operations into large-scale units.[56] British employers between the world wars, wrote the Reid Committee, did not seem to have sufficiently appreciated the need for technical reorganisation. 'There was a tendency to assume that the successes of competing countries would be temporary, and were essentially due to unfair subsidisation,' and hence to ignore the high productivity in Europe. And whereas European mining engineers had designed new developments on the grand scale, in Great Britain 'far too few mining engineers saw the technical problems in a true light, or realised the extent to which accepted systems of mining and traditional practices required to be altered.' The Reid Report attributed this myopia to 'insularity of outlook' and to a poor quality of engineering talent in the industry.[57]

A further drag on the pace of change lay in the miner himself, like his employer a man of the 1820s rather than the 1920s. After his climactic strike and crushing defeat in 1926 he was, as the Reid Report put it in Jeeves-like language, 'generally in no mood for willing co-operation with the employers'.[58] But the miner's tenacious resistance to innovation went deeper than the 1926 defeat, deeper into the tribal memory, the fierce spirit of the pit village *contra mundum*. Said the Reid Report:

> They mostly refused to recognise that their wages, in the long run, must depend upon the progressive efficiency of the Industry. Mechanisation, though seldom encountering active resistance, was not generally received by the men with enthusiasm, no doubt in the fear that more machines meant fewer men at a time when unemployment was widespread; and, where machinery was installed, the potential savings seem largely to have been dissipated by a quiet but effective determination that the number of men discharged should be kept as low as possible. . . . In addition to this, they have steadfastly required the observance of old customs and traditions which are inappropriate to the conditions of mechanical mining, and thus have put a brake upon the modernisation of the industry.[59]

The effects of such luddism were exacerbated by the poor technical training in the British coal industry caused by a failure on the part of managements of 'practical men' to perceive that new machines and methods demanded systematic training rather than the traditional acquisition of rules-of-thumb on the job. In the opinion of the Reid Committee, the thorough German training in the principles of mining and in the working of all equipment (by practice in dismantling and reassembling it) 'ensures better workmanship and greater freedom from breakdown of machinery'.[60]

British coal mining between the world wars therefore had not within it the attributes that make for rapid evolution; indeed quite the contrary. As a consequence, successive governments had to ponder what could be done to hasten the evolutionary process. For the Labour Party the answer was simple, engraved on tablets of coal in the 1918 party programme: full nationalisation. Unfortunately the party, forming only two brief minority governments in the period, could not carry out this programme. To Lloyd George's coalition government of Conservatives and Liberals, and to later Conservative or Conservative-dominated national governments, the problem was ideological as well as practical. For while Liberals and Conservatives believed in the free market and 'private enterprise', they were presented in the coal industry with private ownership which had more and more evidently run out of enterprise. Since their free-market ideology ruled out direct state intervention in peacetime, they were left like a farmer with a sick horse, bewilderedly offering a tonic to the front end and a tentative prod or two to the back end, while waiting for a vet who never came.

The process of quarter-hearted tinkering began in 1919 with the appointment of a Royal Commission under Lord Sankey to consider the future peacetime organisation of the then state-controlled industry. Even the coal owners accepted the principle of nationalisation of mineral rights, the territorial limits of the private ownership of which bore no relation to geology or the technical logic of pit operation. But they argued that nationalisation of the mines themselves 'would be detrimental to the development of the industry and to the economic life of the country'.[61] The miners' representatives naturally called for full nationalisation, as did the chairman's own report. A further proposal, by Sir Arthur Duckham, the engineer and industrialist who had been director-general of aircraft production during the Great War, offered a compromise solution resembling those adopted by European coal industries, whereby the industry would be kept in private hands but compulsorily reorganised, so that the over 2000 colliery companies of every shape and size would be amalgamated into district groupings that made technological and operational sense. It was Duckham's view, based on the experience of state control since 1916, that 'it had not been shown that there [was] an increased output per worker or less industrial strife when undertakings [were] controlled by the state': a diagnosis that post-1946 experience was fully to confirm.[62] But in any event, the Sankey Report duly joined other Royal Commission diagnoses of Britain's industrial shortcomings back to the 1860s on dusty shelves, and the coalition government merely passed a Coal Mines (Emergency) Act in 1920, which limited and guaranteed the industry's profits, and a Mining Industry Act which wholly failed to tackle the question of amalgamations.

In 1925, the year when the demand for British coal finally subsided after a century of growth, Baldwin's Conservative government appointed a fresh Royal Commission under Sir Herbert Samuel. Its report in 1926 contained such encouraging facts as that 73 per cent of British coal was now being produced at a loss; and it called for a reduction of such costs by closing inefficient pits. It also pleaded for greater co-operation between miners and mine-owners, coupling this hope with a recommendation that the industry could not commercially bear the present minimum wage established in 1924. The Samuel Commission Report in its concluding passages was less than a technical and managerial recommendation for the reconstruction of an ailing business than a New Jerusalem sermon before its time:

> we would express our firm conviction, that if the present difficulties be wisely handled, if the grievances of the one side and of the other be remedied, and a better spirit prevail in consequence between them, the mining industry, with the aid of science, will certainly recover, and even surpass its former prosperity. It will again become a source of great economic strength to the nation.[63]

The mine-owners for their part, ignorant of the fact that lower foreign coal prices stemmed from technological superiority, believed that the only cost which mattered was wages, which they now proceeded to cut, so provoking the ten-months-long coal strike of 1926. This, ending as it did in the total and embittering defeat of the miners, rather dampened the Samuel Commission's hope of a 'better spirit' in the industry.

The 1926 Mining Industry Act, passed by Baldwin's Conservative government, shied from such a breach of fundamental Victorian private-enterprise principles as a programme of compulsory amalgamations. Instead it left it to the industry to propose its own amalgamations, the only tooth in the Act being that in the last resort an unwilling owner could be overruled by the Railway and Canal Commission. Not surprisingly the Act made little impact, with only one major amalgamation taking place in 1928 and thirteen smaller ones, covering no more than 191 pits in all.[64] In 1930 the minority Labour government's Coal Mines Act also shrank from compulsory reorganisation, let alone nationalisation. Instead it set up a Coal Mines Reorganisation Commission to promote amalgamations, such 'promotion' being thereafter tenaciously thwarted by owners fiercely jealous of the independence of their own individual businesses. Between 1926 and 1938 only ninety voluntary amalgamations went through, affecting about one-tenth of the original number of colliery companies.[65]

The 1930 Act also set up bureaucratic machinery for regulating output and prices, which the owners liked much better because it gave every company and every region and every type of coal an artificially maintained share of the market.[66] But in this way the Act began to shift the industry towards the worst of all possible worlds – no longer the ruthless free-market competition that could have eventually killed off the high-cost and inefficient, not a forcible state programme of reconstruction either, but, instead, assured survival for all; the unexacting atmosphere of an industrial home for the elderly. For with a world slump now coming on top of the purely national slump that had beset Britain's great traditional heavy industries since 1921, broader social (not to say political) considerations were becoming as important a fact as outdated equipment and attitudes in impeding the coal industry's belated adaptation to the modern world. Sweeping closures of technologically backward or geologically difficult high-cost pits would fall most heavily on regions either solely dependent on coal for employment or already devastated by the collapse of other industries – Durham, Cumberland, South Wales, Scotland. In any case, average unemployment in the mining industry itself stood at about 25 per cent between 1927 and 1939.[67] Governments naturally became more concerned to preserve the current pattern of production and hence jobs than to press for a radical redeployment of the industry in favour of high-efficiency, low-cost districts. Henceforward and for the next fifty years such social and political considerations were to confront the economic and technological realities, and serve as a potent brake on change.

In 1938 Chamberlain's national government limply chipped away a little more at the problem. Its Coal Act set up a Coal Commission with increased (but well short of effective) powers to promote amalgamations, while compulsion by the Board of Trade was to provide an ultimate, very ultimate, sanction. Although the owners objected even to this legislation as introducing 'bureaucratic compulsion', in the event little had come of it by the outbreak of the Second World War. Nevertheless the 1938 Coal Act at least nationalised mineral rights – nearly twenty years after the Sankey Commission had first recommended it.

There lay a further, if so far only potential, threat to the national prosperity in this interwar failure to evolve a modern coal industry. Because of insufficient mechanisation, 70 per cent of British production costs took the form of wages. As a consequence, it had been possible to hold down production costs, and hence the market price of British coal, by paying low wages. If the miner should ever be able to win much better wages the whole British economy would then inevitably incur the competitive handicap of dependence on high-cost energy.[68] It only required the special conditions of the Second World War to bring this about.

The wartime coal problem began to emerge in the spring of 1941. The German conquest of France in June 1940 had deprived the British coal industry of 70–80 per cent of its export market, leading to idle pits and a drift of over one-tenth of the workforce into the armed forces or into other industries. When British war production began to gather high momentum towards the end of 1940 and the beginning of 1941 and the demand for coal rose sharply, this loss of manpower became critical; it was to remain so throughout the war. In a first attempt at remedying it, the War Cabinet issued an Essential Work Order in May 1941 laying down that no miner could leave the industry or be dismissed without state permission through a national service officer. The Order guaranteed the miner a weekly wage for regular attendance whether or not there was work for him to do, and placed the responsibility for disciplining persistent absentees in the hands of the local national service officer, who was to consult first with the local pit or district production committee.

In terms of long-term impact on the industry's ability to change into a high-technology, low-cost operation, this 1941 Essential Work Order marks a decisive step in the wrong direction. Fear of the sack, the one effective tool of discipline and personal productivity in an industry with an alienated workforce and poor leadership, was removed. Instead discipline now came to depend ineffectively on a slow and clumsy state procedure. Moreover the new national guaranteed wage – which the miners anyway thought too low – blurred the connection between varying production efficiency and wage levels in different coal fields. Yet the Order only reflected the decisive turn-about from a pre-war glut of coal and miners to a dearth of both. Henceforward it was to be the miner and not the employer who held the bargaining leverage.

Because of the generations-deep mutual antipathy between management and men, hopeful attempts in 1941 at securing their co-operation through joint pit production committees under a national Coal Production Council foundered dismally. Efforts to increase manpower proved little more successful. Only 16,000 miners could be recalled from the armed forces or recruited by October 1941.[69] By the October–December quarter productivity per man employed had dropped by 7 per cent compared with April–June 1940.[70] Yet this national average disguises a widening of the already vast disparities between high-productivity and low-productivity areas. Whereas the low-productivity districts of South Wales, Durham and Scotland had accounted for 42.73 per cent of national output in 1938, they accounted for only 38.46 per cent in January–June 1942.[71] In terms of the long-term commercial adaptation of the industry this marked an entirely healthy trend in favour of efficient fields worth future investment and development. But in the spring of 1942 the War Cabinet was facing a desperate short-term energy crisis in the middle of a total war: immediate maximum national production was what concerned it, not the distant past or the distant future; and these were the problems which it set up the Lord President's Committee on the Coal Mining Industry in April 1942 to solve.

The committee's expert witnesses saw the human factor in falling productivity as lying largely in a lack of zeal because discipline had been undermined by the 'no-sacking' provision of the 1941 Essential Work Order. In the words of one testimony: 'Collieries could not dismiss an inefficient official. Among the men there was a widespread feeling of independence and managers were finding it difficult to control the men, even on safety matters.'[72] The present machinery for disciplining absentees was, according to the same testimony, too slow; better 'a system of automatic penalties' deducted from wages.[73] With regard to the technical problems behind sinking production, the committee's expert witnesses advocated much the same solutions as those vainly recommended by the Sankey and Samuel Commissions as long ago as 1919 and 1926, and feebly encouraged by the Acts of Parliament in 1926, 1930 and 1938 – that is, the grouping of mines into large operational units, and the concentration of expertise and equipment on the most productive pits and seams.

On 28 May 1942 the Lord President summed up the results of the committee's investigations for the benefit of the War Cabinet. He noted that there was 'a wide variation in the standard of skilled technical advice available to colliery management, and output could be increased if all collieries could secure the advice of the most competent engineers in their District.'[74] Here was a further demonstration, though the Lord President did not say so, of the functional absurdity of the fragmentation in the industry's ownership. The Lord President went on to urge that the workforce should be redeployed to the most successful pits, citing a study by the Mines Department of districts producing 44 per cent of total output and with a manpower of 227,000, which showed that by transferring only 17,800 men from low-productivity pits an average distance of four miles to high-productivity pits, output could be raised by 6.5 per cent. If the same principle were applied throughout the country, output could be boosted by 250,000 tons a week. 'What is needed', wrote the Lord President, 'is not so much fresh [government] powers, as machinery to enable these powers to be exercised effectively. The problem of output is, in the main, one of securing detailed changes in the operation of particular collieries. These cannot be brought about through directions from the centre';[75] and to fill this gap he proposed the setting-up of a new regional organisation for coal production.

A draft White Paper embodying the Coal Industry Committee's recommendations was duly approved by the War Cabinet on 29 May 1942 and presented to Parliament on 3 June.[76] It stands like a double signpost on the long road of the British coal industry's halting evolution, pointing backwards at the historic shortcomings of private 'enterprise' which had eventually led up to the present wartime crisis, and pointing forwards to an ever deeper state involvement that was to bring new disadvantages, new impediments to evolution, even while seeking to remedy the old.

The White Paper advocated two principal means of increasing output – recruiting more miners and 'making the industry more efficient, i.e., by raising output per man employed'. It proposed to raise productivity by 'concentrating effort on the most productive mines and seams', so foreshadowing the strategy to be cautiously pursued by the industry decade by decade after nationalisation in 1946. At the same time the White Paper also perceived the incidental problems that such a strategy would entail, not least tenacious resistance on the part of the miners themselves; resistance which was eventually to culminate in the attempt by the leadership of the National Union of Mineworkers in the great coal strike of 1984–5 to bring the strategy to a complete and final halt:

> There are practical difficulties in transferring men from one pit to another. Apart from the problems of providing transport and arranging that no additional financial burden would fall on the men transferred, there is often reluctance on the part of the miners to move to pits other than those in which they have been accustomed to work. The success of all measures of re-organisation will turn very largely on securing the goodwill of both mine-owners and mine-workers. . . .[77]

Complementary measures to achieve higher productivity recommended by the White Paper included more mechanisation, operational regrouping of pits so that all collieries could benefit from the best technical advice in their districts, and the prosecution of absentees in the courts by national service officers.

Although the White Paper still proposed to leave the ownership of the industry and in some respects the management in private hands, its recommendations for a new command structure otherwise served as the direct prototype of the nationalised coal industry's organisation after 1946. Indeed the fundamental principle inspiring the White Paper was, in its own words, that the government had decided 'to assume full control over the operation of the mines, and to organize the industry on the basis of national service. . .'.[78] At the top, the responsible minister (after June 1942, a new 'Minister of Fuel and Power', Gwilym Lloyd George) was to be assisted in his task of control by a controller-general and four directors: of production, labour, services and finance. A National Coal Board would be set up as the executive body responsible for production, mechanisation, manpower and productivity, supply of materials, and health and safety. A second layer of corresponding regional boards under regional controllers was to conduct operations in the field, and especially to provide that technical grip on the pits themselves that had been previously lacking.

When the House of Commons approved the White Paper on 11 June 1942 by 329 votes to 8, it therefore marked the abandonment at long last of any hope for a spontaneous 'bottom-upward' evolution on the part of the coal industry itself, in favour of a 'top-downward' adaptation to be imposed by the power and authority of the state. It was clearly intended that production strategy in this adaptation should follow the excellent industrial and military principle of concentrating resources and effort behind success rather than failure. Yet paradoxically, and in the long run damagingly, a fresh impulse was also given at this period to the contradictory principle of the 'broad front'. For government policy now sought to even out the financial impact on colliery companies and workforces of the disparities in operating costs and profitability. The process had already begun with the Coal Mines Act of 1930, designed to protect every coal field's markets and employment by means of regulating output, supply and prices.[79] The 1941 Essential Work Order had carried it further by spreading across the entire industry the risk of having to pay the new guaranteed weekly wage when production was locally stopped for technical reasons. This spreading of risk had been achieved through a central fund fed by a small levy on every ton of coal disposed of. Now in June 1942 support of the unfit at the expense of the fit by means of national averaging took a decisive step forward with the creation of a 'Coal Charges Account' under the new Ministry of Fuel and Power. The minister was to enjoy wide authority to make such levies as he thought necessary on coal produced, and to dispose of the resulting funds for any purpose connected with the production or marketing of coal. In the words of the official historian of the industry during the Second World War, this became the method 'by which the rising costs of the coal industry were pooled for the duration of the war and the low cost districts were made to help the high'.[80]

At the end of 1942 the government, through the Coal Charges Account, fixed a standard profit for the industry irrespective of the output or production costs of particular coal fields;[81] and by 1943 efficient areas were having to subsidise an inefficient area like South Wales to the extent of 10 per cent of its total costs.[82]

But the particular rising cost which low-productivity fields could not have met in 1942, and which therefore led to the setting up of the Coal Charges Account, took the form of a generous national wage increase for miners recommended in June by a board of enquiry under Lord Greene, the Master of the Rolls. The government had appointed the 'Greene Committee' to investigate a claim by the Miners' Federation for a general rise of 4*s* 0*d* a shift and a national minimum weekly wage of £4 5*s* 0*d*. The mine-owners on the other hand in their cynical capitalist way wanted increases in miners' rewards to be geared to increases in production. They also opposed a national minimum wage because it would breach the principle of local wage bargaining related to local operating costs and profitability. In its first report, the Greene Committee produced a classic board-of-enquiry fudge by recommending a general increase of 2*s* 6*d* a shift and accepting the need for a national minimum wage, which it fixed at £4 3*s* 0*d*, plus a productivity bonus. In its second report in August 1942 the committee stated its own preference for a bonus scheme based on individual pits, but yielded to the common desire of both employers and miners for a district system because it believed it to be vital, and presumably also possible, to obtain the good will of these parties. The industry itself disliked a pit bonus for exactly the same reason that the committee liked it – because it would discriminate closely between the efficient and the inefficient. The union did not want its members in low-productivity pits to suffer financial penalties, while the owners feared that their workers would drift away from such pits to others where the bonuses would be larger.[83]

In the event the new district bonus contributed to a surge in output for a few months, after which there followed a renewed decline. The Greene Committee's fourth report, in September 1943, therefore returned to its idea of a pit bonus, but, even though the government itself was in favour, the proposal foundered yet again on the joint opposition of owners and miners,[84] united by self-interest instead of divided. This marked the final demise of wartime attempts directly to relate reward to productivity. Henceforth hope reposed instead in a vain expectation that the miner would flex his muscles in response to general boosts in his pay. Thus wage policy too (with the exception of locally negotiated piece rates for particular grades) came to follow the pernicious strategy of the 'broad front'. What was more, in this novel wartime situation of a seller's market for mining labour, the Miners' Federation wished to relate wage levels not to coal production or productivity, let alone profitability, but to wage levels in other industries. Thus was born the 'league table' mentality in coal that was to bedevil the postwar era. Since by the autumn of 1943 the miners had sunk to forty-first in the table from twenty-first after the Greene Award in June 1942,[85] the Miners' Federation duly put in a fresh claim for a national minimum wage of £6 per week for underground workers and £5 10*s* 0*d* for surface.[86] The government referred the claim to a new and impartial National Reference Tribunal under Lord Porter, another senior judge like Greene, which in January 1944, and for the sake of peace in the coal fields at this crucial period of the run-up to the coming invasion of Europe, awarded a national minimum of £5 underground and £4 10*s* 0*d* on the surface. The Miners' Federation graciously accepted the award.

There remained, however, the question of who should pay for it and also for new piece rates yet to be negotiated – the mine-owners, the consumers through higher coal prices, or the government through the Coal Charges Account. With regard to piece rates the mine-owners proceeded to agree to union demands with unwonted generosity in the mistaken expectation that the government would pick up the bill. When in February the Minister of Fuel and Power refused to do so, the mine-owners promptly withdrew their agreements and the miners went on strike. In the first week of February alone no fewer than 178,700 tons of production were lost: the highest figure for the war.[87] In the first quarter of 1944 1,641,000 man-days were lost through strikes, and 2 million tons of coal.[88] Once again miners proved more interested in raising rewards than coal. The confusion and strife were ended only by fresh negotiations presided over by the minister himself, leading to a national agreement on the pay structure of the industry which lifted the miner from eighty-first out of a hundred in the industrial earnings table in 1938 to fourteenth, behind only the best-paid munitions workers.[89]

While this policy of appeasement certainly bought relative tranquillity in the coal fields (only 587,000 tons lost through strikes in the second quarter of 1944, and 210,000 in the fourth)[90] it cost money – money derived from higher coal prices and from government subsidy. By the time the German war ended, the price of coal was more than half as much again as in 1938,[91] and the Coal Charges Account was in debt to the Exchequer to the extent of £15 million; a debt in the event written off by the creditor.[92] Moreover the Coal Charges Account levy per ton of coal had risen to 15 shillings – necessitated by the 'broad-front' strategy of milking efficient coal fields in order to subsidise the inefficient, which otherwise could not have paid the repeated national wage increases. In Harold Wilson's estimate in 1945, 'Taking the country as a whole probably half the pits are kept in existence by the other half. . . . In fact, by the end of 1944, economic laws had ceased to apply in the industry.'[93]

Thus the crying need for maximum coal production in 1939–45 had had the unfortunate consequence of perpetuating the survival of the unfittest and so stalling the industry's evolution. Moreover, by fudging the link between productivity and reward for both the miners and mine-owners it had blunted the keenest of direct incentives to change. And, in terms of the long-term market health of the industry, wartime coal policy had led to the worst of all worlds – high wage costs without any compensating reduction in already high technical operating costs.

For no rise in productivity had taken place in the three years following the 1942 White Paper's radical proposals, even though in January 1943 the

Minister of Fuel and Power, Gwilym Lloyd George, was reporting optimistically on prospects for the coal year 1943–4.[94] By the beginning of October 1943 he was instead warning that a fresh energy crisis lay ahead, and urging that further drastic measures would have to be taken.[95] In fact weekly output had now declined 140,000 tons below the 1942 figure because of a fall in productivity per man employed greater than the minister had expected in the spring.[96] He attributed this fall partly to the growing fatigue of the miner after four years of war, blackout and rationing, and to a shortage of materials like timber or equipment and spares, so leading to more frequent breakdowns. He also believed that allied war successes in the last year, including the recent fall of Mussolini, had led, in his words, to the 'lack (not, I believe, confined to the miners) of psychological incentive and a sense of urgency. . .'. [97] But he discerned a deeper-seated psychological factor – the 'continuing dissatisfaction of the miners with their conditions. This is of long standing and, apart from their antagonism to the mine owners as a body, is chiefly directed at their failure to win recognition for a stable wage basis and working conditions commensurate with the hardship of their work.'[98] It was, of course, this particular grievance that the Porter Award and the subsequent national wage agreement in 1944 were intended to remove. Disgruntlement over pay was not all, however: according to the minister, 'there had been a decline in the standard of discipline. Indiscipline is primarily due to the removal of the fear of unemployment which was the main weapon for enforcing discipline in pre-war days,' wartime disciplinary procedures under the Essential Work Order and via the magistrates' courts being too slow.[99]

Yet he did not blame the disappointing productivity record solely on the native mutinousness of the miner. The scarcity of highly qualified and talented mining engineers and managers had crippled the attempt to fulfil the operational promise of the elaborate organisational chart drawn up in the 1942 White Paper:

> Though the government is theoretically in full operational control of the industry, in practice that control has proved difficult of achievement. The Government has the power to remove managers who are inefficient and to assume control of pits that for one reason or another are not giving satisfactory results. In several cases this has been done. There are, however, 1,600 pits working under my jurisdiction, the managements of which are responsible for day to day operations while remaining the employees of the colliery owners.
>
> The effective operational control of so many pits is precluded by the insufficiency of staff to maintain the close oversight which would be needed. . . .[100]

Indeed, though the minister did not mention it, the shortage of world-class management constituted one of the gravest long-term weaknesses of an industry that had so long cherished the 'practical man'. In the words of the managing director of Powell-Duffryn Associated Collieries in a letter to the Controller-General of the Ministry of Fuel and Power, 'it is not unusual to find Managers who are admirable at handling their labour and other problems, quite unable to lay out a satisfactory scheme of working which must cover the development of a pit for a number of years. . . .'[101]

The Minister of Fuel and Power believed that the failures of 1942–3 had also been caused by the 'dual control' of the industry adopted as a result of the 1942 White Paper: a half-way house to nationalisation which had left ownership in private hands while operational control had been vested in the state. Even though the new regional organisation had proved 'a great improvement',

> operational control had failed to win the confidence of any party within the industry. The men point to dual control as illogical: the managements feel themselves to be open to attack from all sides and are smarting under a grievance through their inability to reply adequately; the owners, without being openly defiant, are sceptical of the merits of control.[102]

Gwilym Lloyd George's new cure for all the continued ills of the industry was to proceed to a full state takeover from the owners, and to organise pits into operational groupings of 2–4 million tons production under technical directors solely responsible to the regional controllers.[103] But he warned that this step alone 'would not provide the output which I am seeking unless explicit pledges were received from the leaders of the mineworkers (and carried out to the limits of their powers) to remove all obstacles on the men's side to increased production'.[104] Outright requisition of the industry was however ruled out in a Commons debate in October 1943; in fact killed by the War Premier, true to his belief that contentious questions such as nationalisation and New Jerusalem should wait for a postwar government with a fresh electoral mandate. Nevertheless, a new Cabinet committee on the coal industry accepted Lloyd George's plans for large-scale operational groupings and other changes in the command structure.[105] Unfortunately for the minister, neither management nor workforce liked the new organisation any better than the previous one set up after the 1942 White Paper – for the very same basic, and to them cogent, reason that it threatened major changes in the way the industry worked. Such changes meant the uncomfortable redeployment of men, managers and machines, together with a consequent rundown of some old familiar pits. Deeply felt local loyalties would be affronted and the existence of dependent mining communities imperilled. And so, although in the course of 1944–5 the grouping scheme came slowly into effect, it achieved little in improving colliery management and less in boosting output,[106] which instead dropped by 4.4 million tons in the second half of 1944 compared with the similar period of 1943.[107]

For it was literally at the coal face, certainly on the colliery site, beyond the reach of grandiose reorganisations of management structure, that the government's wartime hopes of raising productivity finally came to grief. Output per man-shift at the face fell from 2.75 tons in 1943 to 2.70 tons in 1944–5; output per man-shift underground from 1.44 tons in 1942 to 1.33

tons in 1945.[108] The miners did not, as the minister had hoped in his memorandum to the Cabinet in October 1943, remove all obstacles to increased production, but instead clove steadfastly to traditional restrictive practices. Whatever might be their patriotic sentiments, they were motivated in practice more by a sense of past and present grievances, by fear of the future and by ingrained hostility towards 'the bosses' than by the nation's danger or the nation's need. In the words of a socialist sympathetic to the miners,

> It must be fully admitted that, apart from magnificent efforts in particular districts, the miners did not fully co-operate in securing maximum production. Strikes, ca'canny, and a lower effort all proved that more could have been done, in spite of the difficulties and the inefficient lay-out and organisation of the industry.[109]

No less signally disappointed was the 1942 White Paper's expectation of great results from more mechanisation. The first problem had lain in obtaining the actual machinery, the British manufacturers of which had been converted by 1942 to other war work, while American equipment, in any case difficult to get, was designed for the 'room-and-pillar' method of coal extraction and was not really suitable for the traditional British method of 'longwall advancing'. The proportion of coal mechanically cut crept upwards from 66 per cent in 1942 to 72 per cent in 1945; of mechanically conveyed from 65 per cent to 71 per cent.[110] Moreover, British coal management, with its narrow day-to-day outlook and inadequate professional education, failed to grasp that it was not enough simply to slot new machinery into the existing system of operating the pit, but that the system had to be redesigned as a whole round the machinery. In fact, the pit had to be looked upon as a single complex machine in itself. That meant, for instance, an appropriate layout of all communications below and above ground. Yet most British pits had quite inadequate roadways and layouts bequeathed by the Victorian age.

Above all, mechanical loading was needed as the essential link between mechanical cutting and conveying. This had still been an almost unheard-of novelty in Britain at the outbreak of the war, and it remained a bottleneck right through to 1945, partly because of a dearth of the loaders themselves, partly because British workers required considerable training before they could operate them, and that meant first setting up special training centres.[111] In those few cases where American systems could be properly put into operation the increases in productivity were remarkable: in one Derbyshire colliery, up from 6.79 tons per man-shift at the face to 8.09 tons.[112] Yet this marked a further widening – and a potentially far greater widening – between technically élite collieries and the backward mass of pits which, as Wilson put it, 'were kept in operation, often at a serious financial loss and under Government subsidy, simply in order to keep sufficient pit-room available to meet the nation's needs. . .'.[113]

In any event, with some exceptions, neither management nor miners were keen on rapid mechanisation. The mine-owners felt that they were doing all right anyhow without embarking on the expense and possible commercial risk of installing American equipment and methods, because in wartime they were enjoying guaranteed prices for coal and good profits, while after the war there would at least be the statutory price-and-market maintenance schemes that had enabled them to bumble on in the 1930s. In the case of the miners, there was nothing in their traditional nature to make them other than distrustful of new machinery; in particular they feared that owners would use mechanisation as an excuse to upset the existing complicated and hallowed structure of reward rates.[114]

And so the Minister of Fuel and Power had sorrowfully had to inform the House of Commons on 13 July 1944 that 'it is unlikely that a large increase will result from the use of American machinery during the present coal year.'[115] Nevertheless, in the same debate he also pointed out to the Commons, to the general agreement of honourable members, that 'high wages can only be maintained by a high output per man-shift, so that the cost of production permits the supply of coal at a reasonable price to our industries, particularly those manufacturing for export, and to those who buy our coal overseas as coal. . . .'[116]

Here, indeed, was the nub of the problem that the wartime course of the coal industry bequeathed to the postwar era. In the words of *The Times* in its first leader on 11 October 1944:

> British coal is the basic fact, and the basic cost, in British industry. . . . The most telling token of the present emergency is that the current price of British coal would be both a serious hindrance to the regaining of world markets and a grave brake upon British manufacture; and the price is too high because output, in relation to wages and the labour force, is too low. There is no single unfavourable factor confronting the future of the basic British industries which is more alarming than the price of domestic [i.e. home-produced] coal.

Or, as Harold Wilson summed it up in his book *New Deal for Coal*, the coal industry 'is facing the post-war period with higher wages, with costs doubled, and with productivity more than 10 per cent below the pre-war figure'.[117]

It was commonly agreed that the only peacetime solution to this conundrum lay in reducing operating costs by higher efficiency.[118] But the real puzzle resided in how to implement this rather obvious principle. The 1945 Reid Report recommended a 'vast programme of reconstruction of existing mines and the sinking of new ones' in which the mistakes of the past would be avoided, and a concomitant policy of closing down out-of-date low-productivity pits. Even more ruthlessly, the Reid Committee wanted the principle accepted that even new pits should have a strictly limited economic life:

> The output to be raised from a new or reconstructed mine should, in our opinion, result in the exhaustion, within a reasonable period of

time, of the reserves allocated to it. No useful purpose is to be secured by planning an unduly long life for a mine. . . .[119]

Wilson's *New Deal for Coal*, already in the press before publication of the Reid Report, also called for a massive investment programme, costing £150–£300 million in his estimation, and also for a continuation of the wartime attempt to redeploy the resources of the industry: 'concentration would require to be undertaken as part of a national plan which would provide for a progressive programme of new sinkings and widespread development, so that more and more of the unproductive mines could be closed.'[120] Moreover, in his view, wartime 'dual control' must give way to full national ownership – as was in the event brought about by the Labour government's Coal Nationalisation Act of 1946.

While all these optimistic hopes are understandable enough in the context of the time, the realities hardly justified them. In the first place, the very fact of the industry's existence in its present form constituted a colossal handicap, for it meant that the high-technology coal industry of the future could not be constructed on a 'green-field' site, but would demand the shifting of a century-and-a-half's accretion of obsolete capital stock and mental attitudes. Nothing in the wartime experience suggested that this process could be other than painful and prolonged, even given the powers of complete state ownership. Indeed state ownership, which meant ultimate responsibility resting in the hands of a minister who was a party man, could only politicise the key question of closing down outdated collieries and thereby condemning communities to a slow death from the moment when the winding gear stopped. In this way state ownership could only strengthen the miners' traditional dogged opposition to change. Nor was it likely that the fact of nationalisation would lead to a compensating 'born-again' willingness to co-operate in exploiting new technology to the utmost. As the socialist intellectual G. D. H. Cole admitted:

> Men are creatures of habit; and neither among managers nor among workers can the habits of mind established under capitalism be suddenly transcended as soon as an industry passes from private to public ownership. The industrial relations character of capitalist society is bound to leave an evil legacy behind; and in the coal industry, with its exceptionally bad record of relations between masters and men, this legacy is bound to be worse than in most others.[121]

Certainly only faith, or perhaps the prevailing contagion of New Jerusalemism, could have inspired the Reid Committee, in the face of all wartime evidence, to call on miners and their leaders to join with mining engineers 'in an entirely new spirit of co-operation for a united effort to raise the productivity of the Industry to the highest level. . .'.[122]

In the financial sphere, too, the experience of the war did not augur well for the postwar coal industry. As Wilson rightly argued, the natural outcome of wartime measures like the Coal Charges Account was 'a single national financial system',[123] and this would certainly be so under nationalisation. It meant, in other words, finally consummating the existing trend towards lumping high-cost and low-cost coal fields into a homogeneous package of wages, profits and prices. It meant accepting that the subsidising of loss-makers by the profitable and by the taxpayer was to become a permanent feature of the industry. Yet by 1945 the loss-makers had grown even more uncompetitive than before the war. Cumberland coal, for example, now cost more than twice as much per ton as Leicestershire coal.[124] A 'single national financial system' entailed abolishing the last traces of that free-market competition, or process of natural selection through bankruptcy, which might in the end have rendered extinct such coal-mining areas as Cumberland. By instead making possible their continued survival, an 'all-in' financial strategy could therefore only countervail, rather than reinforce, the chosen postwar technological strategy of running down the unproductive and developing the productive.

It therefore followed from the historic nature of the British coal industry, from the record of its performance in the Second World War and from the course of wartime government policy that in the postwar era the industry's evolution into a highly efficient advanced-technology operation could only be difficult, protracted and costly. And it followed as a consequence that the international competitiveness of the British economy as a whole must suffer indefinitely from dependence on expensive energy – and no part of the economy more than the steel industry, the basic sinew of industrial strength.

Chapter Five

'In Great Need of Modernisation': Steel

> I believe that when the full story of the steel trade's contribution to winning the war is made known, it will be a clear vindication of private enterprise, and the policy of improvement and modernisation which was carried out in the national interest just prior to the war.[1]

In presenting this little commemorative ingot of self-congratulation to his shareholders on 3 June 1945, Mr Richard E. Summers, chairman of John Summers and Sons, was singularly well placed, for his company's 60-inch hot and cold continuous strip mill at Shotton, Wales, completed in 1939, was one of only four large-scale integrated steel plants built in Britain in the last twenty years; and then only under government encouragement as part of the pre-war rearmament programme. A joint memorandum by the Ministry of Supply and the Board of Trade to the War Cabinet Reconstruction Committee two months earlier on the postwar prospects of the iron and steel industry took a less robust view. In fact, its only point of agreement with Summers lay in blaming the high cost of British steel on the excessive price of British coal. The Reconstruction Committee was informed that the average cost of British steel 'was now estimated to be at least £2 a ton *above* that of our competitors and the new increase of 3/6*d* a ton in the price of coal would raise it by a further 7/– a ton'.[2] In a nudging reference to wartime wage inflation in coal mining, the memorandum noted that Britain probably had the highest-priced coking coal in the world where she once had the cheapest.[3] It was hardly a consolation to state that new construction and modernisation in the steel industry 'might' reduce the industry's costs by £1 a ton, because this served to indicate all too graphically British steel's own present uncompetitively high costs. And indeed the joint report spent much time in analysing the causes of this uncompetitiveness.

The proof test lay in productivity: 'In real terms as opposed to prices and money costs, there are important differences between the British and American steel industries. American plants need only 60 per cent of the man-hours per ton of output needed in the average British plant.'[4] A broad survey of competitive prices, including those of the rising Australian steel industry, indicated that 'the competitive position of the British industry cannot be regarded as good.' Written at a time when the German steel industry, one of Britain's most formidable pre-war competitors, had been heavily bombed and was about to fall into allied hands, the joint report glumly remarked that much depended on whether Germany retained a strong industry after the war, and, if that were so, 'we will have difficulties in getting export orders. . . .'[5]

The main reason for low average British productivity and concomitant high average costs was obvious enough to the authors of the joint report – over half the total production came out of small and obsolete plants. In 1936, according to the report, eighty out of the hundred blast furnaces in the United Kingdom producing pig iron were out of date, yet they supplied 60 per cent of the output, while just twenty modern furnaces accounted for the remaining 40 per cent. Average annual production per furnace had not yet attained 70,000 tons, and only 45 per cent of total production was being made in furnaces bigger than 125,000 tons annual capacity. The report therefore recommended that after the war Britain should build furnaces with annual capacities of 150,000 to 250,000 tons. This was an order of magnitude that had already been attained in Germany and the United States by the late 1920s.[6] In the case of steel, the report drew the depressing conclusion that 'a significant volume of production is not economic at any probable level of prices and is overdue for replacement by modern plant.'[7] It reckoned that there were not more than three steel mills in the country that could be regarded as efficient, each turning out half a million tons annually – less than half the total production. Even in a good modern British steel works 'it is seldom that every section of the plant is equally up to date and efficient.'[8] Moreover, old plant compromised quality as well as costs, because modern plants made better steel. The report went on to note that whereas American wartime expansion had served largely to increase general steel-making capacity, the £53 million spent in Britain (90 per cent of it government funding) during the war had gone to specialised plant like alloy steels, for which the report saw little future.

In any event, although neither the Board of Trade/Ministry of Supply report nor the chairman of John Summers and Sons chose to mention it, the British war effort had absolutely depended on American supplies of steel. Between 1940 and 1944 no fewer than 14,570,000 tons had made the hazardous sea passage from North America to the United Kingdom[9] – equal to more than a quarter of Britain's own total production in this period.[10] In the second half of 1940 steel shipments had constituted the heaviest single charge on hard-pressed Atlantic shipping capacity.[11] British dependence on America for the special steels demanded by advanced technology rose even higher than for steel in general: 29 per cent for carbon steel; 34 per cent for alloy steel.[12]

The British defence effort had been blunted by inadequate home steel production from the very beginnings of pre-war rearmament in 1936. As early as December 1936 the Admiralty was reporting to the Cabinet

Defence Policy and Requirements Committee that new warship construction was being held up by delays in delivery of structural steel.[13] In April 1937 the Air Ministry also complained about the shortage of structural steel, which was slowing up completion of new airfields and sector stations, with their attendant aircraft hangars and other buildings.[14] By the following month the Air Ministry was reporting that delays in steel deliveries were now causing 'serious anxiety' and that 'the position is now acute'. The lag between ordering and taking delivery of steel had now risen to six months.[15] At the same time the Admiralty reported that the construction of new factories to manufacture naval equipment was also being throttled by late deliveries of structural steel.[16] By now the steel industry was already at full stretch and, according to the Ministry of Labour in May 1937, was unable to accept new orders except for dates 'at some distance ahead'.[17] In June the ministry noted that although monthly production of steel ingots and castings had risen by 140,000 tons since June 1936, it was not enough to satisfy the 'unprecedented demand', so causing complaints from customers that their plans were held up for want of steel.[18] Six months later production was still failing to meet demand, even though steel furnace capacity had now risen by 750,000 tons in the past year and stood at 2.5 million tons more than in 1929. With all existing furnaces producing to capacity, the Ministry of Labour could only look for future rescue to the large new plants being built in South Wales, on the Clyde, in Lincolnshire and elsewhere.[19]

In the meantime, however, Britain had had to look to foreign supplies of both general and special steels to enable the rearmament programme to keep going: to America, Germany, Czechoslovakia. By October 1938, for example, the total order for armour plate for the new aircraft carriers and cruisers placed in Czechoslovakia had reached 15,000 tons.[20]

Nevertheless in 1937 the rearmament programme's demand for steel amounted to no more than 15 per cent of the United Kingdom's current annual consumption.[21] This modest additional load had proved enough to overstrain a steel industry which at the start of rearmament in March 1936 had been suffering from 11.3 per cent unemployment: symptom of unused capacity caused by the then still lingering effects of the world slump.[22] In other countries too – in Germany and the United States – rearmament demanded major expansions of steel-making capacity. But in Britain it demanded something more: the creation of a technologically up-to-date steel industry virtually from scratch. In size and type the new plants a-building in 1937–9 as part of the rearmament programme were novelties in Britain, though long familiar abroad; and without them the 1945 report by the Ministry of Supply and Board of Trade could have contained nothing but gloom. For on the eve of rearmament the British iron and steel industry, taken all in all, was merely a patched-up and added-on relic of Victorian and Edwardian technology, as a report in July 1937 by the Import Duties Advisory Committee (the IDAC Report) on 'The Present Position and Future Development of the Iron and Steel Industry' bleakly described.[23]

In the production of pig iron, the raw material of steel making, Britain had only six blast furnaces with weekly capacities of 3000 tons or over; nine between 2500 and 3000; eighteen between 2000 and 2499; seventeen between 1500 and 1999 – yet sixty-three between 1000 and 1499; and eighty-three under 1000 tons per week. Of the total British average weekly production of pig iron, 73,150 tons was produced in furnaces of 2000 tons a week capacity or over; 122,620 tons in furnaces of less than 1000 tons.[24] In fact, the IDAC Report predicted, even by 1939 the average annual output per furnace in Britain would not have reached the American figure for 1910 and barely two-thirds the German figure for 1929.[25] The report documented a like contrast in the production of open-hearth steel ingot and of sheet steel between a small minority of larger modern plants and a majority of high-cost leftovers from a previous age, some of them hardly larger or more efficient than back-street handicrafts. Whereas there existed only 37 open-hearth furnaces with a capacity of 100 tons or over per 'heat' and 68 furnaces with a capacity of 75–99 tons, together producing nearly 12,000 tons per 'heat', almost 16,000 tons were produced in 335 furnaces with capacities per 'heat' of below 75 tons; and of these, 129 made less than 50 tons of steel per 'heat'.[26] Furthermore the existing twenty-five sheet-steel works and eighty tinplate works in the country could be replaced by 'a very few' large mills like that currently being built at Ebbw Vale.[27] For this reason the IDAC Report registered its approval of the new plant about to be constructed at Shotton, declaring that the new advantages of this kind of operation had already been demonstrated by the United States, and it was clear that Britain 'cannot afford to lag behind foreign practice'.[28]

Outdated equipment also accounted for British iron and steel's high transport costs. In 1938 the Iron and Steel Federation's committee on dock facilities reported that there were only four mechanised grab transporters in the country for unloading iron ore from ships, all on the industry's own wharves, compared with twenty in the port of Rotterdam alone, each double the British capacity. Because of higher handling costs and longer turn-round times it cost 5*s* 3*d* a ton to ship ore from Spain and North Africa to Britain, as against 3*s* 9*d* through Rotterdam,[29] while railway charges for carrying steel products were also higher in Britain than abroad.[30]

So although the IDAC Report of 1937 had remarked that Britain could not afford to lag behind foreign practice, the evidence made it all too plain that British iron and steel had already so lagged, and badly. Nor was this simply because of the effects of the world slump after 1930. Rather, the introduction of a protective tariff on foreign steel under the new Import Duties Act of 1932, coupled with encouragement from the state and the banks, had led to modest projects of modernisation (nearly £5 million worth in 1934 alone). In point of fact the industry had actually been in worse competitive case during the world boom of the 1920s that preceded the slump.

By 1925–9 British exports of iron and steel had fallen to 390,000 tons a year compared with 437,000 tons in 1905–9, although world exports had more than doubled.[31] By 1930 Britain had dropped to fourth in world production of pig iron, and could only tie with France for third place in steel production.[32] In production *per capita*, the index of efficiency rather than sheer size of output, Britain in 1925–9 came fifth in pig iron after the United States, Germany, Belgium and France; in steel, fourth.[33] In 1929 British annual production of pig iron per man employed was only two-thirds the German figure, barely a third the American;[34] of steel, just under two-thirds the German total.[35] And although American wage rates were double the British, American wage costs per ton of pig iron produced were only 60 per cent of British – a stark demonstration of the gulf in productivity.[36] In regard to European competition in particular Britain suffered from doubly high costs, human as well as technological, because British wage rates were higher. It is not therefore surprising that even in a prosperous year for the world economy like 1925, when 84 per cent of German steel plant was being utilised and 79 per cent of American, only 58 per cent of British plant was making steel;[37] nor is it surprising that in the ten years after 1921 no dividend was paid at all by eleven major British steel companies.[38]

To be fair, some factors outside the control of bewildered men in the boardrooms of British steel towns had contributed to this slump in the midst of everybody else's boom. The French and Belgians had radically modernised their steel industries out of postwar reparations from Germany; the Germans modernised theirs out of large loans from the United States. At the same time Britain, in pursuit of Gladstonian financial rectitude and a nostalgic ambition to restore London to its pre-1914 role as the crown pinion of the world economy, was dutifully repaying her own wartime loans from America with interest, returning to the gold standard at the pre-war parity (so overpricing all British exports) and, in pursuit of the dogma of free trade, refusing to erect protective tariffs against foreign steel. The key personage in this neo-Victorian revival was Winston Churchill, the Chancellor of the Exchequer in the Conservative government of 1924–9, who at one point threatened to resign if steel was protected by tariffs.[39] Yet Churchill could justly argue that although British steel was being sold at marginal profit or even at a loss, it cost 30 shillings a ton more than foreign steel because of the inefficiency of the industry itself; inefficiency which tariff protection would only pamper.[40]

For the dismal performance of British steel in the 1920s even in its own home market stemmed above all from its own flaws: plant already mostly obsolescent or even obsolete in date or design, organisation of production and marketing fragmented, leadership outmoded in outlook and often technically ignorant, research and development neglected and underfunded, workforce wedded to traditional methods and demarcations.[41]

The industry had emerged from the Great War with plants expanded to meet the emergency demand. For some three years after the war it had enjoyed a delusive second Victorian honeymoon of prosperity, with demand at home and abroad soaring in the short-lived postwar boom, and with Britain's European rivals weakened by the effects of war and occupation. Enticed by an apparently bright future, British companies borrowed heavily from the banks and invested in much new plant – but unfortunately more often in the form of piecemeal extensions or replacements to existing pre-1914 works than in the form of completely new large-scale integrated operations.[42] The French occupation of the Ruhr in 1923 gave British steel, like British coal, a renewed respite from the fiercest competition. But from 1924 onwards, with the world economy accelerating away on a four-year boom, and Germany, France and Belgium campaigning in international steel markets with modern plants of very large scale, Britain's newly patched and extended but basically obsolescent industry was outclassed. Her iron and steel companies, already deep in debt to the banks for their ill-designed extensions just after the war and currently making no profit at all, were now quite unable to embark on massive reconstructions in order to match the Americans and Europeans plant for plant – even if such a strategy had lain within their professional imagination. They could only make do with what they had, a forlorn and foredoomed competition akin to muzzle-loaders against machine-guns.

The European and American strength did not only lie in large-scale technology; it also lay in large-scale organisation. In Britain the iron and steel industry, like coal mining, still largely adhered in the 1920s to a Victorian pattern of a multitude of individualistic firms competing with each other as well as with the foreigners, and jealously preserving their independence of production and marketing. In 1927 there were no fewer than seventy pig-iron makers and seventy-five steel makers in the United Kingdom.[43] While some amalgamations certainly took place – the United Steel Company dated from 1918, the English Steel Corporation from 1927, four further groupings from 1929–30 – they never matched the scale of such German developments as the *Vereinigte Stahlwerke* of Düsseldorf, founded in 1926, which comprised 151 coal mines, 71 coking plants, 63 blast furnaces, 32 Bessemer converters, 116 open-hearth furnaces, large rolling mills, railways and port facilities. This combine alone produced about the same tonnage of steel as the entire British industry,[44] while its new investment in 1927–9 amounted to double the original total capitalisation of the English Steel Corporation.[45] Moreover, amalgamation in Germany was the prelude, as it was not always in Britain, to ruthless rationalisation of the physical assets, concentrating production round the most efficient plants while closing down the inefficient and shedding superfluous labour. In the first year after its formation the *Vereinigte Stahlwerke* boosted output by 60 per cent.[46] And European international sales operations followed a similar pattern: organisation on the grand scale; coherent, centrally conceived strategies. In all respects, therefore, this was a competition akin not only to muzzle-loaders against machine-guns but also to regiments against army groups.

But in fact by this period the British iron and steel industry was really conducting no more than a somewhat inept and demoralised rearguard action. Its decisive defeat at the hands of foreign rivals had taken place earlier still, between 1890 and the outbreak of the Great War in 1914, when it was toppled from its Victorian pre-eminence as the world's largest producer and greatest exporter. In 1890 British exports had amounted to 73.5 per cent of the combined exports of the five major producing countries (Britain, Germany, France, Belgium and the United States); in

1913 to 30 per cent.[47] In 1890 British production of pig iron stood at 30 per cent of the world total, and of steel at 27 per cent; in 1913 at 13 per cent and 10 per cent.[48] In total production of iron and steel Britain had been passed by the United States by 1890; by Germany in steel in 1893 and in pig iron in 1905.[49] If it was inevitable that these fast-industrialising and much bigger continental powers should overtake Britain in sheer quantity of production, it was by no means inevitable, however, that Britain should be overtaken in competitive efficiency, as measured by production *per capita*. Yet Britain was so overtaken – in pig iron by the United States in 1901, by Belgium after 1908 and by Germany around 1910; in steel by all three by 1913.[50] Ominously, too, British imports of steel as a percentage of exports rose from 10 in 1890 to 45 in 1913.[51]

As early as 1891 the President of the Iron and Steel Institute, Sir Frederick Abel, in his presidential address warned his members up from Sheffield or Durham or South Wales about the nature of the attack they now faced:

> Small armies of highly-trained chemists, who have gained academic honours, and have won their spurs in original investigations, are in constant employment at the magnificent manufacturing establishments in Germany, which constitute successive indispensable links in a great network of exhaustive enquiry. . . . The combined operations of chemistry, physics and mechanics have furnished, and are continually preparing, the foundations for important advances in the industries of iron and steel.[52]

This German deployment of science to serve her steel industry was to grow still more formidable in the future: new research institutes followed in the 1890s and 1900s; systematic investigations were to be undertaken into alloy steels, the thermal efficiency of production, in-plant transportation, and the mechanisation of steel mills; even more copious exchanges of ideas and personnel between universities and the industry were to take place. All this effort was to be closely related to parallel developments in the electrotechnical and mechanical engineering industries, so creating a multiplier effect throughout the German industrial economy.[53] In Britain in 1890 no such deployment of science existed. In the period 1875–95 fewer than 10 per cent of British steel manufacturers had had the benefit of formal scientific training in institute or university.[54] Even though the new British civic universities gradually developed industry-related research of high quality, its quantity by 1914 remained well below the German level, as also did the British output of science graduates into the industry.[55] As late as 1917, in the middle of the Great War and a steel famine, a Board of Trade committee reported that most British ironmasters were ignorant of the scientific principles underlying their own operations.[56]

Scientific ignorance fostered technical conservatism, for men naturally fear to venture beyond their own competence, which in the case of British iron and steel in the 1890s meant rule-of-thumb experience. But the German advantage – or British disadvantage – went deeper than this.

Underlying the German deployment of science and scientific education lay a fundamentally new attitude of mind; a new concept of industry, industrial leadership and industrial progress. The Americans too shared in this mental revolution, inspiring their iron and steel industry to develop improved technologies on a vast scale, and at the same time to plan company strategy and investment in the very long term.[57] Few indeed of British ironmasters in this period – or much later – were capable of such breadth of vision and scale of ambition, such a way of thinking. So technical conservatism went hand in hand with *entrepreneurial* conservatism. British iron and steel makers too often resembled small-town businessmen suffering at the hands of a big-business competitor, but quite unable to comprehend the nature of their competitor's operation or what made it so formidable, let alone to emulate it. Instead, true to the form of small-town businessmen in such a plight they simply struggled to preserve their existing businesses in their present scope; a cautiously defensive strategy conducing to less investment rather than more.

So British iron and steel companies stayed small; they patched and improved their works piecemeal, if at all; and always late. In 1890–1913 they were late in introducing electric-powered charging of furnaces instead of hand-charging; late in introducing large rolling mills; late with mechanical handling; late in promoting new uses for structural steel in building; late in developing electric furnaces; late in installing coke-ovens; late to develop standardised specifications and sections; late to set up central research laboratories; and above all late in replacing obsolescent plant.[58] The small-town businessman's mentality again manifested itself in the habit of asking with regard to new technical developments what they would cost rather than what they would save.[59] One successful Scottish emigrant to the US who returned to give a paper to the British Iron and Steel Trades Federation in 1902 on the superiority of US rolling mills informed his audience that the entire British steel industry had spent less in a decade than the Carnegie Company in two years.[60] He recounted how when he suggested to a British steel maker that the adoption of American methods could help the British industry, the Englishman replied: 'Why should I? I made over 30 per cent on my capital last year, and I am satisfied with that.' This stalwart was producing some 10 tons per shift of hand-rolled ¾-inch bars, the operation being powered by a single engine which 'appeared to have been designed by Watt himself'.[61] Also in 1902 a British exponent of electric power in steel-making operations vainly asked why British works were content to jog on with low-pressure steam boilers 30 years old and 'the same old beam engine constructed in the days of Watt and Stephenson'.[62] A similar inertness prevailed in pig-iron production, as an Iron and Steel Institute meeting was told by a manager from Palmer's Jarrow works in 1901: 'The blast furnace owners in this country were very conservative, and had a very great objection to spending money unless they saw someone else had done so.'[63]

The cumulative results of such attitudes by the time of the Great War are graphically summed up by the official history of the Ministry of Munitions in explaining the shell famine of 1915–16:

> British manufacturers were behind other countries in research, plant and method. Many of the iron and steel firms were working on a small scale, old systems and uneconomical plant, their cost of production being so high that competition with the steel works of the United States and Germany was becoming impossible.[64]

Twenty-nine out of fifty-nine steel firms then produced only 1000–2500 tons per week between them, while some of the ironmakers 'were operating furnaces seventy years old and many quite out-of-date plants'.[65] It was this history's harsh judgement that 'It was only the ability of the Allies to import shell and shell steel from neutral America . . . that averted the decisive victory of the enemy';[66] an appropriate enough epitaph for Britain's defunct Victorian technological supremacy in iron and steel.

Yet the small-town businessman's mentality had led to structural and commercial backwardness as well as productive,[67] for the British iron and steel industry between 1890 and 1914 failed to match the large-scale business organisation and marketing which were already such notable features of the German and American industries, and which gave them the weight needed to create big standardised markets suited to long production runs. As the *Iron and Coal Trades Review* ruefully remarked in December 1909:

> without its vast system of syndication – its almost military-like production and distribution methods – and the organized fostering of export trade by bounties, the German iron and steel industries could hardly have obtained their present status. Germany is going ahead because her manufacturers and merchants are organized. Britain is standing still because her manufacturers and merchants are not organized.[68]

However, less than two years previously the same journal had declared that Germany's success had been bought 'at a price and in a manner alien to British ideas'.[69] And there can be little doubt that large-scale organisation or co-operation whether in production or marketing was indeed profoundly alien to the British managerial mind. Although some mergers and takeovers occurred, especially after 1900, no British iron and steel combine in the period 1890–1913 achieved the size and weight of a contemporary American or German market leader; nor were British attempts at trade associations to fix common prices and carry out co-operative marketing more than half-hearted and short-lived, for always there seemed to be a rogue company which would not conform.[70] Few British firms even possessed their own overseas sales organisation, and instead of aggressively marketing their products, most were content passively to take orders through agents or merchants. This 'system' further conduced to uneconomically diverse short runs.[71] Similarly, the design and dimensions of steel sections had still not been standardised for the sake of economical production even by 1900, whereas standardisation in Germany dated from 1883, in Belgium from 1885, in France from 1896 and America from 1898.[72]

There was therefore nothing 'inevitable' about the scale of the British loss of market share before 1914, or about the British eclipse in productivity in the same period. The rapid success of little Belgium's iron and steel industry demonstrated, moreover, that there existed no 'inevitable' reason either why Britain should have lost competitive cutting edge just because she was an island economy faced with rivalry from new continental economies like Germany and the United States. If, in retrospect, inevitability there might seem to be, it lay in the nature of the vanquished themselves; it lay in the years before battle was really joined, when the future victors were pondering and preparing, and the future vanquished were yielding to a prideful assumption born of current triumph that they had nothing to learn, nothing to change.

For the explanation of the British eclipse in iron and steel in 1890–1913 is to be found in the character of the industry as it was at the peak of its world dominance back in the 1870s. And that character was in turn still set in the mould of a hundred years earlier, when Britain first pioneered the industrial revolution in iron manufacture; the era, as in coal, of the 'practical man'. There had been no question then of applying scientific knowledge and research to the iron industry, since science in the modern sense of an organised and systematic professional study did not take shape until the early decades of the nineteenth century. Instead ingenious and resourceful individuals groped their way to new processes by trial and error: men like Huntsman, the clockmaker who developed the crucible method of making steel in 1750, the Darbys who at the same period originated the coke-smelting of iron, or Henry Cort who hit on the puddling furnace method of producing wrought iron in 1780. Later British technical developments from 1800 to 1860 likewise owed themselves to working makers of iron or steel with a craftsman's knowledge derived from long experience. Even by 1850, according to an authoritative history of iron and steel in Britain, 'metallurgy as an applied science hardly existed':

> Though a few people . . . had carried out extensive laboratory experiments and acquired a deeper insight into the nature and composition of metals than most working ironmasters considered necessary, the amount of theoretical knowledge generally possessed by practitioners in the trade was usually very limited. This was especially true of steel, where trade secrets as to composition and treatment were jealously guarded by individual makers. The production of iron, both pig and wrought, was still regarded as a craft based upon experience and rule of thumb. Puddling, in particular, was in no sense scientific. . . . The quality of the manufactured iron depended on the empirical knowledge and art of the individual puddler, and the skilled men for the most part disliked any threat to their privileged position in the shape of mechanical improvements.[73]

Indeed the last great inventor of the period of British world leadership in iron and steel, Henry Bessemer, was himself an outstanding example of the traditional breed of resourceful 'practical man'. When he took out a patent in January 1855 for his new method of producing steel in quantity which ushered in the age of steel in succession to that of iron, his knowledge of metallurgy was, as he himself wrote in his *Autobiography*, 'very limited, and consisted only of such facts as an engineer must necessarily observe in the foundry or smith's shop. . .'.[74] Yet although eventually his 'Bessemer converter' was to prove an outstanding industrial success, it had to be rescued from initial failure by the advice of a skilled metallurgist, Robert Mushet.[75]

Even in the 1870s a prominent British steel maker, William Menelaus, could advise a board of directors that chemists 'should be kept in a cage until something went wrong',[76] and as late as the 1890s, when most larger British steel works had come to employ a trained chemist, his task was the low-grade one of routine testing instead of the European and American chemist's role of developing new kinds of steel and how to make them.[77] Before 1884 there was no university department of metallurgy anywhere in Britain, no university research; and organic chemistry was little better off.[78] Thus, on the eve of the foreign challenge, science as applied to iron and steel manufacture not only was neglected in Britain, it was scorned. There reigned instead the stultifying authority of customary practice and traditional wisdom.

Yet the colossal pioneering lead built up by Britain, her virtual market monopoly in a period of constantly multiplying demand at home and abroad for wrought iron, above all for the fast expanding network of railways in Europe and America, had made the first half of the nineteenth century a high summer of prosperity for the individualistic British entrepreneur. Wherever the earth of Britain held coal and iron ore, enterprises by the hundred and of every size had bubbled up in the furnace of apparently endless expansion. Pig-iron production had climbed from 3.2 million tons in 1855 to nearly 6 million in 1870, wrought iron from about 1.25 million to 2.6 million,[79] while British success was even more evident in the export totals, with pig iron up from 292,000 tons in 1855 to 1.3 million in 1870.[80] In this climactic year of 1870 Britain produced 50 per cent of the world's pig iron, 37.5 per cent of the wrought iron and 43 per cent of the steel; she accounted for over three-quarters of iron and steel exports.[81] The momentum of this colossal lead was to keep Britain well ahead of her new rivals throughout the 1870s and the 1880s, although their production of both iron and steel was by now climbing much faster than Britain's. In 1885 Britain was still producing well over twice the pig iron of Germany and almost twice as much as the United States; a third more steel than Germany and about a tenth more than the United States.[82]

But even in the 1880s, when the statistics were still apparently attesting to British supremacy, Britain's rivals had already taken that lead in quality of technology and management which was to enable them later to overtake Britain in quantity of production and exports; it was the break-in before the breakthrough. For when they first began to industrialise themselves in the first half of the nineteenth century, they had profited from shrewd observation of the British 'practical man's' shortcomings, which, while true of the whole industrial scene, were especially true of metallurgy. For example, a young French industrialist who toured British industry in 1842 accompanied by a distinguished French engineer reported back to his father on the lack of formal training and scientific understanding they encountered among British managers and foremen. He remarked on how often it was in England that:

> vast manufacturing operations prospered under the direction of passably intelligent foremen, and by workmen taught solely by experience, not to say routine. These works prosper in this way although the managers do not at all understand the important theory involved in the processes, and from the moment they become managers they rest content giving themselves a more or less plausible explanation which thereafter they do not seek at all to probe deeper.[83]

This Frenchman drew the broad conclusion that it was not technical knowledge and capacity that had then made Britain the leading industrial nation, but the bounties of nature:

> with regard to industry the English are placed in favourable conditions which exist nowhere else. You see every metal with the possible exceptions of gold and platinum, with immense coal mines close to the mines that produce these same metals. . . . fuel, in the end the key factor in industry, is so cheap in several counties that in certain works in Newcastle, for example, they do not even know how much coal each furnace burns. Put English workmen and foremen into some part of France or Germany where difficulties can only be overcome with the help of well-informed men and where conditions are less favourable than in this country and you would see them discouraged by the same difficulties.[84]

The Europeans and above all the Germans looked from the very start therefore to organised science and technology, to thorough training at every level, as the necessary instrument of future industrial success. The forging of this sophisticated and elaborate tool began half a century and more before the resulting tempered blade began cutting into world markets: the French *Ecole Polytechnique* for engineers dated from 1794; the Berlin Technical Institute from 1821; technical high schools at Karlsruhe from 1825, at Dresden from 1828, at Stuttgart from 1829. By around 1870 there were already some 3500 students in German technical high schools. Since the 1820s German universities had likewise been developing formidable teaching departments in chemistry, metallurgy, physics and engineering which poured a broadening stream of highly qualified graduates into industry; they established research laboratories as well, to act as the pathfinders to future technological leadership. At a more humble, though hardly less important, level, Britain's rivals made an immense effort to provide themselves with well-trained foremen and workmen who enjoyed a basic understanding of the science underlying industrial processes. By 1851 there were twenty-six trade schools in the German state of Prussia alone giving compulsory post-school training. The metallurgical school at Bochum, for example, which was jointly funded by government, the town and industry, offered a comprehensive three-year course ranging from pure and applied mathematics to physics, chemistry, accountancy and German language.

The technological march thus stolen by Britain's competitors, presaging her later defeat in world markets, and not only in iron and steel, was first alarmingly revealed at the Paris International Exhibition of 1867. Just sixteen years after the Great Exhibition in London had celebrated her majestic leadership in industrial capability, Britain took only ten out of ninety prizes. The disquiet, amounting to shock, at this lamentable performance provoked the appointment of a House of Commons select committee 'to enquire into the Provisions for giving Instruction in Theoretical and Applied Science to the Industrial Classes';[85] the first of repeated voluminous official analyses of defective British education and training for technological success that were to follow over the next century (see below Chapter Eleven). Suddenly the 'practical man' was perceived by enlightened British observers to be no longer adequate. In 1868, for example, another Commons committee, that of the Council for Education, was informed by a witness:

> The Monkbridge Iron Company of Leeds have turned their attention of late to the production of cast steel for the rolling-stock of railways, the manufacture of which was first carried out on a large scale in Westphalia; they are conducting this process under the superintendence of a French engineer . . . and I was assured that they sought in vain amongst Englishmen for a director of works possessing the combination of scientific and practical qualifications. . . .[86]

This want of properly trained personnel provided a major theme of discussion in the new Iron and Steel Institute, founded in 1869 as a product of the aftermath of the Paris Exhibition. An official of the institute reported in 1871 that foreign labour was more intelligent, foreign management more careful and scientific. British iron works by comparison with European were often, he wrote, 'already more or less antiquated upon completion'. Moreover, 'it cannot but be admitted that both our masters and our men have shown themselves equally loath to adopt or encourage improvements until absolutely forced to do so by pressure from without.'[87] Two years later the then president of the institute acknowledged that 'the cultivation of metallurgical science has been much more industriously pursued abroad than has hitherto been the case in this country';[88] and in 1876 it was reported to the institute that many valuable new technical developments were having to be aborted for lack of 'a highly intelligent class of workmen to carry out the practical details'.[89]

The educational revolution that *had* taken place in Britain while the Europeans were founding technical high schools and university research centres could not be of much help in this new situation, since it consisted of the triumph of the classics, religion and high moral idealism in the public schools and at Oxford and Cambridge; and moreover it touched only a tiny upper-class minority, leaving the remainder of the nation in varying shades of dark ignorance (see above pp. 13–14, below Chapter Eleven). In constructing a national apparatus of research, development and training comparable to those now possessed by her rivals, Britain would have to start virtually from scratch. Yet the lead time for accomplishing this, and then staffing industry with its products, could hardly be less than thirty to forty years. This meant, therefore, that even if Britain embarked without delay on construction of such an apparatus the market defeat of her iron and steel industry (and other industries too) had in any case now become absolutely inevitable, for in the meantime she could only field a militia of 'practical men' against modern professionals. But in the event Britain did *not* so embark without delay, either in the 1870s or at any time in the decisive period of British commercial defeat between then and the Second World War; rather there ensued some seventy years of quarter-hearted, piecemeal and always belated improvements in research and education (see below Chapter Eleven).

One effect of this failure was indefinitely to prolong the sway of the 'practical man' in British iron and steel, with dire consequences in terms of the industry's powers of adaptation. For the British problem was not that the commercial and technological capability of those who ran the industry actually *declined* after 1880 in comparison with 1780–1880, but that it remained much the same – and so was surpassed by the new breed of capability evolved abroad. The physical existence of a huge but obsolescent iron and steel industry instead of a 'green-field' site need not by itself have prevented the creation of a modern industry: the examples of Germany and America between 1870 and 1939 demonstrate that continual drastic replacement of plant presents no problem, given only the right outlook and will on the part of management. The real impediment lay in the mind of the 'practical man', which was very far from being a 'green-field' site; rather a cramped space cluttered with old, high-cost prejudices and time-expired self-satisfaction. Rapid loss of market share after the mid-1890s did not succeed in demolishing this mental clutter and clearing the site; it merely served to make the 'practical man' lose his nerve with regard to future investment and expansion.[90] In the face of such a paradoxical blend of the hide-bound and the defeatist, all radical proposals put forward right up to 1939 for remedying the iron and steel industry's decline were to end in nothing but yellowing paper. In fact, the nearer that proposals came to advocating the emulation of such obvious models of success as Germany and America, the less their likelihood of practical adoption.

In 1902 a member of an investigatory team sent to the United States by the British Iron Trades Federation starkly set out the options now before the industry:

> There are three courses open to the British manufacturer. Either he must stand where he is with his old-fashioned appliances, which in many cases, especially in the Midlands, are as old as the iron trade itself, and so incur the chance of being crushed out altogether, or he may more or less adapt his old machinery by the partial installation of

> new, and so greatly improve his existing plant. There is no doubt that this latter plan is being followed to a greater extent at the present time than it ever has been before. . . . Again, the British manufacturer may begin *de novo*, scrap his plant, and discard old-fashioned methods altogether, and put down a first-class, modern, up-to-date plant. This of course involves two things – boldness and confidence in the future, and a considerable amount of capital expenditure.[91]

In fact only one such new integrated plant was completed before the Great War, at Irlam in Lancashire in 1913.

In 1917 the Board of Trade Committee on the Iron and Steel Trades after the war[92] likewise recommended laying down completely new large units at heavy capital cost. It urged that steel makers should combine into large groups with government financial help; that an export sales organisation for the industry should be set up to co-ordinate selling and to distribute the orders won. It wanted the school-leaving age raised to sixteen, with an overlapping apprenticeship and technical education to eighteen. This fundamentally fresh start should be carried out, urged the committee, behind the protection of tariff barriers. The final report of the Committee on Commercial and Industrial Policy after the War[93] similarly called for the replacement of Britain's old individualistic methods by co-operation and combination on the American and German models. It urged that British public opinion should modify its traditional hostility towards the idea of amalgamation and combination. Since these two wartime reports amounted to a copy of the blueprint of the German iron and steel industry's success, they were therefore shelved as soon as the wartime shell fright had been forgotten. For with the return of peace British iron and steel masters instead engaged with alacrity in their early-Victorian-style scramble of piecemeal expansion in pursuit of the short-lived easy pickings of the postwar boom, after which their nerve for doing anything but lying very still was broken afresh by renewed foreign competition, while governments for their part (excepting the brief and impotent Labour administrations of 1923–4 and 1929–31) abandoned wartime ideas of the state's role, in favour of a revival of *laissez-faire* dogma forbidding the erection of tariff barriers or the state reconstruction of industry.

In 1923 an American expert put forward some strictly private-enterprise criticisms of the British iron and steel industry and proposals for its salvation. He found British management 'conservative and unaggressive', and guilty of persistence 'in regarding obsolete plant as assets when in reality they were liabilities'.[94] He recommended building vast new plants of 3-million-ton ingot capacity on sites located on the English and Welsh seaboard, a solution that had to wait until the 1960s for full accomplishment. In 1923 the cost, estimated at £150 million, was reckoned to be excessive: and so, after no 'German' solution, no 'American' solution either. In 1928 a survey of metal industries which was carried out for the Balfour Committee on Industry and Trade did little but wring its hands over the handicap inherited by iron and steel from its origins in the very beginning of the industrial age; this, said the survey, had left it at a disadvantage in adapting the layout and location of plants to new technical conditions.[95] Yet at the time of writing the European industries had carried out, and were still carrying out, massive replacements of pre-war plant that was in any case mostly more up to date than British.

Nonetheless, all was not words instead of deeds in the 1920s. In 1929 the National Federation of Iron and Steel Manufacturers set up its own Industrial Research Council to complement the work now being carried out in metallurgy by British universities – nearly sixty years after the German steel industry had first set up a co-operative research centre, the *Verein Deutscher Eisenhütten Leute.*[96]

In the early 1930s the new Import Duties Advisory Committee, set up in 1932 after the Import Duties Act, proffered some stale old counsel about the need for co-ordination and co-operation in the industry, in order to enable the technical development 'so urgently necessary'.[97] In 1937 the committee in its major report on the industry (the IDAC Report) sadly accepted that the industry's future was likely to resemble its past:

> It was fully recognised that with an old-established and very complex industry which had developed over a long period of time under conditions wholly different from those prevailing today, and (like all the older industries of this country) had until quite recently been very individualistic in its outlook, progress in the new path was unlikely to be very rapid at first. . . .[98]

Worse, and just as with coal mining, there were now potent social and political factors to hinder the emergence of a modern industry out of a Victorian hulk. In the diagnosis of the IDAC Report:

> there is apprehension, particularly among the trade unions concerned, lest the re-organisation of the general lay-out of the industry, which is on all sides regarded as necessary, involving as it may the transference of large undertakings to new areas, the development of new processes and the progress of mechanisation, should proceed without sufficient regard for the social re-actions of the changes involved. Included in these latter are the creation of derelict areas, or the displacement of labour generally. . . .[99]

The IDAC Report urged that the organisation and style of the industry's marketing overseas should also be modernised – virtually on the lines of the large-scale co-operative methods pioneered by the German industry half a century earlier. But it foresaw difficulties because in Britain different manufacturers were selling similar products, and because of the 'diversified character of the existing distributive machinery', which, as the report proceeded to describe, took the form of a bazaar-like web of agents, merchants, clearing-houses and stock-holders. The committee thought that even with bigger steel companies which did possess their own marketing departments 'it would not be easy to find a common basis on which they would agree to pool their selling organisations'.[100] Moreover, even the existing tentative moves towards co-operative marketing arrangements had been attacked by traditional iron and steel merchants.[101]

The IDAC Report was published in the midst of accelerating rearmament; and it was the urgent demands of this which did more to speed the modernisation of the industry than half a century of discussion and proposal. In 1936–9 United Steel constructed new blast furnaces and coke-ovens in Lincolnshire; Colvilles completely rebuilt their Clydeside works to make the first fully integrated iron and steel plant in Scotland; Stewart and Lloyds extended their existing large modern plant at Corby; John Summers completed their 60-inch hot and cold strip mill at Shotton; and Richard Thomas built an American-type continuous strip mill at Ebbw Vale with a capacity of over 600,000 tons a year, which compares with the 1 million tons of the contemporary German *Reichswerke*.[102] The iron and steel industry as it entered the Second World War thus presented striking contrasts between such new British plant, and the relatively large combines that had built them, and the obsolete works and outdated small firms that still accounted for well over half the total production.

Since wartime developments had to be restricted to emergency schemes for producing alloy and carbon steels, it therefore fell in 1945 to yet another British government and yet another set of experts to consider what still needed to be done in order to provide Britain with a world-class steel industry – some seventy years after the industry's basic weaknesses had first become apparent. The Iron and Steel Federation itself submitted a whining report to the Ministry of Supply and the Board of Trade which blamed the industry's interwar troubles on redundant and ill-laid-out plant built during the Great War, and above all on what it plainly believed to have been a malign foreign plot to kill British iron and steel by dumping products at below cost in the period of free trade before the Import Duties Act of 1932. The consequent decline of the industry, averred the federation, had led to a difficulty in recruiting trained and high-quality talent:

> The number of technical students under training in Universities and Colleges fell far below the level necessary to maintain a regular inflow into the Iron and Steel Industry and its associated engineering industry.
>
> Thus in plant and equipment, in financial as well as in human resources, the Industry was rapidly approaching bankruptcy. It was in no condition to stand the added strain of the world's depression of 1931.[103]

This self-justification demonstrates how distant the industry remained even by 1945 from getting to grips with its own deep-seated failings. Indeed the report goes on to speak with evident pride of the £50 million spent on new plant between 1932 and 1939, although this was an average annual rate not much greater than that of the *Vereinigte Stahlwerke* alone in the late 1920s. Nor did the federation's proposals for the postwar era tackle the fundamental and enduring problem of the industry – the ramshackle sprawl of obsolete plants and miniature firms led by 'practical men' that still existed alongside the modern industry created in the 1930s, and which pulled down the British average of efficiency and competitiveness. For, while the federation proposed a five-year programme of modernisation and new construction to expand capacity to 15 million ingot tons, at a cost of about £100 million, the best it could offer with regard to euthanasia of the obsolete was appointment of an Economic Efficiency Committee. This body was to carry out general surveys in order to co-ordinate modernisation throughout the industry, but – in a latter-day manifestation of ingrained individualism – its function was to be only 'advisory and consultative'.[104]

Traditional caution similarly showed in the federation's technical advice that 'on the assumption that the practical target for the Industry is quality and minimum cost of production as distinct from pure technical efficiency, it is not recommended that American practice in the installation of mammoth plants be adopted as general practice in the United Kingdom.'[105] It therefore proposed new steel-making plants from home ores of 500,000–600,000-ton capacity and strip mills of 750,000 tons to 1 million, the largest of these being only a third the size proposed for Britain by an American steelman as long ago as 1923. Nonetheless the federation thought it right to warn that 'The general adoption even of the comparatively small units recommended, demands a greater degree of standardisation of product than exists at present in this country.'[106] Consumers of steel were just as resistant to standardisation as producers, and even by 1950, according to a report by the Anglo-American Council on Productivity, the benefits of widespread standardisation to British Standards were 'greatly reduced by many large steel consumers maintaining their own private specifications'.[107]

The industry's own plan for the postwar era therefore amounted to yet another exercise in tinkering and partial modernisation, albeit more ambitious than any previous schemes to emanate from it. In terms of large-scale organisation both for production and marketing, of standardisation of product, it hardly did more than approach the level of achievement reached by Britain's foreign competitors more than half a century earlier. In particular it offered no root-and-branch strategy for closing down its Victorian and Edwardian relics.

Yet despite all these deficiencies in the industry's postwar plans, the officials of the Ministry of Supply and the Board of Trade, in their own joint report in April 1945 to the Cabinet Reconstruction Committee, did not put forward a policy of drastic state intervention.[108] Even though their report recognised that the industry's future plans were 'a matter of urgency' in view of the importance of steel to the economy and to exports, it still looked to the industry to sort out its own problems with some Whitehall encouragement. The first aim of government policy, it wrote, should be to 'secure the rapid completion of a substantial volume of modernisation and new construction'. The government should therefore request the industry to draw up within six months a five-year plan, with priority given to development at the 'finishing end', to the boosting of exports and to the reduction of fuel costs, and with preference to 'schemes which enable a greater proportion of output to be produced by large-scale production methods'. To enable this strategy to be carried out, the government should offer tariff protection for five years, and also take responsibility for fixing maximum prices based on costs at the most efficient plant. The memorandum accepted that a programme on the scale suggested by the Iron and Steel Federation, at £100 million capital cost, would present very considerable problems in view of heavy competing postwar demands for resources. Striking a note of some desperation, it mooted the possibility of dismantling German steel plants and re-erecting them in Britain, or making the Germans supply new ones.[109] And it remarked that some British iron and steel regions, especially Scotland, were particularly backward.

When the Cabinet Reconstruction Committee discussed this memorandum on 30 April 1945, with the end of the German war only a week away, it had before it a covering note by the Minister of Supply and the President of the Board of Trade which summed up future prospects with gloom enough:

> Thus in general the industry was in great need of modernisation, had large arrears of maintenance, and its competitive position had greatly deteriorated. The average cost of British steel was now estimated to be at least £2 a ton *above* that of our potential competitors and the new increase in the price of coal would raise it by a further 7/– a ton.[110]

In the ensuing discussion, Dalton, the President of the Board of Trade, supported the proposals in the officials' memorandum, while another Labour Cabinet minister, Morrison, the Home Secretary, advocated outright nationalisation. Butler, the Tory reformer and Minister of Education, opposed this on the grounds that there was 'no case for the nationalisation of an industry that had shown itself highly efficient and fully conscious of its national responsibilities'.[111] The discussion thus neatly encapsulated the argument of the next quarter of a century between the nationalisers of the steel industry and its denationalisers. In the end the Reconstruction Committee endorsed the joint memorandum, agreed that the industry should be asked to draw up a five-year plan, but recommended that the government should give no promise of tariff protection.[112] As a national strategy for creating an internationally competitive steel industry, this was more cautious in scope and feebler in the proposed means of implementation than the proposals drawn up during the Great War – in particular by limply entrusting the future to an industry with a past of proven myopic vision and hesitant action.

But in any event, whatever the eventual benefits of the proposed five-year plan, Britain must now enter the postwar era with an iron and steel industry which on balance was currently more of a problem and a competitive handicap than a source of strength. Its physical output would be insufficient to meet the demands of an economic boom. The capital cost of the five-year plan would add £100 million to the even larger investment needs of the coal industry and to all the limitless financial demands of New Jerusalem that were to fall on a bankrupt country. And the high cost of British steel must be reflected in the export prices of all British industries, especially those of the big consumers of steel, and even more especially of industries themselves backward, such as shipbuilding, where hidebound management and obstructive trade unions had helped to imperil Britain's very survival in the face of the U-boat.

Chapter Six

'The Fossilisation of Inefficiency': Shipbuilding

British supremacy in the technology of the first industrial revolution found its quintessential expression in the building of ships from iron and steel. For here metal – wrought, cast, cut, brazed, hammered and shaped – was bolted or riveted together into structures gigantic by the measure of the previous era of wood; structures impelled across the oceans by steam engines of steel, copper and brass that formed the most massive achievements of British mechanical engineering; and guided and controlled by compasses, chronometers, gauges and telegraphs that embodied ultimate precision in the manufacture of mechanical instrumentation. And all this was the work of the 'practical man'. For British shipyards had been founded by entrepreneurs without benefit of theoretical or applied training; carried on by sons and grandsons who had learned what they knew from their fathers and grandfathers. The ships themselves were built and fitted out much as had been medieval cathedrals – by swarms of craftsmen of many skills, and by masses of the unskilled or semi-skilled deployed in working gangs; construction by hand pushed to the ultimate. And like medieval cathedrals British ships were designed and built to the individual order and requirements of each customer rather than standard designs repeated.

Herein lies a paradox. While the iron or steel ship itself represented all the then novel technology of the first industrial revolution, British shipbuilding merely manifests on an unprecedentedly grandiose scale the characteristics of the pre-industrial craft production. There is a further paradox. The industry's rise to domination of the world markets in 1880–1914 took place when otherwise the first industrial revolution had already spent itself, when Britain's industrial supremacy was otherwise already passing. It took place contemporaneously with the emergence of new science-based second-industrial-revolution industries in Germany and America – above all, chemicals and electrical goods. What was more, British shipbuilding's commercial success equally followed an anachronistic pattern, for just like Britain's earlier general supremacy from the 1780s to the 1850s, it was not won against fierce competition, but sprang from being first into the market, from the consequent temporary monopoly until such time as other countries should have developed their own industries. Again like that earlier general supremacy, shipbuilding's success was launched by the fortunate conjuncture of abundant existing advantages: the numerous rivers and estuaries of the British Isles on which to site the yards; the home-market demand from the largest merchant marine in the world; the available resources of the then greatest iron and steel industry and engineering industry in the world; and thereafter an ever more buoyant market for ships as international seaborne trade grew and grew. It could therefore be said that the British shipbuilding industry was an obsolete industrial form even when newly founded around 1870; doomed to eventual eclipse whenever other countries chose seriously to challenge it, unless it proved itself capable of evolutionary transformation, which it did not. In the event it enjoyed a calm sea and a prosperous voyage for only fifty years before it broached to in the blast of competition in the late 1920s and nearly foundered altogether in the 1930s – a much shorter cycle of prosperity and decline than was the case with British coal mining or iron and steel.

For hardly any altogether new shipyards were laid out after 1870; instead shipbuilders expanded their capacity by buying up other yards, by piecemeal extensions or improvements to equipment.[1] But the shipyard sites, the internal layouts and even the contiguous rivers that had been entirely suitable for the size of iron ship of 1870 proved more and more of a handicap as tonnages and dimensions doubled and redoubled. In the judgement of an industrialist's report to the machine-tool controller of the Ministry of Production in September 1942:

> Shipbuilding establishments generally are old established, they started in a comparatively small way. The work has persistently grown from small to larger vessels. . . . the general layout of the yards has been very much dictated by circumstances and has not been easily adaptable to present-day methods. Many of the existing factors cannot be changed under present conditions without seriously interfering with production. . . .[2]

This report also noted that in nearly all cases 'larger ships were being built than those for which the yards were originally designed. . .'; and in the North-east and Scotland this particularly posed problems because the old yards were limited in extent, and could not be enlarged either because of nearby high ground or because they were cramped within urban areas with difficult access.

Moreover, British shipbuilding became fixed to a remarkable degree in the human and technical patterns of the 1870s and 1880s, with continued reliance on the hands and muscles of multitudes of craftsmen and manual workers, and minimum investment in mechanisation except for heavy tackle for manoeuvring very big components. In the short term, up to 1914, these patterns enabled the British shipbuilder to keep his prices lower than those of newer shipbuilding nations like America and Germany which had laid down elaborately equipped modern yards.[3] But the pre-industrial reliance on numerous craft skills, learned on the job by apprenticeship, entailed profound long-term penalties. For as ships became more complicated, so crafts proliferated, until by 1914 there were no fewer than ninety in British shipyards. Each skill defended its corner of the productive process with the tenacity of a medieval peasant defending his rights within the village common field. Two enduring and in the end fatal handicaps of British shipbuilding ensued – the welter of different craft unions and the destructive effect on productivity of the rigid demarcations between them. Even after consolidation in 1906–10 there were eighteen general shipbuilding unions, not counting specialist trades like plumbing and joinery.[4] As two historians of the industry between 1870 and 1914 sum it up:

> The engineers quarreled with the boilermakers, shipwrights, joiners, brassworkers and tinplate workers; the boilermakers with the shipwrights, smiths, chippers, and drillers; the shipwrights with the caulkers, boat and barge builders, mast- and blockmakers, and joiners, and the joiners with the mill-sawyers, patternmakers, cabinet makers, upholsterers, and French polishers. On the Tyne, there was an average of one major strike per month over questions of demarcation between 1890 and 1893.[5]

The worship of minutely differentiated craft skills also carried with it the other long-term penalties of technical conservatism, of resistance to new processes and new machines which threatened a union's 'ownership' of some piece of the existing action; and of veneration of the 'practical man', self-taught on the job in traditional rules-of-thumb. These characteristics were condoned by management; indeed shared by them. For the shipyard owners too continued to be 'practical men' with minimal technical education. The shipbuilding firms passed down in the same families generation by generation; among fifty leading firms in 1914 as many as thirteen still had boards composed solely of members of a single family.[6] In this inward-looking, intellectually incestuous world, the young aspirant to management learned the job by passing time in different branches of the yard, most important of all in the drawing office. Of the professional staff, most builders and designers before 1890 were men without higher education in mathematics or engineering, such qualifications being regarded as luxuries.[7] Even though the best yards gradually switched towards the trained specialist, 'as late as 1914 science and research were still the poor stepchildren of the industry.'[8]

The very nature of British shipbuilding as the hand-construction of enormous machines rendered it the most graphic of all examples of Victorian industrial disdain on the part of workforce and management alike for formal and thorough technical education at any level. Even when towards the end of the nineteenth century and into the early twentieth the more intelligent shipbuilders had come to recognise the threatening quality of foreign research, technical development and technical education, they failed to translate their admiration into action at home – partly because they could not agree on what form technical education should take.

> The primary theme running through their discussions was the need to preserve the 'practical man' while at the same time providing enough technical training to meet the competition from abroad. This adoration of the 'practical man' influenced the decisions of builders and engineers and led ultimately to the unsatisfactory compromises that characterised all British technical education.[9]

Some shipbuilders even saw part-time technical education as of value less in conferring technical understanding than in inculcating the 'moral' values of discipline and hard work.[10] Although, as in other British industries, gradual progress in this field did take place before 1914, especially in more enlightened firms, it came, again as in other industries, nowhere near to overhauling the foreigner. In 1907 Britain had one full-time student of naval architecture per 16,000 tons of ship produced; Germany one per 100 tons. In Sunderland in 1913–14 only 38 per cent of engineering apprentices and 12 per cent of shipbuilding apprentices were attending evening classes.[11]

The consequence of the neglect of research and development and of the need for highly trained management showed itself in lack of innovation both in ship design and in methods of building. By 1914 few firms had yet equipped themselves with laboratories or testing tanks. Major inventions like Parson's steam turbine emanated from outside the industry. The diesel engine was relatively neglected. 'Most progress consisted of many small changes produced by men of little or moderate education. Great improvements, based on a solid knowledge of scientific theory, were few. . . .'[12] By the 1900s British shipbuilding was already beginning to fall badly behind its newer rivals in terms of technology. As a distinguished historian of the industry explains:

> There is little doubt that much of the equipment found in British yards was less advanced than that in America and Germany. British yards had their ancient steam engines to generate power, their lathes and plate-bending machines, but, as far as the installation of hydraulic, pneumatic or electric power transmission was concerned, or the use of mechanical yard transport . . . even electric lights, most of them were years behind their chief foreign rivals, and visiting foreign experts could seldom conceal their astonishment at this backwardness.[13]

Yet in the short term the British shipbuilder was doing all right in regard to market share, profits, productivity; he was making, according to his own criteria, sensible investment decisions, usually to invest as little as possible. The momentum of his enormous initial advantage in being first into the field for ferrous ships still carried him on; his varied army of hand-craftsmen, lower paid than in America, and the sheer volume of orders and production enabled him for the time being to achieve productivity and prices beyond the reach of his competitors. His very lack of elaborate and up-to-date capital equipment kept his overheads much lower than theirs. But all this was *only* short-term – the time-expiring advantages of an obsolescent technology which neither management nor workforce, in their desire for a steady state, wanted to change.

The 'short term' ended abruptly in the 1920s. In 1909–13 Britain produced nearly 60 per cent of world shipbuilding tonnage; in 1924, with the U-boat sinkings of the Great War in the course of being made good, 64 per cent; in 1929, 54.5 per cent of a world total actually bigger than the annual average for 1909–13; in 1931, with the industry on its beam-ends in the hurricane of the slump, only 31 per cent of a world total shrunk by nearly a third; in 1932, near to foundering, less than 26 per cent.[14] In this latter year British shipyards constructed only 188,000 tons, against an annual average of 1½ million in 1909–13. Even by 1938, when the world total had recovered to its highest ever, at over 3 million tons, the British share only reached 34 per cent.[15] This was the 'long term' now, and all those characteristics of British shipbuilding which had once seemed commercial strengths came to be exposed as catastrophic faults. Craft construction methods had fossilised in the structure of unions and their demarcations, so crippling productivity and blocking technical change; for example, from riveting to welding. The 'practical man' in management lacked the new skills of flow-production planning and detailed cost-control development abroad. The capital equipment was inferior in quantity and modernity, especially with regard to machine tools, electric power and sufficient cranage. The tradition established from the very outset of iron and steel shipbuilding in Britain whereby every yard made every kind of ship, often in different berths at the same time, meant that there could be no economies of standardisation and scale by means of specialising. And the ageing family boards of the industry were hardly less flabbergasted by the sinking condition of the industry of which they had been so smugly proud than those on the bridge of the stricken *Titanic.* The events of the early 1930s made cruel mockery of such assertions as that made in 1925 to the House of Commons Commercial Committee by Sir James Lithgow, accounted among the most able of British shipbuilders: 'Shipbuilding is still, as it was pre-war, a strong, well-organized and virile industry, with pre-eminent technical skill. . . .'[16]

Moreover shipbuilding suffered from that universal Victorian industrial hangover in Britain of individualistic fragmentation – one of the factors that militated against specialising yards or regions on particular kinds of vessel. In 1918 a Board of Trade committee had called for greater co-operation within the industry, warning that 'whilst individualism has been of inestimable advantage in the past, there is reason to fear that individualism by itself may fail to meet the competition of the future in shipbuilding and marine engineering.'[17] Yet it was to be another ten years before a trade association for the industry, the Shipbuilding Conference, could be set up. The National Shipbuilders' Security, founded in 1930, was unhappily to have only the negative role of closing down yards in the face of collapsed demand. The 1930s marked a steady shrinking of shipbuilding capacity, a dwindling of the workforce to little more than half the 1920 figure, and very little modernisation. Britain entered the Second World War in 1939 with a shipbuilding industry that was a rusting, partially dismantled and partly unmanned hulk of essentially Victorian technology; and, on the whole, no less rusting were its management and workforce and their operational methods.

As the motherland of a maritime empire and with an economy highly dependent on foreign markets and on overseas sources of food, raw materials and high technology, Great Britain must depend in war for very survival, let alone victory, on her merchant marine and the Royal Navy. This meant providing enough escorts to protect the convoys; enough repair and new construction to make good the damage inflicted by the enemy surface raider and the U-boat. Yet the misguided and bootless pursuit of disarmament from the time of the Washington Naval Treaty in 1922 until the major resumption of naval building in 1935–6 had left the Royal Navy dangerously short of modern ships of every category, but dismayingly so in the case of cruisers and destroyers, as in April 1931 the then First Sea Lord had pointed out in heavy black type in a memorandum to the Committee of Imperial Defence.[18] Furthermore, disarmament had also led to a dereliction in the specialist shipyard resources needed for naval construction that was even worse than in shipbuilding generally. For example, in 1937 after rearmament had begun, Beardmores, once a principal supplier of warships and of their guns and gun-mountings, presented the problem, according to the government's chief industrial adviser Lord Weir, 'of raising what might be termed a scrap-heap to an efficient unit'.[19]

With regard to shipbuilding in general, the problem lay not so much in re-equipment as in bringing back into production resources lying idle since the slump, and that meant human resources even more than technical. For unfortunately many of these human resources had now drifted away to other work, other towns. As early in the rearmament programme as June 1936 the Ministry of Labour was reporting that although the available supply of skilled shipyard labour 'is adequate for present requirements, much of the existing surplus is of poor quality, and there is some likelihood that a sustained increase in demand would create a problem of shortage in certain occupations.'[20] Next month a special enquiry by the ministry into the supply of skilled labour in shipbuilding laid out the stark implications of a shortage of such labour for an industry which had once risen to world supremacy thanks to a plenitude of it:

> it is abundantly clear . . . that a large and sudden demand for naval construction would be certain to overtax the labour capacity of the industry, and could only be achieved at the risk of serious delay or the disorganisation of the labour force ordinarily engaged in the construction of merchant vessels. The results of the enquiry emphasise the importance of any naval programme being envisaged from the point of view of enabling the industry to recreate and train a

skilled personnel by the engagement of apprentices in adequate numbers.[21]

But despite the recruitment of new apprentices, the dearth of craftsmen in the yards continued to worsen in 1936–7.[22] The present-day weakness of an industry that had from the beginning looked more to labour than capital equipment for productivity became dispiritingly evident. By the end of 1937 shipbuilding output had already reached what Whitehall estimated to be its maximum peacetime potential, with 1,125,426 tons of merchant vessels in hand and 547,014 tons of naval.[23] Yet this represented only 65 per cent of available slip capacity.[24] Although the total registered labour force in shipbuilding and ship repairing had now risen to nearly 180,000 from 161,000 before the start of rearmament, and the total actually at work to nearly 140,000 from 93,000, the rate of unemployment still stood at 21 per cent.[25] The bottleneck that prevented unused slips and unused men being brought into production lay in key skilled labour, of which little reserve now remained.[26] This limit on mobilisable resources therefore placed a premium on efficiency and high productivity – not factors which the shipyard trade unions existed to promote. In November 1936 Vickers-Armstrong, the most important of all British naval shipbuilders and armourers, informed the Admiralty that 'the refusal of their workmen, who are members of the Amalgamated Engineering Union and Electrical Trades Union, to work further overtime may cause delays in completing the contracts for hulls and/or machinery for certain vessels.'[27] In April 1937 the Admiralty reported to the Defence Policy Requirements Committee about a strike at Beardmores which had held up production of the new 'Tribal' class destroyers by some six months, and a strike by apprentices on the Clyde which 'must have a general retarding effect'.[28]

Whitehall's final pre-war planning estimate in 1939 for wartime ship production reckoned in the light of all the factors on an annual output of about 1,200,000 gross tons of merchant vessels and 370,000 standard displacement tons of naval.[29] There was, however, another and decisive factor which must inevitably hold down new construction – the deployment of men and yards on the no less vital task of repairing ships and converting others to war purposes. In the event, at least half as many men again would be engaged in these activities throughout the war years as in building new ships.[30] The actual outbreak of war brought a further factor into play, in the destruction wrought by German guns, bombs and torpedoes along the trade routes and in the course of such maritime campaigns as Norway in 1940 and Greece and Crete in 1941. By March 1941 the backlog of damaged merchant ships awaiting repair had reached over 2.5 million tons, while outright sinkings of merchant ships climbed from nearly 4 million tons in 1940 to 4.3 million in 1941 and 4.1 million in the first half of 1942 alone.[31] To offset these statistics of looming catastrophe, British shipyards had turned out 801,000 tons of new construction in 1940 and 1,156,000 tons in 1941. Here was one ingredient in the shipping and shipbuilding crisis that confronted the War Cabinet in the course of 1942; the other lay in the frightening paucity of naval escorts which had so much exposed merchant vessels to German attack. By March 1942 the Royal Navy could deploy little more than half the number operationally needed, the shortfall amounting to 342 ships.[32]

To screw a much higher rate of completion of new tonnage – most urgently of escorts – out of British shipyards had now therefore become a crucial problem of the war effort. With the concurrence of the Admiralty, the Minister of Production, Oliver Lyttelton, appointed a committee under Robert Barlow, a distinguished industrialist, 'to enquire into Conditions of Labour in Shipyards'. The Barlow Committee submitted its report on 24 July 1942, the month when Auchinleck stopped Rommel from reaching Alexandria in the First Battle of Alamein; when Beveridge wrote the first draft of his plan for a welfare state; and when nearly half a million tons of merchant shipping were lost to the U-boat. The committee did not restrict itself to the question of labour in shipyards only, but produced a terse and devastating anatomy of every aspect of the industry in relation to the war effort.

It opened its report by noting the effects of the pre-war slump, which it judged to have been worse than on any other industry. Skilled men had left shipbuilding, many of them irrecoverably, while the experience of unemployment (though the Barlow Report did not mention it, this had reached 64 per cent at its peak in 1932) had bequeathed a 'not unnatural reluctance on the part of the workpeople readily to admit of a future great expansion of the people in the industry'.[33] It had also led, wrote the committee, to a failure to maintain equipment at a high level of efficiency. In the course of its tour of the shipbuilding areas and discussions with the Shipbuilding Employers' Federation and the Confederation of Shipbuilding and Engineering Unions, the committee had noted 'Sharply marked differences in local practices and customs'. More to the point, it may be thought, with ships going down in the Atlantic every day, was the committee's remark that:

> In certain yards we found an atmosphere based upon an inadequate appreciation of the urgency and gravity of the National situation. In some cases the Management appeared content with the existing position and, at the time we interviewed them, did not fully appreciate the necessity for greater effort. A similar outlook was observed also in the attitude of the Union representatives. . . .[34]

The Barlow Committee was careful to say in its report that this was not true of all managements and unions in the industry, but Robert Barlow himself, in a memorandum to the Minister of Production on 27 July 1942, said he was convinced 'that a degree of complacency among all concerned permeates the whole field of production'.[35] The Barlow Committee's answer to this complacency was to recommend that both sides of the industry should be fully informed of the facts.[36]

The second human factor making for poor productivity was, in the committee's judgement, slackness at work:

> We have evidence of a lack of discipline, particularly among the

> younger men, and of a reluctance to work agreed overtime, and our attention was drawn to what has become a custom whereby workers delay starting work until 10 or 15 minutes after the due time and begin making their way to the gates 10 or 15 minutes before stopping time. . . .[37]

The Barlow Committee calculated the cumulative result of this wartime habit to be the loss of 10 per cent of production; and it called for amendment to the Essential Work Order (Shipbuilding and Ship-repairing) so that prompt remedial action could be taken. A further cause of lost production, however, lay in the reluctance to work overtime:

> It is argued that owing to the arduous nature of the work in some trades, the men may be physically incapable of a higher degree of overtime. It is admitted that an undue amount of overtime defeats its own ends; but if it be true that 6 hours during the week and every other Sunday imposes too great a strain, it is a little difficult to understand why the Men's representatives on the North East Coast have submitted to the Employers a proposal [for extra overtime in the long summer days]. . . .[38]

The committee identified the labour bottlenecks as lying in riveting, plating, welding and electrical work. It believed that productivity could be raised by 'dilution', or raising the proportion of unskilled labour, so that skilled labour was not wasted on what ought to be unskilled or semi-skilled operations, but it noted that opposition existed to dilution because the craft unions were fearful lest the Restoration of Pre-War Trade Practices Act proved inefficacious. This Act of Parliament, by which the state formally undertook to restore all that overmanning and those absurd inter-union demarcations throughout all industries which had already done so much to hasten British industrial decline, was the price extracted from the wartime national government in 1940 by the unions for their kind consent, often enough dishonoured in the event, to the removal of these brakes on productivity while the nation was actually fighting for survival. In fact, Ernest Bevin, the Minister of Labour and National Service, had expressed himself far more pungently on the topic of dilution in shipbuilding than the Barlow Committee when, in the course of a letter to the First Lord of the Admiralty in April 1942, he remarked on 'how difficult and backward the shipbuilding industry has been from a labour point of view ever since I have been in office. Everything that has been done has almost had to be forced upon them.'[39] Most of the unions were craft unions insisting on strict control over the numbers of entrants into their trades and on five-year apprenticeships.[40]

The Barlow Committee itself could only express the hope that discussions with 'both sides' might resolve this key question of dilution; a hope the naïveté of which was brutally trampled on by Bevin in a letter to the Minister of Production on 15 August 1942:

> I think . . . it is quite visionary to think that any prejudice against

> dilution will be removed by further discussions between both sides of the industry. Prejudice against dilution exists, in my opinion, because the men remember what happened to them after the last war and do not trust the employers or the Government to prevent the same thing occurring after this one.[41]

The committee's prescription for curing the dearth of skilled labour took the rather obvious form of more training schemes and more apprenticeships, while its remaining final recommendations called for new overtime agreements, a relaxation of the winter blackout to allow better lighting in the yards, modernisation of equipment, new piece-work agreements, and a detailed analysis of the labour in each yard in order to achieve a more economical deployment.[42]

As a consequence of the Barlow Report the Controller of Machine Tools at the Ministry of Production held a meeting on 5 August 1942 which decided to follow up the report with a detailed technical survey yard by yard by a small team headed by Cecil Bentham, the chairman of Messrs Henry Simon. On 17 August Bentham set off to conduct his survey; and on 30 September he put in his report.[43] It made even glummer reading than the Barlow Report. Bentham summarised how the technical history of the industry since the 1870s had bequeathed yards and layouts unsuited to modern methods, and how radical changes could not now be made without interrupting production. 'Under these circumstances', he opined, 'it has been necessary to concentrate on improvement under conditions which are not necessarily ideal or fundamentally sound.'[44] In particular, because the industry had lacked funds before the war for investment, there had been, in his words, no improvements at a time of great technical strides.

Bentham thought little of the management of the industry, which he found on meeting it to comprise on the whole low-spirited and chap-fallen geriatrics with dusty minds stuffed with Victorian managerial and technical prejudices. The pre-war slump had not only discouraged young men from seeking a career in the industry, but also, Bentham was certain, had:

> disheartened and depressed the older men who cannot readily change to other industries. There seem to be fewer young men in managerial positions than is the case in other industries and lacking the urge of young men coming forward it has not been easy even in the war period for the older men to shake off the inevitable lethargy of the slump period. For a time there has been a lack of acquaintance with modern developments or they have been over-impressed by the impossibility of using them. . . .[45]

There was, therefore, a need for new blood in management – not least because of poor day-to-day 'line' leadership: 'The planning of the work and the operation of the shipyard does not appear to have made much progress in the last twenty years. The work proceeds with the maximum effort, and methodical handling of material is rare. . . .'[46]

Bentham remarked on the extraordinary variety of ships built simultaneously in each yard before the war, and called for much greater standardisation both of types of ship and of their component parts and details. He urged that production of certain types of vessel be concentrated on certain yards in order to maximise output. He recognised that the largest shipyards were already best in this respect, but 'others are wedded to variety because that is the way the yard has grown and it is not easy to change. . . .'[47] Nevertheless, even old and cramped yards could, he argued, be better laid out internally. Where there was sufficient space, ships could be prefabricated in sections and then welded together; this, though Bentham did not say so, was standard American practice in regard to merchant ships and German practice in regard to U-boats. But the problem with this and other kinds of assembly work lay in inadequate cranage. Common present practice was for cranes of 3–5 tons capacity, Bentham reported, whereas prefabrication on a large scale could mean 35 tons. Bentham therefore recommended the installation of twenty cranes of 15 tons capacity immediately; a recommendation which may be compared with the existing general equipment of German shipyards with 20-ton cranes.[48] Bentham found fitting-out berths to be a major bottleneck, and he reported that these urgently needed heavy cranes of up to 100 tons capacity for handling major items of ships' equipment (such cranes having in fact for long been a notable feature of German yards, Blöhm und Voss in particular possessing a 250-ton crane tested to 300 tons).[49] As for marine-engine works, Bentham estimated that only 25 per cent of the plant in the North-east was modern, and 50 per cent in Scotland. Yarrow Shipbuilders alone earned any praise in the Bentham Report, on account of their modern equipment and their use of semi-skilled workers where possible in place of highly skilled.

When he turns to the topic of machine tools in British yards, Bentham rather sounds as if he were compiling an inventory of exhibits in the Science Museum. Many large machines were twenty or thirty years old, he wrote, although still 'fairly effectively' used. Nevertheless the intensity of present-day working was taking the life out of them. The cost of replacement and the consequent interruption of production was, continued Bentham, a problem he could not answer. Medium and small machines were 'wearing out rapidly' owing to the high grade of material they now had to work on and the power behind them. He recognised that most firms had put in a few new machines in the last three or four years, but, said he:

> the effect is rather to show up how very much out of date is the remainder of the plant. The bulk of the machines in some works is left over from the last war or previously. Numbers are in use over thirty years of age and are unsuitable for present day cutting speeds, unskilled labour, accuracy, convenience. . . .[50]

Worse, this antique kit seemed to reveal no less antique attitudes towards the nature of skill and training:

> The use of capstan and turret lathes is very limited and there is simply no comparison on this score with other industries. There are in existence large numbers of old centre lathes and an explanation was given to me on several occasions that these were useful for training apprentices, i.e. they are inaccurate and difficult to operate, and this is good training for apprentices. My view is that today there is no necessity to train apprentices on inaccurate or inadequate machines, and such training is likely to inculcate wrong ideas regarding present day methods, and their training would be much better devoted to mastering the intricacies of precision operations and assembly to accurate dimensions. . . .[51]

Bentham drew the conclusion that large numbers of standard and special tools were needed; not an easy requirement to satisfy in the middle of a world war in competition with the needs of the rest of the munitions industries.

Bentham's description of the workshops where the minor internal organs of ships were fabricated evokes a traveller's account of the craftsmen's booths in an Arab *soukh*. In the coppersmiths' shops, where in fact iron as well as copper piping was assembled, and indeed all kinds of plumbing work, 'Much work is done in a very crude manner' and without benefit of standardised components.

> Many of the pipes apparently cannot be decided until the machinery is assembled, whereas in most other industries such work would be decided either on the drawing board or on models. To anyone acquainted with other types of production the pipe work in some cases appears to be done with the maximum difficulty.[52]

Instead of employing grinding machines to produce accurately faced pipe joints, highly skilled craftsmen patiently scraped away at the surfaces by hand. Nevertheless, Bentham doubted 'whether existing prejudices could be overcome'.[53] In the blacksmiths' shops small steam hammers were being used instead of the electro-pneumatic hammers recommended by Bentham, and there was too high a proportion of skilled labour, coupled with a prejudice against employing female unskilled labour. The workshops engaged on repair work were 'most of them equipped with old machine tools, most of them very much out of date'.[54]

On 26 October 1942 (it was three days after Montgomery had launched his offensive against the Axis army at Alamein), Bentham submitted an additional report in which he stated that 800 new machines and nearly 200 cranes were needed within the next year in order to bring yards and shops into first-class order, at a cost of over £2 million.[55] To plan and monitor the execution of Bentham's recommendations a new Shipyard Development Committee was set up, meeting for the first time on 19 November 1942 under the chairmanship of Sir James Lithgow, the eminent shipbuilder and now Controller of Merchant Shipbuilding and repairs in the Admiralty. Lithgow himself resented public criticism of the industry's lack of

'American' mass-production methods, and he had his own astringent views as to the causes of the industry's backwardness:

> It is not expedient at this stage to put the blame for our present obsolete shipbuilding outlook on the shoulders of the craft unions who are so busy blaming everyone else, but with forty years' experience I do know that it is the worship of the status quo, which these people have always insisted upon, that has frozen at their source most efforts to adopt modern methods, simply because the economy in time and money, which is the justification for modern methods, has been absorbed by extravagant claims for compensation in piece-rates and refusal to adapt themselves to a quicker technique. On the other hand, the repercussion of that obstructive attitude has undoubtedly driven the average shipyard manager to the easier course of leaving things alone, so that when a new technique is urged as at present both sides are loud in its denunciation. . . .[56]

Under the auspices of the Shipyard Development Committee the most ambitious programme of capital investment in the new plant seen in British yards for at least half a century was carried out in 1942–4, at a cost of £6 million, of which the government contributed £1.5 million, a sum equivalent to 75 per cent of that part of the programme relating to merchant shipbuilding.[57] As early as the end of January 1943 most of the tools asked for by Bentham (including pneumatic tools from America) had been delivered, though cranes were late in delivery, and not expected before April.[58] In its final report on 3 August 1943 the committee was able to state that 90 per cent of new welding-equipment schemes were complete or would be so by September. Only exceptionally large cranes or machinery would be delayed until 1944. All this constituted a remarkable feat of re-equipment in the middle of a world war. Yet there had been snags. With regard to marine engines, the problem was 'how to introduce mass production methods into small production units. There was a tendency for small units to turn out four or five types of engine, instead of concentrating upon a single type. . . .'[59] The difficulty in introducing new welding equipment resided in inadequate electric power supplies – either varying voltages at different points in the same yard, or power plants with insufficient output to meet the extra demand.[60] And the fragmentation of the British shipbuilding and marine-engine industry is vividly conveyed by the June 1943 schedule of progress reports on re-equipment, which lists no fewer than ninety-six separate firms.[61]

Conceived as it had been at a time of rising peril from the U-boat, this programme of re-equipping British shipyards was completed, ironically enough, only after the Battle of the Atlantic had been essentially won at sea. In November 1942, the month the Shipyard Development Committee began work, over 800,000 tons of merchant shipping had been lost to enemy action; in July 1943, when the committee was winding up its task, less than 120,000 tons.[62] And as the Bentham Report had recognised, only emergency improvements in shipyard equipment that would not dislocate present production had been possible, not the radical reorganisation of layouts and methods, let alone the development of wholly new 'green-field' yards on the German or American model. The character of British shipbuilding, with its historical flaws, still remained therefore as it was; and especially the human flaws. Would management prove competent to make the most of the new equipment and the available labour-force? Would the unions and their members prove willing to work the new equipment to the utmost? They did not; they would not.

In 1943 merchant shipbuilding reached 1.2 million tons as against 1.3 million in 1942, so achieving a reduced target set by the War Cabinet in October 1942 when it decided to give priority to production of naval escorts. Despite this priority, however, warship construction in 1943 at 316,112 tons amounted only to 84 per cent of the Cabinet's target figure. In 1944 merchant shipbuilding failed to meet a target lowered still further to 1.12 million tons, while warship building for the first half of the year dropped to a mere 72 per cent of the target of 218,532 tons.[63] Management for its part stubbornly resisted new methods of building such as prefabrication or flow-production of standard ships. One of the largest Clyde firms had only two sister ships on its slips throughout the war.[64] Although some frigates, some tramp steamers and all tank-landing craft were prefabricated, this in no way matched the American programme of prefabricated 'Liberty' ships or the German mass production of U-boats, where hulls were constructed in sections on inland sites and welded together in the yards in series. The limited progress of prefabrication in Britain owed itself not only to the reluctance of managements to enter into a wholly unfamiliar method of manufacture, but also to the want of the production-management skills needed to co-ordinate the flow and assembly of parts, and lastly from lack of technological resources which the post-Bentham programme of re-equipment could not remedy. In the first place, cramped British yards rarely afforded the extent of flat space needed for assembling large prefabricated components; and secondly, few British yards enjoyed the cranage or the internal transport facilities to manoeuvre such sections. In any event, unlike those in America or Germany, transport facilities outside the shipyards themselves were also too restricted in Britain to enable large-scale sections to be moved from inland places of fabrication.[65]

Yet the principal culpability of shipyard management resided in their incompetent planning of the familiar traditional production in their yards, and their utter failure to make optimum use of their workforces. In April 1943, for instance, the Ministry of Labour was complaining about 'the wasteful use of a large percentage of skilled and unskilled labour in many'.[66] This wastefulness owed itself partly to lack of sheer moral fibre on the part of management in tackling union resistance to dilution. In the judgement of an unpublished study of labour in the wartime shipbuilding industry written for the Cabinet Office Historical Section:

> the expansion of the labour force was primarily at the discretion of the employers, some of whom were reluctant, partly because of the opposition of the unions, to dilute their labour force.

> . . . it is true to say that the yards were never quite as full as they would have been if all employers had been prepared to make the best use of what labour was available, including women, and the unions to agree fully to dilution.[67]

Nonetheless, for all the weaknesses of dim, old-fashioned and often elderly managers, it was the unions and their members who continued to be the real culprits in losing potential production, as was infuriatingly evident to their fellow citizens reaching home ports after crewing merchant ships through the combined ferocities of the sea and the U-boat. A reporter noted down in his diary in May 1943 a ship's officer's opinion of workmen engaged on ship repairing:

> 'There's a group of them always to be seen in the bottom of the hold round a brazier. What they're supposed to be doing, I don't know. They're never working when I see them.' A Government official who accompanied me said, as we walked round this dry dock and ship repair yard [in Liverpool]: 'Just take a look as we walk round and see if you discover anybody working.' He added that he visits these sorts of yards from time to time, and the sight makes him almost weep – he estimates (somewhat satirically) that the men working are one in ten.[68]

Better documented, naturally enough, than such skilled and dedicated avoidance of tiring activity was the effect of continued rigid craft demarcations and overmanning insisted on by the unions, even to the point of threatened strikes or actual strikes. According to a memorandum by the Ministry of Labour in October 1943, interchangeability of work between one craft and another was:

> only permissible in existing circumstances in so far as it is expressly provided for in agreements which have been reached between the Shipbuilding Employers' Federation and certain of the principal shipbuilding unions. . . . This method, however, is cumbersome and it is arguable that, if the skilled labour force in each shipyard is to be kept continuously employed to the best advantage, a much more flexible method should be adopted whereby craftsmen could, where necessary, be transferred to skilled work in another craft where they are more urgently required even though it be only for a short period of a few hours at a time. Few industries require the skills of so many different types of craftsmen (each necessarily working in the same confined area) or experience so much difficulty in keeping them continuously employed; it frequently happens that some of the skilled craftsmen are unable to get their work through to time whilst other types of craftsmen are insufficiently occupied. Owing to the demarcation restrictions, however, the latter cannot help the former, although technically equipped to do so.[69]

In unrelenting pursuit of such absurdities worthy of a weird land of nonsense observed by Lemuel Gulliver, the Amalgamated Engineering Union and the Boilermakers' Society refused to allow appropriately skilled members of the National Union of Railwaymen to work in shipyards; the Electricians' Trade Union in a shipyard refused to work with a non-union electrician, and threatened to strike;[70] the Boilermakers skirmished with the Constructional Engineering Union as to who should do what;[71] and went on strike in December 1944 over a dispute with the Shipwrights over who should operate a flame cutting machine.[72] In the fabrication and installation of ships' ventilators alone no fewer than seven crafts were involved, some more than once.[73] Even day-to-day interchangeability, such as an electrician drilling a hole for his wiring rather than wait for a paid-up driller, 'was not achieved on any scale. The men and the unions objected to it on much the same grounds as they objected to dilution, but more strongly. If any skilled man could do another's job the labourer could do it too, and they feared, at labourer's rates.' There was also the fear of losing the 'ownership' of part of the production process to another craft.[74] Thus while the convoys fought their way through, the shipyards bickered and downed tools about what were to them the really important issues.

'Dilution' spurred the most dogged resistance of all to technological change, and not least because of the potential labour-saving from the new machines or processes introduced under the 1942–3 re-equipment scheme. The core of that resistance was provided by the Boilermakers' Society, that Old Guard which eventually in 1960–80 died rather than surrender. In the words of an official of the Ministry of Labour in May 1943, 'Whenever dilution is raised, we seem to be brought up against this ghostly squad of unemployed boilermakers.'[75] Yet since some shipyard work which was rated as skilled in Britain rated only as semi-skilled abroad,[76] dilution of labour on existing processes or the adoption of labour-saving alternatives offered an essential key to higher productivity. This was particularly true of riveting and its alternative, welding. The Boilermakers therefore implacably resisted recruitment and training of more riveters. A government Riveting Training School at Jordanvale on the Clyde was opened only in April 1942, although first mooted in February 1941 – partly because the Boilermakers demanded a promise that the ratio of apprentices to journeymen should not exceed 1:5. The school eventually supplied some 460 riveters in two years.[77] When and where pneumatic riveting replaced hand-riveting, so in fact requiring only one-man operation, employer and union agreed that an additional man, who would have been needed as a 'mate' on pre-war hand-riveting, should also be employed. As a Mass-Observation Report in 1941 noted, this person 'has nothing at all to do now, except to sit all day beside the riveter. He draws full wages.'[78]

So successful was the union resistance to dilution that virtually no change occurred in the course of the war in the proportion of shipbuilding labour rated as skilled. After a slight drop from 50 per cent in 1940 to 47 per cent in 1942–3, it rose again to 48 per cent by the end of the year – in glaring contrast to the aircraft industry, where those paid at skilled rates dropped from 50–60 per cent in 1939 to some 30 per cent in 1945.[79]

British shipbuilding thus emerged from the Second World War the better off for £6 million worth of new machines, but with its fundamental shortcomings, technological and psychological, still absolutely intact. It is therefore little wonder that the First Lord of the Admiralty, in a memorandum of March 1944 to the Cabinet Reconstruction Committee, reported that 'it is proving extremely difficult to get the industry itself to take the necessary steps to keep its plant up to date'; and that there was a necessity 'to keep a sharp look out for any tendency towards what I may term the fossilisation of inefficiency'.[80] It is little wonder that he pointed out that Keynesian demand management offered no answer to the industry's structural and special problems.[81] And, further, it is little wonder that the Cabinet Reconstruction Committee itself came to the cautious conclusion in July 1944 that while the postwar prospects for British shipbuilding looked promising for the first eight or ten years, this period of grace ought to be employed in improving the long-term efficiency of an industry the management and workforce of which 'tended to be conservative', many of the existing yards of which were 'cramped and ill-sited', and the trade unions in which tended 'to resist the introduction of new methods and to impose demarcation rules to a degree which impeded progress'.[82]

In the event the Cabinet Reconstruction Committee's forecast of eight to ten years' grace for British shipbuilding in the postwar era proved remarkably accurate, for it was to be in 1954 that German exports of ships first passed the British total, and 1955 that the Japanese exports did likewise.[83] For in the event the industry failed to keep its plant up to date, just as the committee forewarned that it might. In the commercially crucial years 1951–4 the industry was to invest in fixed assets only two-thirds the sums necessary even to replace existing equipment, let alone create new yards suitable for the newest types of ship and the newest methods of production. Nor was this to be because of lack of financial resources, as in the pre-war slump, for in the early 1950s the industry was enjoying the biggest order book in its entire history, producing on average £120 million a year.[84] The explanation lies, rather, in that 'fossilisation of inefficiency' to which the First Lord of the Admiralty referred in 1944. Far from abandoning such fossilisation after the war, management and unions were stubbornly to preserve and perpetuate it – even in the teeth of final catastrophe in the 1970s. Thus in the postwar era British shipbuilding was simply to repeat its own history; fulfil once again the predestination encapsuled in its own character, a character which not even a total war had been able to change – prospering without thought for the morrow so long as there was no effective competition; starting to founder from the moment that such competition appeared; and in the end being scuttled by its own officers and crew.

The record of the Second World War thus demonstrates Britain's great traditional industries to have indeed suffered from the same kind of weaknesses that brought about the collapse of the French Army in 1940, from outdated technology and doctrine to poor leadership and to morale so low as sometimes to verge on the mutinous. Industries, however, are more fortunate than armies in that they are not exposed to the sudden shock of battle; defeat comes to them less dramatically. Nevertheless, defeat is implicit in that wartime record, which not only demonstrates the shortcomings of British heavy industry, but also reveals that these shortcomings were so intractable that even the direct intervention of a government vested with extraordinary powers, even the psychological spur of desperate national danger, could do little to remedy them.

Such a record offered no legitimate hope that in the postwar era these industries would prove unqualified national assets, powerful sinews of prosperity, like their German or American counterparts, but instead offered the near certainty that they would continue to present grievous long-term national problems, costly and insoluble. Other means of economic buoyancy would therefore be needed to support Britain's chosen world role abroad and New Jerusalem at home after the war; and these could only be found in the new British industries of the second industrial revolution, the inventions and productive achievements of which were so successfully vaunted by propaganda that they passed into national myth.

Chapter Seven

A Mass Industry Improvised: Aircraft 1936–39

When their wings scrawled victory in trails of vapour across the English sky of 1940, the aircraft of Fighter Command passed into legend along with the pilots who flew them. Who could doubt after the Battle of Britain that the Hawker Hurricane and the Vickers-Supermarine Spitfire were the finest single-engined aircraft in the world? Or that their Rolls-Royce Merlins were supreme among aircraft engines? For once fact accorded with legend. The graceful Spitfire evolved through twenty-four separate marks, its final version at the end of the war being capable of 450 miles per hour compared with the 355 miles per hour of the Mark I that had fought in the Battle of Britain. The sturdy Hurricane too remained in production throughout the war, adapting to the role of fighter–bomber and to an armament of tank-busting cannon. The Merlin engine increased its power output by 100 per cent between 1940 and 1945. Most notably, the Merlin served to transform a disappointingly low-performance American fighter, the Mustang, into the superb long-distance escort which, accompanying Flying Fortress bombers on daylight raids deep into Germany, tore the guts out of the Luftwaffe's fighter defence. And it was the Merlin that supplied the power-plant for the four-engined Lancasters of Bomber Command which from 1942 to 1945 trundled through the night to devastate Germany's great industrial conurbations, and for the all-wood Mosquito light bomber sneaking at high speed through fighters and flak to attack precision targets.

The Lancaster and the Mosquito became legends in their own right too, although never touched with quite the magic of the Hurricane and the Spitfire, which had delivered the nation from the threat of invasion and occupation. If the fighters of 1940 were 'the Few', then the Lancasters – and the Halifaxes and Stirlings – were 'the mass'; coming down the production lines almost like pre-war family cars to swell Bomber Command's offensive strength and make good losses in action that could sometimes amount to 7 per cent of the force despatched to the target for the night. Month after month, year after year, Bomber Command and its Lancasters figured in the headlines of Britain's four-page wartime newspapers and in the BBC wireless bulletins, while cinema newsreels cheered the public with aerial film shot by night of German cities ablaze and shot by day of the same cities roofless and gutted; film too of Lancasters, heavy with bombs, lumbering off the airfields of eastern England into the dusk.

For all these reasons, it was the air war, the Royal Air Force and its aircrews and aircraft that captured the British imagination, to the partial eclipse of the army's episodic battles or the navy's dour far-off struggle against the U-boat. The Spitfire, the Hurricane and the Lancaster came to symbolise Britain's special contribution to the allied victory; and to this day the sight of the surviving specimens overhead at an air display can catch the throat and prickle the eye of onlookers who remember 1940 and the years after. And these potent symbols express a historical truth – that from the very beginnings of rearmament in 1934–5 Britain had given overriding priority to aerial warfare and the RAF over land and sea warfare and the army and navy. For the governments of Baldwin and Chamberlain interpreted the pre-war German menace above all in terms of airpower. It was not what the German Army might do to the French Army that dominated the anguished discussions of Cabinets and Cabinet committees on grand strategy in the 1930s, but what the German air force might do to London.[1] When, as a result of this priority to the RAF and the concomitant neglect of the British Army, France had to fight the German Army in 1940 virtually singlehanded (she fielded ninety-four divisions; Britain ten), and was beaten, thereby depriving Britain of her lodgement in Europe, the British Cabinet came to see air power as the only remaining means by which Britain could effectively strike at Germany itself. Indeed, until Soviet Russia and the United States were dragged into the war in 1941, RAF Bomber Command presented literally Britain's only hope of eventual victory.[2] As a consequence the War Cabinet committed itself to the creation of a vast bomber force,[3] although the planned production targets were to be subject to repeated revisions between 1940 and 1944, and were never fully met. In September 1941 the Prime Minister himself called for an upward revision of the current programme from 11,000 bombers to be produced between July 1941 and July 1943 to 14,500.[4] Nonetheless, in pursuit of such ambitious production targets for bombers as well as for other types of aircraft, the Ministry of Aircraft Production had built up by 1943 Britain's largest industrial operation, with more than 1,700,000 men and women working for it.[5] When the war ended, the aircraft industry and the ancillary firms supplying components had turned out a total of 131,549 aircraft.[6]

It is hardly to be wondered, therefore, that in British minds the Second World War proved Britain to be a world leader in the design and manufacture of aircraft – and not least because of her claimed pioneering lead in jet propulsion. Yet this belief in British aeronautical pre-eminence, however understandable, was by no means justified by the true nature of the British aircraft industry and its performance. In the first place, the industry was almost entirely an artificial creation by government in order to supply the needs of the Royal Air Force, rather than a spontaneous peacetime commercial growth to exploit a new international market. Secondly, with the exception of the jet engine, the technology of wartime aircraft and their manufacture owed itself in large part to foreign innovations and equipment. And thirdly, its broad characteristics as an industrial operation reproduced the same weakness in management, organisation, productivity and labour relations that had so long beset old-established British industries. It might be fairly said that in the case of the aircraft industry the British put old wine into a new bottle.

Britain had been slow to participate in the initial creation of aircraft industries that had followed the Wright Brothers' successful first powered flight in 1903. Even by the outbreak of the Great War there were no aircraft engines of British design and virtually no airframe industry. In the words of the official history of the Ministry of Munitions, 'Both aircraft and aero-engine manufacture were infant industries in England in 1914. Most of the aircraft firms of 1917 were of quite recent growth, their financial position precarious, their works organisation underdeveloped and their equipment small.'[7] Moreover, Britain had failed to develop the manufacture of necessary components such as ball-bearings and magnetos:

> Only one firm was producing magnetos and its output for 1913–14 was 1,140 magnetos of a simple type. In the summer of 1916 the magneto shortage became acute, as the stock of German-built instruments, which had hitherto formed the staple source of supply for the Royal Flying Corps, was rapidly diminishing. . . . repeated failure had attended British magneto production for the first twelve months.[8]

For the first two years of the Great War Britain had to depend on large-scale imports of French aero-engines while it created its own aero-engine industry, and as late as spring 1918 the then plan to create a strategic bomber force was curtailed by 'a serious shortage in the supply of engines'.[9]

Nevertheless British peacetime slowness in exploiting this new technology and new market was remedied during the Great War by an emergency programme funded by the state and carried out under the direction of the Ministry of Munitions. By the end of the war aircraft production had reached a rate of 30,000 per annum.

> aero-engine production was a huge industry . . . and British engines have outstripped the productions of all other countries as to quality and quantity.
>
> The advances made by subsidiary industries were remarkable. The production of magnetos was multiplied a hundred-fold; the research on alloy and steel, the development of strong lightweight metal tubing, and of petrol-resistant rubber tubing, and the improvement in the quality of oil and petrol are all of permanent value to the industry.[10]

It was inevitable, however, that the cessation of wartime demand for military aircraft would compel the newly fledged and rapidly expanded industry drastically to shrink. This was true of all the combatant countries. But Great Britain failed thereafter to make the most of the commercial opportunities in the 1920s for the air transport of passengers and mails, even though she enjoyed the advantage of a worldwide empire with staging-post airfields under her own flag along trans-global routes. In 1930 Britain and the British Empire lagged behind other major nations in air travel, despite headline-making record flights by adventurous heroes such as Sir Alan Cobham, first to fly to Australia and back. The route-mileage of the entire British Empire, at 23,005 miles, was not much longer than the 17,000 route miles operated by Germany, a European power with no overseas possessions. The French, with a smaller and less scattered empire than the British, managed to achieve 19,400 miles. Nor did the performance in civil aviation look any better in terms of volume of passengers, for while the United States carried 385,910 passengers and Germany 93,126 in 1930, the British Empire as a whole carried only 58,261.[11] Even by 1937 Britain had failed to exploit the potential of air transportation. A memorandum by the Air Ministry for the Imperial Conference on a 'Commonwealth Air Route Round the Word'[12] gloomily summarised the achievements of the French, Dutch, Germans and Americans (especially the latter) in developing worldwide and trans-oceanic air routes, including regular commercial flights across the South Atlantic and Pacific. There was a German service to South America, but no British. There was no British trans-Pacific route; no trans-Tasman route. Regular commercial flights from the United Kingdom to Australia via India were not due to start until 1938. The route from the United Kingdom to South Africa remained a mere project. The Air Ministry therefore invited the Imperial Conference – vainly as it turned out – 'to consider the importance of meeting this foreign challenge with a concerted effort made in time to prevent the reputation and rewards of initiative from passing altogether into other hands'.[13]

In thus neglecting the new field of commercial opportunity in the air and in the factory represented by the growth of civil air transport, British aircraft firms and airline companies dismally repeated the contemporary failure of British steel and shipbuilding to display the large-scale enterprise shown in Europe and America. The British government, for its part, again characteristically, failed to promote and back a national 'package' coupling long-distance air-transport development with commercially successful production of modern aircraft.

For the peacetime market for aircraft manufacture and the progress of civil aviation necessarily went together. The comparative British failure in exploiting the potential of civil aviation led not only to weak demand for British air transports but also to lack of innovation in their design, for which such 'shop-window' triumphs as the outright winning of the Schneider Trophy in 1931 by a Vickers-Supermarine single-seater seaplane offered no compensation. An Air Ministry paper in 1937 noted that the British aircraft industry produced virtually no large, long-distance airliners of modern design, and so the empire had to buy from Europe or the United States.[14] The 'new' British airliner for imperial routes in the mid-1930s was the slow biplane Handley-Page Heracles, which owed more to the technology of Great War bombers than to the new technology developed in America and Germany since the war of the all-metal, low-winged monoplane.[15]

For it had been on 25 June 1919, three days before the signing of the Treaty of Versailles appeared to seal the German eclipse as a power, that the first all-metal cabin monoplane, the Junkers F–13, had made its maiden flight in Germany. The F–13, with accommodation for six passengers, became the most widely used transport aircraft in the world during the 1920s. It was followed in 1931 by the Junkers 52 three-engined all-metal monoplane; one of the most commercially successful air transports of the 1930s, and the workhorse of German air supply throughout the Second World War.[16] In 1927 the Lockheed Vega, designed by a German engineer, pioneered light monocoque construction. In 1932 appeared in the United States the ancestor of all modern airliners, the Douglas DC–1, a fast, twin-engined, low-winged, all-metal, stressed-skin monoplane, with an eventual sales total of 190.[17] This was the technology that was to lead to the first generation of high-speed all-metal monoplane military aircraft, such as the Junkers 87 dive-bomber, the Heinkel 111 and the Dornier 17 medium bombers, all of which reached squadron service with the Luftwaffe in 1936, and were faster than biplane fighters then forming the frontline strength of the RAF.[18]

Although some British aircraft firms continued to manufacture civil aircraft in the 1920s and early 1930s, and even exported around 20 per cent of airframes and nearly 40 per cent of engines, the trade took the form of small batch orders to a variety of countries, and mostly of light aircraft.[19] The British aircraft industry as a whole had to be artificially kept alive by means of Air Ministry orders for military aircraft and engines, rationed out between the various firms, and then only in tiny quantities because of the partial unilateral disarmament then being pursued by British governments under the combined influence of moralising internationalism and financial stringency. Moreover, the aircraft industry in Britain conducted no central research of its own, but entirely depended on state research agencies such as the National Physical Laboratory and the Royal Aircraft Establishment at Farnborough. According to a memorandum by the permanent under-secretary to the Air Ministry in November 1935, all technical advances in aviation were pushed by and paid for by the state.[20] This fact renders even more pertinent the second question in a list of fifty-six on armament questions submitted to the Prime Minister in January 1938 by Attlee, the Leader of the Opposition:

> Why is [it] that despite the vast sums spent on research at Farnborough and elsewhere, all the principal inventions seem to come from abroad, e.g., the retractable undercarriage, variable pitch screw, blind flying apparatus including the artificial horizon, enclosed cockpits, power-driven turrets, landing lamps etc?
>
> Why, although abroad the biplane was being discarded for the monoplane, did this country continue with the biplane?[21]

A similar backwardness existed in the British aero-engine technology, as the air member for research and development on the Air (Ministry) Council, Air Marshal Sir Hugh Dowding, reported to his colleagues on 20 January 1938 after a visit to the German aircraft industry. In his view, 'the failure to keep pace with developments in Germany lay primarily with the aero-engine designers and not with the light alloy firms', for engine designers had failed to consult the light-alloy firms on such matters as the design of crankcases. Nevertheless, he reported, Sterling Metals, the source of 75 per cent of the aircraft industry's supplies of light alloys, was 'behind in technique'. With better liaison with regard to research and development, 'we could attain the high level of technique which has been achieved in Germany and which was entirely the result of close liaison between the designers and producers.'[22]

On the eve of major rearmament in 1936, therefore, the British aircraft industry remained a cottage industry with obsolescent products; sleepy firms with factories little more than experimental aircraft shops employing hand-work methods, and centred on their design departments.[23] Yet despite this small size the industry was fragmented into as many as fifteen firms on Air Ministry work, the largest having fewer than 2000 employees.[24] This almost first-industrial-revolution picture of workshop enterprise is complemented by the nature of the leadership and management of the industry – self-made 'practical men' of strong personality at the top like Sir Frederick Handley-Page or Sir Geoffrey de Havilland; chief designers who had begun as junior technicians, draughtsmen or mere 'hands' like Sydney Camm of Hawkers, originally an apprentice in the carpenter's shop; their education merely part-time technical courses or evening classes.[25] These self-taught men could sometimes be, and in the case of men like Camm (the Hurricane) and Mitchell (the Spitfire) were, designers of genius, happy at the drawing board or at the bench, but, like their employers, too often qualified neither by training nor by experience to design for, or to plan and direct, large-scale industrial operations. There was an almost total lack of the qualified production engineers and managers or cost accountants found in American and German industry, and produced in such quantities by the American and German education systems.[26]

When after 1934 the aircraft industry was flooded, and later deluged, with Air Ministry orders, it coped well enough with the *design* of new aircraft like the Spitfire, the Hurricane and the Blenheim medium bomber by profiting from the technological breakthroughs already made abroad. The Director of Technical Development at the Air Ministry had brought back information on the latest developments from a visit to the United States in 1934; designers from the aircraft firms too had visited the United States at this period, returning not only with ideas but also sometimes with complete designs of aircraft and engines.[27] Mitchell, later to design the Spitfire, was for his part profoundly influenced by the eliptical-winged Heinkel 70 light bomber, one of which was bought by Rolls-Royce in 1933 and tested by the RAF at Martlesham Heath.[28] Rolls-Royce themselves had drawn heavily on American engine development in the late 1920s in evolving the R 1/31 which powered the aircraft that won the Schneider Trophy outright in 1931, and which was one of the precursors of the Merlin.[29] As the Air Member for Research and Development, Air Marshal Sir Hugh Dowding, summed up the state of the art in August 1935:

> The recent sudden advance in the technique of aircraft has come about mainly on account of the enormous sums of money which were poured into American aviation during the boom which preceded the present depression, and the improvement manifested itself primarily in connection with civil aircraft.[30]

It was therefore not design that posed the crucial difficulty for the British aircraft industry after 1935 in meeting the future needs of the RAF, but the large-scale expansion at breakneck speed of the industry itself – planning new factories and production lines, masterminding their installation, and thereafter managing mass production of aircraft and engines. Here were problems of scale and complexity of organisation utterly new to the industry and, for several years, beyond it. From senior and middle management down to routine design staff, draughtsmen and skilled labour there was a critical shortage of appropriate training and experience. This revealed yet again the deep-seated British weakness in technical education and training that had already crippled Britain's older industries; a weakness once more both of demand (hitherto) and supply. Beyond a handful of university-educated aeronautical engineers of high quality there was no British equivalent, for example, to the phalanx of college-trained engineers apt for bread-and-butter design and development roles which abounded in the American industry.[31] All this applied equally to the industry's sub-contractors, upon which it critically depended. Moreover great contrasts existed between firm and firm. In 1936, for example, while A. V. Roe were highly regarded in the Air Ministry for their quality of organisation and management, they just had no good new designs for the future. Blackburns on the other hand were inventive designers but hopeless production managers.[32]

But in terms of large-scale series output, Britain had in any event not so much to expand her aircraft industry as create a new one. This immense task of capital development was tackled partly by adding fresh plant to the existing works of the aircraft firms; partly by building 'shadow' engine and airframe factories to be operated by those motor-vehicle firms which were already accustomed to mass production – such as Rover, Austin and Morris. The whole operation was financed by state capital and carried out under state supervision; a programme of investment in new technology on a scale unparalleled in Britain in peacetime, and amounting by 1938 to nearly £10 million.[33] To this primary task was added the further complication of the switch-over from producing simple fabric-covered biplane aircraft of essentially Great War type to the new generation of monoplane aircraft like the Spitfire or the Wellington bomber: far more complex in themselves, with new armaments, instruments and navigation equipment; far more complex in their fabrication because of all-metal design that demanded special alloys and advanced techniques of shaping and assembly. The new generation of aircraft engines, like the Merlin, also involved novel complexities that made fresh demands on the accuracy and sophistication of the manufacturing process.

In turn, this hectic development of the aircraft industry between 1936 and the outbreak of the Second World War threw an immense burden on Britain's general industrial resources and skills – on the steel and construction industries; on the machine-tool industry, without the products of which a factory is merely a large shed; on precision engineering in various forms for the production of instruments, weapons and components; and, pervasively, on skilled management and labour. Moreover, the aircraft industry was competing for these limited resources with the smaller-scale but still important rearmament demands of the army and the Royal Navy. Nonetheless, until after the Munich crisis of September 1938 the government refused to sanction any redeployment of industry from peacetime production and exports, cleaving to its original 1936 decision that the demands of rearmament must be met from surplus or newly created capacity. The combined consequence of all these factors was to expose what the Defence Policy and Requirements Committee (DPRC) in its major report on rearmament plans in February 1936 called 'the limited output of our existing industrial resources'.[34] Indeed Lord Weir, the government's chief industrial adviser, reckoned that Britain was 'short of fundamental facilities for making certain articles'.[35] The soundness of these judgements was borne out by the progress reports rendered by the Air Ministry and the Ministry of Labour to the DPRC in 1936–8 – a gloomy catalogue of delays in constructing the new 'shadow' factories and getting them into production, of the aircraft industry's own muddles and missed delivery dates, and of a critical dependence on imported high technology in order to allow the rearmament programme to go forward at all.

The leitmotiv throughout lay in a dearth of skilled manpower. According to the minutes of the DPRC, Lord Weir declared as early as May 1936, 'there was no effective reserve of fully trained men upon which the Services could draw. Industry was faced with the same problem. . . .'[36] This was not a handicap exclusive to the aircraft industry, of course; it affected all modern high-technology production in Britain, serving as a fresh indictment of the inadequacies of British technical education and training. Just as was again to be the case fifty years later, acute shortage of skilled manpower existed amidst mass unemployment, as the Ministry of Labour made clear in its second progress report to the DPRC in June 1936:

> there is a widespread shortage of fitters, turners, capstan setters and operators, machinists, toolmakers, millers, universal grinders, coppersmiths, sheet metal workers, welders and aircraft riggers. In all the [ministry] divisions, with the exception of Wales, there is an unsatisfied demand for certain classes of skilled operatives. . . . In many areas the shortages are greatest in the branches concerned with armament work.

> Although in all divisions, with the exception of the South-Eastern, there is an apparent surplus of skilled labour, much of this surplus consists of men of poor industrial quality. . . . Inability to read blue-prints and/or work to fine limits makes many of them not readily acceptable to employers. . . .[37]

Nonetheless the Amalgamated Engineering Union at its recent annual conference, reported the Ministry of Labour, had 'adopted a resolution expressing stern and uncompromising opposition' to the introduction into the engineering industry of trainees from government training centres.[38]

By November 1936 the ministry was reporting that only 1800 skilled engineering workers of all kinds in the country remained unemployed:

> The supply of labour for the three 'Shadow' factories at Coventry is likely to constitute a problem early next year [when they would have come into production]. The Daimler Motors Limited scheme alone will require 1,000 workpeople of whom 750 should be highly skilled and it is stated that the firm cannot hope to provide a nucleus of more than 5 per cent from their existing staff.[39]

By February 1937 the ministry was warning that 'as the "shadow" factories reach completion, the problem created by the shortage will be still further accentuated.' In fact no more than 200–300 unemployed fitters able to work to very fine limits now remained in the entire country.[40] In June 1937 the ministry reckoned that the national total of all kinds of skilled engineering workers suitable for employment either immediately or after some training amounted to 4500, against a requirement of 70,000 when rearmament reached its peak.[41] By October 'the lack of skilled men is preventing men [*sic*] employing a larger number of the semi-skilled and unskilled men who are available and is hindering the expansion of the [engineering] industry.'[42] In particular the lack was currently causing delays at Fairey Aviation. In the next two months the Ministry of Labour was reporting that some aircraft firms in its south-western division were limiting acceptance of contracts to the capacity of their existing labour-force, owing to the inability to recruit more skilled men.[43]

Although the Cabinet had approved the 'shadow' factory scheme in February 1936, it was not until September 1937 that the first factories began to produce parts, and not until early 1938 that production of complete engines and airframes got under way. Operating contracts with the motor-car firms had not been finally agreed until late summer 1936, owing to some unseemly haggling on the part of the automobile magnates.[44] Thereafter the construction and tooling of factories went ahead steadily if slowly. Yet the requirements of this tooling, along with the tooling of new extensions to existing aircraft firms and of new factories supplying equipment for the army and navy, served to expose the limitations of the British machine-tool industry, both in design and quality of production. In 1933–7, when Germany enjoyed 48.3 per cent of the world's trade in machine tools, and the United States 35.3 per cent, the

United Kingdom's share was a mere 7.1 per cent.[45] And so, just as in 1914–15, the expansion and re-equipment of British industry compelled Britain to turn to foreign suppliers for advanced machine tools, whether sophisticated designs for special purposes, or highly accurate semi-automatic tools for general precision-engineering work. United Kingdom imports of machine tools leaped from 7765 tons in 1935 to 20,058 tons in 1936 and 31,591 in 1937.[46] By contrast, as Vice Admiral Sir Harold Brown, director of munitions production at the War Office, pointed out to the DPRC on 22 October 1936, the Germans had not only provided themselves with their own machine tools, but now enjoyed a surplus for export.[47]

Furthermore, it was tardy deliveries on the part of the domestic machine-tool industry that was delaying the process of getting new factories or new aircraft into production. In December 1936, for example, it was reported to the Secretary of State for Air that hold-ups in the British supply of tools and jigs for production of the Vickers Wellington bomber were such that Vickers had decided to send a man to Switzerland to see if the tools and jigs could be manufactured there.[48] Next month the DPRC also took note that machine tools ordered six months previously were now two months late in delivery, and that, because of this, orders for them had been placed in Switzerland.[49]

The bleak historical truth is that those great symbols of British myth, the Battle of Britain Spitfire and Hurricane and their Merlin engine, were largely fabricated on foreign machine tools; more, their armaments and much of their instrumentation too were foreign in design, and, in the case of earlier production batches, foreign in manufacture as well.

For from the beginning of rearmament Britain found herself compelled to buy key items of aircraft equipment abroad until such time as she would have completed her own factories to manufacture them under licence. The very first progress report to the DPRC in May 1936 by the Air Ministry, noting that more than 20,000 machine-guns would be needed by March 1939, stated that while the Browning fixed machine-gun, an American design, was in due course to be manufactured by Vickers and BSA under licence, in the meantime 'a limited order for Browning guns has been placed with the American company to cover requirements until the British firms get into production.'[50] Although the supply of radio sets offered no problem, wrote the Air Ministry:

> the firms producing ancillary equipment [i.e. instruments] are not well organised for a large-scale increase in production owing to the dearth of orders in the past. Active steps are being taken to extend facilities and obtain new sources of supply, since it is essential that the delivery of the numerous and vital items required should synchronise with the aircraft programme. . . .[51]

In the short term this was not going to prove so easy, as the Air Ministry's second report began to make plain:

> Agreements have been concluded with Messrs Kelvin, Bottomley

> and Baird, under which the firms are establishing a new factory at Basingstoke for the manufacture of a new type of altimeter. This should be capable of meeting the full requirements by March 1939, but for immediate purposes the firm are obtaining 4,000 instruments from the United States.[52]

In October 1936 the DPRC took note that large contracts had been signed with American firms for the supply of aircraft instrument panels, while in April the following year the Air Ministry was reporting that orders had had to be placed for 'Link' trainers for blind flying with the J.V.W. Corporation of America, and for reserve parachutes with the American Irving Company for delivery by 31 March 1939.[53] Next month it recorded that a further 1000 Browning machine-guns had been ordered from the USA, and also that:

> Owing to difficulty in obtaining from home sources the quantities and type of 'Rate of Climb' Indicators required, contracts have been placed with Messrs S. Smith and Sons for 700 Indicators of American manufacture to meet urgent requirements up to October 1937, and for the manufacture at home of a further 3,400 Indicators of the American type.[54]

In January 1938 the ministry informed the DPRC that an order had been placed with Goertz of Vienna for 150 track recorders, 'no suitable design being available in this country'.[55] A year later the Air Ministry, in reporting that a contract had been placed for British-made aircraft dashboard clocks, remarked:

> Production of Clocks of this standard involves the setting-up in this country of new manufacturing technique [*sic*] and in consequence effective production is not expected until the beginning of 1941. Hitherto clocks of Swiss manufacture have been obtained.[56]

It is noteworthy that some of those United Kingdom sources on which the Air Ministry *could* rely for key items of equipment were in fact local out-stations of American companies and expertise, such as the Sperry Gyroscope Company, of the Great West Road, London, contracted in August 1936 to supply 2500 artificial horizons and directional gyroscopes,[57] and Standard Telephones, given a contract for ground transmitter sets a year later.[58]

Yet the Air Ministry's difficulties by no means amounted to the whole sum of British dependence on imported industrial equipment during pre-war rearmament. All through this period the army's and the Royal Navy's own programmes were further exposing the narrowness of Britain's manufacturing base in new technologies, and especially in sophisticated machine tools.

Even the setting up of straightforward mass production operations, like a new factory to make simple petrol cans, compelled a resort to American automatic or semi-automatic machine tools,[59] while specialised processes in shell and gun manufacture saw Britain turn mainly to her major potential enemy, Germany, to enable her rearmament to go forward. In October 1936 the War Office warned that the bottleneck in producing all calibres of shell larger than 3 inches lay in forging capacity:

> The majority of the existing forging capacity, however, employs methods which are not in accordance with the latest practice either as regards production or economy in labour and materials. It is proposed, therefore, that German or Hungarian types of presses, which are designed specifically to meet these requirements should be used.[60]

Next month the War Office noted that while so far the machining of shell cases had presented no problems, one firm 'has been authorized to install a German machining plant'.[61] From Germany too came a new lathe which, according to the War Office, had speeded up bomb production thanks to its capacity to absorb seven times the horsepower of any other lathe in the world.[62]

Furthermore, the army and navy, like the air force, found themselves forced to buy large quantities of actual military equipment and components 'off the shelf' from foreign suppliers because adequate designs or manufacturing resources were lacking at home. The Bofors light anti-aircraft gun offers the most notable example of this. As early as spring 1937 it had become clear that the Vickers design for a light anti-aircraft gun was no good, while in any case no jigs existed for its manufacture.[63] In March Lord Weir expressed himself to the DPRC as 'very perturbed' at the 'limited and inexperienced' capability in the United Kingdom for fabricating automatic guns and their mountings; and in April the DPRC therefore authorised the purchase of 100 Bofors equipments from Sweden, together with 500,000 rounds of ammunition, thus saving at least a year in delivery time before British facilities for manufacturing the guns under licence could be brought into production.[64] In December 1938, after the Munich crisis, a further 180 Bofors equipments had to be ordered abroad, this time from Belgium, Poland and Hungary.[65]

Without a fuse a shell or bomb is, as Lloyd George once pointed out, a harmless steel vase, and its explosive content merely an inert stuffing. Anti-aircraft shells in particular required clockwork time-fuses. Unfortunately effective British designs of such mechanical fuses were lacking, along with firms able to manufacture them or even powder-fuses to the exactitude required. As a consequence the supply of shells to the army and navy and of bombs to the RAF were seriously bottlenecked. The problem became acute at the end of 1936 when fear of the bomber led to the decision to order an extra 300 3.7-inch anti-aircraft guns, for no industrial capacity then existed to produce the large quantities of clockwork time-fuses required for their ammunition.[66] In January 1937 the War Office therefore proposed the building of three new factories for fuse manufacture:

> A large number of the requisite machine tools are of foreign origin, and it will, in the initial stages in the latter case [of the Swiss Tavaro fuse] be necessary to purchase the fuse mechanisms complete abroad for assembly in this country. Eventually, when the proper equipment is available, the whole fuse will be manufactured here.[67]

Nonetheless, as the Secretary of State for War reported on the 20th of that month in a memorandum devoted to this topic of fuses, since no fewer than 100,000 would be required by the end of the year, there was no prospect of achieving this figure by production at the three British centres, and therefore the Tavaro fuse would have to be bought from Switzerland until a new factory should have been constructed in two years' time. Six months later, however, a fresh decision was taken to build a new factory to make a British design of fuse, and buy Swiss to fill the gap meanwhile.[68] But by February 1938 the new fuse factory at Blackburn had still not progressed beyond the stage of issuing tenders for the site work and preparing contract drawings for the building.[69]

The Admiralty too had its disappointments over fuses, reporting in April 1937:

> The unsatisfactory state of supply of Fuse No 206 is due to the intricate nature of the mechanism and difficulty experienced by the manufacturers in producing fuses which will satisfactorily function at proof. Additional sources of supply are being developed, but owing to manufacturing difficulties a considerable period must elapse before effective deliveries can be expected from new sources.[70]

However, nine months later the Admiralty was still grappling unavailingly with the same technical problems.[71]

Just as with the Royal Air Force, so with the army and the Royal Navy, high-technology instrumentation offered another bottleneck in supply because of scant British manufacturing resources in this field. Rangefinders and gun-sights, sound locators and heightfinders for anti-aircraft defence, fire-control gear for the main and anti-aircraft armament of warships, anti-submarine sonar equipment – all became critical problems during the pre-war rearmament period. The earliest report by the War Office to the DPRC in May 1936 remarked that the production of optical and scientific instruments 'is very limited, mainly on account of the shortage of skilled operatives. . .'.[72] With regard to predictors and heightfinders, wrote the War Office in September that year, 'sources of supply in this country are very limited and the maximum prospective outputs are below estimated requirements. The possibility of obtaining supplies of suitable instruments from foreign firms is to be investigated.'[73] By the beginning of 1937 purchase of these items from abroad had passed from the realm of possibility to that of urgent action, with the order of eighty predictors from the United States and fifty heightfinders from France. In April 1937 an order for another fifty heightfinders was placed in Austria; and in June 1938 followed yet a further order for fifty from Austria.[74]

Meanwhile deliveries of radio-telephone sets to the army by British suppliers had been worthy of the standard of reliability to be set by British exporters in post-1945 international markets, with only 457 sets delivered by the beginning of February 1938 out of 775 sets due by March.[75] The Admiralty was encountering similar problems with the supply of radio equipment, and also with sonar, on which it was relying to defeat the U-boat in the event of war; and by November 1937 it was groaning to the DPRC that deliveries of radios and sonars 'have, for a considerable period, been in arrear, and although there have been some signs of improvement in recent months, the position is still not satisfactory.'[76] But the Admiralty's special anxiety stemmed from persistent hold-ups in production of fire-control gear (which directs the fire of a ship's guns), without which a warship is no more effective in acquiring and destroying targets than a liner. In October 1936 the Admiralty had to report to the DPRC that new cruisers due for completion in June–August 1937 would have to remain for a year afterwards only partially equipped with fire-control because the high-angle systems would not be ready in time.[77] A year later the situation had worsened rather than improved, for the Admiralty now reckoned that delays over fire-control gear had become the factor most affecting the construction of new ships. It warned the DPRC that ships would be delivered without their second or third high-angle systems. Although the Admiralty did not say so, this meant that the defects of British technological resources were temporarily rendering the fleet vulnerable to high-level German or Italian air attack. The Admiralty went on to inform the DPRC in tones almost of despair: 'The Country has been scoured to find firms willing to undertake the work, but without success.'[78] Of two firms discovered which were up to the task, one turned out to be a manufacturer of toffee-wrapping machinery.[79]

As late as October 1938 the Minister for the Co-ordination of Defence, in surveying the whole scene of rearmament for his colleagues in the wake of Chamberlain's presentation to Hitler in Munich of the strategic keys to central and eastern Europe, reported that 'the real bottlenecks consist of highly specialised products, e.g., fire control gear, gun mountings, predictors and the like', the problem being sharpened by a shortage of the right kind of skilled labour for instrument factories.[80]

Even the production and installation of the 'Chain Home' radar system that was to enable Fighter Command to win the Battle of Britain, and which was later to take its place in the national folk-myth about British technological leadership, was held up by a bottleneck in the production of thermionic valves owing to British manufacturers lagging behind in research. Supplies had to be obtained from the United States and from Philips of Eindhoven.[81]

Meanwhile the British aircraft industry was reneging on its production promises in terms both of quantities and of delivery dates as it struggled to overcome the combined problems of massive expansion and development of new types of aircraft. This failure in 1936–8 of the industry to deliver was responsible for the critical weakness of the Royal Air Force during the

Czechoslovakian crisis; a weakness which, because of the prevailing fear of the German bomber, provided in turn a major factor in Chamberlain's policy of yielding to Hitler rather than risk a war. In March 1938, in a formidable report on the unwarlike condition of all three services that was to serve Chamberlain as the authoritative text in justifying appeasement to his colleagues, the Chiefs of Staff enumerated the various deficiencies in the air force's combat effectiveness, and drew the discouraging conclusion: 'The net result of these deficiencies . . . is that the air force cannot at the present time be said to be in any way fit to undertake operations on a major war scale.'[82] Of twenty-seven mobilisable squadrons of fighters, twenty were composed of obsolete fighters too slow to catch modern German bombers; of thirty-five mobilisable squadrons of bombers, ten were light bombers useless against modern fighters.[83] Yet it was now nearly *four* years since the Cabinet had first given approval for deficiencies in the RAF's strength to be made good within, yes, four years; it was now *three and a half* years since the Cabinet had ordered this programme to be speeded up for completion within *two* years; and it was *two* years since the Cabinet had decided to embark on large-scale rearmament, including the construction of 'shadow' aircraft and aero-engine factories.

In particular, the industry had failed to deliver the new all-metal monoplane fighters on which the successful air defence of Great Britain against the bomber must depend. By now their German equivalent, the Messerschmitt ME 109, had already been in squadron service in small quantities with the Luftwaffe for twelve months, even though its original specification was issued in the same year, 1934, as the Air Ministry specifications for the Hurricane and Spitfire. The prototype ME 109 had first flown at the end of October 1935. The prototype Hurricane had been expected to fly in June 1935, but did not do so until November. The prototype Spitfire had been expected to fly in September 1935, but did not do so until March 1936.[84] In August 1936 the Air Ministry was hopefully estimating that Spitfires would be delivered at a rate of twenty a month from September 1937, and that fifty-two Hurricanes would be produced in July–September 1937, sixty-five in October–December and seventy-eight in January–March 1938.[85] In the event only ten Hurricanes had been delivered by January 1938, and not a single Spitfire.[86]

The Merlin engine had itself provided one delaying factor, in regard not only to the Spitfire and Hurricane but also to the Boulton-Paul Defiant fighter. The Air Ministry was reporting in August 1936 that no figures were yet available as to Merlin production: 'The contractor has been constantly pressed for complete and detailed delivery proposals but nothing tangible is as yet forthcoming.'[87] Next month the Air Ministry noted that production of the Fairey Battle light bomber was held up because additional cooling was needed for its Merlin engine, 'which has failed to pass its type test as originally designed. It may therefore be necessary to provide larger radiators which would involve important alterations in the design of the aeroplane.'[88] In October 1936 the ministry was hoping for nearly 100 Merlins between the beginning of November and the end of the year, but in a note of caution added that Rolls-Royce 'are still being pressed to give a more detailed programme'.[89] By November, however, the Merlin had not gone beyond limited production prior to a further type test:[90] 'The contractor has been informed of the Department's requirements and his proposals are still awaited.' Even by April 1937, of 3350 Merlins on order, just 10 were expected in June, 100 in September and 150 in October.[91] Next month the ministry diagnosed the current shortfalls in Merlin output as being 'chiefly due to Rolls-Royce making insufficient allowance for the effect of holidays when estimating deliveries'.[92] In October 1937 a further shortfall of twenty-five was attributed to 'continued difficulties in commencing production of a new mark of engine'.[93] In the first two weeks of November production reached just 36 engines, as against Air Ministry hopes of 100 in the November and December of the *previous* year.[94] Not until the beginning of 1938, roughly fifteen months behind the original schedule, could the Air Ministry report that deliveries of Merlins were up to forecast, with production from now on of 115 a month.[95]

While persistent slippage in the planned production targets for the Hurricane might perhaps be generously attributed to inevitable teething troubles and to over-optimistic estimates on the part of Hawkers, the failure of the Spitfire even to begin to reach the squadrons until late summer 1938 clearly owed itself to the incompetence of Vickers-Supermarine and their components suppliers. By February 1937 the Air Ministry was admitting to the DPRC that it could now give no estimated delivery dates for the Spitfire at all, even though the whole order for 310 aircraft was due for completion by March 1939; and the ministry noted in the 'Comments' column of its current progress chart: 'Whole of Supermarine situation being overhauled. Revised programme still under review.'[96] Seven months later the ministry reported that though there had been further delays owing to difficulties with sub-contractors, these difficulties had been now 'mainly overcome, but that first aircraft unlikely before February 1938'.[97] In December 1937, however, the ministry's report again struck a gloomier note: 'Firm state they are unable to forecast deliveries at present.'[98] The persistent problem offered by Spitfire production was discussed at one of the Secretary of State for Air's progress meetings on 3 February 1938, when the Director of Aircraft Production voiced the opinion that it was not the sub-contractors who were at fault, but Supermarine themselves. Supermarine indeed appeared to be so much of a shambles that the meeting considered whether 'it might pay us to provide the capital to put the Southampton factory on a thoroughly efficient basis.'[99] Later that month an extra 300 Hurricanes had to be ordered for completion by October 1940 simply because of this failure of Spitfire production.[100] And as late as May 1938, when Hitler had already stoked up the Czechoslovakian affair to an urgent crisis of peace and war, the Air Ministry still had to report that no forecasts of Spitfire deliveries were yet possible.[101]

Nonetheless, Vickers-Supermarine was not the only incompetent aircraft firm in this period; the Spitfire not the only aircraft to suffer from acute production problems. The DPRC was told in February 1937 of the inefficiency of Vickers Aviation, causing production of their aircraft to be extremely unsatisfactory.[102] In September that year Lord Swinton, the Air Minister, informed his DPRC colleagues that the management of Faireys was 'totally unsatisfactory': hence delays in deliveries of the Battle light bomber so serious as to merit a threat to cancel the contract.[103] In Lord Weir's view Faireys possessed no good production manager.[104] These harsh judgements on Vickers and Faireys certainly seem to be borne out by their production records. Of ninety-six already obsolescent Vickers Wellesley bombers due for delivery by April 1937, only twenty-two had been delivered by June.[105] The first Vickers Wellington medium bombers, the specification for which had been issued as far back as 1932, had originally been expected in June 1937, but that month the Air Ministry reported that the aircraft was not expected to fly before the end of 1937. Come October 1937, and the Wellington's advent from the production line had to be put off again to May 1938, when a single aircraft was expected to be delivered; this monthly total would rise, it was hoped, to nine by January 1939.[106] In fact the first Wellington finally arrived in October 1938 – sixteen months late.[107] As for the Fairey Battle, already set back in 1936 owing to late delivery of machine tools and what the Air Ministry delicately called 'slowness of labour',[108] only 84 had been delivered by December 1937 out of a contract of 155 due for completion by the previous June.[109]

Nevertheless, even aircraft firms that earned official approbation, such as Handley-Page – 'now completely equipped and organised to ensure effective production of large metal stressed skin airframes', according to Lord Weir in November 1936 – had their difficulties too. By July 1937 only 34 Handley-Page Harrow bombers had been delivered out of 100 due by June. In December the Air Ministry reported that, of Bristol Blenheims and Armstrong-Whitworth Whitleys due for delivery the previous June, only 34 out of 80 and 117 out of 140 had even now been delivered.[110]

But in any case completion of bombers depended on the supply of power turrets for the defensive armament. As early as September 1936 the Air Ministry was reporting that forward and central gun turrets for the Whitley had proved unsatisfactory on test and would have to be redesigned, and that machines would have to be accepted without turrets in order to allow flying training.[111] Six months later Blenheims, Harrows and Whitleys were being delivered without defensive armament because no satisfactory turret design was yet available.[112] It had originally been intended that the Armstrong-Whitworth Whitley should be equipped by a turret manufactured by the same firm, but it had now been discovered that this turret was only structurally suitable for one out of the three gun positions, and as a consequence the remaining two turrets would have to be of Frazer-Nash design (actually based on a French design) and manufacture. In the case of the Handley-Page Harrow, none of Handley-Page's own designs of turret was satisfactory, and so the Harrow would also have to be fitted with one Armstrong-Whitworth turret and two Frazer-Nash. Unfortunately Frazer-Nash, according to the Air Ministry, was 'a brilliant designer, but his firm were not good enough at production.'[113] Hence there ensued a prolonged bottleneck in the supply of turrets, which was rendered even worse because Bristol's prototype design of a turret for their own Blenheim bomber was also not up to the job and needed modification.[114] Thus by a unique double achievement of British technology some of Britain's new bombers in 1937 as well as some of her new warships would be temporarily defenceless against attack by enemy air forces.

While production of combat-worthy new-generation aircraft was thus being delayed into 1938, the industry had been delivering large quantities of obsolescent or obsolete types ordered back in 1934–6 in pursuit of the government's then faith that sheer numbers of aircraft and squadrons would serve to cool Hitler's fevered ambitions. The consequent inventory of some 4000 out-of-date aircraft and 6000 out-of-date engines delivered since April 1935 proved no more than costly lumber in 1938 when the Chiefs of Staff came to weigh the RAF's fitness for war.[115]

Only in the course of 1938 did the problems of developing and producing advanced combat aircraft really begin to be overcome, but, even so, it was not until 1939 that these aircraft were being turned out in quantity, with cumulative totals of 600 Hurricanes and 300 Spitfires delivered by August and September respectively.[116] Indeed in 1939 British aircraft production at nearly 8000 of all types virtually reached parity with the German total of nearly 8300, even though this impressive British figure was bulked out by continued manufacture of now obsolescent and operationally dubious aircraft like the Battle, Blenheim and Whitley.[117]

Yet with the advent of the Second World War in September 1939 and the British commitment to ever more vast production programmes, the aircraft industry and the constellation of other industries such as radio and radar that centred on it were to be subjected to new and sterner trials of their technological capability and their productive efficiency.

Chapter Eight

New Technology and Old Failings: Aircraft 1939–44

Even before the Second World War began, the rearmament programme – most of all, the creation of a great aircraft industry – had been running Britain towards that balance-of-payments predicament with which she was unavailingly to grapple between 1945 and the advent of North Sea oil at the end of the 1970s, and in which the key factor lay in an unhealthy dependence on foreign technology. The huge purchases abroad of machine tools, weapons and equipment since 1935 had helped to change a current balance-of-payments surplus of £32 million in that year into a deficit of £18 million in 1936 and £56 million in 1937.[1] Chamberlain's government therefore appointed a committee under Sir Thomas Inskip, the Minister for the Co-ordination of Defence, to tackle the question, in Inskip's own words, of 'how are we to reconcile the two desiderata, first, to be safe, secondly, to be solvent. . .'.[2] In February 1938, in the second of two reports reflecting much anguished haggling in Whitehall between the three service departments and between them and the Treasury, Inskip put forward a compromise by which a limit of £1600 million was to be set on rearmament over the next five years, while the services were invited to bring as much of that expenditure forward into the next two years as was feasible, in order to give Britain's diplomacy some military weight as quickly as possible. As Inskip admitted, all that this compromise achieved was to postpone as long as possible a choice between providing adequate defence and imposing 'a breaking strain' on our resources.[3] But, Inskip went on, if the international scene in fact failed to become more tranquil in the future, 'we shall be faced within two years with a choice between defence programmes which we cannot afford, and failure to make defence preparations on an adequate scale.'[4]

In the event, the international scene had grown so much grimmer by the autumn of 1938 that the Cabinet was having to ponder still further increases and accelerations in rearmament, which caused Sir John Simon, the Chancellor of the Exchequer, to wring his hands piteously – especially over the expansion of the RAF. 'The Air Ministry's programme is . . . so costly', he told his colleagues, 'as to raise serious doubts whether it can be financed beyond 1939–40 without the gravest danger to the country's stability.'[5] With a fall of a quarter in Britain's total gold and convertible currency reserves since the previous year, national bankruptcy, a distant iceberg on the horizon in 1937, now began to loom huge and jagged in the offing.[6] Simon warned that even the existing rearmament programme was leading to rising imports and reduced exports: 'Our balance of payments – already a serious problem – will become more and more serious.' Our monetary resources were already being heavily depleted, and 'might be still more rapidly exhausted and we should have lost the means of carrying on a long struggle altogether.'[7]

By the spring of 1939 the contrast between Britain's self-perpetuated role of first-class world and imperial power and her backward industrial economy had brought her within the zone of icy chill that spelt inevitable shipwreck. For while the Chiefs of Staff asserted that Britain could only hope to win a *long* war, the Treasury warned that she could only afford a *short* one.[8] It was an interesting dilemma. Nearly a year later, in February 1940, when the 'phoney war' was still granting Britain an unexpected respite, the Treasury reckoned that, even if carefully husbanded, British resources could last at the current rate of dollar expenditure no longer than two years.[9]

Yet in August 1940, after the collapse of France had left Britain alone and with a vulnerable empire to defend, Winston Churchill and his Cabinet made the deliberate decision not to tailor British war-making down to the weak resources of the British economy but instead to create and equip an army of fifty-five divisions and expand aircraft production to 2782 a month by December 1941.[10] The consequent purchases from the United States of steel, machine tools, aircraft, aero-engines, motor transport and other war and industrial equipment of all kinds would, so calculated the Chancellor of the Exchequer, amount to $3200 million over the next twelve months. But remaining British resources in foreign exchange and American securities amounted, he wrote, to only £490 million and as a consequence Britain would exhaust her gold and dollar reserves by December 1940.[11] In other words, Britain would then go bankrupt; incapable either of waging war or of sustaining her national life.

This moment of final wreck did not in the event occur until March 1941, when Britain's own reserves were utterly at an end, and payments currently due to America for war supplies could only be met thanks to a loan of gold from the Belgian government in exile.[12]

On 11 March 1941, however, the United States Congress passed an 'Act to promote the defense of the United States', or, as it was to become better known, the Lend–Lease Act, the effect of which was to transform Britain from a bankrupt into an American pensioner. For henceforth American food and raw materials, American military and industrial equipment, flowed to Britain free of payment, to the cumulative gigantic total by 1945 of $27,023 million worth.[13] Because of Lend–Lease Britain no longer needed to earn her own living, nor wage war within her own means. Instead she was able to turn her economy over to war purposes to a degree impossible for any other belligerent – exports down by 1944 to 31 per cent of the 1938 figure; 55 per cent of her labour force in the armed forces or war employment compared with only 40 per cent in the United States.[14] More, access to America's colossal productive and technological resources enabled Britain to expand her war factories far beyond the limits of British industry's own ability to equip them. Here was the essential basis for that grand scale of British war production which so misleadingly impressed public opinion, and which prophets like Beveridge took as providing practical justification for their vision of New Jerusalem. For the truth is that Britain's war economy was in its fundamental nature artificial: as dependent on American strength as a patient on a life-support machine and this was especially so of the aircraft industry.

By the end of 1943 the creation had been completed of Britain's largest industrial operation from the cadre of the little aircraft industry of 1935, with its mere 35,000 employees and £14 million worth of output per annum. According to the Minister of Aircraft Production, Sir Stafford Cripps, in a report in November 1943 on 'The Future of the Aircraft Industry', 1,750,000 people were now working on his ministry's contracts, in the light-metal industry, armaments, equipment, instruments and radio as well as airframes and engines; and that expenditure on production in the current fiscal year amounted to £800 million.[15] The professional aircraft industry, wrote the minister, now comprised twenty design firms (of which six were associated in two groups), employed nearly 300,000 people, and was responsible for developing the thirty-two main types of airframe currently in production. The five important aero-engine firms (three of these were either part of airframe firms or associated with them) employed 110,000 people, of which three-quarters worked in just two companies. These airframe and aero-engine firms directly controlled nearly a quarter of the total output for which the Ministry of Aircraft Production (MAP) was responsible. The 'shadow' factories, mainly managed by the car industry but provided at state cost, accounted for another 100,000 employees. But the sub-contracting of components manufacture had reached into all branches of the engineering industry, and here again state funds had often provided the tools and paid for the new factory space. On airframes alone, the minister noted, sub-contractors were employing 400,000 in 14,000 factories. Nevertheless, just fifty firms, together with their sub-contractors, accounted for three-quarters of all the ministry's contractual work.[16]

The Ministry of Aircraft Production had now therefore become the biggest customer of the engineering and allied trades, giving employment to around 40 per cent of this industrial group, the overall workforce in which had more than doubled since 1935.[17] Six out of every ten engineering factories took some aircraft work, and, measured in terms of labour, over 6000 of them were contributing half or more of their capacity to working for the ministry. Of the 650 larger engineering firms in Britain with more than 1000 employees each, four-fifths did some aircraft-production work.[18] The capital cost of creating this huge industrial complex between 1935 and June 1943 amounted to £350 million, of which

£150 million had been laid out on new buildings and £200 million on plant.[19]

Here then was an industrial development without parallel in British history in terms of scale, speed and cost – and of state participation. Here was the centre of gravity of the entire British war effort. But how efficient really was this great new industry? How good were the professional airframe and engine firms in designing and developing new types of aircraft? How well did the industry meet its production targets? How well was it organised? What was the industry's productivity record?

The simple production figures look impressive enough: 26,263 aircraft delivered in 1943 as against 2827 in 1938; 26,461 in 1944.[20] The total output in 1939–45 amounted to 796,750,000 lb of structure weight.[21] But comparison with Germany and the United States in terms of output per man-day, even though such a comparison can only be approximate, presents a less inspiring picture. Perhaps expectedly, but nonetheless ominously with regard to postwar market prospects for the aircraft industry, the United States far outstripped Britain in productivity, with a peak annual average of 2.76 lb of structure weight per man-day in 1944[22] compared with the British peak annual average of 1.19 lb in that year.[23] But even Germany's peak annual average productivity, at 1.5 lb per man-day in 1943, was a fifth better than Britain's.[24] Moreover, this German productive superiority constituted more of an achievement than the bare figures indicate. For whereas German production overwhelmingly concentrated on fighters, a large proportion of British output took the form of bombers, which required fewer man-hours per structure weight to produce. In the words of a calculation in the Air Ministry in 1940, 'a ton of heavy aircraft represented less added value and a smaller industrial effort than a ton of lighter aircraft.'[25] The German industry further suffered from the dispersal of some of its factories to new underground sites because of heavy allied bombing, and from the chaotic nature of Nazi war administration, with either want of clear policy or devastating changes of policy. Specifications and production priorities suffered from the same twin effects of Nazi muddle, that pervasive handicap about which German professional management was to complain bitterly to allied interrogators in 1945.[26]

The British wartime record in the design and development of new types of aircraft, and in the speed at which they were put into production, was also markedly inferior to the American or even the German, despite those external handicaps under which German aircraft firms laboured. As against two designs completely disastrous in production, in the four-engined Heinkel 177 and Junkers 288 heavy bombers, the German aircraft industry put into production the Focke Wulf 190, a fighter superior to later marks of the Spitfire and Hurricane and the newest British fighters; the ME 262 and Ar 234, the first jet aircraft in squadron service; and the ME 163, the first rocket-propelled fighter, and the first with the swept-wing configuration common to all high-speed jet aircraft today. It had flown an experimental helicopter. But the tally of British botches well outnumber the famous successes, and include such now largely forgotten names as the twin-engined Westland Welkin fighter, the Bristol Buckingham medium bomber, and the Vickers Windsor and Warwick bombers, the latter described by official historians as 'the most spectacular failure of all'.[27] The Typhoon, the designated replacement to the Hurricane and Spitfire, proved inferior to the latest mark of Spitfire as well as to the Focke Wulf 190 when it at last reached the squadrons late in 1942, and it finished up as a platform for rocket attack on tanks. Its offspring the Tempest, appearing in October 1943, also proved inferior to the latest Spitfire and to the FW 190.[28] Both the Typhoon and the Tempest suffered from an engine that had turned out as much of a design and production disaster as the Merlin was eventually a triumph – the Napier Sabre.[29] Of just two unquestioned British post-Spitfire-generation successes, only the de Havilland Mosquito's all-wooden fabrication can be claimed as technologically original, while the Gloster Meteor jet fighter remained conventional in its airframe design though revolutionary in its power plant. Nor had the wartime British aircraft industry any designs either flying or on the drawing board to compare with the American Boeing B–29 heavy bomber with its pressurised cockpit, or the Lockheed Constellation long-distance transport aircraft with a pressurised cabin, of which no fewer than 260 were on order by spring 1943.[30]

The truth was that in regard to design the British aircraft industry had enjoyed a brief creative period from 1933 to 1937, borrowing from earlier technical breakthroughs abroad, when the Spitfire, Hurricane, Manchester (precursor of the Lancaster) and Halifax came off the drawing boards, but that thereafter this creativity was largely spent. In January 1943 the Air Minister himself acknowledged this when he noted on a report by Air Vice Marshal Sorley (about Sorley's recent visit to American aircraft factories) that Great Britain was now behind on aircraft design and production and technical achievements, and that 'soon we shall be out of date.'[31]

While the jet-engined aircraft provided the one shining exception to this, the speed of its progress from the drawing board to the squadron evokes the turkey rather than the jet.[32] Jigs and tools for production of eighty Gloster F9/40 (later the 'Meteor') fighters a month were ordered as early as January 1941, well before the first successful flight by an experimental aircraft powered by the Whittle engine in May; and the production order to Glosters was confirmed in August, with engine manufacture to be phased accordingly. Yet the Meteor only began to reach the squadrons in very small numbers in July 1944. In Germany, although an experimental jet aircraft had made its first flight in 1939, the first operational prototype, that of the ME 262, did not fly until 1942. Nevertheless the ME 262 came into service a month earlier than the Meteor and in larger quantities; by July 1944 monthly production of the ME 262 had already risen to fifty-nine aircraft.[33] Nor was the sluggishness in developing the Meteor exceptional. Though the specification for the Typhoon was issued in January 1938, it did not reach the squadrons until late in 1942, whereas the Focke Wulf FW 190 specification was issued in spring 1938 and the aircraft reached the squadrons in July 1941. The Halifax took four years from specification to first deliveries; the

Manchester-into-Lancaster five years. Despite a thoroughgoing investigation in the summer of 1942 into the length of time needed to design and produce new types of aircraft carried out by Sir Ernest Lemon, the Director-General of Production at the MAP, the ministry was warning at the turn of 1943–4 that it would take not less than five years to design and bring into service a new heavy bomber.[34]

The reasons why the wartime British aircraft industry failed to achieve a better comparative record in design, development and productivity are twofold: despite its now formidable size and central place in the war effort, the industry still suffered from profound defects inherited from the nature of its small-time origins in 1935, while yet further weaknesses had resulted from the scrambling haste of its expansion ever since – a corner shop that suddenly found itself a Harrods. There was, however, a third factor, common to all branches of engineering in Britain, indeed all manufacturing industry: the retarding force exerted on production even in wartime by the trade unions by means of restrictive practices on manning and demarcations.

The first of the inherited defects lay in tiny design staffs which could not be multiplied rapidly because no reservoir of trained talent existed. The British education and training system simply did not turn out enough engineers (let alone aeronautical engineers), technicians or draughtsmen, and could not easily be adapted in the middle of a war to do so. Moreover because of traditional Air Ministry policy the small available cadre of design talent had been split up between sixteen design firms; and because of the jealous independence and commercial secrecy cherished by these firms no less than by firms in older British industries like steel, each little design team had worked largely in its own mental box before the war. Even in wartime the MAP found it difficult to persuade the aircraft firms to abandon rugged individualism for the pooling of talent and ideas.[35] The scant design resources were fragmented even further because of the plethora of overlapping new types or marks of aircraft in each category – bomber, fighter, naval aircraft.[36] The 'boys in the backroom' approach was also reflected in the equally 'backroom' nature of equipment for research, design and experimental testing.[37] And the British 'boys-in-the-backroom' themselves, because of their professional origins in small handwork set-ups, did not always bear in mind the need for ease of eventual large-scale series manufacture when designing new aircraft. For example, according to a contemporary British calculation, the airframe of Mitchell's Spitfire Mark V C demanded over 13,000 man-hours to build, as against approximately 4000 man-hours for the Messerschmitt ME 109G, while even later the Tempest and Typhoon took twice the man-hours of the Messerschmitt.[38] Indeed according to an American team of investigating experts in 1945, German designers were better even than American in designing 'for easy production with means at hand. American designs were, by comparison, unsuited to large-scale manufacture at reasonable cost.'[39]

But in any event Germany and the United States were alike in maintaining vast design departments, lavishly staffed and equipped. A team of British experts to America in September and October 1942 headed by the Controller-General of the Ministry of Aircraft Production, Sir Alexander Dunbar, and including the chairman of the Society of British Aircraft Constructors, Sir Charles Bruce-Gardner, reported after visiting twenty-nine plants that there was a much higher proportion of engineering (that is, design and development) staff to production staff than in Britain; and that, thanks to the much larger university output of engineers in America, this engineering staff was mostly recruited from universities, 'not shop-trained ex-apprentices as is generally the rule in the United Kingdom'.[40] Furthermore, the mission found much closer integration between the design and production departments than in Britain. It therefore recommended that British designers and production engineers should be sent to the United States in order to study how to achieve this closer integration, because this was the way to simpler production methods and faster output: 'If anything is to be learned, no lesson could be more valuable.'[41]

A later mission to America headed by Sir Roy Fedden, special technical adviser to the Minister of Aircraft Production, reported in April 1943 after visiting five airframe, four engine and two propeller firms that it had been struck by the 'size, scope and experience' of the combined technical and engineering expertise deployed by the companies themselves and by the US Navy and Army Air Corps. The mission found that the design and development staffs in American aircraft firms were about five to seven times larger than in Britain, thus making possible the faster evolution of prototypes and thereafter faster development to the production stage.[42] But it was not only a matter of the huge scale of American research and development. American techniques of design and experimental testing were themselves, according to the Fedden mission, far in advance of British, with standardised drawing-office procedures, the photocopying of drawings for direct printing on to metal, and the 'lofting' of designs as in shipbuilding.[43] Like the Dunbar mission, Fedden's team pointed out that this whole American approach was only made possible by the wealth of engineering talent, thanks to engineering education in the United States being, in the words of the Fedden report, 'undoubtedly planned in a far-reaching way'.[44] Fedden and his colleagues therefore looked to the future with some trepidation: 'It is sufficient . . . to say that we cannot hope to compete in this country in the future, unless immediate steps are taken to deal with the matter of training engineers. There is not a moment to be lost.'[45]

When two years later Sir Roy Fedden led a similar mission to defeated Germany, his team found that Germany too had equipped itself with superior resources in research and development, in terms of both facilities and talent. 'It is believed', said this second Fedden report, 'that Germany possessed aeronautical research and test equipment in advance of anything existing in this country or America at the present time.'[46] A 'scientific approach' to engine developments had led to techniques 'in certain respects' ahead of British.[47] By way of treasure trove, the mission had found a 'plethora of excellent [research and development] equipment' which it thought might be secured for the proposed new British aeronautical college. The report of another British technical mission to Germany in 1945, led by Sir Roy Farren, Director-General of the Royal Aeronautical Establishment at Farnborough, and comprising nine senior members of major aircraft and equipment firms, only served to provide more evidence that backrooms and the boys in them were not enough. A German technical director, according to the Farren mission, enjoyed more numerous and better-qualified staff than his British opposite number, while the design and drawing-office organisation was much larger in scale than in Britain.[48] For example, the mission discovered that the experimental side of the Messerschmitt company was double the British scale. They also pronounced themselves impressed by the calibre, 'relative youth' and energy of the staff.[49]

The conclusions reached by the Fedden and Farren teams are, moreover, fully borne out by a third British report, by a technical team of three led by R. M. Clarkson of de Havilland, on a visit to the Messerschmitt plant at Oberammergau in June 1945. It was this team's judgement that Germany had been ahead of both the UK and the US in certain technical developments. The team estimated that the Messerschmitt R and D organisation, with a total staff of 1400 (including 600 pure R and D personnel) equalled in scale those of the big American firms; and it was particularly impressed by the great practical and operational knowledge of the staff they interrogated, and by the strong emphasis in the design process on ultimate ease of production. The team's summing-up serves to emphasise how lucky Britain had been during the war that incompetent Nazi administration and vacillating Nazi policy had done so much to dissipate the German aircraft industry's technical talent and resources; and how lucky Britain was also to be in the postwar era in not having to meet German as well as American competition in air-transport manufacture:

> The scale on which science and engineering have been harnessed to the chariot of destruction in Germany is indeed amazing. There is no shortage of technical personnel or material facilities, no stinting of financial resources even for apparently long term and complex developments.[50]

In Germany just as in America the essential foundation for such advanced design techniques and lavish facilities and staffing was provided by superb engineering education at all levels. The Farren mission particularly admired the German training system for technical staff, with graduates directly recruited from the technical high schools (of which no true equivalent yet existed in Britain) after a three-year diploma course which included one year's practical training; and juveniles recruited as apprentices at the age of fifteen from junior technical schools (of which again no true equivalent existed in Britain). Outstandingly able apprentices were, Farren reported, sent on to university at either the firm's expense or the government's.[51]

So it was that, no matter how brilliant might be individual British aircraft designers or how outstanding the particular achievements of the best British companies like Rolls-Royce, the overall British effort in the design and development of new aircraft presented an all-too-typical picture of the piecemeal, the inadequate and the under-funded. Here was the Victorian-style 'practical man' living again in a new technology, and already being outclassed by foreign professionalism. And this was equally true of the field of production, thus partly accounting for the fact that British productivity in terms of structure weight per man-day was only four-fifths of the German and little more than a third of the American (see above p. 147).

In the first place Britain failed to achieve the economies of scale in regard either to size of plant or to length of production run exploited by the American aircraft industry. To be fair, this failure is partly to be attributed to the compulsion of circumstance. The menace of air attack had rendered it prudent to disperse productive resources in many factories rather than concentrate them in a few gigantic plants of the American type; this was true of Germany as well, especially after the allied bomber offensive got really under way in 1943. Then again, the wise practical decision taken in 1936 to site 'shadow' airframe and engine factories alongside existing automobile plants had also necessarily entailed dispersion, since the British car industry was itself so geographically scattered.

Nevertheless the fragmentation of the professional aircraft and engine industry over many sites, some of them cramped and awkwardly laid out, was the result of the Air Ministry's charitable but curious interwar policy of keeping as many as sixteen principal design firms alive, rather than concentrating the industry into a few strong groups. Moreover, the multiplicity of aircraft types and marks in production in Britain as compared with America (or even Germany by 1944) further prevented the kind of production economies which gave the United States such an enviable output record. In 1943, for example, Britain was manufacturing four different designs of single-seat fighter as against Germany's two; four different heavy bombers as against America's three. To make matters worse, the British industry continually introduced piecemeal improvements to aircraft in the course of production, whereas in America the assembly-lines were allowed to pour out a particular mark of aircraft in vast quantities before a halt was called for major 'saved-up' design changes. Equally the Americans would completely stop production of an obsolescent model, proceed to retool and rejig the factory for a new model, and then resume mass production, while the British 'spliced in' new models gradually while production of the old still continued, simply because Britain could not afford any pause in the flow of aircraft. All these factors resulted too often in batch production, with the consequent wasteful use of scarce skilled labour in making continual adjustments on the factory floor. Thus even in so new a technology and so recently created a manufacturing complex the hallowed patterns of the British industrial tradition had already asserted themselves.

It is therefore perhaps not surprising that the Dunbar and Fedden reports of 1942–3, when they turn to the question of production, should make comparisons between British and American aircraft factories that call to mind those drawn for half a century past between the steel and shipbuilding industries in Britain and abroad. The Dunbar mission in particular was struck by the organisation of the American industry into large factory units, the biggest four to five times larger than the biggest in Britain, where 'dispersal into smaller units [was] forced upon us by conditions in the United Kingdom'.[52] Sir Roy Fedden's team reported similarly in April 1943 on the scale, boldness and financing of new US production facilities.[53] Both missions wrote of American aircraft factories with something of the wonder of men transported from a nineteenth-century red-brick industrial town into the world of 'Things to Come'. Here were vast structures permanently blacked out and brilliantly lit by fluorescent tubing; air-conditioned, spacious, clean, even elegant. In the words of the Dunbar report:

> We are convinced that the better lighting, the painting of walls and plant in light colours are valuable aids to production, and we should like to see American practice followed in the United Kingdom so far as consideration of cost and fuel economy permit.[54]

The greater floor space per man 'makes for tidiness, better supervision and transport within the factory'.[55]

The conclusion reached by both missions that plant 'housekeeping' was of a much higher standard in America is confirmed by the report of an engineer commander of the Royal Navy after a visit to the United States in 1943,[56] and also by an American expert visiting Britain in July of that year who found plant housekeeping good at only two British aircraft factories, and inferior to American standards in all the rest.[57] In such British slovenliness on the working site was freshly manifested yet another of the nation's old industrial traditions. And slovenliness, as General Brooke so rightly divined when he inspected Corap's Ninth Army in 1940, offers an accurate clue to the state of morale and efficiency. But so equally does smartness. Within the bright and clean American aircraft factories, the Dunbar mission found a bright and clean workforce:

> The impression of the condition of the workers was very favourable. They are generally of good physique, alert, clean and well-groomed. The women in particular are of a good type. The wearing of trousers is compulsory for women, and some plants had employed experts to design well-cut and becoming standard uniforms.[58]

American aircraft companies provided their workers not only with couturier-designed trousers, but also with better training than in Britain – a government course to begin with, followed by four to six weeks' training in the aircraft plants themselves in special training shops.[59]

Nevertheless, no matter how smart, well trained and well cared for the rank and file of a force may be, they cannot perform their best unless they be well organised and directed by first-class staff-work; staff-work based in turn on sound operational doctrine, indeed a sound professional philosophy. The wartime British aircraft industry, again true to an older industrial tradition, had no clear operational doctrine as such, no coherent professional philosophy; its way of doing things was the cumulative outcome of countless *ad hoc* answers by 'practical men' to the incidental problems posed by rushed pre-war expansion and then by the urgent demands of war. Such pragmatism, however, had its functional costs, in that too high a proportion of the industry's scarce resources in skill were deployed well forward in steering the production process itself – adjusting for modifications, fixing local hold-ups, arranging the transitions between one batch of aircraft and another; day-to-day crisis management because production had not been carefully organised with the very object of avoiding crises. It was otherwise in the United States, where the abundant engineering and management talent was heavily concentrated in preparatory planning before the assembly-lines began to roll. According to the Fedden mission:

> The various production operations are broken down into stages and planned more elaborately in America than in this country. Much time and effort is put into pre-preparation work of scheduling, process planning, machine loading, labour loading and shop layout and this is carried out in greater detail in America than is customary in many of our factories. This is considered to be an essential part of obtaining efficient production. Time study is extensively used as a means of obtaining adequate data for this work.[60]

What the British 'practical man's' ad-hockery could mean at its worst is revealed by a report on Vickers-Armstrong (Aircraft) in July 1943 by five Ministry of Production experts who had thoroughly investigated all the factories and operations under the company's supervision. Of the management they wrote:

> The important executives have little competent assistance, and each and every one has too much detailed work to do. It is our considered opinion that assistants should be provided to enable them to carry out their proper function of policy and general control.[61]

The assistant to Vickers' production manager turned out to be a solicitor with no engineering experience, while the production manager himself refused to delegate and insisted on trying to control everything personally.[62] Labour relations were poor, as was productivity, with skilled workers employed on simple operations and much idle time. Shifts completed their quotas by 3.30 p.m., so leaving a slack period, including overtime, up to 7 p.m.:

> It was agreed that in general the tempo of the workpeople was poor and that, in particular, the night shifts were lacking in supervision and in a large number of cases was not warranted, (with a potential capacity of at least 60 men, in one Hangar in the Experimental Section, the total night shift consisted of 2 machinists and 1 canteen worker).[63]

The five investigators found that the personnel department of Vickers was 'largely ineffective and has very little control over labour demands'; that the stores department suffered 'severely' from lack of central control; that the planning and rate-fixing department suffered likewise, and 'does not permit of any continuous utilisation of labour'.[64] Their damning final judgement was that there existed 'no system of line production throughout the whole organisation'.[65] It was no wonder, then, that Vickers' production of aircraft had fallen from twenty-one per week after Dunkirk to only nine in the early part of 1943 despite 5000 extra workers and a total labour-force of more than 14,250.[66]

Unfortunately Vickers-Armstrong (Aircraft) did not constitute the only extreme case of managerial incompetence serving to offset the achievements of efficient companies and pull down the national average of productivity. In 1943 the development of the jet engine had to be removed from Rovers and placed in the hands of Rolls-Royce because of, according to an unpublished official study,[67] the 'chaotic condition of the production organisation assembled at Rover's shadow factory' for manufacturing the Whittle W2B engine off the drawing board. No engines of sufficient power output had yet been built. This had meant that no flight trials of the Gloster F9/40 (later Meteor) were possible, so completely upsetting plans for the prototype and ultimate production. In any event, Glosters, the makers of the airframe, were, according to the same study, equally chaotic.[68] Earlier the same year inspectors from the MAP reported after a visit to the Bristol-Group parent aero-engine factory at Bristol that the factory was badly organised, with no proper layout of production lines and what another unpublished official study called 'knife-and-fork methods' predominating.[69] The result was that 'machined parts perambulated the shops on a vast scale', while elaborate machine tools were either misused on simple operations or allowed to stand idle. The general atmosphere was 'one of lassitude'.[70]

But poor productivity could not always by any means be solely blamed on bad management. For example, in attempting to start up production of their infamous Sabre engine at their Acton Works in 1942, Napiers, incompetent though they were, ran into unavoidable trouble with the local type of labour, who were 'notorious for truculence, slackness and readiness to enter into industrial disputes'.[71] For whereas in the United States the workforce and the unions co-operated with management to achieve maximum utilisation of plant, in Britain the jealous sense on the part of unions and their members of their 'rights' supplied another of the factors, and a crucial one, that held down productivity in the aircraft industry.

There were, of course, strikes. All of them were wildcat, since official stoppages had been made illegal under the Essential Work Order; all of them of the trivial and parochial kind that were to become so drearily familiar during Britain's long postwar industrial decline. Out of the eight or more serious strikes in the aircraft industry between February and May 1943, for instance, six were over wages; one because of objection to an efficiency check on the use of a machine; and one because of objection to two fitters being transferred by management to a different section in the same shop.[72] The remaining twenty-eight stoppages in this period were caused by such questions of overriding importance in the midst of a total war as arguments over piece rates; complaints about canteen facilities; the alleged victimisation of a shop steward; the use of females in riveting work; the refusal of Amalgamated Engineering Union members to work with non-union employees; a refusal of management to allow collections for the Red Army during working hours; and a sit-down strike to prevail on other workers to join an embargo against payment by results.[73] Although the actual time lost by these stoppages in February–May 1943 amounted only to one-fiftieth of 1 per cent of hours worked, the knock-on effect on the production process was incalculable. MAP statisticians warned furthermore that the tally of actual strikes took no note of the effects of 'widespread' (*sic*) go-slow movements.[74] Just two go-slows in 1943, at Austins and at the Rootes factory at Speke, Liverpool, are known to have cost fifty-seven aircraft in lost production.[75] According to an internal MAP memorandum in October 1943, at the height of the bomber offensive against Germany, 'ca'canny' (i.e. go-slows) in production of Halifax bombers at Speke had caused a shortfall of forty-nine aircraft in the two months August and September.[76] A strike at Rolls-Royce at Hillington, Glasgow, in November 1943 alone cost over 730,000 man-hours.[77]

During 1944, the critical year of the invasion of Europe, the 'lads' were out at Rootes, Hawkers, Short Brothers, Fairey Aviation, A. V. Roe, Vickers-Armstrong and Austins of Longbridge, to name the most notable out of thirty strikes.[78] They struck at Hawkers at Langley over rate-fixing for new machines; they sat down at Faireys in a demand that a certain inspector should be removed.[79] At Airspeed, Portsmouth, in August 1944, they downed tools on the score that the time allotted to finish pressed panels was too fast. In fact, at fifty minutes, it exceeded by eleven minutes the time allowed for this task to female labour by de Havilland.[80] The secondary cause of this strike lay in the dismissal of a man who refused to continue work under the fifty-minute time allocation; and no one would return until this man of principle had been reinstated.[81]

It is true that time and production known to have been lost in the aircraft and engine industry through strikes amounted to no more than 0.5 per cent of man-hours worked in the period July 1942 to December 1944,[82] so in no way competing with the coal miners' outstanding record (see above pp. 67–8, 80–1). But stoppages and go-slows themselves, like absenteeism at double and more the American rate in 1942–3,[83] were merely the obvious whiffs of sulphurous smoke, the bubbling up of small gouts of lava through the cracks, that indicated the subterranean reservoir of unwillingness, suspicion and hostility smouldering away below; and which otherwise manifested itself unquantifiably in slackness of effort and poor discipline. As early as April 1941 this malaise of slackness had become a general problem.[84] A report on de Havillands at Castle Bromwich, for example, referred to 'a marked absence of discipline', 'slackness' and 'difficulty in controlling shop stewards in some factories'.[85] In March and April 1943 the new Production Efficiency Board investigated Coventry firms engaged on MAP contracts, and reported that there would be no need for extra labour if only the existing labour-force did its stuff, which it was not encouraged to do because times and prices for piece work made it possible to enjoy 'high earnings without a corresponding high effort'.[86] Wrote the Production Efficiency Board:

> in each factory there is evidence of slackness and lack of discipline. Operators are slow in starting work at the beginning of each shift and after each break, and there is a complete stoppage of work from 15 to 30 minutes before each break. . . . Our discussions show that managements are aware of these weaknesses but feel themselves powerless to remedy them. Trade Union representatives agree that the weaknesses exist.[87]

The prize must surely however be awarded to the sheet-metal workers at Hawksleys of Gloucester, who went on strike in August 1942 because one worker would not 'go slow' and earned 7*s* 9*d* an hour by piece work when the union limited earnings and work to 4*s* 6*d* an hour.[88]

Thus in the high-technology industries as in the old Victorian staples the war, with its soothing drug of lavish but only partly earned wages and secure jobs, served as the midwife of the bogus full employment and the notorious low British productivity of the postwar era. Part of the problem of the 'fully employed' shop-floor card-players no doubt lay, as an unpublished official study argued, in the poor quality, low status and inexperience of the personnel managers in the aircraft industry.[89] But the real explanation is to be found, once again, in that deep reservoir of resentment and hostility which impelled the workforce to take as much as it could while giving as little as it could get away with. Jack Tanner, the national president of the Amalgamated Engineering Union, said it all in 1944:

> It must not be forgotten that before the war and indeed well into the war, the disorganisation in industrial production, the waste of man and machine power, of raw material and human skill were largely a matter of indifference to the worker. He observed them as he observed other evidence of an inefficient social system, his prime concern being to fight for better wages and working conditions.[90]

Here too lies the explanation for a resistance to 'dilution' in the high-technology industries such as aircraft manufacture no less obdurate than in shipbuilding. In Germany the skilled craftsmen resisted dilution out of a mistaken belief that it would mar the superb quality of the German engineering product;[91] in Britain they resisted it simply in defence of privilege. The problem had first emerged during the pre-war rearmament period, because dilution offered the obvious short cut to getting more production out of limited industrial resources. But in the face of anticipated bitter hostility on the part of the craft unions, the government thought it prudent to leave the matter dormant. In the words of the Ministry of Labour to the DPRC in August 1936:

> It raises an industrial issue of first-class importance. It is considered that the adoption of any such measures is a matter which should be left entirely to employers and workpeople, and that it would be unwise in present circumstances for the Government to be in any way involved.[92]

Less to be expected – at least at first sight – is the opposition of management itself in the aircraft industry in the 1930s to dilution. But a report by the Air Ministry's area officer for the north-west region makes it all too clear why: 'the whole force of conservatism and laziness was against dilution and the unions' objections were sometimes a welcome excuse for inaction.'[93] For this reason and for technical reasons dilution proved easier to introduce in the new shadow factories.[94]

In August 1940, at the height of the Battle of Britain, the Parliamentary Secretary to the Ministry of Supply was reporting that 'some dilution was taking place, but this had not gone very far . . . and the goodwill of the local Trade Union authorities had not yet been entirely secured.'[95] Even after the passing of the Restoration of Pre-War Trade Practices Act in 1940, guaranteeing the craft unions that they would be given back their privileges once the war was won, sheet-metal working – so basic to aircraft production – remained the battleground for a last stand against dilution. Of all absurdities, the sheet-metal unions sought to maintain that because for centuries metal had been shaped by craftsmen banging away with hand and bench tools, then metal shaping for a Spitfire or Lancaster fuselage and wings by the power press and automatic tool in a mass-production aircraft factory must be rated as craftsmen's work and manned and paid as such.[96] The unions especially objected to the presses and tools being operated by women. As the Ministry of Labour reported in October 1943:

> The Sheet Metal Unions refuse to admit that any sheet metal work of a semi-skilled character exists, though a Committee of Investigation appointed by the Ministry of Labour and National Service in June 1942 to investigate the problem reported that the Committee was of the opinion that a very considerable proportion of the work in sheet metal shops in the aircraft industry was of a semi-skilled character and could be performed by women.[97]

In point of fact the rise in British aircraft production from 1939 to the end of 1942 (though never up to target) was achieved not by a revolution in productivity, but by simply deploying 111,500 extra machine tools and over 1 million extra workers.[98] In January 1943 Ernest Bevin, the Minister of Labour and National Service, repudiated any idea that a shortage of labour had been responsible for the failure to fulfil aircraft production programmes, and with characteristically brutal candour put a large finger on the true reason for the failure: 'The aircraft industry was the one industry which had failed to improve its output in proportion to the amount of labour supplied.'[99] It was only in 1943–4, when plant and labour-force reached their limits, that improved productivity came to be seen as a necessary key to higher output.[100] But this presented a novel problem, because, in the absence of the detailed time-and-motion studies of all production processes enjoyed by American management, no means existed for measuring productivity. In November 1942 a meeting of civil servants agreed that measurement of productivity would be too difficult; and that a more practical approach would be to monitor absenteeism – with the result that from June 1943 accurate figures for absenteeism became available for the first time.[101] It was not until 1944 that the Ministry of Aircraft Production issued 'An Introduction to the Theory and Application of Motion Study'[102] and began training courses in production systems and layout. In the few aircraft-industry firms where motion study was carried out and production tasks reorganised accordingly – in the face, naturally, of fierce opposition from shop foremen – productivity increased by 60–130 per cent.[103]

But across the whole industry, according to a draft memorandum prepared for the Chief Executive of the Ministry of Aircraft Production in April 1944, the figures had shown no upward trend in productivity since early 1943; the apparent rise being due to the increasing emphasis on heavy bombers, more economical to produce per structure weight.[104] This pessimistic contemporary assessment is confirmed by comparing British, German and United States productivity. In 1944 Daimler-Benz manufactured a total of 28,669 aero-engines with a workforce of 63,502; Rolls-Royce at its own factories 18,100 aero-engines with a workforce of 56,000 – a productivity only 71 per cent of that achieved by the German firm under heavy bombing and enforced dispersal.[105] The British peak monthly production of aircraft in terms of structure weight, in March 1944, amounted to 1.28 lb per man-day – compared with a German monthly peak of 1.93 lb, and an American peak, in May 1944, of more than 3lb.[106] As late as November 1944 a Whitehall memorandum is found freshly diagnosing a basic reason for this poor productivity: 'Probably the most outstanding single cause of failing to reach a maximum production efficiency in wartime is scarcity of skilled management.'[107]

To the end of the war, therefore, the British aircraft industry failed to find answers to the cluster of problems involved in wringing American or even German levels of output from given numbers of men and machine tools.[108] Yet the aircraft industry's difficulties were by no means special to it alone. They were shared by the remaining 60 per cent of the British engineering industry not working for the Ministry of Aircraft Production, but producing for the other armed services; shared too by such branches of advanced-technology production as radio and that epitome of self-congratulating national myth, radar.

Chapter Nine

The Dependence on America: Radar and Much Else

'Give us the tools, and we will finish the job!' proclaimed Winston Churchill in a broadcast on 9 February 1941 partly directed at American ears. With the passing a month later of the Lend–Lease Act the United States duly began to 'give' the tools which Britain could no longer afford to buy, so that month by month, year by year, they would continue to make the slow Atlantic voyage through the hazards of weather and U-boat: and not only the weapons of war which Churchill had in mind, but real tools for industry. In 1939 the United States had supplied Britain with 8364 machine tools; in 1940 (the peak) with 33,111; in 1941 the total was 32,044. Thereafter, with the equipping of British war industry gradually approaching completion, the numbers fell away to 24,023 in 1942, 20,514 in 1943 and 8416 in 1944.[1] But in the peak years of 1940 and 1941 American supplies of machine tools amounted to about half the total British output; that is, about a third of Britain's total requirements. It marked a lamentable state of dependence for the one-time 'workshop of the world'. Indeed, to lack, as Britain did, the ability to tool her own factories was to lack a fundamental characteristic of an advanced industrial economy. This inability was the more serious because of the condition of the existing machine tools in those factories. 'The general-purpose tools already available in industry', an unpublished official study wrote of the situation early in 1941, 'were usually old and worn, not capable of great accuracy and high cutting speeds, and the rapid machinery necessary for rapid output.'[2] Moreover, during the war as in the pre-war rearmament period Britain depended on the United States for certain kinds of specialised or highly sophisticated machine tool even more than in general. The peak annual imports of automatic lathes, in 1942, were two-and-a-half times British production; of turret lathes, nearly three times; of vertical drillers, twice; of boring and gear-cutting tools, equal to British production.[3] In 1941 Britain found herself *totally* dependent on America for over twenty types of advanced machine tool.[4]

Thus British wartime output of high-technology products, from aircraft to radar, guns to instruments, would have been quite literally impossible without free access to the American machine-tool industry. Rolls-Royce continued to make the Merlin and later engines on American tools. Aircraft propellers and the navy's Oerlikon guns were fabricated on special-purpose American tools. Fuse production of all kinds was 100 per cent dependent on American automatic machines.[5] British manufacture of thermionic valves for radios and radar sets also crucially relied on American tools; and in May 1943 a senior official of the Radio Board was calling for an approach to the United States authorities 'on a high level' because of Britain's desperate need for valve-making machines.[6]

Nevertheless, from the very beginning of rearmament in 1936 governments had made strenuous efforts to expand Britain's own machine-tool output, partly from existing manufacturers, partly by drawing on new firms. By 1939 the existing manufacturers had doubled production compared with 1935 – by dint of doubling the workforce rather than by improving productivity.[7] The outbreak of war, and even more the great scare of summer 1940, spurred these endeavours to create new capacity in the industry (especially for making substitutes for foreign tools) and to extract more productivity from plant and personnel. By January 1943 the workforce, at 70,000, had nearly trebled over the 1935 figure, while output had slightly more than trebled.[8] At first sight this might appear to be a considerable achievement, even though it still of course left Britain critically dependent on American supplies. But management and men in the British machine-tool industry proved no better at exerting themselves efficiently than their confrères in other industries old and new. By March 1941, when the 1940 invasion fright had worn off, a 10 per cent fall in the utilisation of the industry's plant had taken place, equivalent to losing 50,000 tools.[9] In July 1941 6 per cent of tools were not manned even on main shifts, and 50 per cent were not manned on the second shift.[10] It is hardly surprising that a visiting team of American experts at this period voiced scathing contempt for the British machine-tool industry's flaccid productivity, especially since Britain was then pleading her dire need for American tools to help her out.[11] A further explanation for this poor record lay in wasteful use of scarce skilled labour (or labour which was paid as skilled) – 62 per cent of its workforce being rated as skilled in 1944, as against 27.5 per cent in the German machine-tool industry.[12] For in British machine-tool manufacture as in other kinds the craft unions proved as much help to the war effort as a powerful brake fitted to every machine.

In 1942, the peak year for British productivity, each operative turned out an average of 1.5 tools; in 1943 the average dropped to only 1.2 tools per operative.[13] The German machine-tool industry in its peak year of 1940 achieved an average output of 1.7 tools per employee, even though neither in that year nor at any time during the war was it run anywhere near its full potential capacity.[14] For so rich were the German industry's resources that without needing to stretch itself it was able comfortably to produce all the machine-tools required by the German war effort, including replacements for those destroyed by allied bombing, with the exception of some special single-purpose models.[15]

But in any case, Churchill's broadcast promise in 1941, that if America gave the tools Britain would finish the job, turned out in the event to have been a false prospectus, if the word 'tools' is taken to mean industrial machines as well as weapons. For over a regrettably wide range of weapons, war equipment and components Britain proved unable to finish the job in large enough quantities, or even at all. Thus the pre-war process of buying in finished products, military and industrial, continued in wartime on an even larger scale.

In the history of British tank development for the Second World War there are no equivalents of the Spitfire or Hurricane, only of the Westland Welkin or Bristol Buckingham or at best the Typhoon. With few exceptions, such as the Matilda, a heavily armoured but slow infantry-cooperation tank, British tanks until late in the war were mechanical abortions that foreshadowed the disastrous car models launched into world markets by the British automobile industry in the postwar era. Not all the blame attaches to the manufacturers, for the War Office itself was responsible for the failure to evolve clear design specifications to fit clearly conceived battlefield doctrine; a failure every bit as damaging and time-wasting as those which critical historians attribute to Nazi munitions administration.[16] The War Office was responsible too for the persistent under-gunning of British tanks compared with their German opposite numbers. Nevertheless, the mechanical failings of British tanks were largely the fault of commercial firms incompetent at design, development and manufacture.

Pre-war British development of a 'cruiser' tank (that is, a fast tank forming the backbone of an armoured division) had started with an experimental chassis demonstrated by an American engineer named Christie in 1936–7. Christie's creative contribution lay in the all-independent suspension system which the Russians adopted with conspicuous success. Unfortunately the British not only adopted the suspension system but also the engine that powered the experimental chassis. This was an American Liberty aero-engine, the design of which dated from the Great War. The Liberty combined impressive output of power when in the mood with appalling unreliability when not. The task of developing a cruiser tank round the War Office specification, the Christie chassis and the Liberty engine was given to Nuffield Mechanizations and Aero. There followed over-hasty, botched piecemeal development instead of thoroughgoing preliminary design and testing; exactly the same calamitous pattern as with the new models of British cars after the war. The gearbox of the prototype gave out after only 70 miles, while the steering brakes had a life of only 127 miles. After two months of trials at the end of 1937, no fewer than forty-seven mechanical defects had been reported.[17] The engine's carburettor and ignition system had to be redesigned; so too the air-cleaner, piping, fuel-pump, cooling and starting systems, which nevertheless were still to give endless troubles. Fresh designs of track, clutch and brakes were also needed. Heavier gear-box components had to be developed.[18] When the eventual production model, now named the 'Crusader', eventually reached the Western Desert in 1941 (coming off the ships with nuts and bolts only hand-tight; another tribute to British manufacturing standards) it proved mechanically unreliable to such an extent that the Commander-in-Chief Middle East had to reckon on having 25 per cent reserves to cover those in the workshops.[19] The British steel industry made its own distinctive contribution to the Crusader: firing tests in 1942 showed Crusader's armour to give less protection than should have been expected from its thickness; less in fact than comparable American armour.[20]

Meanwhile a parallel attempt to develop another cruiser tank, later to be named the Covenanter, had proved a complete and abysmal failure. Its extraordinarily mongrel parentage included a Thorneycroft engine (soon dropped in favour of a new design to be developed), a hull designed and made by the London, Midland and Scottish Railway Company, and a turret designed by Nuffield Mechanizations. The chief engineer of the London, Midland and Scottish Railway, no doubt on the analogy of one of his steam locomotives, placed the engine radiator inside the tank's fighting compartment, so accomplishing, in the words of a tank expert, 'the dual role of cooling the engine and roasting the crew'.[21] When the production models of the Covenanter emerged from the construction shops (to say 'off the assembly-lines' would be to flatter) in the summer of 1940 its defects were 'so numerous and so fundamental' that it had virtually to be redesigned and remade in most of its parts.[22] In particular its newly designed horizontally opposed twelve-cylinder engine suffered from grievous faults only belatedly cured when the tank was already obsolete. The Covenanter, of which 1900 were made, never fought in a battle.[23] Yet Covenanter's sorry story was eclipsed by those of Centaur and Cavalier, wartime designs that failed even to get as far as production.[24]

Moreover, such ultimately fairly successful wartime tank designs as the Churchill and the Cromwell also suffered from needless technical teething-troubles. The broad specification for the Churchill was issued in summer 1940. A year later the prototype's Bedford engine was found to perform markedly less well in the tank than it had on the bench, while faults in the suspension limited its speed to 8–9 miles per hour. In November 1941 the War Office was reporting that the Churchill was unfit for sustained operations in the Middle East or even in the United Kingdom unless sixteen modifications were carried out on the transmission, suspension and steering. As late as July 1942 (all this time, it should be remembered, the armoured campaign in the Western Desert had been ebbing and flowing in hard-fought battles), Churchills were failing their acceptance tests at mileages of only about 150 miles. Not until early in 1943 were its defects really cured.[25] The Churchill too, despite being largely the responsibility of Vauxhall Motors, a British out-station of the American firm General Motors, suffered from the classic disease of British automotive development; that is, lack of thorough organisation and proper planning of the whole design process, leading to the putting into production of what was still really only an unsatisfactory prototype[26] – the customer as tester. Only with the Cromwell (specification early 1941; ready in time for the Normandy landings in 1944) did the British wartime fumbling after a mechanically reliable, combat-worthy, all-purpose tank culminate in success. Yet even with the Cromwell there took place a prolonged dispute as to whether it should have a Rolls-Royce Meteor engine or the Nuffield-built Liberty engine for which, incredibly enough, Leyland Motors, the tank's 'parent' manufacturer, had tenaciously argued.[27]

In this whole dispiriting story other besetting British industrial sins manifested themselves yet again. An amazing ragbag of firms was jointly engaged in the design and manufacture of tanks, from armaments concerns like Vickers through mass-production car-makers like Nuffield and Vauxhall to positively Victorian institutions like railway and railway-carriage workshops. As for the mass-production motor-car manufacturers themselves, they had grown rich before the war by turning out mechanically simple vehicles, and therefore the design and development of a tank proved a novel and taxing experience for their exiguous design departments. Some of the older engineering firms had no modern conception of design and development at all. The Vulcan Foundry, charged in 1936 with designing a complex new heavily armoured tank, put two draughtsmen on the job. In November 1939 Harland and Wolff bettered this performance by being able to find 'two or three' to work on their own new tank design contract.[28] True to British form, these inadequate design and production resources were further dispersed over too many projects – no fewer than thirty separate designs of tank in hand between 1935 and 1944. While one or two of these aborted on the drawing board, others were unfortunately monsters that lived too long.[29] Given this double fragmentation of resources, it is not surprising that British peak productivity in actual tank manufacture amounted to only 80 per cent of German measured in numbers of vehicles produced per employee and only 65 per cent of German in terms of tonnage per employee.[30] Moreover, total British output of tanks and self-propelled guns was lower in proportion to German than the disparity of national populations would warrant. In her peak year of 1942 Britain produced 8611 tanks and self-propelled guns; Germany in her peak year of 1944 turned out 19,002 tanks, self-propelled guns and assault guns, of which tanks alone numbered 8334. In terms of total tonnage, British peak output in 1942 amounted to 204,000; German in 1944 to 548,000.[31]

Yet even these comparisons are flattering to the British performance, in that mere quantities take no note of fighting quality. Only a minority of the British total production could be said to be battleworthy; and some of it, like the Covenanter, was literally junk. Virtually all the German production consisted of first-class combat vehicles, even if the Tiger did present some maintenance and transporting problems because of its size and complexity. As is well known, German production of tanks was based on a very few thoroughly well-developed designs entrusted to a few large and technically first-class manufacturers like Henschel, M.A.N. and Daimler-Benz, and engine-makers like Maybach. From the Pz III and IV of 1940–1 to the Pz IV Special of 1942–3 and the Panther and Tiger of 1943–5, the German Army enjoyed mechanically rugged, superbly made, well-armoured and well-gunned tanks that outclassed their allied opposite numbers of the time.[32] Not only this, but the designers of German tanks had kept in the forefront of their minds from the first the need for ease of manufacture and thereafter ease of maintenance in the field. The latter aspect, embodied in the system of unit assembly, particularly impressed British soldiers when they came to inspect captured enemy tanks. But here the Americans too designed better than the British; for example to remove and replace the engine of the Grant took a fraction of the time needed for a Crusader engine.[33]

And it was to the Americans again that the British had to turn for rescue from their own failures in design and production. By summer 1942 the armoured divisions of the Eighth Army were equipped with nearly twice as many American Grants and Stuarts as British Crusaders;[34] and the arrival of the Grants was regarded by Middle East Command as 'a resounding event . . . for it provided the means of killing German tanks and anti-tank gun crews at ranges hitherto undreamed of. And this could be done from behind the heavy armour of a reasonably fast and very reliable tank.'[35] By the time of the Second Battle of Alamein in October 1942 it was the American Sherman that provided the Eighth Army with its hardest punch, numbering 252 out of the 1029 tanks fielded at the start of the battle, with Grants and Stuarts pushing the American contribution up to over half the total.[36] In Normandy in 1944 two-thirds of the tanks with British armoured divisions and independent armoured brigades were Shermans, despite the advent of the Cromwell and the Churchill.[37] Taken in all, American supplies of tanks to Britain in the years 1939–44 amounted to more than the total of Britain's own production.[38]

Even in the case of workaday military wheeled motor-transport the United Kingdom had to look to North America because of the limited production and primitive designs of her own automobile industry. Before the war that industry had concentrated on small family cars and light vans, suitable for a sedate Sunday outing to the seaside and deliveries of groceries around town, achieving a total average output in 1937–8 of 285,000 such vehicles. Production of trucks capable of carrying heavy loads amounted only to 85,000.[39] It was quite impossible that such an industry could supply the motor transport to move an army of fifty-five divisions, as projected in the summer of 1940, unless it was enormously expanded. Instead the industry's expansion went, by government choice, into aircraft and aero-engine 'shadow' factories and to a lesser extent into tank production. By switching the weight of its existing resources from light cars and vans to trucks the industry managed to achieve a peak production of 137,339 trucks in 1942 (of which a fifth were needed for civilian use) and 23,183 cars and vans.[40] This compares favourably enough with the German automobile industry's peak output in 1943 of 126,447 trucks and half-tracks.[41] Yet, unlike Britain, Germany had decided to limit the motorisation of her army to the capacity of her motor industry, leaving the mass of the infantry divisions reliant on horse transport. She had no difficulty therefore in supplying from her own resources the vehicles needed by the panzer and panzer–grenadier divisions – robust Mercedes-

Benz and Magirus-Deutz trucks and towing vehicles, the Volkswagen *Kübelwagen*, German equivalent of the 'Jeep'; makers' names that were to flag West Germany's triumphs in world motor-vehicle markets in the 1950s. Britain, however, in the peak year of her output, 1942, imported more trucks from Canada and the United States than she produced herself – 187,723 to 160,522.[42] In 1943 she imported over a third more than her own production. For very heavy trucks (four tons and over) Britain in 1944 relied on the United States for as much as two-thirds of her needs.[43] Over the five-year period 1940–4 imports from North America exceeded British production by 744,195 vehicles to 700,746.[44]

But once again quantities do not tell the whole story. North American trucks and gun-tractors were produced by a few large firms like Chevrolet, Ford, Dodge, Chrysler and Mack, with excellent R and D organisations and vast plants. Here were powerfully engined vehicles, ruggedly built, well suspended and comfortable to drive; apt for long distances over bad terrain, and easy to maintain. Although the British ends of American companies, such as Ford and Bedford (General Motors), made a significant contribution to British output, the remainder of United Kingdom production emanated from technically backward native firms like Morris Commercial and a rabble of small and today mostly extinct makers. No one who, after driving in a North American Ford or Chevrolet 15-cwt truck, experienced the Morris Commercial version could forget the Morris engine, quiet as a pneumatic hammer, or the transmission, smooth as if filled with gravel, or the seats and springing, as cushioning as the road surface itself, and the entire vehicle straining fit to explode or disintegrate when pushed beyond 45 miles per hour.[45] The British motor industry developed no equivalent of the indispensable Jeep or *Kübelwagen*. This was, after all, the same motor industry excoriated by a Whitehall committee in March 1945 for its poor pre-war export record, its division into '*too many, often small-scale units, each producing too many models*', and its unreadiness – unwillingness – to exploit the coming postwar export opportunities.[46] And it was true that in 1937 the six leading British producers of cars had made some 300,000 vehicles with more than forty different types of engine; the three leading United States producers had offered fewer different engines in a total production ten times larger.[47]

Even the influx into Britain of foreign motoring accessories in the postwar era was foreshadowed by the 'import' in 1942 of the German 'jerrican' design of petrol container, and its manufacture in new plant costing more than £1.5 million.[48] The problem of evolving a functional design for so simple an artifact had proved beyond British talent, which had originally only been able to conceive the infamous two-gallon petrol tin, flimsy, leaky and cursed by soldiers up and down the Western Desert. Yet in the midst of this obsolete technological culture of the 'practical man' there paradoxically thrived a constellation of scientific R and D establishments unsurpassed in the world for brilliant innovation.

The common *raison d'être* of these establishments lay in national defence; their wartime excellence pre-eminently demonstrated in aeronautics, radio and radar. Their earliest progenitors are to be found back in the nineteenth century, in the Admiralty's Experimental Establishment at HMS *Excellent*, the gunnery school, and the Design Department of the Board of Ordnance. The Boer War's chastening demonstration of defects in British weaponry gave birth to a new interdepartmental Armament Research Committee; and during the same era the more general British alarm about German and American application of science to industry led to the creation of the National Physical Laboratory in Teddington in 1900. This new body was charged with conducting basic research into matters relevant both to the defence and to the industrial prosperity of the realm. The Great War, a far bigger fright than the Boer War, jerked the British into radical fresh developments in state-sponsored research. The year of the battles of Verdun, the Somme and Jutland (1916) saw the setting up of a new Department of Scientific and Industrial Research and the transformation of the Royal Aircraft Factory at Farnborough into the Royal Aircraft Establishment, to be concerned henceforth with research instead of manufacturing. It was to be on the Royal Aircraft Establishment and the National Physical Laboratory that the 'practical men' of the aircraft industry would rely in the 1920s and 1930s for original research and discovery in aeronautics (see above p. 129). In the aftermath of the Great War, while the memories of the British failure to annihilate at Jutland and of the U-boat's near-victory in 1917 still lingered, the Admiralty created the Admiralty Research Laboratory. This developed gyroscopic systems for searchlights, new gunnery predictor sights based on the latest optical science, and a complete fire-control system for the 40-mm Bofors gun later adopted by the United States. It also investigated methods of protecting ships against the magnetic mine, swinging lethally on its mooring towards the steel mass of a passing vessel, and of reducing the noise made by ancillary machinery inside a submarine that could give away its whereabouts to enemy sonar.

The 1930s' rearmament period and in particular the prevailing fear of the bomber gave rise to a fresh generation of research institutions, this time especially concerned with radio and radar. The Admiralty created its Signal Establishment; the War Office its Radar Research and Development Establishment and Signals Research Establishment. In 1935 the Bawdsey Research Establishment at Orfordness on the Suffolk coast was specifically set up to explore and develop the possibilities of using radio echoes as a means for locating enemy bombers. It was at Bawdsey that fewer than a dozen scientists from the Department of Scientific and Industrial Research led by Sir Robert Watson Watt evolved the original designs of the 'Chain Home' radar stations that made possible Fighter Command's victory in the Battle of Britain. And the work of Watson Watt's team demonstrated a common feature of all these proliferating defence-research organisations – intimate links with university science departments and the deploying of the most distinguished living academic scientists on the development of the future technology of war.[49]

These links had first been forged during the Great War, when scientists had been mobilised in haste to tackle the desperately urgent problems posed by Britain's lack of many advanced technologies, from chemicals to optics and aeronautics. This task the scientists had discharged with outstanding success, so that the white coat could rank with the khaki and the blue as a garb of national salvation. New processes for making high explosive, acetone, poison gas; new optical systems for gun-sights and periscopes; new methods of making optical glass – these were just a few among the contributions of university science. The universities also conducted basic research into radio, into the mathematics of aircraft structure and of stable flight, even research into the cold storage of food. Thus for the first time the science departments that had been gradually built up in British universities since the 1870s became national assets deployed on national problems. As an authority on the linkage between the universities and British industry sums it up:

> While the technological activities of the civic universities played their vital role, some of the cleverest strokes came from scientists moving from their pure disciplines to consider with a fresh eye technological problems they would not normally be involved with.[50]

The mobilisation of university science was renewed with the advent of rearmament in the mid-1930s. Professor Cockcroft and his team in the Cavendish Laboratory at Cambridge, Professor Oliphant and his colleagues Randall and Boot at Birmingham, Professor Lindemann and the Clarendon Laboratory at Oxford, all contributed to the development of the first operational radar, and to the later evolution of short-wave (10 and 3 cm) radar, already under way by 1939. This web of science departments and state research establishments was intermeshed in turn with the technological branches of the armed services, through bodies like the Committee of Air Defence Research chaired by Sir John Blackett, and through the services' own directorates of research and development.

The Second World War fed fresh energy into this diverse effort: the pace of mobilisation of scientific talent quickened; new research establishments sprang up. In 1943 the Admiralty founded the Naval Construction Research Establishment, complete with a structures laboratory, to investigate the strengths of ships – a somewhat tardy development provoked by the disquieting proneness of British warships to succumb to enemy fire, whether in the form of shells, bombs or torpedoes. Bawdsey was replaced by a new institution, the Telecommunications Research Establishment (TRE), which, in its ultimate home at Malvern, became at once the power source and the control panel for the entire complex circuitry of British research into radar and radio development. In order to staff TRE the Cavendish Laboratory had to be robbed of much of its personnel.[51] With so many agencies in being and so many projects afoot there proliferated Whitehall committees charged with supervising and co-ordinating the work, and with conducting particular items of equipment from the stage of research and testing into factory production. The summer of 1940 saw a Centimetre Valve Measurements Committee set up; in 1941 followed the Interservice Technical Valve Committee, the

Interservice Valve Production Committee and the Interservice Cathode Ray Tube Development Committee, to cite some of the more tersely titled bodies in just one field of science applied to war.[52]

Walled in by the strictest secrecy the brains and the laboratories of this ramifying scientific apparatus developed the technological marvels that when revealed long afterwards would serve to swell the British heart with pride. There was 10-cm radar, installed in very-long-distance aircraft and undetectable by U-boats' anti-radar warning devices, which pinpointed hapless German submarines cruising on the surface for the allied navies to destroy, and so provided the essential tool of victory in the Battle of the Atlantic in the spring of 1943. There were the electronic devices which from 1942 onwards enabled Bomber Command to find and hit a German city through the darkest night and thickest weather. First of them, in spring 1942, came Gee, a major advance on the German radio-beam system that had directed the Luftwaffe to British targets like Coventry during the Blitz of 1940–1. Tiny time intervals between electronic pulses transmitted from three widely separated ground stations enabled an aircraft's navigator to calculate his position accurately on a special gridded chart. It was Gee that made possible the 1000-bomber raid on Cologne on 30 May 1942. Next, in December 1942, followed Oboe, whereby an aircraft flew along an electronic beam forming the circumference of a circle centred on a ground transmitter and passing over the centre of a German target city. A signal from a second electronic beam aligned on the city from another ground transmitter and intersecting the beam along which the aircraft was flying told the navigator exactly when he was over the target. Finally, in January 1943, H_2S reached the Pathfinder Force – a cathode-ray screen on which a type of airborne 10-cm radar produced an outline image of the terrain beneath, especially coastlines, rivers and lakes. Thanks to H_2S Bomber Command could now very roughly 'see' its targets even through darkness, cloud or industrial haze.

At the same time other radar devices developed by British science were changing warfare in perhaps more humdrum ways. The Royal Navy found its Italian enemy at night in the Battle of Cape Matapan in March 1941 by radar; and sank that enemy by radar-directed gunfire. In November 1941 the Fleet Air Arm located the ships of the Italian battle-fleet in Taranto by radar and bombed them by radar. The German fast battleship *Scharnhorst* was located by radar in Arctic darkness on Boxing Day 1943, and sunk by radar-directed gunfire. By 1943 the army and especially the Royal Artillery had come to depend on Forward Area radars to locate enemy defences or troop concentrations and to direct the consequent bombardment. Radar multiplied the effectiveness of any weapons system by at least a factor of five,[53] and transformed the entire operational conduct of war by land, sea and air. The pioneering of these developments was therefore a triumph for that loose confederation of state and university scientific research bodies created by Britain; even, it might appear, a triumph for British ad-hockery.

There was, however, a shadow on this glowing image. It emanated from a disharmony between scientific genius and industrial backwardness. For while Britain could devise all these technological wonders, she could not make them quickly enough or in large enough quantities. The development of centimetre wave radar in 1941–2 was held up for want of the right kind of thermionic valves.[54] The Mark III IFF (Identification Friend or Foe) radar originated as an idea at Bawdsey in 1939; it was ready for mass production at the end of 1941; but over a year later, it was still meeting, according to a Whitehall committee, a 'serious setback' owing to 'delays in production of certain vital components'.[55] Throughout 1942 the large-scale production of H_2S was held up by all kinds of teething-troubles and factory delays, and Bomber Command had to content itself with 200 hand-built sets by the beginning of 1943, with the promise of mass delivery in the course of 1943.[56] Similar delays occurred with the improved 3-cm version of H_2S towards the end of 1943. In October the Chief Superintendent at the TRE was complaining sourly to the Ministry of Aircraft Production that The Gramophone Company was making feeble excuses for failing to start work on the receiver and indicator for the new model despite receiving a technical brief from TRE in July.[57] On 28 December 1943 the Director of Communications Development at the Ministry of Aircraft Production was writing to the chief superintendent at the TRE about the lack of valves for the few test sets now put together at The Gramophone Company, describing how the ministry had managed to get hold of twelve valves ('quality unknown') in order 'to avoid a crisis in the Company's production'.[58] Trouble in getting the improved H_2S into production rumbled on into 1944.

In the case of the Mark VIII AI airborne interception radar for night fighters, production was held up in 1942 for want of magnets and magnetrons.[59] As late as April 1944 Sir Robert Watson Watt was submitting a blistering memorandum to the Ministry of Production about the consequence of late delivery of radio and radar equipment. HMS *Coventry* (sunk in September 1942) had been lost to air attack, according to him, for want of one additional radar. The air cover of the fleet, he wrote, was 'far below requirements' because Fighter Direction equipment was six months behind schedule, while airborne radar for carrier fighter-aircraft was also held up by production problems. So too, according to Watson Watt, were the radio proximity fuse for anti-aircraft shells, the radar observation of the fall of shot, the gun-laying radar for the anti-aircraft defence of the United Kingdom. The Royal Air Force was short of Gee equipments and was still using H_2S on obsolete 10-cm wavelengths instead of the superior 3-cm version because of delays in production. Bomber Command lacked VHF radio-telephone equipment and the army lacked lightweight radio-telephone equipment because production was bottlenecked by want of miniature valves.[60]

Delays and difficulties in producing new equipment in the factory were, however, merely a facet of the basic British problem with radio and radar – the sheer inadequacy of scale of the industrial base in this technology. This inadequacy when coupled with the fast-growing demands of war finally confronted the War Cabinet with a major crisis in production in 1942–3 – ironically enough, also the years of the production crises in coal and shipbuilding, Britain's old technologies. It was not so much the assembly of radio or radar equipments that presented the problem as the supply of the components and thermionic valves. In December 1942 the Production Planning and Personnel Committee of the newly created Radio Board reported on valve manufacturing capacity in relation to demand in 1943, and calculated that United Kingdom production plus American imports were 'unlikely to exceed' 35 million valves, as against a total service and civilian requirement of 50 million.[61] In April 1943, the Paymaster-General, Lord Cherwell, again analysed service and civilian demands against possible production, and found that British output at 26 million valves would be only 56 per cent of the total needs of 46 million. After suggesting further and ruthless cuts in service requirements, Cherwell still found himself left with a shortfall: 'The main conclusion arising from this investigation is the vital need for an increased output of valves and radio equipment in general.'[62] Science, he wrote, was developing new equipment vital to the modern navy and air force, without which they would be 'grievously handicapped'. There could be no second best. But Cherwell could only recommend that an 'urgent enquiry should also be made into the possibility of obtaining greatly increased imports from North America, particularly Canada, in 1944.'[63]

Here then is a familiar pattern – and just as familiar too the pattern of a particular British reliance on North America for highly sophisticated items, in this case magnetrons.[64] In January 1941 the capacity of firms belonging to the British Valve Association for making special valves amounted only to 3 per cent of total capacity.[65] But British dependence on North America went wider than valves alone, for the production of components too constituted a 'real bottleneck' according to Cockcroft.[66] On the basis of British production costs it was forecast in April 1943 that imports of radio components and equipment of all kinds from the United States that year would equal four-fifths of the value of Britain's own production.[67]

Several factors go to explain Britain's failure thus to realise in production the promise of her scientists' innovation; this British lapse into dependence on America in yet another field of high technology. First and foremost among these factors is, however, the nature of the British radio and electrical industry itself. For by 1939 it had already acquired too much history of the wrong kind.

From the very start of the age of electricity, in the 1880s, Britain had failed to seize a world lead in the new technology as once she had with steam during the first industrial revolution – and even though her scientists, men such as Faraday, Kelvin and Lodge, had contributed so much to the primary discoveries and to the early development of electricity's industrial applications.[68] By 1913 Britain's share of world exports of electrical machinery and apparatus (including telegraph cable, Britain's technically undemanding staple) amounted to 23.4 per cent compared with Germany's 48.5 per cent.[69] She was importing a fifth of the generators she needed for her factories and power stations. She had become heavily dependent on imports of electric lamp bulbs, and entirely dependent on imports of wireless valves – mostly from Germany.[70] She had hardly begun to develop her own range of domestic electrical equipment like cookers and kettles, although these were by now a major sales field for the German AEG combine. It was perhaps even more demonstrative of Britain's laggardliness that in 1913 her electrical industry was largely a colony of the German and American industries. The biggest British firm, British Thomson-Houston, employing 12,000 people, was a subsidiary of the Thomson-Houston Company of Schenectady, New York (later General Electric or GE). The other major United Kingdom producers were the British Westinghouse Company, subsidiary of the Westinghouse Corporation of Pittsburg, and the British end of Siemens,[71] the latter company being expropriated by the government during the Great War and sold to the British public.

As in so many other technologies the shock of the Great War jolted through the fat of British lethargy with enlivening effect. Led by the Ministry of Munitions and backed by state funding the electrical firms added to their factories or built new ones, quadrupling their output of basic products like lamp bulbs. They developed for the first time the capability to manufacture radio valves and radio apparatus. Electric power generation doubled in Britain between 1914 and 1918; and, even though decades later than in Germany and America, the gas-light and the factory steam engine driving a jungle of clacking belts began to disappear.[72] Furthermore, the British electrical industry never again slipped back into its pre-war condition of limp acquiescence in foreign domination of world markets and even the United Kingdom home market – thanks partly to the temporary switching off of competition from Germany in the wake of her defeat. By the mid-1930s British exports in all types of electrical goods were 45 per cent greater by volume than in 1913, and comfortably exceeded imports.[73]

Nevertheless, with the exception of Marconi, the dominant British companies across the whole range of electrical goods, from radios and gramophones to washing machines and vacuum cleaners, continued to be the out-stations of great American corporations and American industrial culture – Hoover, AEI (Associated Electrical Industries, formed in 1928 by merging British Westinghouse and British Thomson-Houston), GEC, Electrical and Musical Industries (formed in 1931 by merging the British ends of Columbia Records and the British Gramophone Company). Another American out-station, Erie Resistor, accounted for most of Britain's capacity for making this essential component. These companies of American parentage not only displayed the American approach to research and development in themselves but also could tap the immense resources of their associated firms in the United States. It was an American research team led by a Russian *émigré* to the US, Vladimir Zworykin, which in the 1920s developed the iconoscope, the invention fundamental to all subsequent developments in television and radar; and in 1931 developed the first electronic camera for television work. It was a research team at EMI, a British concern of part-American parentage, which independently evolved a superior electronic camera in 1934. The all-British John Logie Baird's electro-mechanical television system proved a complete dead-end, rather than the starting-point of modern television as British national myth would have it. In a final trial against the EMI electronic system in a BBC studio in 1936, his enormous and cumbersome camera apparatus had to be bolted to the studio floor, and gallons of water circulated round it to keep it cool. Baird is of historical importance only because of his successful publicising of the idea of television, and perhaps as an example of a romantic British admiration for slightly dotty individualist inventors in backrooms rather than professional research teams in large corporations. It was in fact the Marconi Company which made the biggest indigenous British contribution to the new technology by developing the first VHF television transmitters in collaboration with EMI.

But not even the British companies of American ancestry had the international market weight or research facilities of their United States associates or of great German combines like AEG or Telefunken. Most indigenous British radio manufacturers merely assembled bought-in components into simple equipments – a long way indeed from the world of the Bawdsey Research Establishment or the Cavendish Laboratory. Thus on the eve of the Second World War the British radio and electrical industry, though prosperous, was in no sense a world leader, a creator of new markets, as was the contemporary American industry, as the German industry had been before 1913, or as the Japanese industry was to become after 1970. Rather, it was a follower, technically and commercially – and even in terms of productivity, for output per man-hour in radio production in 1935 was less than a quarter of the American figure.[74] How limited were the resources, capabilities and mental horizons of the pre-war industry, and how inadequate a base it was for war expansion, is documented in the reports commissioned by the government during the production crisis of 1942–3. According to one report to the Minister of Production in March 1943,

> A large proportion of the peace-time Radio Industry was concerned with the mass-production of broadcasting receiver sets. Except in the case of a few firms a considerable proportion of the labour of the Radio Industry was seasonally employed and included a high percentage of unskilled employees.
>
> With the advent of War conditions, the nature of the Radio Industry underwent an extreme change. The mass-production of broadcast receiving sets was curtailed drastically. In its place grew up a demand, from the Services, for equipment of a highly technical nature (transmitting and receiving sets), which increased and are still increasing in complexity.[75]

Production of such highly technical equipment required that up to 40 per cent of the workforce should be skilled. Moreover, according to another report, in April 1943, peacetime production of valves had been only 11 million, 'the majority of which were the simpler types used for broadcasting receivers. In 1942, 16 million valves were delivered to the Services, together with 5.4 million valves to meet the demands of broadcasting, the GPO, Mercantile Marine etc. . . .'[76] In any case, up to 40 per cent of radar equipment took the form of precision-engineering components;[77] and precision engineering, as opposed to bolting things together with 2-inch nuts, constituted another weak area of the British industrial economy, its resources competed for by all branches of war production. For example, with regard to the navy's fire-control machinery, the trouble was, according to an officer in the Directorate of Naval Ordnance interviewed in 1946, that 'while our designs were as good as the Germans, our machine tool industry was neither so large nor so skilled as theirs, so that it took us six years to put a designed instrument into production, whereas it took the Germans only two. . . .'[78] By 1942–3 precision-engineered components for radar equipment therefore came to present as much of a bottleneck as valves, and for similar reasons: 'Many components now in use are of special types which were not in production before the war and for which special manufacturing capacity has had to be provided.'[79]

Nonetheless Britain's limited pre-war electronics industry provided only one among the factors causing the crisis of 1942–3. There was a general failure to foresee the colossal wartime rise in demand for radio and radar equipment. When a mission led by Professor Tizard went to the United States in 1940 to solicit American co-operation in radio and radar development, Watson Watt went on record as saying that British productive capacity would be adequate for all future needs, and that 'the USA has nothing to offer.'[80] Sir Frank Lee, the Director of Communications Development, was also against asking for American aid.[81] The armed services, for their part, simply put in their orders without any comprehension of the British radio industry's restricted resources. In the words of the chairman of the Production Planning and Personnel Committee of the Radio Board in April 1943, 'Though the illusion of limitless capacity has long been dispelled, the Services till quite recently still appeared to be basing their demands upon that illusion. . . .'[82]

But the major *wartime* cause of the 1942–3 crisis was that from 1939 onwards this newest technology had suffered from a galloping attack of the classic British industrial disease – fragmentation of resources and effort, overlaps in product design, batch production virtually by hand, utter want of standardisation of parts and components. While in the case of the old technologies the disease had stemmed from an excess of private-enterprise individualism, here it stemmed as much from the confusions and redundancies of government agencies and government direction. Each of the three service departments and the war production ministries had been pursuing its own development of radio and radar equipment, evolving its own specifications for components, and its own production programmes. As Lord Justice Du Parcq pointed out in a major report on radio production in August 1942, with regard to overlapping research 'it must be remembered that the supply of persons competent to conduct research is limited, and that the field of necessary research is very extensive and continues to grow rapidly. . . .'[83] The first annual report of the new Radio Production Executive in June 1944, referring to the state of affairs up to 1943, talked of 'the chaotic state of non-interchangeable and unidentifiable service numbers [for parts]. The waste of productive effort alone in this sphere must have been considerable.'[84] Some components had as many as fourteen different references for the same item. Standardisation of parts and components to British Standard Specifications was – typically – still only being studied by the industry in 1939; and completion of the task had been halted by the war. Now standardisation had to be resumed for the most urgent of reasons, for it was calculated that a preferred list of components could by itself raise production by a quarter. Up to 1943, for example, there were no fewer than 1100 types of transformer laminations and 800 types of resistor; 15 different kinds of magnetron.[85]

The production process itself was fragmented between plants, at heavy cost in efficiency. According to a report to the Minister of Production in March 1943 on the utilisation of labour in the radio industry,

> Security has been given to us as the reason for the manufacture of equipment in three, and in some cases four, factories, where it would be possible to mass produce in one factory with far better utilisation of labour.
>
> The manufacture in four different factories necessitates four different sets of jigs and tools which have to be made by just those skilled personnel of whom we have indicated the greatest shortage exists.[86]

Thus already handicapped in these various ways, production further suffered from muddles in scheduling and from Whitehall's ignorance of industry. The same 1943 report to the Minister of Production remarked that ministries did not understand 'the Time Cycles' for acquiring raw materials and components and feeding them into the production process.[87] This only bore out Lord Justice Du Parcq's evidence the previous year that orders for components were not placed until after the armed services had ordered the final equipments; an idiocy true even of bulk items like condensers (now called 'capacitors'). What was more, wrote Du Parcq, the services were prone to insist on special designs and specifications requiring special manufacture when a standard component would do. He reckoned that delivery delays for components were then running at about twenty weeks, sometimes six months.[88] According to a report to the Radio Board in April 1943, the method up till then of allotting components and valves to makers of sets:

> is largely a hand to mouth system under which the allotment or refusal of valves to manufacturers may not show up in the real production position till too late. And it exposes us to the danger that manufacturers holding contracts for sets far in excess of the components available, will in the months ahead lodge requisitions for valves and components accordingly. . . .[89]

This report was of the opinion that the armed services actually preferred shortfalls in deliveries because 'the stuff is not there' to shortfalls accepted and planned for in advance: 'This more haphazard system is clung to all the more tenaciously because of the combination of complexity and swift changes which make advance planning of requirements an arduous and intricate job with the staffs available. . . .[90] After all, modern equipments could have up to 1000 and more components – a tricky task of scheduling for those to whom Critical Path Analysis (to use the modern term) was a novelty: and few British civil servants or military men had attended an American business school (there being no British) to learn such mysteries.

Yet sheer operational need forced the British into fragmenting production between small batch orders enormously wasteful of plant and restrictive of overall output. In Du Parcq's words in August 1942 200 Gees now were worth more than 1000 in nine months' time; and he actually recommended 'progressive tooling' rather than a six-month pause to tool up.[91] The penalties of such a policy had been pointed out to the Air Supply Council in the previous May by the Parliamentary Secretary to the Ministry of Aircraft Production, when he wrote that the need 'to enter at once into small-scale production so as to meet urgent operational requirements' meant orders 'for a large number of items *in very limited quantities* which results in an abnormally heavy demand being made on the resources for development, model shop production and limited tooling.'[92] Instead of long American runs, the British radio industry found itself struggling with what were called 'crash programmes', like literally hand-building 200 H_2S chassis in 1943.[93]

The impact of 'crash programmes' on efficiency of production was the more damaging because the industry's overall resources in scientific and engineering skills were so thin, in contrast to the brilliant and growing array of highly qualified talent deployed on research in government establishments and in universities. In May 1942 Professor Tizard was reporting to the Aircraft Supply Council that 'the ratio of 2,500 engineers in Government employment to 864 in the radio industry was definitely too high.' In February 1943 there were 541 research workers on radio and radar in government establishments; only 236 in the entire radio industry.[94] On basic research, the staff at the Telecommunications Research Establishment numbered thirty-four as against only fifteen in the radio firms.[95] Moreover, the industry's development and model-shop staff, the key men who had to carry a TRE design through the prototype stage into production and grapple with the problems of 'crash programmes', were far from being the kind of university or technical high school alumni to be found in such roles in Germany or the United States. According to the 1943 report on the utilisation of labour in the radio industry, their knowledge had been acquired 'by practical experience in the Industry, though they may have no academic qualifications. A period of training in development work preceded by some practical experience in the Industry are the criteria in these departments.'[96] It might have been a Victorian Royal Commission talking about the shipbuilding industry. Even the assistant staff in the research departments of radio firms had acquired their technical qualifications merely 'by years of service'.[97] Thus the newest of technologies mirrored old British industrial habits and longstanding British weaknesses in technical education.

If the 'practical men' of the radio industry found it hard to cope with crash programmes for manufacturing novel and sophisticated equipment, the mandarin researchers in the government establishments for their part were often too intellectually remote from the realities and constraints of production engineering. Their education and background made them more at home with the civil service élite than with production engineers. According to one veteran of pre-war radar development, 'It needs to be remembered that the Orfordness team did not contain an engineer and they tended to minimise the enormous gap between a demonstration of early warning and a full-scale scheme. Watson Watt was less guilty than some others in this matter. . . .'[98] Even in wartime there still existed a mutual lack of understanding between mandarin science in its laboratories and the self-educated practical man in the model shop.[99] It was a lack of understanding which the lopsided concentration of most of the best-trained talent into government research centres could only have deepened. Indeed, Lord Justice Du Parcq in his 1942 report found a similar 'unfortunate gap in co-ordination' between the scientists and the armed services because they did not jointly discuss policy and operational needs.[100]

As a result of all these factors, and despite piecemeal extensions to existing radio and electrical factories and a few new plants built since 1939, Britain had therefore by 1942–3 failed to match either Germany's achievement in radio and radar of precision manufacture to the highest scientific standards (owing partly to superlative and abundant German technical education) or the American creation of a huge new mass-production capacity backed by proportionately lavish research laboratories, made possible by America's size and wealth (by 1944, 4000 personnel in the Radiation Laboratory of the Massachusetts Institute of Technology alone).[101] For reasons avoidable and not so avoidable she found herself stuck once more in the classic British industrial pattern of batch production by the 'practical man'; of too few resources too much divided.

When in the spring of 1942 the War Cabinet confronted the problem posed by the gap between service needs for radio and radar and the predicted production, especially with regard to valves, it resorted to the traditional British governmental device of an enquiry headed by a distinguished personage. Since the topic in question related to electronic technology, the Cabinet selected a senior judge, Lord Justice Du Parcq, to conduct the enquiry. He was appointed on 2 May 1942, four weeks before Gee led a thousand bombers to Cologne. Charged with investigating the whole question of 'Radio Communication and Equipment in the Fighting Services', Du Parcq submitted his report[102] on 11 August, after two and a half months. He pointed a judicial finger at the overlaps in research, development and manufacture, as already cited. He noted the bottlenecks in producing valves and components, and recommended as the necessary key to solving all these problems that a Radio Board be set up to pull the present disorderly and sprawling effort together. Du Parcq remarked that everyone interviewed by him agreed in principle about this idea, which had been first mooted by Oliver Lyttelton, the Minister of Production. On 22 September, a mere six weeks after Du Parcq's report, the War Cabinet duly created the proposed Radio Board,[103] with the function 'to ensure that there is a single coherent policy on the development of radio equipment, on scientific research for that purpose and on such questions of inter-service radio policy as may be determined by the Chiefs of Staff'.[104] The new board was also to take responsibility for forward planning of production and standardisation of finished equipment and components. This responsibility it delegated on 23 October (opening day of the Second Battle of Alamein) to a new Production Planning and Personnel Committee.[105] The Radio Board similarly delegated responsibility for research and development to a new Operations and Technical Radio Committee (OPTEC).[106] Thus the second stage of the standard British governmental cure-all was now in hand: the creation of a network of committees to debate, report and pass papers to each other: and finally to hand decisions to civil servants to execute. In December 1942 the existing Whitehall interservice committees on new developments in valves and cathode-ray tubes were revamped and brought under OPTEC,[107] so completing the major, but by no means the last, components in the new bureaucracy some eight months after Du Parcq's first appointment.

The real world of radio production took even longer to rearrange. Not until the end of March 1943 did the Minister of Production receive the basic report (by yet another committee, this time specially convened to enquire into 'the Utilisation of Labour in the Radio Industry') on what needed to be done in order to render manufacture more efficient.[108] This committee, as also already cited, traced all the faults and resistances in the existing production 'system'; it went on to call for better production planning, with a properly phased flow of components, arguing that no contracts for complete radio or radar equipments ought to be placed until balanced programmes for the constituent parts and assembly work had first been drawn up. Such 'better planning, co-ordination and standardisation', the committee reckoned, would bring about higher production from existing resources. All this constituted sound if elementary production-engineering principles. Nonetheless, it was not until May 1943, now a year after Du Parcq's appointment, that a new Radio Production Executive was created to carry out the policies of the tidied-up Whitehall committee structure. The executive's task, to quote its own first annual report in 1944, was 'to ensure that the Radio effort of this country is directed as a whole where it is most needed instead of being divided between competing users, each concerned with gaining their own ends'.[109]

By the middle of 1944 this elaborate new bureaucratic apparatus of a board, an executive and various committees had not only generated much paper and many discursive meetings but also, perhaps less expectedly, had succeeded in rationalising the entire process of designing and production. In the first place many components had been standardised: to take two outstanding examples, the number of types of transformer laminations had been reduced from 1100 to 30, of resistors from 800 to 225.[110] A common interservice catalogue of radio parts and reference numbers had been compiled – 'All work which will carry its usefulness into peace-time,' wro the Radio Production Executive in its first annual report, 'and never aga should we be caught in the chaotic state of non-interchangeable ar unidentifiable service numbers.'[111] Standard working schedules had bee devised and issued as guides to production planning. A new central sta organ had been set up to integrate the needs of all radio users and relat these to production capacity; a valuable function only made possibl thanks to American Hollerith tabulating machines.[112] Major productioı bottlenecks, as in metal laminations, had been cleared. Component output had been boosted by an average of over 30 per cent in the first fou months of 1944 compared with the equivalent period of 1943, while valv production in May 1944 amounted to 3,436,000 as against 2,486,000 ir June 1943.[113] What may be termed 'functional mergers' had beer promoted between 'parent' firms responsible for the final production of an equipment and subsidiary firms supplying the components, so repairing to some degree, and if only temporarily, the fragmentation of the industry into many companies each with a limited range of technical resources. All this achievement in the course of hardly more than a year stood much to the credit of the coherent industrial strategy and staff-work that had belatedly superseded piecemeal ad-hockery.

Nonetheless, Britain's fundamental weaknesses in radio technology remained. The praiseworthy production increases of 1943–4 had still crucially depended on American industrial equipment and American techniques. For instance, Erie Resistor, the British end of the American company of the same name, accounted for 75–80 per cent of the total British output of carbon resistors and ceramic condensers, those basic components of radio and radar; and in March 1943 it was foreseen that the planned upsurge in radio production would require that special plant be obtained from the parent US company.[114] In October that year, marking a considerable delay, the managing director of the British firm was sent off on a visit to the American parent in order to pick up the latest technical information about methods of producing the new 'hot moulded' resistor and 'ceramicon' condenser. Only now were these new American developments to be introduced in Britain, with the aid of the new American plant to give 'high speed machine controlled production'.[115]

But it was in production of the ubiquitous thermionic valve that Britain continued most to depend on American technology. At the end of April 1943 the chairman of Radio Board's Production Planning and Personnel Committee had called for 'a special approach to be made to the USA at a high level for supply of a schedule of machine tools for valve production. . .'.[116] Nevertheless, even with the aid of American valve-making machines, and despite a rise of nearly a third in valve production between 1943 and 1944, Britain could still nowhere near satisfy her own fast-rising national requirements; in August 1943 it was calculated that output for the year would amount to just over 70 per cent of needs.[117] So Britain continued to rely on North America to make up the shortfall. Whereas in 1944 British valve production came to 35.5 million, imports from Canada and the United States came to 17.5 million.[118] Worse, Britain continued to rely even more heavily on America for certain special types of valve, such as the 725A Magnetron and its associated 723A local oscillator used in radar.[119] Britain was lagging behind in production of magnetrons because of the time needed to erect the necessary plant; and in August 1943 it was estimated that production for the year would number only 100,000 as against a demand of about 150,000.[120]

The advent of miniature valves and components, making possible a new generation of lightweight, compact radio and radar equipments, found Britain wanting all over again. It was in January 1943 that the controller of physical research and signals development at the Ministry of Supply pointed out to OPTEC the importance of miniaturisation, especially for jungle and airborne use. He noted that much research and development would be needed – and emphasised that the question of the supply of miniature components was 'a vital one'. It was, he wrote, 'essential that production of these components on a suitable scale should be ensured if the scheme – with all its attendant advantages to production as well as to the user – is to be realised'.[121] In autumn 1943 a mission was belatedly sent to the United States to study the latest methods for producing these miniature valves.[122] But even six months later, in March 1944, the Air Supply Board was being told that 'The specialised plant for making these valves has been developed in the USA. . . . The capacity for making such plant in the UK is limited and will be fully occupied in producing such items as must be designed here. . . .' It was therefore necessary to order plant from the United States 'without delay' at a cost of $1 million.[123] Given all the delays, given this failure thus far to create new capacity, it is not surprising that by the spring and summer of 1944 Britain had run into yet another valve-production crisis, this time over miniatures.

On 9 June (it was three days after the D-Day landings in Normandy) the chairman of the Production Planning Committee informed the Radio Board that 'there is likely to be a considerable disparity between the scale of miniaturisation in the British and USA programmes. . . .' Whereas the US (which had now been making miniature valves for some three years) was expected to produce at least 22 million of them in 1944 and 45 million in 1945, the United Kingdom, he wrote, would not manage more than 500,000 miniature and midget valves in 1944 and 4 million in 1945.[124] 'We hope to receive from USA and Canada 800,000 miniatures in 1944 and about 7 million in 1945.'[125]

The British inability successfully to solve the technical and industrial problems of producing miniature radio equipment, demanding as it did much higher standards of skill and precision than the standard sizes, entailed very serious consequences for the armed forces – despite the inflow of North American supplies. The Royal Air Force wanted lightweight radios and radars for use in light aircraft, especially in South-east Asia. The British Army had developed a complete new range of lightweight 'tropicalised' radio sets for use in jungle warfare against the Japanese, as well as a lightweight mine detector, but, as a War Office memorandum warned the Radio Board in May 1944,

> All these new sets are dependent on the availability of the miniature valve and unless the latter are in large-scale production in this country in the near future the War Office will be unable to meet its obligations in 1945 to supply our troops in the Far East with equipments best suited to that theatre.[126]

What was perhaps even more ominous than this lagging behind in miniature valve and component technology was that by 1944 Britain had lost her original pioneering lead in radar research. That this loss of leadership owed more to shortage of national resources than to a falling off in scientific genius only emphasises that discrepancy between British pretensions as a first-class world power and the realities of Britain's second-class size which the British nation and their leaders were unable or unwilling to recognise. In the event, her shortage of scientific resources, exacerbated by loss of physicists to atomic research, left Britain no alternative but to consent to the United States taking over much of the responsibility for further radar research and development. In discussion with a visiting American 'Special Mission on Radar' in May 1943, a working party of the Radio Board chaired by Professor G. P. Thompson agreed that the United States should undertake the main research work in the pulse Doppler field. It agreed that the US should also continue to be responsible for K-band research and development, and the provision of related components and valves, with the question of a possible British share in manufacture being deferred until later. The development of tunable magnetrons, of magnetrons in the X-band above 150 kilowatts, and low-voltage magnetrons in all frequency bands was to be 'entrusted entirely' to the United States. Only the future development of H_2S and 2-megawatt S-band transmitters were to be joint ventures.[127] Nor was this all: the klystron valve was also being developed in America, as was the 'TR box' combining transmitter and receiver units.[128] By October 1943 Sir Robert Watson Watt, chairman of OPTEC, was reporting that a recent conference presided over by him had concluded that a review 'of the present excessively small provision of basic research in radar was now desirable'.[129]

Thus by a paradox British leadership in radar discovery had already dimmed in reality even before it began to glow in national myth.

On that other frontier of science and technology – nuclear physics and the development of an atomic bomb (code-named 'Tube Alloys') – shortage of human and material resources extending from research, development and testing to ultimate manufacture had compelled Britain to hand over the project entirely to the United States, including her key discoveries and the best of her scientists; even to the extent of abdicating her future share in the peaceful commercial exploitation of atomic energy to the good will of the American government, as she did by the Quebec Agreement of 1943.[130]

By 1944 the only field of technology where the British R and D effort still matched the American, where Britain still unquestionably remained in the lead over America, was jet propulsion.[131] It was also the only field of advanced technology in which Britain was competing on even terms with Germany, which otherwise was pioneering on its own the new age of rocketry in all its forms, as well as developing the 'Schnorkel' submarine, the 'Walther' submarine propelled by hydrogen-peroxide which could travel fast and deep under water, radio-controlled glider-bombs, homing torpedoes and an experimental helicopter. For, as Professor R. V. Jones reported to the War Premier in December 1944: 'The Germans have been consistently fertile in producing new weapons, and in several directions temporarily outshine us. The most notable examples are the new submarines and fuels, rockets, and jet propulsion generally.'[132] But whereas British R and D work with regard to the gas turbine was solely concerned with its application to the jet propulsion of aircraft, the Germans were already exploring its potential use to drive ships and tanks, and to generate power. For example, M.A.N.-Lurgi had developed a design for a 12,000 kilowatt turbine to burn gas supplied by the high-pressure gasification of brown coal (or lignite) – a complete technological–industrial package without parallel in Britain.[133]

And even in the restricted sphere of aircraft jet engines, whereas Germany fabricated all her own components despite shortages of certain metals like nickel because of the allied blockade, Britain had temporarily to turn to the United States for such essentials as turbine blades and impellers, because she was encountering technical problems with making components to Whittle's design specification that would not distort or fail.[134] In any case, the development stage and organisation of series production proved beyond the resources of Rovers, the main contractor; and it was not until Rolls-Royce – in Professor Jones's judgement, one of the few British firms to equal German standards in precision engineering[135] – took over the whole production side of the project (as well as Rovers' modification of Whittle's design) from Rovers that jet propulsion in Britain really began to make progress.

Apart from Rolls-Royce engines and a few specialised products like high-speed cameras for aerial reconnaissance, there was in fact only one branch of second-industrial-revolution technology where the Second World War did not find Britain to a greater or lesser extent wanting – the chemical industry, and, in particular, ICI, the huge combine which dominated it. From the beginnings of rearmament in 1936, when new plant had to be put in hand to meet potential wartime demand for explosives, propellants and poison gas, ICI coped efficiently with all the loads that the nation laid upon it. As the largest of all government contractors it undertook to construct and manage no fewer than twenty-five factories; it produced every kind of war material, from the obvious, like ammunition, to the less so, like light alloys or drugs such as the anti-malarial 'Mepacrine', or aviation fuel from the hydrogenation of coal.[136] Here indeed was the single British industry, the one British enterprise (apart from Rolls-Royce) of world class. In the judgement of an authority on the history of the chemical industry, ICI was:

> the first large enterprise in Great Britain which could fairly be described as 'science-based'. In the late 1930s there were nearly 500 scientists employed on ICI research, and many managers outside the research establishments had also a scientific background. This concentration of scientific talent, allied with skill in large-scale technology and in management, was a combination which no other organization in the country could match.[137]

In view of this untypical record, it is not surprising that ICI should also be untypical of the British industrial scene in its very ancestry. When four companies merged in 1926 to create ICI, the dominant among them was Brunner, Mond, which owed its foundation back in 1873 to a German Jew, Ludwig Mond. Mond himself had been trained as a chemist at Kassel Polytechnic and Heidelberg University, and he brought with him to England German technicians and the new German business philosophy of applying science to industry. Here then, in this imported German professionalism, lay the fundamental strand in forming the management character of the future ICI. The Great War provided the second moulding influence. For one other of the companies which were merged into ICI in 1926, the British Dyestuffs Corporation, had been created by government initiative in 1918 as a result of Britain's wartime effort to manufacture its own drugs and dyes in place of former German imports. Indeed Brunner, Mond itself, as well as Nobel Industries (a third party to the merger of 1926), had also greatly expanded in size and in range of products under the stimulus of the Great War. As a historian of the industry sums it up:

> The British chemical industry as it stood at the outbreak of war in 1939 was a direct product of experience in the war that ended in 1918. It had come into existence because businessmen and politicians, looking at the matter from very different points of view, had come to the same conclusion: that the deficiencies revealed in the chemistry industry of 1914 must be made good. The foundation of ICI in 1926 was as much an act of State as a commercial transaction. . . .[138]

Furthermore, the immediate spur for founding ICI was supplied by the creation in Germany in the previous year of the even bigger chemicals combine of IG Farben. Thus ICI was the child of a marriage between the tradition of German technological culture imported by Ludwig Mond and the experience of the Great War. It was in no sense the product of a spontaneous British commercial response from the 1870s onwards to the opportunities of a new world market, as were the German or American chemical industries.

By reason of its very uniqueness and its very success, therefore, the example of ICI serves starkly to illuminate all the shortcomings of other British industries old and new. But more than that, it suggests that those shortcomings, as revealed by rearmament and war between 1936 and 1945, cannot be explained solely in industrial or economic terms, any more than defeats in the field like that of the French Army in 1940 can be explained solely in military terms. For industrial institutions and military institutions alike are, in general, expressions of their parent national society and its culture. And therefore, just as military historians look beyond the immediate defects of the French Army and seek the root causes of defeat in the years before, in the slow onset of political and moral rot in French life, so the explanation of the 'British disease' has to be sought beyond the confines of industry, in the nature of British society itself, its attitudes and its values.

Part III

Reality – The Human Resources

I consider then, that I am chargeable with no paradox, when I speak of a knowledge which is its own end, when I call it liberal knowledge, or a gentleman's knowledge. . . .

(*Cardinal Newman, 1852*)

That which our school-courses leave almost entirely out, we thus find to be that which most nearly concerns the business of life.

(*Herbert Spencer, 1861*)

these are not scrofulous and verminous children . . . they are the bud of the Nation.

(*the Minister of Health, 1939*)

Chapter Ten

The Legacy of the Industrial Revolution

In a powerfully romantic metaphor the novelist Joseph Conrad likens the island of Britain to 'a mighty ship bestarred by vigilant lights – a ship carrying the burden of millions of lives'.[1] However, the industrial Britain of the 1930s and 1940s rather more resembled a *Great Eastern* anachronistically fitted out with radar and a cinema – not only because of her Victorian structure and machinery, but also, and more profoundly, because of the nature of the human society aboard her. The First and Second Class passengers, the ship's senior officers – the relatively well-educated few – occupied agreeably spacious surroundings far removed from the clank of the engines and the heat and dirt of the boiler rooms; sunshine and fresh breezes blessed their days. Obedient to their service the engineers, coxswains and artificers – too few in number for so huge a vessel, and their training sometimes as antiquated as the ship itself – kept the ageing engines turning and watched the helm. Below this small and layered élite existed the 'millions of lives' of Conrad's metaphor – the mere hands and the Steerage passengers; their only resource their muscle, their only knowledge what they gleaned from toil, hardship and subordination; their families living in unhealthy confinement; their fresh air the down-wafting funnel-smoke.

And yet in these millions of lives, descending generation by generation, lay the nation's most important and only lasting asset. Whether Britain in the postwar era was to prove, in Conrad's phrase, 'stronger than the storms' did not depend on natural bounty like coal and iron-ore, or on the once heaped-up and now dissipated wealth of the past, or even on the present condition of her industries, but on the intelligence, energy, zeal and adaptability of the mass of her industrial population. Unfortunately this mass lacked such qualities in marked degree. Of all the grievous long-term handicaps bequeathed to modern Britain by her experience in the first industrial revolution from 1780 to 1850, one of the most pervasive and the most intractable was that of a workforce too largely composed of coolies, with the psychology and primitive culture to be expected of coolies.

*

It has long been the British habit in discussing what the Victorians called 'the condition of the people' – that is, poverty, ignorance, slum housing and consequent ill-health – to interpret the evidence from a moral or humanitarian standpoint. The tone from the days of Dickens and Shaftesbury has been that of the tender heart moved to pity, the Christian social conscience awakened. This is but a further aspect of that revolutionary change of sensibility brought about by the religious revival of the early nineteenth century – another manifestation of the romantic emotion which in due season would go to produce the 'New Jerusalem' movement of the Second World War. But in the long perspective of British decline it is more fruitful to abjure the indulgences of pity, guilt, remorse and moral indignation, and to adopt the detached and analytical approach of the physician towards a case, or the engineer towards a malfunctioning machine. It is better to forego that sentimentalising of the industrial worker as a kind of 'noble savage' to which, as Richard Hoggart points out in his book on the British working class, *The Uses of Literacy*, 'middle-class intellectuals with strong social consciences' are especially prone;[2] and instead evaluate him as a military historian might evaluate the rank and file of an unvictorious army. For it is time that the evidence on 'the condition of the people' be freshly interpreted with the purpose in mind of casting light on Britain's efficiency as an industrial power.

It is impossible to exaggerate the long-term consequences, social and psychological, of the experiences of the new industrial workforce in the raw factory settlements of the late Georgian and early Victorian England under conditions of ferocious competition and unbridled exploitation. It was in that era, when men, women and children were flooding into these settlements from the countryside and exchanging the slow, natural rhythms of the land or self-employed crafts (however hard that life might have been) for the harsh mechanical discipline and the pace and clamour of the mill, exchanging the village for the back-to-back terrace, that the British industrial working class, with its peculiar and enduring character as a culture apart, an alienated group often embittered and hostile, was created. It happened that water power and coal and iron largely existed in the bleak, wild landscapes of northern England, South Wales and lowland Scotland – regions hitherto lacking the numerous population and rich civilisation of the south; indeed regions traditionally turbulent and remote from the government of the Crown since the middle ages. Rare it was for the new factory settlements to cluster round an established city, as later would German industries develop round Leipzig and Dresden, Düsseldorf and Cologne: instead villages like Manchester, Birmingham, Leeds, Huddersfield, Bradford, Halifax, Middlesbrough proliferated into vast brick-built industrial camps; nothing but mean dwellings, drink-shops and 'works'. The population of Leeds, already up to 53,000 by 1801, more than doubled by 1831; Manchester and Salford too more than doubled in the same period from 95,000 to 238,000.[3] At the extreme, Oldham grew from 300–400 inhabitants in 1760 to some 30,000 in 1801; Middlesbrough, a late starter on the road to breakneck industrialisation, from 25 inhabitants in 1801 to nearly 350,000 in 1931.[4]

Except in rare cases such as Robert Owen's paternalistic management at New Lanark, the brutality of indoctrination into the life of a coolie in a vast camp for coolies, performing coolie work in service to machines, was unsoftened by positive care and control by the state. Not until the great uprooting and resettlement had been largely completed did Parliament belatedly begin to mitigate the squalor, chaos and exploitation by reforms in local government and public health, and by regulating working conditions by successive Factory Acts (Municipal Corporations Act 1835; central board of health set up by an Act of 1848; the Factory Acts of 1833 and 1847).

This was the environment, then, which moulded the character of the new British working class: a home life in a mean brick hovel without piped water in an unpaved street with open drains, much like the townships in which the Bantu coolies of South Africa still live today; a working life at the mercy of a 'practical-man' master who believed that the profitability of his business depended on low wages and long hours. It was, after all, from the study of the *British* working class that Marx and Engels principally derived their conception of the alienated proletariat. For, as the Marxist historian E. P. Thompson justly observes in *The Making of the English Working Class*:

> The process of industrialisation is necessarily painful. It must involve the erosion of traditional patterns of life. But in Britain it was unrelieved by any sense of national participation in communal effort, such as found in countries undergoing a national revolution. Its ideology was that of the masters alone.[5]

From the very beginning the machine was perceived by British workpeople as an enemy; technical progress as the destroyer of status and independence.

> The gap in status between a 'servant', a hired wage-labourer subject to the orders and discipline of the master, and an artisan, who might 'come and go' as he pleased, was wide enough for men to shed blood rather than allow themselves to be pushed from one side to the other. . . . In 1797 the first steam-mill was built in Bradford to the accompaniment of menacing and hooting crowds.[6]

Yet in this same era the advance of *laissez-faire* economic doctrine caused the steady repeal of old paternalistic legislation, however moribund, that had protected craft, employment, status and wages. There seemed nowhere for workers to turn for legitimate redress of their oppressions. Even trade unions in Britain began their existence as illegal, undercover organisations, for they were prohibited under common law and later under the 1800 Combination Act as 'combinations' in restraint of trade. Not until 1825 were they legalised. Other repressive legislation of the 1790s and 1800s, born of governmental fear of revolution on the French model, fell equally hard on the emerging working class, bequeathing to successive generations a sour and profound suspicion of the role of law and the courts in labour relations. As a consequence of *laissez-faire* unbridled by government yet coupled with state repression, the workforce, in Thompson's words, 'felt that the bonds, however ideal, which bound them to the rest of the community in reciprocal obligations and duties were being snapped one after another. They were being thrust beyond the pale of the constitution.'[7]

By the 1830s the character of the British working class as a tribe apart, with its own values, had matured. Those values were highly collectivist, 'with sanctions against the blackleg, the "tool" of the employer or the unneighbourly, and with an intolerance towards the eccentric or individualist. Collective values are consciously held and are propagated in political theory, trade union ceremonial, moral rhetoric.'[8] And this character was to endure down the generations, along with the bitter ancestral memories passed from father to son to grandson to great-grandson. Richard Hoggart, writing of the working class of around 1950, notes that the predominance of the group over the individual 'imposes on its members an extensive and sometimes harsh pressure to conform'[9] – a truth crudely demonstrated on the grand scale thirty years later during the coal miners' strike of 1984–5.

No less enduring was the internal class solidarity forged by the 1830s, even though many fine distinctions between the status of different crafts or even streets were to exist within that solidarity. Hoggart, himself from a working-class family, defines working-class consciousness in the mid-twentieth century as a 'sense of being in a group of their own, and this without there being necessarily implied any feeling of inferiority or pride; they feel rather that they are "working-class" in the things they admire and dislike, in "belonging".'[10] This aparthood had been also strongly fostered by the sheer physical segregation of the working class in the 'coolie' districts of British industrial towns; rather as in the British Empire in India the Indians lived in the crowded native quarter of a city remote from the ruling English in the bungalows and gardens of the cantonment. As a research study on the town of Middlesbrough in 1944 noted, class neighbourhoods could be clearly differentiated by the overlapping of a variety of indices – rateable value, age of buildings, type of housing by ownership and density, rates of truancy from school, the prevalence of 'poverty shops' like pawnbrokers.[11] 'The sharp contrast between the different groups of neighbourhoods is accentuated by the lack of variety within most of them. Poverty and prosperity have their entirely different quarters. . . .'[12] Nonetheless, neither the poorest nor wealthiest quarter offered 'merely isolated extreme cases, they represent the broader, entirely opposite groups to which each of them belongs. . . .'[13] Indeed, the widespread building of council estates in the twentieth century on the windy outskirts of industrial cities to house families from the slums served to perpetuate this physical and social aparthood in a novel guise.

Moreover, whereas American workers during the industrialisation of the United States after 1850 never accepted that they were permanent members of a coolie class, but believed instead that, true to the American myth, they were merely passing through on their way to prosperous middle-class status, British 'coolies' came early to accept that working-class they were, and working-class they and their children would always remain; and proud of it. In Hoggart's judgement in 1957, 'Most working-class people are not climbing; they do not quarrel with their general level; they only want the little more that allows a few frills.'[14] In fact it was an aspect of their conformism that social ambition was positively discouraged as 'giving y'self airs',[15] quite apart from an individual's fear anyway of becoming isolated from social roots and family.

It is apparent that none of these lasting characteristics, beliefs and attitudes of the British urban working class make for maximum industrial productivity or for maximum speed in adapting to new technologies; indeed the very opposite. Was it not the boss's factory, the boss's product, the boss's market and the boss's profit; and in the boss's interest to bring in new machines? Did not the boss exact – or try to exact – the most work for the least wage? It followed that the worker's only connection with the productive process was to fight the boss as best he could through trade unions or through simple skiving, in order to do as little for as much money as possible; or to protect his job or craft by restrictive practices. So deeply ingrained in the worker was this sense that the productive process, let alone success in the market, was no responsibility of his that it determined his actions even in the midst of the Second World War (see above Chapters Four to Eight). This refusal to look beyond his own job and his own wage to the larger interest of his industry and its future arose not only from class alienation, however, but also from the intense narrowness of life in a factory town, with horizons hardly wider than the nearby 'snickets' or 'ginnels', and a forward view hardly extending beyond the end of the current week.[16] In Hoggart's informed diagnosis the core of working-class attitudes is 'a sense of the personal, the concrete, the local: it is embodied in the idea of, first, the family and, second, the neighbourhood. . . .'[17] And hence working-class people, 'with their roots so strongly in the homely and personal and local, and with little training in more general thinking', found it hard to bring the 'outer world' and their own personal world into focus.[18]

The Victorian British Army and Royal Navy had succeeded in capturing this instinct for the immediately local, for the family or the tribe, by means of regimental loyalty or the loyalty of a ship's company. Nineteenth-century German and Swiss industrialists had enlisted their employees' commitment to the enterprise and the product by paternalistic good management, supported by a state and civic paternalism far more enlightened than the grim and grudging *laissez-faire* policies of early-nineteenth-century Britain.[19] But with few exceptions Victorian British entrepreneurs never sought in such ways to win their workers' enthusiasm. In Britain the pattern was early established, and forever continued, whereby at best management and workforce confronted each other in a state of suspended hostilities, like armies of observation: hardly a pattern that encouraged spontaneous zeal at the bench. In 1879 William Morris, himself a romantic and a socialist, could write:

> It is true, and very sad to say, that if anyone nowadays wants a piece of ordinary work done by gardener, carpenter, mason, dyer, weaver,

> smith, what you will, he will be a lucky rarity if he gets it well done. He will, on the contrary, meet on every side with evasion of plain duties, and disregard of other men's rights; yet I cannot see how the British Working Man is to be made to bear the whole burden of this blame, or indeed the chief part of it. I doubt if it be possible for the whole mass of men to do work to which they are driven and in which there is no hope, and no pleasure, without trying to shirk it. . . .[20]

It was Hoggart's judgement in the early 1950s that fundamentally nothing had changed since Morris's day.[21] And certainly the cumulative evidence about lacklustre output, absenteeism, stoppages and go-slows during the Second World War in industries ranging from coal and shipbuilding to aircraft manufacture bears this out (see above Chapters Four to Eight), as does the appalling record for low productivity, strikes and shoddy workmanship which in the 1970s helped to destroy the British motor-vehicle industry. So the degree of motivation explains the performance; the performance demonstrates the degree of motivation; and the nature of the historical experience of the working class accounts for both.

But this experience determined more than simply the pitch of enthusiasm and commitment brought to the production process by Britain's industrial rank and file; it determined too their human quality – their all-round capability and effective intelligence, their aptitude for new and more sophisticated tasks. For the working class of the Second World War was the end-product of several generations of conditioning by life in the same original brick camps for industrial 'coolies'.

Just as the overlapping of various indices of health and housing plainly demarcated the working-class districts of a factory town from the rest, so did similar indices delineate nationally the dense groupings of the working class in those conurbations created by the first industrial revolution in the Midlands and North of England, in South Wales, in Scotland, where more than 50 per cent of the population of the United Kingdom now lived.[22] In the first place, a plot on a map of comparative pre-war rates of growth in new and most successful technologies between 1923 and 1937 would show up as lightly shaded areas in the North-east and Scotland with only 4 per cent and Lancashire, Yorkshire and the Midlands with 10 per cent, in contrast to the dark patch of London and the Home Counties with 32.2 per cent.[23] Secondly, a similar plot of unemployment figures in 1938 would by contrast show London and South-eastern England lightly shaded at under 8 per cent of insured employees, that is, within Beveridge's wartime definition of 'full employment'; and darkly shaded, Scotland at 16.8 per cent, the English North-west at 17.7 per cent, and darkest of all, South Wales at 25.9 per cent.[24] Here were the twin factors which together marked out on the map of Britain the 'Special Areas' or 'Depressed Areas' of Whitehall terminology – regional problem cases that had once been the power and pride of British world industrial leadership.

Plotting of health statistics also plainly delineates these same groupings. It does more; it begins to describe the human quality of the British working-class people who lived in them. A survey in 1926–9 discovered that at age thirteen Christ's Hospital schoolboys were 2.4 inches taller than council-school boys; at age seventeen, 3.8 inches taller than 'Employed Males' of the same social origins as the council-school boys. These were the age-groups which by the time of the Second World War would be forming the 'prime-of-life' sections of the industrial workforce. Such disparities in physique between the classes only reflected a long-established national pattern: in 1883 British Association data showed that boys aged thirteen and a half in an industrial school were on average 5.8 inches shorter than boys of the professional classes.[25] Then again, in 1942, out of every 1000 babies born in South Wales, the North-west and the North-east of England, 61.5 died as against 40.2 per 1000 in South-east England.[26] In every 1000 children aged one to two in these industrial areas seven died, compared with four per 1000 in the South-east; three children per 1000 aged two to five died compared with fewer than two per 1000 in the South-east. Even in the age-group five to fifteen the death rate in South Wales and Northern England was nearly half as much again as in the South-east,[27] while in 1944 deaths from measles among children aged one to fifteen ran at four times the rate of the South-east. In sum, 70 per cent more boys of school age and children under five died in South Wales and the northern regions of England than in the South-east; 78 per cent more girls aged five to fifteen.[28] In the case of adults, the rate of tuberculosis in 1944–5 among women aged fifteen to forty-five was well above the national average in the industrial areas; below in the South-east.[29] Between 1940 and 1944 twice the percentage of men and women in South Wales and northern England died of bronchitis as in the South-east.[30]

Moreover this stark contrast between the health of the two Britains, the one industrial and strongly working-class, the other rural, market-town, suburban and more middle-class, remained little diminished despite the wartime improvements in medical care and welfare services that had brought the infant mortality/still-birth rates in the North down from 67 per 1000 live births in 1938 to 51.2 per 1000 in 1943–5.[31] For the health statistics do not only reveal deficient standards of medicine in the industrial regions (and indeed in inner London), which Beveridge and the other New Jerusalemers intended that their new National Health Service should put right; they also reveal the long-term consequences of bad housing, of poor diet, of dirt and – both result and cause – of domestic incompetence. For in the words of a 1943 Ministry of Health survey of working-class diet which found that 10 per cent of the sample of 600 people investigated were 'ill-nourished', 'There was no evidence that an adequate diet was not available, but many of the people had lived for years past in poverty and unemployment and had given up the struggle to maintain a decent standard of housekeeping and cooking.'[32]

Indeed the abysmal pre-war level of nutrition analysed by Professor John Boyd Orr in his famous work *Food, Health and Income* (half the population was below the ideal standard specified by the United States Government Bureau of Home Economics) owed more to housewifely incompetence and unwise family priorities in expenditure than to outright poverty. He reckoned that an increase of some 12–25 per cent in the consumption of milk, eggs, butter, fruit, vegetables and meat would bring the diet of the lowest of the six groups in his classification (4.5 million people) up to the level of the best.[33] Yet a comparison between Orr's estimated consumption of different kinds of foodstuffs for families spending per head about the same amount of money pre-war as the total cost of wartime rations (generally agreed to have assured a healthy if spartan diet) clearly shows that the cause of the pre-war failure of Orr's lower social groups to enjoy a healthy diet lay in their own ignorant choices.[34] For pre-war meat consumption even in the lowest group was a fifth higher than the 1943 ration, and in the next lowest group more than two-thirds higher; pre-war consumption of fats in Orr's lowest group was a third higher than the 1943 ration, and of sugar getting on for twice the 1943 ration. Furthermore Orr's lowest group had consumed per head in peacetime almost as much jam, jelly and syrup as his highest group. These were all expenditures that could have been trimmed back in favour of milk, eggs and greenstuffs – as they were by *force majeure* under rationing. Richard Hoggart's comments in his 1957 book on working-class culture bears out that poor diet was indeed a matter of inept housewifery or improvident spending. He describes how the children were stuffed with food as babies, with even the dummy dipped in syrup, and how the man of the household 'must have money for cigarettes and beer, perhaps even for an occasional bet; the amount regularly spent each week, even by men out of work, would seem in many cases excessive to, say, the professional middle classes.'[35]

It is hardly surprising that ignorant and incompetent housewives made unskilled mothers. To inculcate a skill in child-rearing perhaps lost in the generations that lay between Georgian villages and the industrial-town life of the 1940s was the endeavour of the new wartime day-nurseries. In Middlesbrough in 1944:

> The Matron of one of the northern nurseries stated that the mothers knew very little about child-care and were extremely grateful for advice. The contrast between the children in that nursery and those of the same age who were seen on the street was certainly remarkable. Those in the nursery were bright looking, clean and usually rather well dressed. Those in the streets were covered with dirt and ragged.[36]

But still more conclusive evidence of widespread domestic incapability is to be found in the reports of surveys into the state of working-class homes in the 1930s and 1940s. Thus research carried out in Glasgow, Cardiff and Liverpool in 1937–9 by the Carnegie United Kingdom Trust found nearly a quarter of homes in all kinds of districts (ranging from middle-class residential areas through modern council estates, 'good' or 'fair' working-class housing, to slums) were to be classified as 'dirty and untidy', with nearly 50 per cent 'fairly clean and tidy', and less than a third 'very clean and tidy'. Even on new council-housing estates there were 16 per cent of homes 'dirty and untidy' compared with less than 7 per cent in 'residential' (i.e. middle-class) areas.[37] According to this Carnegie Trust Report:

> It is difficult to convey how very 'dirty and untidy' were the 25 per cent of the houses so classified. . . . It seemed, very largely, their women-folk who had lost all pride in personal appearance and appearance of the Home. . . .
>
> Quite often father and son were unemployed; they hung about the house in the morning and were 'in the road'; the mother had no fixed routine for household duties; with late rising, the making of the beds could stand over till the afternoon, and, when the afternoon arrived, there seemed little point in doing them, since they would be used again in the evening. They seldom had visitors; but when they did, these people were like themselves, who bothered little whether beds were made and saw nothing unusual in the breakfast dishes still lying unwashed. A most common sight in these homes, at any time of the day, was a loaf of white bread, a pot of jam, and a saucer with a piece of margarine lying on the table. This was ladled out intermittently as an effective silencer of the children's whimperings.[38]

And of the new council estates the report stated: 'That one in six of the houses visited had to be classified as dirty and untidy is regrettable. The houses were new; but the people were not. . . .'[39] How hard it was to expunge the mark of the working-class ancestral experience even by providing a fresh start in a clean and spacious environment is explained by the Middlesbrough survey report of 1944:

> many of these families could not easily shake off the habits engendered by their former environment. Hardly any houses in the northern neighbourhoods have baths, and many only cold water laid on. Soot and dirt continually cover clothes and furniture. Unless the housewife is very strong and very house-proud, she is defeated by these difficulties and gives up the struggle for cleanliness. And even though furniture is disinfected when the family moves to the new estate, dirt and disease may continue.[40]

Had a malevolent conqueror wished to pursue a long-term policy of degrading the British industrial population into a physically, intellectually and technologically inferior race of 'natives' posing little competitive threat, he could hardly have succeeded better than the unwitting effects of *laissez-faire* dogma, shortsighted exploitation of cheap resources by 'practical-man' capitalists and sheer want of effective public administration in the Britain of 1780–1840. To cite a by-no-means untypical example, the Glasgow of 1844, as described at the time by an expert on epidemic disease:

> In all districts of the burgh, and in the suburbs, there is a want of sewerage and drainage. . . . the streets, or rather the lanes and alleys, in which the poor live are filthy beyond measure. . . . The houses, in the disease-haunted areas, are ruinous, ill-constructed, and, to an

> incredible extent, destitute of furniture. In many there is not a single article of bedding, and the body clothes of the inmates are of the most revolting description; in fact, in Glasgow there are hundreds who never enjoy the luxury of the meanest kind of bed, and who, if they attempted to put off their clothes, would find it difficult to resume them.[41]

Or a contemporary description of the recently run-up quarters for the 'industrial classes' in Manchester in 1844, which lacked even foundations:

> The walls are only half brick thick, or what the bricklayers call 'brick noggin', and the whole of the materials are slight and unfit for the purpose. . . . they are built back to back; without ventilation or drainage; and, like a honeycomb, every particle of space is occupied. Double rows of these houses form courts, with, perhaps, a pump at one end and a privy at the other, common to the occupants of about twenty houses.[42]

Such a description would hold good for most of the new workers' districts in Lancashire, and across the Pennines in Yorkshire and the North-east; in the Midlands too.[43] Consider the state of the great port of Liverpool in the middle of the nineteenth century, as described to the Barlow Royal Commission in 1940 by the city's medical officer of health:

> There were no Infectious Diseases Hospitals, and sewage disposal arrangements in the slum areas were non-existent. There was no piped water supply in general use, no provision for the cleansing and paving of streets and passages, and an enormous population, drink-sodden and degraded, was living in the conditions of the utmost misery in the slum areas near the docks.[44]

In the telling phrase of Edwin Chadwick in 1844, the new industrial populations of Britain were living like 'an encamped horde', but unlike such hordes of the past, they did not soon move off to fresh and unsullied camp sites, but stayed on generation by generation like latter-day refugees; and, as Chadwick also pointed out, unlike an encamped *army*, this horde was at first governed by no sanitary rules and discipline whatever.[45] The later reforms in local government and the great advances in public health from the mid-nineteenth century on into the twentieth century could only mitigate, not re-make, this appalling environment. At the time of the Great War nearly a third of the British nation lived their entire lives in conditions as bad as, and in some respects worse than, the dug-outs of the Western Front,[46] as comparative eyewitness descriptions well illustrate. The middle-class novelist, Frederic Manning, for example, on life in a dug-out: 'Each of the guttering candles had a halo round it. The smoke from them, and tobacco, and acrid fumes from the brazier, could not mask the stale smell of unwashed men, and serges into which had soaked and dried the sweat of months.'[47] Or the same writer on the primitive trench sanitation of the pole latrine: 'while they sat there they hunted and killed the lice on their bodies. . . .'[48] But turn to Seebohm Rowntree's classic study, *Poverty:*

A Study of Town Life, published in 1910, for a picture of family life that remarkably echoes Manning's account: 'Two rooms, seven inmates. . . . Dirty flock bedding in living-room placed on box and two chairs. Smell of room from dirt and bad air unbearable.'[49] Or: 'There is no water supply in the house, the eight families having to share one water-tap . . . with eight other families who are living in other houses. The grating under this water-tap is used for disposal of human excreta. . . .'[50]

Even the general environment of the war zone behind the front line appeared hardly more desolate and dilapidated than the surroundings of a British industrial town. Thus Edmund Blunden on the war zone of northern France: 'The red-brick hollow of a station marked "Cuinchy" told us that we were almost at our journey's end: other ruins of industrial buildings and machinery showed through the throbbing haze; the path became corrupt, and the canal dead and stagnant.'[51] And his fellow officer Siegfried Sassoon writing about the scene round his camp on the outskirts of Liverpool: 'the smoke-drifted munition works, the rubble of industrial suburbs, and the canal that crawled squalidly out into blighted and forbidding farm-lands. . . .'[52] Indeed, in even broader terms, Sassoon's own description of the Western Front trench zone as 'a place of horror and desolation . . . where a man of strong spirit might know himself utterly powerless'[53] hardly exceeds in dread that of the social investigator, R. H. Sherrard, on returning to a great English city in peacetime: 'I never set foot in Manchester without a shrinking at the heart, an instinctive and irrepressible feeling of pale terror. Is it on account of its almost perennial gloom? Is it because I am familiar with the dreadful squalor and surpassing misery of its slums?'[54]

Even by the late 1930s all too little of this had changed; the bulk of the industrial population were still living in the same grim 'camps' first run up to house their great-grandparents. To step from the railway station into any northern factory town was to step back straight into the mid-nineteenth century: sights, sounds – and smells. In Middlesbrough, for example, a third of the entire existing housing stock had been built seventy years earlier to shelter a vast influx of manual labour, and crammed together at fifty houses per acre. Even by 1939 only a tenth of such dwellings had been fitted with baths.[55] Slum-clearance schemes between the world wars had only chipped at this domestic legacy of the first industrial revolution, sometimes leaving unsightly wastelands amid the remaining terraces, which worsened rather than improved the dreary urban scene.

The state of this grimy world – so far removed from that of Nobel prizewinners and the Cavendish Laboratory and radar and the jet engine, or, for that matter, from the country retreats of the intelligentsia – in which the bulk of Britain's labour-force still lived was summed up in 1940 by the Barlow Report in the studiedly cool language appropriate to a Royal Commission:

> unfortunately the existing large towns and areas of industrial concentration in Great Britain are not well planned, and it is for that

> reason that their inhabitants suffer certain disadvantages due to bad housing, lack of space for recreation, difficulties of transport, congestion, smoke and noise. These disadvantages . . . are the result of the haphazard manner in which urban development has proceeded in the past, and which has been marked by:–
>
> a) densely built inner areas of badly constructed and unplanned housing;
> b) an increasing density of industrial and commercial development and consequential transfer of land from housing to industry and commerce in the cores of the towns.[56]

In surveying the standards set by cities and city planning in other countries, an appendix to the Barlow Report remarked with regard to Germany that 'the general tidiness of the towns, the care that has been taken to blend old and new . . . are all impressive features.' It noted that, as long ago as the 1870s, Germany had introduced comprehensive building regulations and the zoning of cities, with the obligation to obtain permission from the local authority before building, while a complete regional planning authority for the Ruhr dated from 1920. Similar town-planning and regulation measures had long ago existed in Sweden and Holland too, even the United States.[57]

How deep-seated and hard to eradicate were the human consequences of long generations of living in Britain's industrial areas, despite further advances in public health, housing and welfare since the Great War, is shown not only by the differing mortality rates (already cited) within the United Kingdom, but also by comparing rates in urban Britain with, for example, urban Holland. Liverpool's infant mortality rate per 1000 live births in 1936 was nearly two and a half times higher than that of the comparable Dutch port city of Rotterdam, and its crude death rate per 1000 living nearly twice Rotterdam's.[58] Birmingham's infant mortality in 1936 ran at twice the Dutch city's, while Tyneside's annual average for 1931–4 was nearly three times Rotterdam's rate for 1936.[59] Perhaps an even more telling comparison is that Glasgow's infant death rate in 1937 was higher than Tokyo's.[60]

What kind of a generation, then, was emerging from Britain's 'coolie' districts around the outbreak of the Second World War – from the more-than-two-thirds of homes found by the Carnegie Trust enquiry to be less than 'very clean and tidy', let alone the quarter found to be 'very dirty and untidy'? What kind of children were being brought up by defeated mothers lacking in the basic skills of housewifery and childcare? The Carnegie Trust enquiry of 1937–9 found that out of its sample of 1800 young people aged between eighteen and twenty-five in three cities, more than a third in Glasgow were 'so deficient in physical and mental qualities' as to be totally unfit for training in a government training centre, and nearly a third in Liverpool. When the other city in the survey, Cardiff, is included, no fewer than two-thirds of the entire sample proved to be unskilled labourers, nearly a third semi-skilled manual workers, and only 7 per cent skilled tradesmen. Of the unemployed in the sample, seven out of ten were unskilled; and lack of skills and unemployment were both found by the enquiry to be related to the quality of the home background.[61] The Carnegie Trust Report drew the conclusion that the data 'suggest the operation of a vicious circle of social and economic determinism, the boy being the father of the man. All things work together – education, occupational skill, home circumstances – in a conspiracy for good or evil in terms of less or more employment according to the status of the father.'[62] This conclusion is borne out by surveys of Glasgow youth after the Second World War, carried out in 1947–50 and 1952, which found that fewer than one man in three was in skilled employment by the age of twenty-two; that one in five were still living in slums or near-slums; and that the drop-out rate for those who actually began apprenticeship was 36 per cent.[63] And again the investigators linked the condition of the home to school achievement, and then these factors to the type of ultimate skills and employment.

Just as the historian is entitled to take the demoralised and incompetent troops of Corap's Ninth Army on the Meuse in 1940 as revealing in extreme form a general malaise that prevailed in the French Army at the time, even though not every formation was as bad and some were actually good, so he is similarly entitled to take the low domestic and personal capabilities of such a large section of the British industrial workforce as demonstrating in exaggerated degree characteristics prevailing in the whole. Even so affectionate and understanding a writer on the working class as Richard Hoggart acknowledged:

> There are many thrifty working-class people today [1957], as there have always been. But in general the immediate and present nature of working-class life puts a premium on the taking of pleasures now, and discourages planning for some future goal. . . .[64]

And he goes on to comment on the unplanned, day-to-day nature of the working-class approach to existence; its contentment to drift on a familiar stream of experience as long as possible; its priority for smoking and drinking over saving, or for buying showy new possessions like an elaborate photo-frame before essentials like new bedsheets or other replacement household gear.[65]

In the light of all the cumulative evidence, it is little wonder, then, to find the Ministry of Labour in a 1943 memorandum commenting on the pre-war labour-force's unwillingness to look for jobs far from home or far from the existing rut, owing to 'the strength of local ties and commitments and regional patriotism', and to 'the ability to live on unemployment allowance in the absence of local employment';[66] little wonder to learn that the experience of the Ministry of Supply, according to its spokesman on a Cabinet committee that same year, 'had shown the great difficulties of starting new industries, particularly those requiring special skill and managerial ability, in South Wales and similar areas. . .'.[67]

Yet it was the mass evacuation of working-class children to the countryside in 1939–40 because of the German bomber threat which revealed the worst to a horrified nation. For example, of 31,000 children in Newcastle registered for evacuation, 4000 were deficient in footwear and 6500 in clothing.[68] In Manchester a fifth of the children arrived for evacuation rehearsals wearing plimsolls, while Liverpool became known in the early months of the war as 'the plimsoll city'.[69] Welsh local authorities who received evacuees from Liverpool spoke of 'children in rags', in a personal condition which 'baffles description', and with clothing so verminous that it had to be destroyed. In country areas taking in Merseyside evacuees the proportion of children found to be infested with nits ranged from 22 per cent to 50 per cent, and it was much the same with Scottish city children.[70] In March 1941 a special investigator appointed by the Board of Education and the Ministry of Health found in Britain's cities 'a state of affairs that is a disgrace to a civilised country', with about half the girls under fourteen in industrial areas having lousy heads, and the proportion of infested boys ranging from nearly half at age two to a fifth at age fourteen.[71] Such were the children which an impenetrably complacent Minister of Health described to the House of Commons in March 1939 as 'the bud of the Nation'[72] – a bud hardly promising to flower after the war into the best high-technology workforce in the world.

There was another aspect to this progressive erosion of personal capability in the course of generations of life in overcrowded and insanitary housing; yet another cause of the primitiveness of the British urban working class. Only very belatedly had these phenomena been combated by proper schooling, even of the most basic kind. And even by the Second World War the rank and file of British industrial society were still worse trained for work than those of Britain's chief technological competitors; far worse than Germany's.

Chapter Eleven

Education for Industrial Decline

Of that depressing sample of unemployed youth in three British cities in 1937–9 portrayed in the Carnegie Trust Report, *Disinherited Youth*, only one in every eleven in Cardiff had gone on from elementary school at the age of fourteen to benefit from either secondary or technical education; only one in thirty-three in Liverpool.[1] Three-quarters of the Cardiff youths who claimed to have been to a secondary school in fact had not stayed there longer than two years.[2] In Glasgow one in thirteen had begun secondary education, but only one in sixty-four had finished the course.[3] Lumping the samples of the three cities together, probably no more than one in a hundred had emerged from the education system with any paper qualification whatsoever, scholastic or vocational. It is not therefore very astonishing to find that only one in sixteen finished up in the category of the 'skilled';[4] and even this by no means implied having passed out from a formal course of instruction. Nor can it astonish that this sample should have remained unemployed even during the period when pre-war rearmament was gathering pace and the Defence Policy and Requirements Committee was wringing its hands over the crippling national dearth of technical skills. Had the sample dwelt in Hamburg, Cologne and Essen they would all, at the very least, have gone on from primary education to compulsory part-time further education and vocational training under the Weimar Republic's *Berufsschule* law of 1924, and all have entered the job market with some kind of recognised qualification, rather than have to return that answer of the already defeated so frequently given to the Carnegie Trust investigators: 'I'm *just* a labourer.'

The Carnegie Trust sample constituted an extreme case, but by no means a special one: it reflected the broad British picture. Only one in five children leaving elementary school at age fourteen in 1937–8 received any kind of further full-time education, while the remainder were pushed off the plank straight into the job market.[5] Of nearly three million youngsters in England and Wales between the ages of fourteen and eighteen who were therefore receiving no kind of full-time education, only one in 25 were even on part-time courses, and only one in 123 in voluntary day-continuation schools (for part-time education). There was no more than a single compulsory day-continuation school in the whole country, at Rugby, with 1280 pupils.[6] The 40 voluntary day-continuation schools existing in England and Wales, with a total pupil strength of about 20,000, may be compared with the 3199 *Berufsschulen* (vocational training schools) in Germany, with a total of over 1,800,000 pupils, almost all of them on compulsory courses to the age of eighteen.[7] Over a million of these German pupils were working in industry and commerce, and their courses consisted of two-thirds general education and one-third vocational instruction. Upon completion of their course they received a leaving certificate giving entry to more advanced technical education.[8] As the Permanent Secretary to the English Board of Education pointed out in a memorandum in May 1942 (initialled as read by the president of the board, R. A. Butler), over a wide range of German industries there was 100 per cent vocational training, as against 10 per cent for the United Kingdom.[9] Thus while most young Germans were learning a trade as well as continuing their education, most young Britons had been dumped out of school to look for work in obsolete, failing industries situated in decrepit 'depressed areas' – the educational orphans of the Carnegie Trust Report.

The fortunate one in five British children who did go on from elementary school at fourteen to some kind of further full-time education were in any case themselves not particularly well served. In the first place the proportion entering actual secondary schools rather than other institutions was only one in eight for boys and one in ten for girls.[10] In fact the secondary-school population aged fourteen to eighteen equalled less than a tenth of the entire national age group.[11] Of the 80,000 who went to a secondary school at fourteen, only 47,000 remained after the age of sixteen, and only 19,000 after the age of seventeen. In terms of qualifications, five-eighths of the original entrants emerged with only the School Certificate, a mere sketch of a 'liberal education', valueless either as equipment for a career or even as a leaving certificate, for it led nowhere in terms of further education or training. It was of importance only in order to show a prospective employer taking on clerks.[12]

Of the 19,000 pupils who did complete a full secondary education to age eighteen in 1937 (one in 132 of the total national age-group fourteen to eighteen), only 8000 emerged with the Higher School Certificate, the potential passport to university or other higher education;[13] and just over half of these actually got to university; or one in 570 of the total national fourteen-to-eighteen age group.[14] In sum, of the 80,000 pupils who began secondary school only a twelfth finished up with the Higher School Certificate; only a sixth went on to some form of further education (and a twentieth to university); and in any case four-fifths of them all fell out into the job market with no vocational training or vocational qualification whatsoever.[15] Of the grand total of 663,000 school-leavers in 1937 at all ages from all kinds of state-funded school, only the 13,000 who had attended junior technical schools from thirteen to sixteen had received any kind of career training.[16]

This half-cock education meant that it was the potential talent of working-class children that was being the most neglected, given their inherent social handicaps, for all too few of them hurdled all the competitive obstacles and reached the terminus of a secondary education. In Middlesbrough in 1944, for example, the odds of a working-class child getting into a secondary school varied from one in 8 on new council estates to one in 177 in the oldest and poorest district.[17] In fact, the national chances of an elementary-school child actually getting to university were no more than one in 170.[18]

But it has to be remembered that the state-funded elementary and secondary schools were educating the lower-middle classes as well as the working classes. Hence these schools were responsible for intellectually forming, and preparing for careers, the broad mass of the British nation – the country's principal reservoir of ability. One 1930s estimate, for instance, reckoned that elementary schools alone contained 73 per cent of the nation's stock of children of high intelligence.[19] From this reservoir, therefore, must be drawn not only the rank and file but also the 'NCOs' and most of the 'officers' who would run Britain as an industrial society. Yet here was an education system that was largely turning out 'coolies' – or at best white babus, as indicated by the fact that while nearly a sixth of secondary-school leavers in 1937 went into local government and nearly a third became bank or insurance clerks, only an eighth entered skilled trades, and only one-sixtieth were recorded as entering industry.[20]

Other advanced technological nations, however, recognised the importance of secondary education as the nursery of technical and managerial talents; none more so than Germany, Britain's trade rival for eighty years and in the Second World War her formidable enemy for the second time. Since even elementary schooling in Germany was designed to prepare children for further education and skill-training, it followed that her secondary schooling was also designed to be a preparatory stage rather than the kind of academic dead-end it represented for the majority of British secondary-school children. Even the German equivalent of School Certificate, the *Zeugnis der mittleren Reife*, although obtained by a smaller proportion of the population, provided a passport into technical education or career training.[21] In any case proportionately twice as many German secondary-school youngsters as British stayed on until the age of eighteen.[22] What was more, proportionately two and a half times as many obtained the senior *Zeugnis der Reife* (or *Abitur*) as British youngsters obtained the equivalent Higher School Certificate.[23]

But what counted in respect of school-leavers at all ages was whether the intelligence and talent so far fostered would now be further developed or instead allowed to go to waste. For individual and national capability alike depends on the nature of full-time technical and professional training. And here, in comparison with Germany – or America; or Sweden and Switzerland, for that matter – Britain on the eve of the Second World War resembled an army with only the sketchiest of training establishments and altogether lacking a comprehensive training programme.

In the first place she possessed no national system for further education and training; all depended on the initiative, or sloth, of local authorities. The result was a rummage-bag of institutions under differing titles unevenly spread over the country. For instance, Middlesbrough, an old industrial town of 350,000 people, had only one junior technical school and one technical college, with 'rather narrow scope'.[24] Wolverhampton, part of the Midlands industrial complex of more up-to-date metal-working and engineering industries, was equipped with just two technical colleges, with a total of fewer than 200 full-time students even as late as 1948.[25] The seven biggest technical colleges in the country were all in London.[26] The lack of a national system, to say nothing of the confusions and overlaps, was such that even the classification of institutions and the given student numbers vary from one official document to another.[27]

For the age-group thirteen to sixteen, England and Wales provided just before the war 214 junior technical, junior commercial, trade and nautical schools, with a total of about 30,000 full-time pupils.[28] This compares with 1233 *Berufsfachschulen* (full-time training colleges) in Germany in 1937 with 138,055 full-time students on a wide range of technical, craft and commercial courses.[29] For older youngsters in England and Wales there were 149 technical institutions thought worthy to be classified as 'colleges',[30] with just 9000 full-time students, mostly aged sixteen to twenty-one, as against 26,056 students of similar ages being given advanced vocational training in 303 German *Fachschulen* (technical colleges), of which 62 specialised in engineering or machine-construction – or one in 4500 of national population in England compared with one in 2600 in Germany. The forty-six German engineer schools alone turned out over 2000 fully qualified practical engineers every year.[31] Thus when full-time vocational education from sixteen to twenty-one is taken as a whole, Germany was proportionately training more than twice as many young people as Britain.[32]

Yet this gruesomely adverse British balance takes no account of training courses within industry itself, widespread in Germany but limited to a few enlightened firms in Britain. Even more important, it takes no account of the advanced technical education of superb quality in the ten German *Technische Hochschulen* (technical high schools), ranking as universities and awarding their own degrees, which formed the very dynamo of German technological prowess because of their high professional standards and prestige, and their use of courses designed to prepare for careers in industry.[33] In Britain there was no equivalent of these institutions before the Second World War with the single exception of Imperial College, London. Instead science and technology to degree level were taught exclusively by the general universities. But in any case their limited capacity was heavily skewed towards the arts: in 1938–9 only a quarter of all the degrees awarded in the United Kingdom were in scientific and technological subjects, and even then technology came a very bad second to 'pure' science, with only half the number of graduates.[34] In the five years before the Second World War the number of full-time university students in the arts in Britain amounted to 46.5 per cent of the total student roll; in pure science to 16.3 per cent; and in technological subjects to a mere 9.7 per cent.[35] In round figures the British output of graduate engineers just before the Second World War amounted to some 700 a year; the German to over 1900.[36] The German figure for mechanical engineers alone, at 662, almost equalled the British total for all kinds of engineer. The German output of graduate electrical engineers (by this period a key category) in the one year of 1937, at 448, was more than half the cumulative British total for the fourteen years 1925–39 of 781.[37] This colossal German superiority in university technological education and in output of graduate engineers of all kinds, as well as of chemists, physicists and metallurgists, was only partly offset by the British 'Higher National Certificate' scheme, open to part-time students already at work, and whose previous education was often limited: a second-class qualification for people of second-class standing.[38]

Such then was the anatomy of British education for capability (to use the modern term) on the eve of the Second World War; such was the crushing inferiority of British output of well-educated and well-trained personnel at every level – an inferiority not just with regard to Germany, it must be said, for Britain would emerge quite as discreditably from similar comparisons with the United States or Sweden or Switzerland.[39] This inferiority held gloomy enough implications for the quality of Britain's workforce and its leadership a decade or so later.[40] But in terms of the late 1930s and the war years of the 1940s, what mattered was the huge accumulated backlog of inferiority that lay behind so miserable an annual output; a backlog with ramifying effects so evident in Britain's pre-war and wartime industrial record. Here was complete fulfilment of a diagnosis and a prophecy made as long ago as 1868 by a Royal Commission:

> we are bound to add that our evidence appears to show that our industrial classes have not even that basis of a sound general education on which alone technical education can rest. . . . In fact our deficiency is not merely a deficiency in technical education, but . . . in general intelligence, and unless we remedy this want we shall gradually but surely find that our undeniable superiority in wealth and perhaps in energy will not save us from decline.[41]

How was it, then, that the first, and for long the greatest, industrial power in the world came so to neglect its most important and only permanent asset, the capability of its own people?

It had not been for lack of warning. For a hundred years prior to the Second World War private individuals and official bodies had attempted to convince public opinion and government that the battle for export markets was being lost in the school-yards and quadrangles of Britain. As early as 1835 Richard Cobden wrote after a visit to America that 'our only chance of national prosperity lies in the timely re-modelling of our system, so as to put it as nearly as possible on an equality with the improved management of the Americans.'[42] Just after the Great Exhibition of 1851 had seemed to consummate the triumph of British technology, Dr Lyon Playfair wrote in his book *Industrial Instruction on the Continent* that European industry was bound to overtake Britain if she failed to alter her outlook and methods.[43]

In 1861, the Royal Commission on the State of Popular Education in England (the Newcastle Commission), rendering the first-ever comprehensive survey of this subject, reported that of those children who did go to school a large proportion 'do not even learn to read; at least, their power of reading is so slight . . . as to be of little value to them in after-life and to be frequently forgotten as soon as school is left.'[44] Three years later the Clarendon Royal Commission reported on the education of the upper classes in nine renowned public schools – and found a similar state of affairs, in that:

> natural science . . . is practically excluded from the education of the higher classes in England. Education with us is, in this respect, narrower than it was three centuries ago, whilst science has prodigiously extended her empire. . . . This exclusion is, in our view, a plain defect and a great practical evil. . . .[45]

Then in 1868 came the already cited Schools Enquiry Royal Commission, on all types of education lying between the elementary school and the élite public school.

In the same year a House of Commons Select Committee on Scientific Instruction reported in detail on how professional and technical ignorance at all levels of British industry was already beginning to rot British industrial supremacy at the roots:

> the foremen are, almost without exception, persons who have been selected from the class of workmen by reason of their superior natural aptitude, steadiness and industry. Their education, and that of the workmen, during their school age, has been received in the elementary schools; and owing both to the defective character of the instruction in some of those schools, and to the early stage at which children go to work, it is rarely sufficient to enable them to take advantage of scientific instruction at a later period.[46]

The select committee found the knowledge of the smaller manufacturers and the managers to be no better: 'Unfortunately, this division may be disposed of in a very few words. Its members have either risen from the rank of foreman and workmen . . . or they are an offshoot from the class of smaller tradesmen, clerks etc. . . .'[47]

Even – and worst of all – the owners and managers of great industrial undertakings themselves were found by the committee to be deficient in professional education. If they had risen up from the ranks, 'Any knowledge of scientific principles which they may have acquired is generally the result of solitary reading, and of observation of the facts with which their pursuits have made them familiar.'[48] However, 'more generally . . . the training of the capitalists, and of the managers of their class, has been that of the higher secondary schools'[49] – and that, as the Clarendon Commission had pointed out four years previously, practically excluded science. In the 1870s and 1880s when the foreign challenge was becoming more and more evidently threatening, two fresh Royal Commissions carried out elaborate investigations of British and European technical and scientific education. The Devonshire Royal Commission on Scientific Instruction and the Advancement of Science, reporting from 1872 to 1875, remarked with some bitterness that 'still no adequate effort has been made to supply the deficiency of Scientific Instruction pointed out by the Commissioners in 1861 and 1864. We are compelled, therefore, to record our opinion that the Present State of Scientific Instruction in our schools is extremely unsatisfactory.'[50] The Samuelson Royal Commission on Technical Instruction (reporting in 1882–4) visited France, Germany, Austria, Switzerland, Belgium, Holland and Italy before framing its bleak comparisons between the technical education at different levels in Britain and Europe, and its bleaker inferences from this to Britain's industrial future. But hardly less significant in the long perspective of British industrial history are the commission's incidental comparisons between the human quality of the British and European workforces. Thus in Switzerland the commissioners on visiting an elementary school 'were especially struck with the clean and tidy appearance of the boys, and there was difficulty in realising that the school consisted mainly of children of the lower classes of the population.'[51]

Of Germany they noted: 'The one point in which Germany is overwhelmingly superior to England is in schools, and in the education of all classes of the people. . . . the dense ignorance so common among workmen in England is unknown. . . .'[52] They approved the evening schools in Europe where workers could continue part-time scientific and technical studies:

> the evening science teaching was conducted by professors of higher standing than, and of superior attainments to, the ordinary science teachers who conduct courses in some of the largest and most important of the manufacturing centre [*sic*] of this country. In the case of machine construction, the models and materials for instruction were superior to those found in similar schools at home.[53]

They remarked that technical higher elementary schools like those on the continent 'are singularly wanting in our own country';[54] and were especially struck with European advanced technical education for managerial staff – the polytechnics:

> To the multiplication of these polytechnics . . . may be ascribed the general diffusion of a high scientific knowledge in Germany, its appreciation by all classes of persons, and the adequate supply of men competent, so far as theory is concerned, to take the place of managers and superintendents of industrial works.
>
> In England, there is still a great want of this last class of person.[55]

Even humble members of European industry were by now well aware of growing British technical backwardness because of want of proper education. A German foreman in a chemical works told the Samuelson Royal Commissioners: 'There is a great lack of chemical knowledge even among the foremen and managers of English dyehouses, and thus, in dealing with new colours and new effects, they are compelled to rely on "rule of thumb" experience, which is often at fault.'[56]

The Samuelson Royal Commissioners concluded their report with yet another impassioned, but in the event virtually unheeded, cry of alarm:

> it is our duty to state that, although the display of continental manufacturers at the Paris International Exhibition in 1878 had led us to expect great progress, we were not prepared for so remarkable a development of their natural resources, nor for such perfection in their industrial establishments as we actually found. . . .

And:

> Your commissioners cannot repeat too often that they have been impressed with the general intelligence and technical knowledge of the masters and managers of industrial establishments on the Continent.[57]

In the 1890s and 1900s the interlinked topics of British defeats in world markets for technology and want of professionally qualified personnel were shoved under the nose of public opinion by various popular campaigns. In 1894 there was a bestseller called *British Industries and Foreign Competition*; in 1896 a 'Made in Germany' press panic followed the appearance of a book of that title. The *Daily Express* ran a series entitled 'Wake Up England!' In 1901 the *Daily Mail* followed suit with a series on 'American Invaders'. In 1900–1 *The Times* itself ran a major series of articles on 'The Crisis of British Industry' and 'American Competition and Progress'.[58]

In 1909 it was the turn of general education for the adolescent in Britain to be indicted. A consultative committee of the Board of Education reported that three-quarters of the young between fourteen and seventeen years of age in England and Wales were under no form of education, nor of physical training:

> The Committee finds that at the most critical period of their lives a very large majority of the boys and girls in England are left without any sufficient guidance and care. This neglect results in great waste of early promise, in injury to character, in the lessening of industrial efficiency, and in the lowering of ideals of personal and civic liberty.[59]

The warnings were resumed as a result of the Great War. In 1917, a departmental committee of the Board of Education wrote of the schooling of the broad mass of the nation:

> The story amounts to this . . . public education after the Elementary School leaving age is a part-time affair. And there is very little of it. In 1911–12 there were about 2,700,000 juveniles between 14 and 18,

> and of these about 2,200,000 or 81.5 per cent were enrolled in neither day schools nor in evening schools. . . .[60]

The committee therefore called – in vain, as it turned out – for compulsory day-continuation classes of the kind in fact to be introduced in Germany in 1924. In 1927, an unofficial investigating committee, made up of representatives of different industries and professions and of the teachers' associations, reported on the fragmented nature of British technical education, with, for example, fourteen institutions of university rank offering courses in mining engineering to just 200 students, whereas in Germany there were three times as many students in just four mining colleges. It harshly criticised the dismal penny-pinching with regard to equipment in British technical institutions compared with their foreign counterparts. In one college:

> The equipment for the practical study of electrical engineering is meagre, and the room in which the electrical machines are housed is very small and dingy in the basement. . . . The lecture room is so badly lighted that it is impossible to see anything on the blackboard, and in the laboratory the lighting is so poor that volumetric or colorimetric work is impossible. . . .[61]

In 1924–9 came the largest and most exhaustive of all investigations into British industrial failings, the Balfour Committee on Industry and Trade; and what its final report had to say on the broad topic of technical enlightenment and British management shows how little had changed in sixty years:

> Before British industries, taken as a whole, can hope to reap from scientific research the full advantage which it appears to yield to some of their most formidable trade rivals, nothing less than a revolution is needed in their general outlook on science. . . . [62]

And as late as 1939 a consultative committee on secondary education is found deploring the failure since 1900 'to foster the development of secondary schools of quasi-vocational type designed to meet the needs of boys and girls who desired to enter industry and commerce at the age of 16'.[63]

Why, then, had these repeated heavyweight warnings been so little heeded as to leave Britain on the eve of the Second World War still without an education and training system worthy of a first-class technological power? The answer to this question lies in the workings yet again, from Britain's formative era as an industrial society in 1780–1840 onwards, of three factors, this time in combination – the cult of the 'practical man'; romantic idealism; and the profound British dislike of coherent organisation, especially if centrally administered, especially if under the aegis of the state, and especially if a charge on public funds.

*

In 1850 *The Economist* proclaimed that 'the education which fits men to perform their duties in life is not got in public or parish schools, but in the counting-house and lawyer's office, in camp or on board ship, in the shop or factory.'[64] Herein was encapsulated the by now immutable faith of self-taught ironmasters, coal owners, engine-builders and masters of textile mills that the native British genius of the 'practical man' had put Britain in her place as the world's greatest industrial power, and would keep her there. The 'practical man' had learned how to make things or carry on his business by experience on the job; and he passed on his knowledge to the next generation orally or by example in much the same way as a medieval craft 'mystery'. From boardroom to workbench this was the British way; this was seen as the secret of British success. Yet the 'practical man' was only practical in a very primitive sense, as might be expected in what was only the primitive first stage of industrialisation. Even the minority of British entrepreneurs in the late eighteenth century who took an interest in the 'science' of their day were no less so, since 'science' itself then partook of the character of amateur dabbling, and awaited the German university of the early nineteenth century to develop it into a profession systematically concerned with research and theory. The British 'practical man' was therefore the very opposite of the *educated* practical men who were to emerge from American and European technical schools to challenge him. Indeed the cult of the 'practical man' in Britain carried with it a positive mistrust of the application of intellectual study and scientific research to industrial operations; a deep suspicion of the very kind of theoretically grounded professional for which Britain's rivals looked right from the start. Such suspicion is, after all, a natural reaction of the self-taught towards the man with the certificate.

This suspicion of formal professional and technical education (at best it was indifference) extended equally to schools for the shop-floor workforce and to technical institutions and universities, as is well demonstrated by the histories of the Victorian iron and steel, coal and shipbuilding industries (see above Chapters Four to Six). In the first place, primary education and evening classes were seen as instruments of promoting docility and duty rather than competence; and as late as 1918 there was widespread opposition from industry to proposed day-continuation schools, on the grounds that they would reduce the hours spent by young people on productive work, and that, in the words of the Federation of British Industries, 'a large percentage of children were incapable of benefiting by education beyond the elementary stage.'[65] Vocational training out of public funds for school-leavers was denounced at the same time as 'Prussian'.[66] Even in the mid-1930s employers remained indifferent or hostile to day-continuation schools, while the Education Act of 1936, in raising the school-leaving age to fifteen, made exception for young people already in 'beneficial [i.e. full-time] employment'[67] because of pressure from employers.[68]

This shortsighted failure to appreciate the benefit of a well-educated, effectively intelligent workforce extended to the question of systematic skill training. The 'practical man's' longstanding attitude was well expressed by the president of the Sheffield Chamber of Commerce in evidence to the 1886 Royal Commission on the Depression in Trade and Industry: 'My apprentices get . . . no technical training whatever except what they learn in the factory.'[69] In answer to a commissioner who asked, 'You let him pick up his trade in the best way he can?', the witness replied: 'No, he is apprenticed to a workman. We masters have nothing to do with him.'[70] Such Victorian indifference to proper training either on the firm's premises or in a technical school, except in rare and therefore conspicuous cases (such as Mather and Platt, the Manchester engineers, who set up an excellent works technical school) is widely documented (see above Chapters Four to Six). And it was still persisting on a large scale even by the time of the Second World War. In January 1942 the Deputy Director of the Ministry of Labour and National Service was writing of British industry's 'ingrained prejudice against institutional training for the higher grades of skilled labour, e.g. setters, tool makers and the like'.[71] In Manchester in 1942, where there was an acute shortage of tool-setters, fewer than a quarter of the available high-grade places at the government training centre had been taken up, and none by local firms.[72]

Nor did the 'practical man's' widespread neglect to train his own workforce change much between the 1840s and 1940s. In 1941 the Director of Labour at the Ministry of Labour was complaining that despite appeals to industry since September 1940 to repair this neglect, not enough had been done.[73] Although there were, as ever, bright exceptions, such as A. V. Roe at Trafford Park ('first-class'), it was the more disturbing that this reluctance either to undertake proper training on the firm's premises or to make full use of outside institutions was just as evident in the aircraft industry as in the old Victorian staples, so demonstrating afresh how the 'practical man's' outlook survived even in new technologies in Britain. For the Ministry of Aircraft Production found a 'Reluctance on the part of employers to train seriously', so that organised schools of instruction for green labour were 'the exception rather than the rule'.[74] The ministry's lamentations continued through 1942 into 1943. In February 1943 a MAP official found Vickers-Armstrong at Castle Bromwich 'resistant and difficult' about training: 'I had a bad reception at this firm – contemptuous, patronising.'[75] In October it was reported to the ministry that Vickers-Armstrong at Broughton had accepted 300 women workers but 'could provide no training for them except to sort and match up nuts and bolts'.[76]

For a hundred years a similar general indifference to formal training on the part of the 'practical man' had extended to higher technical education and to university science and technology – and even although individual industrialists had philanthropically founded university colleges in their own towns; men such as John Owens, whose bequest of £100,000 at his death in 1846 led to the creation of Owens College, the nucleus of Manchester University, or Josiah Mason, who founded Mason's College, precursor of the University of Birmingham, in 1880. For the handful of such enlightened individuals did not redeem the mass of 'practical men' whose interest in higher technical education ended with a gift to the local endowment for the sake of reputation. Indeed, the wave of founding new colleges in Britain after 1870 is judged by an authority to owe more to the 'enormous pride of the Victorian city' and its determination not to be outshone by rival municipalities than to 'any fear of competition they might all have felt collectively from the Germans'.[77] How little overall impact the scattering of foundations by the enlightened across the country made is shown by the fact that the total number of graduates per annum in all subjects from all provincial universities just before the Great War had only reached 500–600, while just a third to a half of these actually joined industrial firms.[78]

Similar considerations apply to the establishment of technical schools or colleges by individual local industrialists, for their farsightedness too was in no sense representative of the well-attested indifference of employers in general. In 1910, more than twenty years after the Samuelson Royal Commission had tried to awaken opinion to Britain's backwardness in technical education, the Board of Education in its report for 1908–9 pointed out:

> The slow growth of these technical institutions is, however, in the main to be ascribed to the small demand in this country for the services of young men well-trained in the theoretical side of industrial operations and in the service underlying them.[79]

Twenty years later still, in 1929, the Balfour Committee on Industry and Trade reported that the 'practical man' still dominating British industry had hardly modified his hostility to the products of technical colleges or universities:

> The available information makes it clear that the present response of the leaders of industrial and commercial enterprises to the educational efforts made to train candidates for entry into the higher grades of these organizations is much less certain and widespread than in certain foreign countries, e.g., Germany or the United States.[80]

By the interwar period the prejudices of the 'practical man' had led to a peculiarly disastrous paradox: British industry was desperately short of well-educated and skilled personnel of all kinds compared with its rivals; the British education and training system was still only turning out a fraction of the trained talent produced in other countries; and yet, and yet, this fraction was actually more than British industry wished to employ. The Balfour Committee noted, for example, of the iron and steel industry that 'it may be said that of recent years the supply of engineers and chemists has exceeded the demand.'[81] With regard to the cotton industry, the committee reported that:

> except for relatively few men with scientific qualifications required in the finishing trades and the research departments, there is very little demand for staff technically trained in the sense that they must have passed through some course in the schools.[82]

In engineering and metal-working generally the committee reckoned it likely that:

> the number of men trained in the universities and larger technical colleges will not only suffice for senior technical posts, but will also extend to posts of lower grade, such as foremen and inspectors, which formerly were recruited from the ranks of skilled workers.[83]

The Balfour Committee's diagnosis was confirmed by the report of the Malcolm Committee, a contemporaneous official investigation specifically concerned with the relationship of education and industry, which wrote of technical education in general:

> We have had little or no concrete evidence of an unsatisfied demand on the part of industry for the product of a full-time system. It would be deplorable if any such development . . . should result in the output of a substantial number of highly-trained young men whom industry was unable to absorb.[84]

Unfortunately the 'practical man's' lack of interest in education and training since the 1840s and earlier had been all too completely matched by the lack of interest in industry and industrial success displayed over the same period by the dominant British educational establishment. Indeed, this displayed positive scorn for anything so low as 'trade' – horror at the very thought that education might actually prepare the young for a working life and the gaining of an income rather than pursue other, nobler, purposes.

*

> I consider then, that I am chargeable with no paradox, when I speak of a Knowledge which is its own end, when I call it liberal knowledge, or a gentleman's knowledge, when I educate for it, and make it the scope of a University. . . .

Thus spoke Cardinal Newman, one of the most influential voices in the Victorian debate about the proper purpose of education, in 1852. And:

> You see then, Gentlemen, here are two methods of Education; the one aspires to be philosophical, the other mechanical; the one rises towards ideas, the other is exhausted upon what is particular and external. Let me not be thought to deny the necessity, or to decry the benefit, of such attention to what is particular and practical, of the useful or mechanical arts; life could not go on without them; we owe our daily welfare to them; their exercise is the duty of the many, and we owe to the many the debt of gratitude for fulfilling it. I only say that Knowledge, in proportion as it tends more and more to be particular, ceases to be Knowledge. . . .

Therefore:

> Liberal education makes not the Christian, nor the Catholic, but the

> gentleman. It is well to be a gentleman, it is well to have a cultivated intellect, a delicate taste, a candid, equitable, dispassionate mind, a noble and courteous bearing in the conduct of life; – these are the connatural qualities of a large knowledge; they are the objects of a University. . . .[85]

The Victorian liberally educated 'gentleman' traced his ancestry back through the renaissance ideal of the 'Courtier' to Plato's 'guardians'; the former made possible by the peasants, artisans and businessmen of Italian city states; the latter by an economy founded on slavery. Newman and the intellectual élite within and outside the universities to whose convictions he gave such eloquent utterance likewise grandly assumed that a mass of rude mechanicals would always maintain that fabric of material prosperity which supported their own rarefied pursuit of cultural excellence. Yet Newman's 'gentleman' was not simply a renaissance courtier or Platonic aristocrat dressed up in a frock-coat and side-whiskers. He was also the 'gentleman' of Kenelm Digby's *The Broad Stone of Honour* and the Eglinton Tournament; the parfait knight, pure of face and blank of loins, depicted by the Pre-Raphaelites; in other words, a figment of the romantic imagination. Moreover he was, of course, a *Christian* gentleman. And the real driving force behind the Victorian crusade against a useful or technical education lay in the religious revival. Newman himself, once a member of the Oxford Movement, later a Cardinal of the Roman Church, perfectly exemplifies the interwoven strands of medievalising romanticism and religious emotion.

The capturing of the future of British education by religion and the classics began with the public schools, which by the first decades of the nineteenth century had sunk into pits of anarchy and bullying; and it was Dr Thomas Arnold, headmaster of Rugby from 1827 until his death in 1841, who led the attack. Arnold manifested in his own stormy personality all the moral obsessions and emotional fervour of the revivalist movements of his time; and through the medium of disciples who went on from Rugby to become leading figures in other schools, he was more responsible than any other single person for the nature of later Victorian élite education and the character both of the revamped ancient public schools and all the numerous new ones that opened between 1840 and 1900 to cater for the swelling middle classes. Religion for Arnold was the most important element in education; and he went as far as to resign from the governing body of the new London University because religion was not to be a compulsory examination subject: 'An University that conceived of education as not involving in it principles of moral truths would be an evil.'[86] Christian morality was thus very much more important to him than scientific knowledge:

> rather than have it [science] the principal thing in my son's mind, I would gladly have him think that the sun went round the earth, and that the stars were so many spangles set in the bright blue firmament. Surely the one thing needed for a Christian and an Englishman to study is a Christian and moral and political philosophy. . . .[87]

It was Arnold's belief therefore that a 'thorough English gentleman – Christian, manly and enlightened – is . . . a finer sentiment of human nature than any other country, I believe, could furnish.'[88]

The new romantic ideal of Christian education went on from Rugby and other freshly reformed public schools to capture the universities of Oxford and Cambridge. Dr Moberly, the headmaster of Winchester, remarked on this spiritual revolution:

> the tone of the young men at the University, whether they came from Winchester, Eton, Rugby, Harrow or wherever else, was [in his own day as an undergraduate] universally irreligious. A religious undergraduate was very rare, very much laughed at when he appeared; and I think I may confidently say, hardly to be found among public-school men. . . . A most singular and striking change has come upon our public schools. . . . This change is part of a general improvement of our generation in respect of purity and reverence.[89]

It was in this same period that the exponents of what Newman called 'liberal knowledge', i.e. knowledge unrelated to what is 'particular and practical' and enshrined in such disciplines as the classics or mathematics, won a particular success which was to determine the character of the British state bureaucracy for the next century. For, thanks largely to a coterie of Oxbridge alumni, the entrance examinations for the newly reformed civil service were framed on the assumption that governing an industrial nation required exactly the same kind of 'liberally educated' intellects as might otherwise seek a career in the Church or even the university.[90] Thus in the early 1850s was born the Whitehall mandarin, able at a touch to transmute life into paper and turn action to stone. Henceforward the British governing élite was to be composed of essay-writers rather than problem-solvers – minds judicious, balanced and cautious rather than operational and engaged; the temperament of the academic rather than the man of action. Moreover, this was to be an élite aloof from the ferocious struggle for survival going on in the world's market place; more at home in a club or senior common room than a factory. And where would such mandarins be recruited other than from Oxford and Cambridge, their original breeding grounds? The cosiest of symbiotic relationships had thus been established.

The takeover bid for the soul of British education in the mid-nineteenth century by the highminded liberal-studies lobby did not go without challenge. As early as 1809 Sidney Smith had observed in the *Edinburgh Review* that an 'infinite quantity of talent is annually destroyed in the Universities of England,' and proceeded to argue that it was vain 'to say that we have produced great men' by means of stuffing them with Greek and Latin; rather, 'classical learning is supposed to have produced the talents which it has not been able to extinguish.' He could see, however, why the ancient universities might be reluctant to change their ways:

> When an University has been doing useless things for a long time, it appears at first degrading to them to be useful. A set of lectures upon

> political economy would be discouraged in Oxford, probably despised, probably not permitted. To discuss the enclosure of commons, and to dwell upon imports and exports, to come so near to common life, would seem undignified and contemptible.[91]

In 1861, when Oxbridge and the public schools had already given themselves over to producing liberally educated 'Christian gentlemen', and six years before the Paris Exhibition made manifest Britain's loss of technological leadership, Herbert Spencer percipiently remarked on the incompatibility between the stained-glass and white-marble ideals of British education and the iron foundries, and cotton mills and gas works that sustained British prosperity.

> That which our school-courses leave almost entirely out, we thus find to be that which most nearly concerns the business of life. Our industries would cease, were it not for the information which men begin to acquire, as best they may, after their education is said to be finished.[92]

Turning on its back Newman's argument about the priority of 'philosophical' knowledge over practical, Spencer averred:

> it is one thing to approve of aesthetic culture as largely conducive to human happiness; and other to admit that it is a fundamental requisite to human happiness. However important it may be, it must yield precedence to those kinds of culture which bear directly upon daily duties.[93]

Spencer indeed thrust his argument into the heart of the question of what kind of service was rendered to the national life by the type of élite education that by now prevailed:

> And here we see most distinctly the vice of our educational system. . . . It neglects the plant for the sake of the flower. In anxiety for elegance, it forgets substance. While it gives no knowledge conducive to self-preservation – while of knowledge that facilitates gaining a livelihood it gives but the rudiments, and leaves the greater part to be picked up anyhow in after life . . . it is diligent in teaching whatever adds to refinement, polish, éclat.[94]

But the mid-Victorian tide of moral and intellectual highmindedness, the romantic yearning for the pure and the ideal, swept over such utilitarians as Spencer. In 1867, the very year of the fateful Paris Exhibition, John Stuart Mill asserted in his inaugural address as rector of St Andrews University:

> The proper function of an University in national education is tolerably well understood. At least there is a tolerably wide agreement about what an University is not. It is not a place of

> professional education. Universities are not intended to teach the knowledge required to fit men for some special mode of gaining their livelihood. Their object is not to make skilful lawyers, or physicians, or engineers, but capable and cultivated human beings.[95]

Mill was condescending enough to acknowledge:

> It is well that there should be Schools of Law, and of Medicine, and it would be well if there were schools of engineering, and the industrial arts. The countries that have such institutions are greatly the better for them; and there is something to be said for having them in the same localities, and under the same general superintendence, as the establishments devoted to education properly so called.[96]

But:

> these things are no part of what every generation owes to the next, as that on which its civilization will principally depend. They are needed only by a comparatively few, who are under the strongest private inducements to acquire them by their own efforts. . . .[97]

Thomas Huxley's attempt in 1874 to controvert Mill by putting forward science as an alternative vehicle to the classics as a means of cultivating the mind and intelligence – a suggestion of wonderful promise – fared no better than Spencer's blunt utilitarianism. Even Matthew Arnold, who knew the excellence of European education and training for capability at first hand, and who in 1871–2 had pointed out the connection between the Prussian education system and the recent Prussian victory over France, was arguing by 1882 that 'knowledges' that cannot be directly related to our sense of conduct and our sense of beauty are mere 'instrument knowledges', whence followed in his view the overriding importance of Greek as part of our culture.[98]

The debate thus being won by the Arnoldians and Newmanians, the natural consequences followed. In the public schools the classics continued to dominate the curriculum, especially for the 'high-flyers', until after the Great War, and even although science and 'modern' subjects such as modern languages, history and English literature had crept in from the 1860s onwards, often in the first place as extras out of school hours, for long they were regarded as refuges for the second-rate. In the words of a late-Victorian assistant master at Harrow, 'most Classical boys leave school knowing little or nothing of . . . the two chief modern languages, and the rudiments of history and English literature.'[99] With most masters and all the cleverest boys classicists, it is hardly surprising to find that to the end of the century, and after, most candidates for the Class I Civil Service Examinations chose to offer classics as preferred subjects.[100] Although the late nineteenth and early twentieth centuries were times of intense scientific progress, of the vast technological developments of the second wave of the industrial revolution, and of Britain's more and more evident failure to ride the crest of that wave, little or no awareness of all this penetrated into the public schools. The growing threat to British industrial predominance from new competitors did not lead to a comparative examination for the benefit of pupils of the kind of evidence contained in the Devonshire or Samuelson Royal Commission Reports, but rather – in some schools – to a romantic and uncritical patriotism in the style of Henry Newbolt's verse, whereby other great powers were to be humbled by 'pluck' and team spirit.[101] Modern history in the schools remained strong on political, constitutional and ecclesiastical topics, but weak on economic and social history; weaker still on the history of technology.

Even the experience of the Great War did not shake the fundamentals of the Arnoldian tradition. As late as 1929 the headmaster of Harrow, Dr Cyril Norwood, could write in his influential book *The English Tradition in Education*:

> For what has happened in the course of the last hundred years is that the old ideals have been recaptured. The ideal of chivalry which inspired the knighthood of medieval days, the ideal of service to the community which inspired the greatest of the men who founded schools for their day and for posterity, have been combined in the tradition of English education which holds the field today. It is based upon religion: it relies largely upon games and open-air prowess, where these involve corporate effort. . . .[102]

It is noteworthy that Dr Norwood allotted three chapters out of twenty to religious teaching, and only ten pages to British technological backwardness and lack of trained managerial talent, at a time when interim reports from the Balfour Committee on Industry and Trade were already appearing, and when Britain's great Victorian industries lay in long-term slump in the midst of a world boom.

Given the intimate connection between the public school and Oxbridge, it is not surprising that the ethos and curricula of the two ancient universities even up to the Second World War should also have been inspired by the victory won by the Victorian liberal-education men. Both universities for long successfully defended the medieval disciplines of the classics and philosophy against the encroachments of science; and for longer still the encroachments of technology. Greek remained a compulsory subject at Cambridge even for scientists until 1919; at Oxford until 1920. In 1900, according to one analysis, only a tenth of the fellowships in Oxford colleges were held by natural scientists; and their share amounted to only a quarter of the share enjoyed by classicists alone.[103] Moreover in the previous seventy years not a single head of an Oxford college had been freely chosen from the sciences.[104] In 1900 Cambridge even forfeited the chance of a school of naval architecture when the prospective donor withdrew his offer on learning that all the students would have to qualify in Greek.[105]

In the face of such stubborn resistance, science could make but slow progress. Although both Oxford and Cambridge had created schools in the natural sciences as early as 1848–50, the student numbers for long remained miniscule. The Clarendon Laboratory for physical research at Oxford and the Cavendish Laboratory at Cambridge were not founded until the 1870s, some forty years after comparable European developments. In any case, Oxford science remained virtually stillborn until after the Great War, for the professor of physics for fifty years until 1915 was 'entirely opposed to research', with the result that the Clarendon Laboratory was bereft of necessary equipment, even electric power, while the professor of chemistry thought it demeaning to appear in the laboratory and beneath his professional dignity to conduct research.[106] It is true that the Cavendish at Cambridge swiftly grew into a world centre of excellence in original discovery, but right up to the Great War its work lay so much at the frontiers of research as to be of little direct benefit to British industry. Thus even at its best Oxbridge science became another intellectual mandarinism to place alongside the traditional mandarinisms of the classics or mathematics.

Technology, or 'applied science', took even longer to win footholds in Oxbridge. Although a chair of engineering was created at Cambridge as early as 1875 (something like half a century later than comparable European developments) it was not until 1894 that engineering became an examination subject, to be taken that year by fewer than 3 per cent of undergraduates undergoing examination.[107] At a private conference held in Cambridge in 1903 to discuss the gulf that had at last been recognised to exist between the university and industry, the professor of chemistry said he agreed:

> with all the Vice-Chancellor had said as to the complaint of men engaged in business of various kinds that the University does not provide an education for their sons suited to their needs. . . . We ought to pay far more regard to the future careers of our students, and interest them by making them feel that what they learnt would serve them in after life. A contempt for trade is not justifiable, and to express it is unworthy of a philosopher. . . .[108]

Oxford, however, was still far from making such recantations. In 1903 a professor at the Royal College of Science indicted her for her continued highminded aversion from Britain's needs in the real world:

> It is not only that Oxford keeps aloof from technical education, but she keeps aloof from the very much greater thing of which this movement is only a symptom, namely the phenomenon that trade and manufacture are no longer left to themselves as they used to be; they are being organised on scientific lines in all countries. She has always ostentatiously held herself aloof from manufacture and commerce. It is almost incomprehensible that a university aiming at breadth of culture should scorn those things which keep England in her high position.[109]

Not until 1908 did Oxford set up a chair in engineering; and in the first honours-school examination in the subject in 1910 it was taken by just two undergraduates. Not until the interwar period did the Cambridge engineering department develop into a centre of excellence with growing industrial links, but even so it was not until 1945 that Cambridge created a chair in electrical engineering, and not until 1963 that the tripos in electrical sciences followed.[110]

This victory of the Victorian lobbyists for a 'liberal education' in the public schools and ancient universities must be accounted one of the crucial factors in Britain's loss of technological leadership between the 1860s and the 1940s. In the first place, their arguments posed – and thereafter established – an entirely false antithesis between the subjects fit for enriching the mind, cultivating the reason and inspiring the moral sense, and those other subjects held to amount to no more than the mundane nuts-and-bolts of a narrow professional training. The antithesis was false because a classical education was itself extremely narrow and specialised, a minute study of a handful of texts, and also because in the nineteenth century (as since the middle ages) a classical education too was a vocational training – for clerics. Just as German technical high schools existed to turn out engineers to run German industry, so mid-Victorian Oxbridge existed primarily to turn out clergymen to run the Church of England, or to become public-school schoolmasters and dons, while late-Victorian Oxbridge (in particular Oxford) came to exist to turn out public servants. Furthermore, the antithesis was false in assuming that professional education could not be made the vehicle for a general cultivation of the mind, but must always remain a mere cramming of facts. It is hard to see why study of some aspect of the world in which the student would have to live and work should be less likely to make him capable, wise, cultivated and moral than study of a dead world of which only partial records survived. Similar considerations apply equally to the moral sciences and mathematics, Cambridge's own particular versions of a properly 'pure' medium of education.

This false antithesis, once established, was to become a self-fulfilling prophecy – with profound ill-effects on all British education and culture, beginning with the apex of the pyramid, the universities. For it meant that subjects in technology and commerce in Britain were relegated to the academic second class, recruiting the socially and often intellectually second class, studied in second-class (in the snobbish sense) 'red-brick' universities with chairs in jam-making (to cite one Victorian Oxbridge sneer); and hence indeed sometimes tending to partake more of the nature of nuts-and-bolts technical training than a broad cultivation of the mind. Huxley's vision of science as the grand alternative to the humanities in forming the outlook of the nation was lost. On the contrary, as the president of the Royal Society argued in his anniversary address in 1903:

> Expenditure by the Government on scientific research and scientific institutions, on which its commercial and industrial prosperity so largely depend, is wholly inadequate in view of the present state of international competition. I throw no blame on the individual

> members of the present or former Governments; they are necessarily the representatives of public opinion, and cannot go beyond it. The cause is deeper, it lies in the absence in the leaders of public opinion, and indeed throughout the more influential classes of society, of sufficiently intelligent appreciation of the supreme importance of scientific knowledge and scientific methods in all industrial enterprises and indeed in all national undertakings. . . . In my opinion the scientific deadness of the nation is mainly due to the too exclusively medieval and classical methods of our higher public schools. . . .[111]

There was, however, more to the triumph of the romantic ideal of a 'liberal education' than neglect of science and technology in themselves; more than a pervasive intellectual and social snobbery. For just as it was the factory town that had made the British working class, so it was the Victorian public school and Oxbridge that had made the British middle classes of the late nineteenth century and twentieth century. Here amid the silent eloquence of grey Gothic walls and green sward, the sons of engineers, merchants and manufacturers were emasculated into gentlemen. Here the children of wealth were taught that the pursuit of wealth was vulgar, ignoble and unknightly, not to say the mark of the cad and the bounder; and that the more estimable career lay in 'public service'. With a secure mandarin career to be crowned by a knighthood in one of the proliferating imperial orders of chivalry, it was possible to despise, and socially humiliate, the 'box-wallahs' from whose activities derived the mandarin's salary, perquisites and pension.[112]

This governing class moulded by the public school and Oxbridge saw British power less in terms of industrial competitiveness and technological prowess than of worldwide imperial possessions, the pink on the map. And they saw the British Empire itself less as a repository of resources to be exploited than as a great instrument of civilisation and enlightenment, the successor to Greece and Rome; their own role as being that of super-prefects, administrating the empire justly in the interests of the governed. As late as the 1920s, for example, the officer in charge of recruitment to the Colonial Service regarded the public school 'as the spiritual child of chivalry', producing exactly the kind of person he wanted for 'really a crusading service'.[113] The values and the world view of this British governing class were thus profoundly pre-industrial, conservative, nostalgic. Nor were its human characteristics and patterns of behaviour any more appropriate to leading a technological society through rapid evolutionary change and against formidable and unscrupulous competition. The romantic ideal of knightly gentleness and honour, the academic ideal of balance and detachment, hardly made for ruthless and single-minded maximisers of world market share or gross national product; rather for a deep instinct to fudge in order to avoid the harsh decision – to *appease*, in domestic questions as much as in international relations.[114] Moreover, the governing class's whole ethos and conditioning made it static in outlook rather than dynamic, seeking continuity before change.

The public school and Oxbridge did more than shape the British governing élite itself; they acted as the nursery of the intelligentsia which wrote and painted from the early nineteenth century onwards against the fact of Britain's existence as an industrialised society, seeking escape in those visions of beautiful alternative worlds, medieval or rural, and suffused by Christian love and fellowship. In large part they acted as the nursery too of that kindred 'enlightened' Establishment which was ultimately to bring forth the New Jerusalem movement of the Second World War, and of which the leading names read as if gold-lettered on the Gothic cloister wall of some all-embracing *alma mater*.

Yet this was still not the whole of it. Directly or indirectly the influence of the victory won by Victorian apostles of a 'liberal education' ramified far wider yet. In the first instance it provided one major reason why the new 'red-brick' provincial university colleges founded from 1870 onwards became as strong in the arts as in science and technology, rather than develop into technical universities on the German model. John Owens, founder of Owens College, Manchester (later Manchester University), the first of these provincial colleges, deliberately chose to emulate the liberal arts education of Oxford and Cambridge,[115] and only later did this bias become modified by the founding of the new departments of science, engineering and chemistry. Liverpool, founded in 1881, aimed from the beginning to cover the arts as well as science, not least because certain rich local industrialists of Unitarian faith (the religious revival again) chose to support subjects like classical history, Egyptology and archaeology as well as technology.[116]

In the case of those provincial colleges which had been distinctly intended by their founders to be overwhelmingly technical in character, such as Mason's College, Birmingham (now Birmingham University), Leeds, Sheffield and Nottingham, powerful outside factors compelled them eventually to conform to the prevailing British pattern of a 'liberal education'. The first of these factors lay in London University's examination requirements for external degrees (for which initially the new provincial colleges had to enter their students), which demanded literature and the classics as a necessary part even of a science degree.[117] In the second place, the new 'Victoria University' of 1880, a federation of northern colleges dominated by Manchester, insisted that purely technological institutions like Sheffield and Leeds should broaden their coverage to the arts if they wished to be admitted. Then again, when the state in Britain at last began to give financial support to university education in 1889, the body which dispensed the funds (the ancestor of today's University Grants Committee), being weighty with Oxbridge high minds, required that remaining overly technical institutions like Birmingham and Southampton should strengthen their teaching in unuseful knowledges if they wanted government money. And finally there was the pressure of demand for the arts from students intending to become school-teachers, wherein was manifested another aspect of the wider influence exerted by the triumphant 'liberal-education' lobby; indeed the operation of a closed loop.

These developments did not, it is true, prevent the provincial universities serving British industry even before 1914 with first-class technological research far beyond Oxbridge's contribution, and in *quality* the equal or superior to the work of German universities.[118] Nonetheless the large-scale channelling of resources into the arts greatly damaged the potential *quantitative* contribution to technological research and education made by the provincial universities; relatively the more so because their overall numbers were so much smaller than those of their German equivalents. In 1910 there were nearly 17,000 students in German technical high schools alone, to say nothing of ordinary universities – almost equal to the total number of non-Oxbridge university students of all kinds in Great Britain in 1913–14, at 19,000.[119] At Birmingham there were then 185 students in engineering and other technologies, 396 in the arts; at Manchester, 70 in engineering, 385 in the arts; at Liverpool 122 in engineering and technology, 270 in the arts. In any case more students were studying 'pure' science than engineering and technology, a clear manifestation of the British scale of academic snobbery.[120] Between 1920 and 1939, the balance actually changed to the disadvantage of science and technology, with students in all British universities studying technologies falling from over 13 per cent of the total to less than 10 per cent, 'pure' science staying steady at around 10 per cent, and those studying the arts rising from nearly 40 per cent to over 46 per cent.[121] Newman, Mill and Arnold would have much approved.

On state-funded elementary and secondary education in Britain the long-term impact of that triumph of 'liberal education' in the Victorian debate was clear and decisive: the intellectual and emotional stream can be traced from its spring in the romantic movement, especially religious revivalism, all the way down to the broad current of British national schooling on the eve of the Second World War. It was not just a question here of the general influence exerted by the convictions that had come to prevail among the intelligentsia and informed public opinion at large by the second half of Victoria's reign, although this was important enough. It was that the development of state education in Britain at critical junctures fell directly to members of that governing élite which had been moulded by the Arnoldian public school and Newmanian Oxbridge. The outstanding figure in this regard is Sir Robert Morant, the civil servant who was largely responsible for preparing and implementing the 1902 Education Act, the most important single piece of legislation in the field before the Butler Act of 1944. Born in 1863, of a mother who was a devout Evangelical, Morant was educated at Winchester, in Dr Moberly's house, studying classics, and New College, Oxford, reading Hebrew as well as classics. He was an evangelising activist in the Inter-Collegiate Christian Union, and conducted Sunday School classes. Morant completed his Oxford career by taking the Final School of Theology. Hardly surprisingly, he was to set out in office not to provide England with education for capability (either general or technical) that could match that of her rivals, but to demolish what little had been gradually built up by his time.

However, the bias of British élite values had already made its mark on state-funded education before then. Elementary education for the masses under the 1870 Education Act concerned itself as much with religious indoctrination as with the basic skills of the three Rs; and in 1888 a Royal Commission on Elementary Schools made a special point of stating in its summary of recommendations:

> That while we desire to secure for the children in the public elementary schools the best and most thorough instruction in secular subjects, suitable to their years and in harmony with the requirements of their future life, we are also unanimously of opinion that their religious and moral training is a matter of still higher importance, alike to the children, the parents, and the nation.[122]

Moreover the commission was also persuaded that:

> the only safe foundation on which to construct a theory of morals, or to secure high moral conduct, is the religion which our Lord Jesus Christ has taught the world. That as we look to the Bible for instruction concerning morals, and take its words for the declaration of what is morality, so we look to the same inspired source for the sanctions by which men may be led to practice what is there to be taught. . . .[123]

In the field of state-assisted secondary education between 1870 and 1900 the prestige of the public school's classical curriculum and academic approach enticed the reformed grammar schools into mimicry. It also helped to turn to wastepaper the Schools Enquiry Royal Commission's recommendations in 1868 that a network of 'modern' schools, on the pattern of German *Realschulen*, should be set up to prepare the middle classes for working careers; it helped likewise to ensure that systematic provision of trade and technical schools remained dead paragraphs in yellowing reports.

Nonetheless, in a haphazard English way, post-elementary technical education did make some progress before 1900. The Science and Art Department (a body created in 1853 after the Great Exhibition) began ladling out funds to elementary schools which set up science and technical classes for older children; which in fact provided a 'modern' education of a secondary character otherwise lacking. It was this particular development that Morant, as an official in the Department of Education after 1895, successfully set out to smash, ostensibly on the grounds of legal principle, arguing (as the court was to agree in a test case inspired by him in 1901: the 'Cockerton judgement') that such senior classes were *ultra vires* the powers granted by the 1870 Education Act. By now the liberal-education lobby in the country had become generally fearful lest the Science and Art Department, that hot-bed of believers in a useful education and in 1899 incorporated into the new Department of Education, might actually become influential enough to impose a 'technical' character on all secondary schooling in England and Wales in the future. There were alarmed criticisms that non-scientific subjects were already being neglected in some state-assisted schools. Oxford and Cambridge and the leading public schools raised afresh the banner of Arnold and Newman, and their sympathisers-cum-alumni within the Department of Education rode out accordingly to destroy the infidel. In the van was J. W. Headlam (later Sir James Headlam-Morley), a veritable paladin of Victorian Oxbridge culture – son of a canon, educated at Eton and King's, Cambridge; later a fellow of King's, and later still professor of Greek and ancient history at Queen's College, London. In 1901 he submitted a highly influential report on 'the Teaching of Literary Subjects in some Secondary Schools' which drew the conclusion that to exclude 'liberal' subjects must in the end 'damage the intellect and character of the nation'.[124] This sage opinion was quoted to the House of Commons in July 1901 by the Parliamentary Secretary to the board, while the board itself later made a point of publishing the full text of Headlam's report.[125]

But these marked only the preliminary skirmishes. It was Morant, as the Permanent Secretary to the Board of Education from 1903 to 1911, who fought and won the decisive battle. For when the 1902 Education Act ushered in the era of greatly expanded secondary education, including for the first time secondary schools directly set up and managed by public authorities, it fell to Morant and his staff to frame new Board of Education regulations for both elementary and secondary schools. Morant's closest colleague, J. W. Mackail, the man who actually drafted the regulations, was a former scholar and fellow of Balliol who had married a daughter of Sir Edward Burne-Jones (the Pre-Raphaelite and noted depictor of knightly behaviour), and whose own contributions to British enlightenment included a life of William Morris and *Select Epigrams from the Greek Anthology*. In 1906 Mackail was to be elected professor of poetry at Oxford, and as late as the grim year of 1938 his mind was still to be happily dwelling on such topics as *Studies in Humanism* and *The Sayings of Christ*. It is thus hard to imagine that the shaping of British state education at a crucial point in its development could have fallen into the hands of men more sublimely oblivious, or dismissive, of Britain's urgent educational needs as an industrial society already outmatched by its rivals. And it is no wonder that Morant and Mackail in devising the new secondary-school code looked to the public schools as 'the models of liberal education as the second half of the nineteenth century had come to understand it', to quote the author of an unpublished official history of education;[126] nor that as a consequence the Board of Education 'set its face against any technical or vocational bias and in general the effect of the new regulations was to broaden and liberalise the education in all schools under state supervision.'[127] This far-reaching victory was completed by the simple device of providing no new general system of post-elementary technical education to replace the illicit developments destroyed by the Cockerton judgement; for only a relatively few junior technical schools were founded piecemeal from 1913 onwards.

It remained for Morant's successors to preserve what he had won; and in the early 1920s the then permanent secretary to the Board of Education, Sir Lewis Selby-Bigge (Winchester and New College, Oxford; former lecturer in philosophy), is found urging that the term 'secondary' be reserved for those schools whose tradition was to train character and intellect by giving 'a liberal education unhampered by premature specialisation' (the old false antithesis again), and that to apply the term to other kinds of post-primary education could only delude the public.[128]

In 1938 the Report of a Consultative Committee of the Board of Education on Secondary Education with Special Reference to Grammar Schools and Technical High Schools (the Spens Report) devastatingly summed up what the tradition of Victorian highmindedness running back through Morant to Arnold had done to the development of British state-funded education. Of the many new secondary schools set up since the 1902 Act, the 'most striking feature' was 'their marked disinclination to deviate to any considerable extent from the main lines of the traditional grammar school curriculum'.[129] This 'conservative and imitative tendency' the report saw as having been 'greatly re-inforced, and in a sense fostered' by the regulations issued in 1904–5 under Morant's aegis, and later by the new School Certificate Examination as set up in 1917.

> the Board took the existing Public Schools and Grammar Schools as their general *cadre* or archetype for the secondary schools of all kinds. The further development of post-primary schools with traditions somewhat different from those of Grammar Schools, such as the Higher Grade Schools, the Organized Science Schools and the Day Technical Schools which had sprung into existence in the last quarter of the nineteenth century, was definitely discouraged and the new Secondary Schools were in effect compelled to take as their model the curriculum of the existing Public Schools and Grammar Schools.[130]

And in a condemnation stronger still:

> on a dispassionate retrospect of the history of post-primary education since 1900 we cannot but deplore the fact that the Board did little or nothing . . . to foster the development of secondary schools of quasi-vocational type designed to meet the needs of boys and girls who desired to enter industry and commerce at the age of 16.[131]

It was in fact an absurd by-product of the overriding priority given to an academic liberal education with university entrance as its ultimate prize for a very few that, because of curricula angled to examination requirements, every child in the system was receiving a smudgy carbon copy of such an education, however irrelevant it might be to his inclinations and abilities, and however early he might leave school, instead of receiving a training which would actually be useful and interesting to him or her. As the Spens Report put it, 'although 85 per cent of pupils did not remain at school beyond 16', the curriculum was 'still largely planned in the interests of pupils who intended to go to a University', so that too much of the work was intended as a foundation for further studies which in fact were never undertaken.[132] The order of preference of subjects offered by candidates in

1937 for the School Certificate (the examination which weeded out those academically not good enough for the sixth form) fully bears out this judgement.[133] Every 'failure' who left school at sixteen or seventeen (to say nothing of those who left at fourteen) with a smattering of Latin and of English literature, a smidgin of religious knowledge, some history learned by heart and a few dry morsels of the laws of physics and the formulae of chemistry was therefore a living tribute to the success achieved over the hundred years by the evangelists of an academic 'liberal education'.

*

> we are left with nothing but our system of checks, and our notion of its being the right and happiness of an Englishman to do as far as possible what he likes, we are in danger of drifting towards anarchy. We have not the notion, so familiar on the Continent and to antiquity, *of the State*, – the nation in its collective and corporate character, entrusted with stringent powers for the general advantage, and controlling individual wills in the name of an interest wider than that of individuals.[134]

Thus did Matthew Arnold in 1869 identify those national characteristics which supply the third key factor in causing the tardy and scanty growth of all kinds of education and training in Britain, and the failure to articulate them into a coherent system. However, they are national characteristics already deeply ingrained by the time the industrial revolution first began in the late eighteenth century. For the whole trend of British constitutional and social developments in the Stuart and Georgian periods had lain in weakening the role of the state, as represented by the monarch, either in favour of mercantile freedom and corporate self-regulation, or by fragmenting administration among the parishes and county justices of the peace. Central government, in the form of precarious cabinets, was reduced to the functions of tax-gathering, foreign policy and defence (though even then not the militia); and its power was further limited by parliamentary caprice and by corruption, disorganisation and inefficiency.

It was exactly this self-adjusting anarchy of autonomous interests which to eighteenth-century Englishmen both constituted and safeguarded English 'liberty', an Englishman's right and happiness to do as far as possible what he liked, in contrast to the servile lot of continentals whose lives were subject to ubiquitous supervision by the state. Liberty had become indeed, as it was always to remain, the English measure of all questions political, social and industrial; the supreme English value.

From the time of Charles I onwards, and with the example of Louis XIV before them, the British had therefore identified strong central government with the absolute monarchy to which Englishmen never, never would be slaves. State action to foster industries or set up training institutes for artisans or engineers, as taken by France and other European monarchies in the seventeenth and eighteenth centuries, was seen as just another manifestation of continental tyranny. The example offered by Bonaparte in creating a complete centrally directed education system only served freshly to awaken the British to an active suspicion of the state's role in this sphere as a menace to individual liberty. And so, intellectually fortified by the *laissez-faire* ideas of Adam Smith and his successors, the British went through their industrial revolution convinced that education must be a matter solely for individual initiative or private charity. By contrast, European states, given their very different historical traditions, found it perfectly natural to assume leading roles in encouraging their countries' industrial progress, not least by the provision of adequate education and training institutions.

So it was that the French revolutionary régime created the *Ecole Polytechnique* in 1794 for the production of engineers, first of the *Grandes Ecoles* giving career-orientated higher education; and a structure of primary and secondary education soon followed. In Prussia, universal state primary education was inaugurated in 1806, becoming compulsory between the ages of seven and fourteen in 1826. As well as the *Gymnasien* specialising in the humanities, *Realschulen* were founded in every German town to provide a secondary education in science and 'modern' studies. By 1863 Prussia had 63,000 pupils in secondary education compared with a total for England and Wales of 11,000, even though Prussia's population was then the smaller. An enthusiastic partnership between the state, local authorities and local businessmen in Europe led to the proliferation of trade and technical schools in all the main centres. By 1851 there were already twenty-six trade schools for school-leavers in Prussia alone. In the 1820s the first German technical high schools (later to be universities) were being founded. In 1855 the first of all the world's polytechnics, the Zurich *Polytechnikum*, was set up in Switzerland, a country which had already introduced compulsory day-attendance at trade schools for children who had left elementary school.

In the meantime, and led by the German example, Europe had been fast expanding its universities, especially their teaching and research in science. By 1830 there were 16,000 students in German universities, a figure which bears comparison with the 19,000 total for England and Wales only reached eighty years later. The United States largely followed the German model in her own rapid nineteenth-century expansion of higher education. The Massachusetts Institute of Technology was founded in 1865, forty years before the British equivalent, Imperial College. It was this staggeringly impressive provision of education and training abroad that the British parliamentary committees and Royal Commissions of the 1860s to the 1880s documented in great and alarming detail for the benefit of a country which had not even *begun* to create comparable institutions. For Britain was already by then up to fifty years behind.

It was not ignorance of foreign developments that had caused this backwardness but, in the first place, plain unwillingness to emulate them. As early as 1834, in evidence to a parliamentary committee, Lord Brougham, the Lord Chancellor, pronounced strongly against compulsory free primary education funded and administered by the state, on the ground that they 'who argued in favour of such a scheme from the example of a military government like that of Prussia, have betrayed, in my opinion, great ignorance of the nature of Englishmen. . .'. He could not see how a national system of education could be established 'without placing in the hands of the Government, that is of the Ministers of the day, means of dictating opinions and principles to the people. . .'.[135] In 1861 the Newcastle Royal Commission on the State of Popular Education in England reported on similar grounds of national tradition that 'we have not thought that a scheme for compulsory education to be universally applied in this country can be entertained as a practical possibility.'[136]

But in any case such a proposal posed an administrative problem that was insoluble in the short term. Whereas European countries already possessed complete systems of municipal and other local authorities to run schools as well as other public services, Britain was not to give herself a modern network of borough and county councils until 1888. Before that date the only local authorities apart from those for large towns set up by the Municipal Corporations Act of 1835 were the myriad parishes and the county magistrates. Therefore practical administrative considerations as well as national prejudice impelled Britain to embark from the very start on a 'permissive' course of offering financial support to existing bodies that already gave elementary schooling, instead of embarking on direct provision of schools by the state. The existing bodies in the 1830s being the churches, and especially the Church of England, it was to them that the government began allotting subsidies so that they could open more schools. From this fatal, if politically inevitable, first step there grew an ever more powerful vested interest which was to complicate and obstruct educational reform right the way down to the Butler Education Act of 1944.

The immediate effect of very modest state support to church schools from 1833 onwards was small enough: in the 1860s there were still fewer children in grant-aided elementary schools of efficient standard than there were children receiving no form of education whatsoever. Secondary education in the 1860s consisted of a random patchwork of ancient and often decayed grammar schools, with a total of only 11,000 pupils; and there was not a single one of these schools over which the state enjoyed any control. Britain thus still remained the only advanced country in Europe making no systematic effort to educate its people.

In 1868 the Schools Enquiry Royal Commission therefore advocated a well-designed national system of education adapted from the Prussian model. At the bottom layer of the pyramid was to be an improved and extended provision of elementary schooling; next up, a network of 'modern' schools in every town, like the German *Realschulen*, to give a career-orientated education to children of the 'shopkeeper' middle classes; and at the top a similar network of efficient grammar schools equivalent to the German *Gymnasien* for the intellectual and managing élite. The commission made clear that in its view the existing endowed and non-endowed grammar schools could not possibly fulfil the roles of their top two educational tiers, for many English towns lacked a grammar school altogether.[137]

But these proposals proved altogether too Prussian for British political taste. The Endowed Schools Act of 1869 looked no further than to piecemeal reform of existing endowed grammar schools; it continued to restrict the state's role in secondary education to handing out grants-in-aid. Elementary education was dealt with quite separately by the Forster Education Act of 1870. This at last took the radical step forward of embarking on the creation of state elementary schools to make good the grossly insufficient numbers of church schools. Since Britain still lacked a modern system of local government, the Act had to set up elected school boards to administer the new schools. Yet only by 1880 had enough 'board schools' been opened to permit universal compulsory elementary education – fifty-four years later than in Prussia. Only in 1891 did elementary education become free to all – ninety-one years later than in Prussia. It was the mid-1890s before more children were being educated in 'board schools' than in church elementary schools. Meanwhile secondary education was making even slower progress: by 1895 there were 218 grant-aided grammar schools in England and Wales, giving an education of approved standard to some 30,000 pupils, a figure which compares with Prussia's total of 63,000 some thirty years earlier for a population less than two-thirds as big.

All this time the development of technical schools and colleges in Britain had been stultified by the same combination of prejudice against state intervention and lack of local government organs. In vain did the Royal Commissions of the 1860s, 1870s and 1880s amass their evidence about the excellence of European technical education and call for Britain to repent of her neglect before it was too late. The nearer a proposed blueprint approached the Swiss or German model, the less acceptable to political and industrial opinion it proved. The 1868 Commons select committee on scientific instruction for the industrial classes, for example, wanted science taught in all elementary schools; the conversion of some existing endowed schools into regional science centres; courses in science and technology in teachers' training; co-ordination of various government science institutions in London into a single scheme. The result was nil. The Samuelson Royal Commission of 1884 recommended well-equipped technical schools and colleges in all large towns; more 'modern' subjects in secondary-school curricula. The half-cock result, five years later, was the Technical Instruction Act of 1889, another exercise in 'permissive' rather than positively interventionist legislation, by which the new local authorities set up under the Local Government Act of 1888 were empowered to create technical schools and colleges if they so wished and to levy a penny rate to pay for them. After 1890 revenue from the whisky duty was diverted to local authorities to help in the good work. Unfortunately the degree of enlightenment and initiative displayed by individual local councils only sufficed for a highly uneven development of largely mean institutions, so that, in the words of one authority, British technical education by 1902 amounted to 'little more than congeries of technical and literary classes; a small number of polytechnics mainly in London; a rather larger number of organised science schools and evening science and art classes . . .'.[138]

And in the case of new provincial universities there was no question at all of central or local government taking the initiative in creating them or running them; these were functions entirely left to the hazards of private philanthropy.

Moreover, it was not only that educational developments in Britain of all kinds since the 1860s had been so uneven and tentative, but also that they were entirely unrelated to each other. In the judgement of the 1895 Royal Commission on Secondary Education (the Bryce Report) the growth of the state's concern with education:

> had not been either continuous or coherent; i.e., it does not represent a series of logical or even connected sequences. Each one of the agencies whose origin has been described was called into being, not merely independently of the others, but with little or no regard to their existence. Each has remained in its working isolated and unconnected from the rest. . . . The Charity Commissioners have had little to do with the Education Department and have still less with the Science and Art Department. Even the borough councils have, to a large extent, acted independently of the school boards, and have, in some instances, made their technical instruction grants with too little regard to the parallel grants which were being made by the Science and Art Department. . . . The University Colleges, though their growth is one of the most striking and hopeful features of the last 30 years, remain without any regular organic relations either to Elementary or to Secondary Education, either to school boards or county councils.[139]

And so:

> This isolation and this independence, if they may seem to witness to the rich variety of our educational life, and to the active spirit which pervades it, will nevertheless prepare the observer to expect the usual results of dispersed and unconnected forces, needless competition between the different agencies, and a frequent overlapping of effort, with much consequent waste of money, of time, and of labour.[140]

The 1902 Education Act went as far as politically practicable towards sorting out the mess. The school boards were abolished and responsibility for elementary, secondary and technical education alike placed in the hands of county and county-borough councils. For the first time there were to be state secondary schools to supplement the inadequate number of grant-aided grammar schools – but this new departure too was 'permissive' rather than obligatory, and depended for success on the zeal of local authorities. Yet the Act's attempt to tidy up the results of British ad-hockery still left the church schools with their independence, although brought within local government's overall responsibility in terms of inspection and financial support, for here was a vested interest now too powerful and vocal to be overturned. Moreover the 1902 Act actually weakened the existing central executive authority of the Board of Education by devolving the positive power to initiate (rather than merely regulate) educational policy down to the county and county-borough councils: the British instinct for localism yet again. Further expansion of technical education too was left to the enterprise – or not, as the case might be – of local authorities, despite their poor past record.

Although in terms of the British tradition the Education Act of 1902 marked an immense stride forward, the piecemeal results in all fields produced through its purely 'permissive' strategy proved by no means enough for Britain to catch up with her competitors. Despite the opening of 500 new county secondary schools by 1914, over four-fifths of young people between fourteen and eighteen remained under no kind of full-time or even part-time education. In 1908 the number of full-time students at technical schools *and* provincial university colleges had not yet reached 3000.[141]

In 1917 H. A. L. Fisher, President of the Board of Education, on introducing a new Education Bill to the House of Commons, referred to the growing consciousness that:

> there is a lack of scientific correlation between the different parts of our educational machinery. We find an important and populous centre without a secondary school in any shape or form. We find an older and less important centre with four secondary schools. . . .
>
> There is not even a reasonable probability that the child will get the higher education best adapted to his or her needs. The Act of 1902 no doubt contemplated area schemes for higher education, but the duty of considering the whole need of an area was left hanging in the air.[142]

But Fisher's proposals for a co-ordinated expansion masterminded by the Board of Education were opposed by the local authorities as smacking of 'centralisation',[143] while industry (as already described) resisted the idea of day-continuation schools, and other sections of opinion, especially members of the House of Lords, objected to vocational education being paid for out of public funds – all in all, a revelation of how little British prejudices about the role of the state in national education had fundamentally changed since the 1830s. In the event the Education Act of 1918 left the Board of Education still with only weak powers of co-ordination, while the Act's proposed day-continuation schools fell victim to the economy cuts of 1922. Elementary, secondary and technical education all continued to follow the British pattern of hesitant and patchy piecemeal improvement: the number of secondary schools of grammar-school type crept up from 1123 in 1914 to 1307 in 1931; of junior technical schools from 84 in 1920 to 177 in 1931.[144]

In the interwar period two more great educational reports attacked over the same ground as their predecessors back to the 1860s, and, like them, failed in the 'devil's gardens' of vested interests (especially religious and local government), of reluctance to expend more public funds, and of instinctive British dislike of clear organisation. The Hadow Report of 1926[145] called for the school-leaving age to be raised to fifteen, and for all children to receive a secondary education after the age of eleven. This meant creating 'modern secondary schools' alongside existing grammar schools, in order to provide education with a more 'practical' and 'realistic' bias – really a fresh statement of the Schools Enquiry Commission's proposals as long ago as 1868, themselves borrowed from the then already existing German system.[146] Instead of the Hadow proposals being implemented as a whole by legislation and without delay, there followed a gradual creation of 'modern' schools by administrative action. The Spens Report of 1938[147] went still further than Hadow and advocated a tripartite system of secondary education composed of 'modern' schools, 'technical high schools' and existing grammar schools, all enjoying parity of esteem. Nothing had been done to implement this system by the time the Second World War broke out.

Although the Education Act of 1936 legislated for the school-leaving age to be raised to fifteen in 1939 (in fact postponed because of the outbreak of the war), by 1938 two-thirds of the necessary building work had still to be carried out; and only a quarter of the new places needed for the extra senior pupils had been provided.[148] And it was only the urgent demand of the rearmament programme for skilled manpower which belatedly speeded developments in technical education, with eleven new junior technical schools being built in 1938–9, and nine major extensions to existing technical colleges completed.[149] Even these improvements left the general standard of buildings and equipment in technical education, in the words of a wartime report, 'deplorably low'[150] – a suitable valediction for a century of limping progress in the teeth of the combined hostility of the 'practical man' and the liberally educated 'gentleman', and against the hardest grain of national prejudice. In the context of British war production and British postwar hopes the words of the Schools Enquiry Royal Commission of 1868 come echoing back with a grimmer resonance:

> our deficiency is not merely a deficiency in technical education, but in general intelligence, and unless we remedy this want we shall gradually but surely find that our undeniable superiority in wealth and perhaps in energy will not save us from decline. . . .

Part IV

The Limits of the Possible

The question is – what is possible; and what is our order of priority?

(R. A. Butler, 1942)

Chapter Twelve

New Jerusalem or Economic Miracle?

If Britain after the war was to earn the immense resources required to maintain her cherished traditional place as a great power and at the same time pay for New Jerusalem at home, she had to achieve nothing short of an economic miracle. Such a miracle could only be wrought through the transformation, material and human, of her essentially obsolete industrial society into one capable of triumphing in the world markets of the future. Had all the most powerful groups and institutions in that society been willing enthusiastically to throw themselves behind the process of transformation, it would still have been difficult enough to achieve, given the scale of the inherited problems. But instead of such willingness there existed the massive inertial resistance to change which was so manifest in the history of Britain as an industrial society; a resistance that not even the shock of war had proved strong enough to budge more than a little. In planning for the postwar era the wartime coalition government therefore confronted a truly gigantic task, not the least aspect of which was that, as R. A. Butler observed to a colleague at the time, politics is the art of the possible.

The task had to begin with Britain's immediate and desperate economic plight. For by 1944 her visible exports were only sufficient to buy one-seventh of the food and raw materials and other goods she needed from abroad. The Treasury calculated that at the end of the war with Germany British foreign debts would be fifteen times greater than Britain's remaining reserves of gold and foreign exchange; that Britain's current-account balance of payments in the first three years of peace would be £1000 million in the red.[1] An earlier Treasury estimate, in 1942, had reckoned that the quantity of imports for which Britain herself could actually pay 'might suffice to keep the population fed and to provide raw materials at the present rate of use per head' – in other words, wartime austerity indefinitely prolonged without hope.[2] But beyond such immediate economic peril lay the vaster long-term problems of restructuring the British industrial machine. Such restructuring would need to go much deeper than merely modernising out-of-date and uncompetitive traditional 'heavies' like coal, iron and steel, shipbuilding and cotton. It meant swinging the whole balance of the economy in favour of newer industries and the newest products; it meant a social and environmental restructuring as a necessary aspect of such an altered balance; it meant at the deepest, at the longest-term, the creation of a new kind of workforce – of society even – with the developed intelligence and the specific skills, the motivation, that in ten or twenty years' time would enable Britain to outpace the best of foreign competition: hence a remodelling of the entire education and training system. Yet all this profound change must be set on foot in the midst of short-term crisis and at a time of a griping shortage of national resources.

'Politics is the art of the possible' – but judgement in 1942–5 of what would be politically possible had to take account of the popular yearning for New Jerusalem, and the ever more manifest popular demand that New Jerusalem should be built at the end of the war without tedious delay because of anything so trivial as national insolvency. Then again, politics had to bear in mind that the old industrial areas were dense concentrations not only of obsolete and worn-out industries, but also of parliamentary votes and seats. In any case New Jerusalem had its own powerful lobby within the wartime coalition government, in the form of Labour ministers much concerned with 'reconstruction'. For all these reasons there is evident throughout the Whitehall debates and reports and eventual policy decisions on 'reconstruction' up to the end of the war a conflict between two contrasting and competing priorities – New Jerusalem versus a realistic national 'corporate strategy'.

It was of course the publication of the Beveridge Report on social security as a White Paper in November 1942, and the prospect of a parliamentary debate on it in the following February that had induced the Cabinet in January 1943 to set up a special Committee on Reconstruction Priorities to ponder the whole question of the likely national income after the war and the various calls to be made on it. Herbert Morrison, the Labour Home Secretary and Minister for Home Security, eloquently put the New Jerusalem case to this committee in a memorandum on 20 January based on a highly optimistic guesstimate of the country's postwar resources, by which military expenditure was to halve in ten years, while thanks to a rise in national income the Exchequer's receipts in revenue would increase over twenty years to almost double the increased cost of the Beveridge Plan over the same period.[3] Wrote Morrison:

> I am entirely against allowing ourselves to be driven by the pressure of public opinion into disastrous courses. We must deal in full honesty with the people and not encourage them to expect financial impossibilities. But I question whether we could claim as a good reason for not adopting the Beveridge Plan the fact that the Government had chosen to make pessimistic assumptions about the post-war future. . . .
>
> I can see no need to make or act upon such assumptions. I should certainly not like to have to expound and defend them to a nation bearing the full burden of total war.[4]

'Pessimistic assumptions' of the kind to which Morrison referred were graphically set down that same month in a paper by Kingsley Wood, the Chancellor of the Exchequer, in which he pointed out that the taxpayer would have to bail out Beveridge's welfare state to an incalculable and unlimited extent, because it was only partly financed by insurance contributions. Such a bailing out would constitute 'a prior charge' on national resources 'in good or bad times alike'.[5] In Wood's opinion there were 'lying in the future, so far as it can be at present dimly discerned, doubts and uncertainties suggesting that large financial commitments cannot at this stage be undertaken without misgiving'.[6] The British national income might, he wrote, increase greatly over the next twenty years, as many prophets asserted, but also possibly not; possibly the British economy might be in great difficulties owing to an adverse balance of payments and because of a slow switchover to new technologies.[7] In any case the Beveridge Plan charge on the Exchequer could only be met at the expense of other state expenditure.[8] This last point was banged home to the Prime Minister by Lord Cherwell in a personal note on 11 February 1943 saying that if the Beveridge Plan were accepted, there would not be enough resources for everything else, such as housing, education, higher wages and what not.[9] Kingsley Wood's diagnosis concurred with earlier studies of the Beveridge costings in 1942 by the Government Actuary, who reckoned the immediate extra cost of Beveridge over existing welfare arrangements – and not including a national health service – at £160 million per annum. If such a service and all other welfare schemes were added in, he calculated that the total cost to the Exchequer would amount to £367 million in 1945 and £541 million in 1965.[10] Wood himself reckoned that the initial cost to the taxpayer of the Beveridge insurance scheme alone would probably come to £400 million a year.[11]

It was the British Employers' Federation who, in a paper circulated to the Committee on Reconstruction Priorities, pointed out other aspects of the Beveridge Plan which did not make sense as 'corporate strategy'. Beveridge, in pursuit of a characteristically idealistic principle of 'equality' and a related wish to remove the stigma of 'the Poor Law' and the means test from those in receipt of welfare aid, had based his scheme on universal membership by every citizen, whether he needed state welfare handouts or not. While the British Employers' Federation expressed itself in favour of abolishing Want, it argued against thus ladling out benefits to those who were *not* in want, a process which it believed to be wasteful and unessential, and which 'rather calls for consideration from the standpoint of its *desirability* in relation to the country's post-war obligations generally and its available resources'.[12] Noting the pre-war economic record of declining exports and a rising visible balance-of-payments deficit, as well as Britain's immediate economic difficulties, the Employers' Federation was none too sanguine about the likely available resources. And it argued, like Cherwell, that the full implications of the cost of the new welfare state could only be realised 'when it was borne in mind that the improvement of the Social Services is only one of the post-war social betterments which the people of this country are looking forward to', such as education and housing, and that out of the available resources would also have to be found defence, pensions and the interest on the National Debt.[13] The federation had other cogent points to make. The Beveridge Plan must ultimately form a charge on export prices. Its proposed handout to the unemployed really amounted to a minimum wage which would deter people from accepting jobs at a slightly higher figure.[14] For all these reasons the federation wanted the 'non-Want' aspects of the scheme to be related to other postwar obligations and demands as well as to Britain's postwar industrial performance.[15]

Underlying this whole debate about Beveridge and indeed the rest of New Jerusalem lay an insoluble puzzle – no one could know, although they could argue about, the postwar performance of the British economy, and the amount of resources this would yield. Nor, for that matter, could anyone know how fast and how far the costs of the welfare state and a national health service would grow. The Treasury did its best to guesstimate the performance of the economy. In a major paper in June 1943 in conjunction with the Central Statistical Office and the Economic Section of the Cabinet Office, it identified six factors as determining real national income per head. The first four comprised the ratio of 'occupied' wage-earners to the total population; the proportion of the 'occupied' who found work; the hours of work; and finally productivity; that is, the output achieved by an hour's work:

> Productivity . . . is itself the result of many factors: the health, skill, education and technical training of the workers; the efficiency of the management; the amount and quality of the capital equipment with which labour and management operate; the attention which is devoted to industrial research; the freedom of industry from restrictive practices; the ease with which new technical methods are spread through the industrial system; shifts from occupations of low to those of high productivity; and the sex and age composition of the labour force.[16]

The last two of the six factors were even harder to predict accurately, being the terms of international trade, and the income from overseas investments.[17]

As the memorandum acknowledged, changes in the calculations of any of these factors could produce major variations in the final out-turn, and in any case there were, it went on, wide divergences of view over such matters as the future level of unemployment, whether productivity had been speeded up by the war thanks to new factories with new equipment and greater standardisation, or whether dilution, blackout, problems with wartime transport and other factors had actually lowered efficiency. The memorandum averred that the best firms working for the Ministry of Aircraft Production and Ministry of Production, thanks to American methods and machines, now equalled American levels of productivity, and remarked that this had inspired the 'optimists' to guess at a 2½ per cent per annum increase in productivity during the war. On the other hand the 'pessimists' expected future 'friction' in adopting new methods, and saw no sign that the efficiency of the older industries had improved at all in wartime.[18] Groping around among all these imponderables, the Treasury paper finally came up with a total national income in 1948 of £6800 million, allowing for 35 per cent inflation 1938–48. Keynes in a dissenting note expressed his belief that the paper underestimated wartime improvements in productivity, and remarked that if the national income fell much below £7000 million, savings would not be enough to meet the cost of the building programme and other contemplated capital programmes. Kingsley Wood himself in a covering note said he would settle for £7000 million as a working basis: about equal in real terms to the national income in 1938. In the event, the net national product in 1948 in real terms was to prove about one-seventh greater than in 1938.[19]

The 1943 Treasury guesstimate of future national income constituted sober enough guidance to the planning of national 'corporate strategy'. Its very caution, coupled with all the unresolvable uncertainties, implied a strategy in which expenditure was restricted to the essential, and in which even the essential was carefully ranged in order of priority according to the relative contribution to national output and productivity. Yet in this context the Beveridge Plan made little sense, except as a future dividend from that Golden Age which might be achieved decades hence as the result of a British economic miracle. Politics being, however, the art of the possible, and the people's desire for Beveridge's welfare state being so urgent, corporate strategy had to yield to New Jerusalem: the government's White Paper offering a watered-down version of Beveridge (nevertheless costing public funds £240 million a year) eventually appeared in September 1944; and in 1946–8 the Labour government was finally to pass the legislation which created the free National Health Service as well as a virtually complete embodiment of the welfare state as conceived by Beveridge.

In the event the cost of the National Health Service alone, originally to cost £53 million a year extra, was nearly to double between 1949–50 and 1951–2,[20] so entirely vindicating Kingsley Wood's apprehensions, while the Labour government's creation of the welfare state was in any case only made possible by the American loan of $3.75 million negotiated by Keynes in 1945. In fact the most chilling wartime predictions of postwar penury and danger of economic collapse were to come true between 1945 and 1950, from the 'economic Dunkirk' (in Keynes's phrase) in late 1945 after the abrupt American ending of Lend–Lease, on through the first perilous postwar balance-of-payments crisis of 1947 to the great emergency of summer 1949 when actual national bankruptcy seemed all too possible.[21] And in the long term the welfare state would become, just as Kingsley Wood forewarned, a prior charge on the national income of ever more monstrous size, and finally 40 per cent of all public expenditure, uncontrollably guzzling taxes which might have gone into productive investment and spewing them out again indiscriminately to the poor and the prosperous.[22]

*

The second far-reaching victory of New Jerusalem over corporate strategy in 1943–5 was won in the field of national resources for building and construction. From the very inception of the New Jerusalem movement, housing had supplied almost as inspiring a theme for its evangelists as social security from crib to coffin. MOI films,[23] *Picture Post*, ABCA *Current Affairs* booklets and assorted architectural prophets had all vouchsafed a vision of families each happy in its own bright labour-saving home in the garden-cities that would replace soot-begrimed Victorian slums. To New Jerusalemers it was no longer tolerable that a huge mass of the British population should continue to live in nineteenth-century 'camps for coolies', often sharing lavatories with several other families; and bringing up children in the squalor documented by the 1930s' social studies of such towns as Middlesbrough. They therefore pressed for an absolute national commitment to build enough new houses in the immediate postwar era to replace all such dwellings. The aim was desirable enough; the intention laudable enough. It was the timing that lay in question: the timing in relation to the crying need to repair and reconstruct Britain's productive apparatus and the infrastructure on which an efficient economy depends – the need for new factories and plants; new roads, new docks, a modern road and railway system; new schools and colleges. Was a commitment to a great programme of house building another example, like the Beveridge Plan, of declaring a dividend on the Golden Age before that dividend had been earned in fact?

The opening of the argument inside the coalition government over these crucial questions coincided at the beginning of 1943 with the parallel debate over the Beveridge Plan. A report on 'Post-War Housing Policy' by a committee of civil servants[24] reckoned that an additional 1 million houses would be needed after the war to replace slums and the houses destroyed or damaged in the war. By the year 1954 another 400,000 would be needed because of the expected increase in the number of families. At the same time decaying older properties would need steady replacement. All this would raise the total of new houses needed over ten to twelve years to 3½–4½ million.[25] To cope with such a programme as well as other new construction a labour-force of 1¼ million would be required by the fourth year of peace.

When the same committee came to consider the cost of all this construction and repair work, the reckoning amounted to £670 million, of which nearly half was in respect of new housing. The committee glumly drew the conclusion that to allocate more than £600 million to building construction, given a national rate of saving of less than £800 million, would starve other national needs, such as industry, of capital.[26] Despite this consideration and despite also the committee's estimate of the cost of new housing at well over twice that of all other new building, the Minister of Health (Health being the ministry then responsible for public-sector housing) was not dismayed. After consulting other departments, he wrote:

> It is certain that the country will expect an even more vigorous policy after this war [than before the war]. The next four million dwellings

> must be built more quickly than the last, and the work must be carried out, not haphazardly, but to a planned programme. . . . Every family who so desires should be able to live in a separate dwelling. . . .[27]

On 28 January 1943 the whole question came before the new Cabinet Committee on Reconstruction Priorities. The committee's mind was wonderfully sharpened by the need to decide a final draft of a White Paper on recruitment of a building labour-force, for it followed that this document would need to state the government's postwar housing target. Kingsley Wood, the Chancellor of the Exchequer, did not like the proposed building programme any more than in the same month and in the same committee he liked the Beveridge Plan. He pronounced himself against the 'formal declaration of Government policy involved in presentation of a White Paper. This would be interpreted as a definite commitment of a contractual nature between the Government and the industry.' If however his colleagues decided that such a declaration was necessary, 'he must ask for the deletion from the present draft of the statement that the postwar building programme would employ a labour force of 1,400,000 men within three years after the war.'[28] Such a labour-force implied a programme of new capital expenditure of about £570 million for building alone: 'This must be found out of a total of national savings estimated . . . at somewhere between £700 million and £800 million. This meant that the building programme was only possible at the expense of depriving other industries of their capital.'[29] It would therefore be 'most unwise' to make any declaration implying a capital allocation of a size required to employ 1,400,000 building workers. The Minister of Labour, Bevin, for his part asked for an 'authoritative statement' on the size of the programme and the labour-force so that he could persuade the building-craft unions in good time to accept dilution and the novel kinds of training. After discussion he eventually agreed to settle for a figure of 1,250,000 workers.[30]

When in July 1943 the Cabinet Committee on Reconstruction Priorities came back to this topic of postwar building priorities and resources the Minister of Works (Lord Reith, formerly director-general of the BBC, stern Presbyterian and improver of public taste and morals, a notable of the 'enlightened' Establishment) remarked that for the purposes of calculating possible new house building in the first two years after the war:

> it has been assumed that no factory construction would be allowed during this period, and that industries would be compelled to make use of existing factories constructed for the purposes of war production. In practice it might not be possible to apply this principle without some qualification. . . .[31]

However, although this overriding priority for house building was by now tacitly accepted as the basis for allotting construction resources, it was challenged in September 1943 by the President of the Board of Trade, Hugh Dalton, wearing on this occasion his homburg as a minister of commerce and industry rather than his shovel-hat as a prominent believer in New

Jerusalem. He averred that 'in many cases industrial building – e.g., the rebuilding of bombed factories, the conversion of war factories to peace-time purposes and some new factory building – would be no less urgent than the building of new houses.'[32] The meeting got no further, however, than blandly agreeing that a plan for the postwar control of building was needed, with priority allotted on the basis of relative urgency irrespective of the type of construction.[33]

The argument rumbled on through 1944. On 11 January yet another committee within the elaborate and cumbrous Whitehall machinery for milling reconstruction problems[34] noted in a report:

> If the attempt is made to meet all the housing deficiencies within the first few years, there is the possibility that the consequent absorption of resources may be such as to embarrass the execution of other desirable forms of capital construction. . . .[35]

But eleven days later a memorandum by the Minister of Reconstruction himself, Lord Woolton, called for targets of 100,000–200,000 permanent houses by the end of the first year after the war with Germany, and a further 180,000–200,000 by the end of the second year. Lord Woolton (Manchester Grammar School, BSc at Manchester University), the former Fred Marquis and chairman of the Lewis department stores, had once been a warden of a dockland social settlement in Liverpool, and having seen slums at first hand his nonconformist social conscience got the better of his businessman's hard-headedness over housing.

Only a couple of months later, however, in March 1944, a committee on postwar building came up with some less appealing accountancy, by which it reckoned that repair of war damage, making good accumulated arrears of maintenance and removing defence works would alone cost £480 million and demand 1,405,000 man-hours of labour. This, according to the committee, would reduce new house building to a total of 194,000 completions in the first two years of peace.[36] Nevertheless this committee still recommended that two-thirds of the available labour-force should be deployed on building new houses; and its view was to carry decisive weight in a fresh outburst of debate in June and July 1944 about the fundamental strategy of construction priorities. The Paymaster-General (now C. G. Crookshank) feared that the total labour-force fixed by the 1943 White Paper was too ambitious at 1,250,000; he wanted it dropped to 1 million. A powerful memorandum by the Secretary to the Department of Overseas Trade, Harcourt Johnstone (and therefore a person close to the frontline realities of the coming export battle), attacked the current assumptions over housing policy, on the fundamental grounds that the contemplated programme was too large and too rapid. Why, he asked, tear down and replace good houses, involving the 'wholesale ejection of people from their homes'?[37] The British, he added, had no wish to see the appearance of their familiar towns transformed. Having thus prophesied, and warned against, the social catastrophe to be wreaked by the arrogance of town planners and city councils in the 1960s, Johnstone proceeded devastatingly to point out the inconsistency of the current housing programme with the realities of Britain's postwar situation and the dictates of sound 'corporate strategy':

> We shall have many calls upon our available resources. More may have to be devoted to arms for international policing; we shall undoubtedly have to export many more goods in order to acquire the pre-war level of imports; the social security plans entail spending resources to provide goods for those otherwise in 'want'; the condition of badly paid labour is to be improved; all these extra payments are not to be mere pieces of paper but are designed to increase the quantity of goods that the classes affected will consume and require to have produced for them. . . .[38]

In his view there would as a consequence be no spare building labour for unnecessary purposes. Johnstone then proceeded to the question of financing the proposed building programme – which would fall mainly on the middle-class taxpayer: 'The annual capital expenditure proposed [in a joint memorandum by the Ministers of Works and Labour in July 1943][39] exceeds by a considerable amount the total consumption in excess of £500 p.a. of all people in Great Britain with more than £500 a year. . . .'[40] Labour generally too would be short after the war with Germany, especially while the Japanese war continued, and so 'it would surely not be justifiable to send new recruits to the [building] industry to be trained. This would have to be at the sacrifice of some urgent need – such as additional manpower for the export industries.'[41] Johnstone therefore asked for these points to be cleared up before the government gave approval to plan to build 3–4 million houses in ten to twelve years.

But the Minister of Health and the Secretary of State for Scotland, in memoranda of their own,[42] wanted no amendment to the March 1943 White Paper on training for the building industry, no reduction in its proposed labour-force of 1,250,000. They argued that agreements had already been made with the building industry for a new apprenticeship scheme, while a new adult training scheme was now coming into operation. When the Reconstruction Committee came to discuss these contrary views on 3 July 1944, it simply took note of all three memoranda and agreed that there was no need to alter the policy enunciated in the White Paper. Thus far, then, the realists or corporate strategists were losing the argument. Yet in an each-way bet characteristic of committees, the minutes of this meeting also record a conviction that at least in the first postwar decade more building labour would be needed than before the war on industrial construction or adaptation 'in order to secure better conditions for the workers and more efficient production'.[43] The committee remained uncertain, however, 'whether this increased demand for industrial building would extend into the second post-war decade'.

On 8 September the Minister of Reconstruction again told his committee that he regarded housing as the most urgent of problems, especially in London; and the Minister of Health backed him by saying that there should be no reduction in the agreed proportion of two-thirds of building resources to be devoted to housing.[44] In January 1945 the whole question of priorities was analysed afresh in a joint memorandum by the Ministers of Reconstruction and of Works. As blessed by the War Cabinet Reconstruction Committee at a meeting on 29 January, this memorandum provided the final strategy bequeathed by the wartime coalition government to its successor for apportioning the national resources in construction. It allotted 127,000 man-years and £56 million in the first year of peace to building new houses; 81,000 man-years and £36 million to all other types of new building – industrial, infrastructure, public utilities, educational buildings, health, R and D establishments.[45] The joint authors of the memorandum had therefore to carve up the £36 million with the finesse of surgeons. Trade and industry received a meagre portion of £14 million – a quarter of housing's ration. Even so, the Minister of Health in the course of discussion on the paper asked that the proportion of resources going to housing should be raised from the present 66⅔ per cent to the 70 per cent originally agreed in March 1943.[46] The Reconstruction Committee nevertheless decided to approve the allocations recommended in the memorandum, with the proviso that the Minister of Works should review the possibilities for housing after six months.

Thus did the wartime coalition finally choose a construction policy of parlours before plant. In March 1945 there followed the White Paper on housing policy which publicly nailed postwar governments to a minimum target of 3–4 million new houses in ten to twelve years.[47] Even this figure proved too mean and modest for the Labour Party, surfing its way to victory in the general election of June 1945 on the sweeping wave of New Jerusalemism, and it grandly raised the bidding to 4–5 million. Given that Gallup Polls revealed that housing came second only to social security in the minds of voters, the gesture proved shrewd as well as grand. Yet this was only the beginning of two decades of competitive huckstering between the Labour and Conservative parties in promising new houses to the electors, always at the expense of new industrial construction, new infrastructure and a new communications network; and Macmillan's successful house-building drive as Minister of Housing in Churchill's government of 1951–5 was to be particularly damaging in this respect, since this was the period when West Germany and Japan, with freshly re-equipped industrial machines, were making their initial breakthroughs in world markets.[48]

It was of course to be one of the favourite British 'wooden legs' excusing Britain's relative industrial decline after the Second World War that Germany and Japan had been fortunate in having to rebuild their industries from the foundations upwards thanks to the destruction wrought by the allied air forces, whereas Britain, cursed by victory, had been forced to struggle on with her existing factories and infrastructure. The wartime documentary record gives the lie to this comforting British myth. It was Britain's own free choice – the choice of governments and electorate alike – to relegate the physical re-creation of her industrial base to a very poor second place in her order of building priorities. Instead of starting with a new workshop so as to become rich enough to afford a new family villa, John Bull opted for the villa straightaway – even though he happened to be bankrupt at the time.

The problem could be dissected geographically, in which case it appeared to be that of the 'distressed areas'. It could be dissected industrially, in which case it appeared to be that of decayed heavies like iron and steel and shipbuilding. It could be dissected in terms of employment, in which case it appeared to be that of 17–25 per cent out of work before the war. It could be dissected socially, in which case it appeared to be that of the unhealthy, ill-housed, ill-nourished and ill-educated working mass. But it still remained the same problem, the most intractable of all mid-twentieth-century Britain's handicaps – in other words, the problem represented by the entire legacy of the first industrial revolution.

There were at base two possible broad strategies of response. The problem could be attacked frontally by a comprehensive programme of industrial and social reconstruction at stupendous cost in national resources. Or it could be outflanked by using those resources to promote a new technological revolution elsewhere in 'green fields' unencumbered by the material and psychological detritus of the past. The pattern of natural evolution had already become clear enough between the world wars, with the 'distressed' or 'Special' areas more and more evidently a species at the end of its evolutionary line,[49] and with a new species, in the form of second-industrial-revolution industries, spontaneously evolving in southern England better fitted for survival in the prevailing world-market environment. As early as 1928 the Industrial Transference Board had percipiently concluded that the answer to the problem of the old industrial regions was not state encouragement of new industries within them, but emigration from them:

> It is a bad thing to tell numbers of men and even whole counties that unless they leave all their familiar surroundings they will not be able to earn a living, but we should be shirking every inference from the fact, if we did not emphasise this as the first and strongest of the lessons that our work has provided.[50]

All the experience of the 1930s in state policy aimed at bucking the natural evolutionary trend by bribing industry to set up operations in the Special Areas went to confirm this judgement. Down to September 1938 the Special Area Commissioners for England and Wales spent nearly £17 million, nearly half of it on amenities and services, with nearly £3 million going on direct inducements to firms, and yet all this resulted in just 15,000 jobs.[51] Down to 1941 the measures to promote industrial development in Special Areas in England, Wales and Scotland had created employment for only 35,000.[52] To examine a particular specimen in the form of a perennial problem area, Liverpool, the city corporation had laid out at its own expense a model estate at Speke, offered firms land on 999-year leases at a peppercorn rent and at a quarter to a half of the market value, with credit of 65 per cent towards the purchase of the lease and up to two-thirds the value of new factory buildings at 4 per cent interest over twenty years. This colossal bribe had brought in to Speke by March 1939 ten new factories, plus eighteen buildings – at a cost to Liverpool Corporation of a sum equal to the entire budget of the National Industrial Development Council of Wales for a year.[53] Despite all such efforts, only 17.5 per cent of new factories in the United Kingdom were built in the Special Areas in 1938 as against 40 per cent in greater London.[54] And indeed it hardly needed much insight to see why a company wishing to set up, say, a radio factory would choose outer London rather than Liverpool or Tyneside. In the dry language of a Board of Trade report in 1943 on the location of industry:

> Before the war, when remedial measures were applied to the Special Areas, they were already suffering from the handicaps, resulting from unemployment and poverty, of sub-standard social services. The land was cluttered with industrial waste and ruin. Such conditions were forbidding to industrial enterprise. . . .[55]

In the face of this clear pre-war evidence as to the natural evolutionary trend, the Royal Commission on the Distribution of the Industrial Population (chaired by Lord Justice Barlow) in a report of far-reaching importance in January 1940 came down decisively in favour of government restriction on industrial development in the South-east by means of licensing.[56] The Barlow Commission wished thereby not only to halt the strong spontaneous drift of population in this direction, but also to buttress efforts to induce firms to set up new operations in the old Victorian conurbations. It desired, so it wrote, a reasonable balance and diversification of industries throughout the country. At the same time, the Barlow Report did take note of certain contradictions that were in the event to bedevil wartime government evolution of policy with regard to the Special Areas:

> Undoubtedly a principal national consideration is the successful conduct of industry: any control which fatally hampered or handicapped industry would in any Western nation, especially in one so highly industrialised and so dependent on manufactures as Great Britain, deal a blow of the gravest character to the national existence. . . . But while making all necessary allowances on that account, when conditions affecting the health or well-being rather than the wealth of the State demand attention, when slums, defective sanitation, noise, air pollution and traffic congestion are found to constitute disadvantages, if not dangers, to the community, when the problem, in fact, becomes social in texture rather than economic, then modern civilisation may well require a regulating authority of some kind to step in and take reasonable measures for the protection of the general and national interests. . . .[57]

The report moreover had its own contradictions, for it called not only for effective measures to promote new industries in old conurbations by means of limiting development in the South-east, but also, on social and environmental grounds, for the large-scale dispersal of industry and population from these same old conurbations – a neat double that was to perplex the report's Whitehall readership. Nonetheless the Barlow Report remained a basic text within the government postwar-planning machinery – just as in the country at large it was to provide another of the major blueprints brandished by apostles of New Jerusalem in their crusade against the limiting nature of reality.

And in grappling with the core problem of the Special Areas and employment combined, the wartime coalition government in fact found itself torn yet again, just as over social security and building resources, between the opposing pulls of New Jerusalem and corporate strategy, or, in the words of the Barlow Report, the 'social' and the 'economic'; torn as well between perpetuating the industrially old and pursuing the new. When early in 1941, the new Cabinet Committee on Reconstruction referred the Barlow Report to a special sub-committee on the location of industry, Arthur Greenwood, the Minister without Portfolio, a working-class Labour Party intellectual sitting for the industrial seat of Wakefield, favoured this sub-committee with a memorandum on the topic in which he pronounced against any policy that would depopulate Britain's Victorian industrial areas:

> I think it must be accepted as a general principle that the long accepted industrial centres cannot be uprooted. In these centres there is a century-old accumulated wealth of resources. They have developed their industrial facilities, supported by a transport system, public utility services, power supply and labour. Behind all this stands organised municipal life with all its social services and amenities. . . . We must, I suggest, safeguard what we hold. . . .[58]

Given the actual condition of that 'wealth of resources' to which Greenwood referred, he was in danger of making on a grander scale an error like the one of which an American steel expert had accused the British steel industry in the 1920s – 'regarding obsolete plant as assets when in reality they were liabilities' (see above p. 101). In pursuit of this howler Greenwood proceeded to rule against new 'green-field' development:

> A policy of general dispersal would . . . involve the country in unnecessary capital construction at a time when its resources are depleted, and would postpone and would indeed imperil the restoration of national prosperity. [It would] cause indefensible hardship (leading to demands for compensation) to persons who have invested capital in the older industrial centres.[59]

His sub-committee on the location of industry agreed with him, opening its report on 25 June 1941 by enunciating two general principles: one, 'that the long established layout of the industrial field should be accepted'; and two, 'that future industrial creation should be controlled with a single eye to broad national interests. . .'.[60] It was left to later Whitehall bodies to argue about what constituted 'broad national interests' in regard to industrial development, about the order of priority in which such interests ought to be ranged, and, for that matter, to argue about the contradictions at the heart of the Barlow Commission's own recommendations. In June 1943, for instance, in a meeting which also disputed the relative priority of house building and factory building, a committee of senior civil servants on postwar internal economic problems remarked that it 'would be difficult to take into account at the same time both the new need for avoiding local unemployment (a short-term problem) and the need for dispersing congested areas (a long-term problem), since these two aims were to some extent in conflict.'[61]

It was in the spring and summer of 1943, when the Whitehall arguments over the proposed welfare state were also at their height, that the battle was really joined between the New Jerusalemers and the corporate strategists over the whole question of the location of industry and the Special Areas. Hugh Dalton, an ambiguous figure in the whole debate over postwar domestic policy, wore on this topic his shovel-hat as a Christian and socialist rather than as on a previous occasion the homburg of a trader. In a paper in May 1943 linking the questions of unemployment and the depressed areas,[62] he argued that Keynesian boosting of total demand would not solve the unemployment problems of the depressed areas, but that special steps would be needed, otherwise the pre-war problem 'will repeat itself with appalling exactitude. All the old "Special Areas", with the possible exception of West Cumberland, will be depressed again, and there will probably be some new depressed areas as well.' And he noted that outside such areas Britain had attained in peacetime 'full employment' as defined by Beveridge. Dalton averred that emigration of labour from the depressed areas could not offer an answer:

> That the inhabitants should move to other areas, in sufficient numbers for the desired result, would involve migration on such a scale as to leave derelict not merely a multitude of small villages, but many fair sized towns. Local purchasing power would continually decline by reason of the emigration. Ruin and unemployment would spread, ever more widely, among those who remained. Local rates would crush the residue of ratepayers, and fixed capital, – in the form of buildings of all kinds, roads and public utilities, – would either be left unused or used to only a small fraction of capacity. . . . Pressed far enough to be 'effective', 'mobility' means murder of whole townships. Such a policy opens up very grim prospects. It cannot, in my view, be accepted.[63]

This reads remarkably like clairvoyance of the actual fate of such urban regions as Liverpool, Clydeside or the North-east in the 1970s and 1980s, once the postwar boom had become finally spent; a fate in spite of every expedient of Special Area policy and the ladling out of rising quantities of state aid.[64] Dalton clearly accepted that, left to the natural course of events, all this was bound to happen; that, given the evidence, the depressed areas must be accounted an outmoded industrial-cum-social species on the way to extinction. But here was a reality which, because of his beliefs and background, he could only reject. He therefore vehemently attacked a paper by the Chancellor of the Exchequer, Kingsley Wood, that scourge of utopians, on the maintenance of employment exactly for accepting that 'there is some ideal geographical distribution of industry, in which deliberate state control of location plays no part,' and which is achieved by mobility of labour:

> This assumption seems to me to be largely unreal. It leaves out of account many vital national interests. To act on it, without much qualification, would bring disastrous social consequences. . . . If we do nothing to control location, I should anticipate, for example, that there should be a strong drift of industry and population to an ever-greater London and an ever-greater Birmingham, with corresponding depopulation elsewhere. . . . I cannot believe that this is the best setting for the next chapter of the English Saga.[65]

The alternative first proffered by the Barlow Report and thereafter by New Jerusalemers like Dalton was for the state artificially to perpetuate the endangered species in the industrial equivalents of zoos or wild-life reserves.

In October another weighty report on the location of industry, this time prepared by Dalton's own department in consultation with the Ministries of Labour and Town and Country Planning and the Scottish Office, thumped down on to the desks of Whitehall.[66] It was based on thorough field investigations in the depressed areas, into their industries and their general social scene, which only served to confirm how dim were their future prospects, how guttering the flame of indigenous enterprise, capability and adaptation. As the report admitted, 'the surveys do little more than confirm our present knowledge.' But it hoped that if a general expansion of the economy took place after the war, the task of shoring up the Special Areas 'will not be so formidable as it appeared in the despondent era before the war'.[67] Nonetheless:

> If, however, measures are not taken to induce industrialists to go to the depressed areas or to direct production to them, there is danger that those areas will be drained of their mobile workers, while immobile workers may be left unemployed in them even during a time of active trade in the country as a whole. . . .[68]

The Board of Trade therefore laid out detailed proposals along the lines of the Barlow Report for thwarting this natural process, on the assumption that pre-war Special Area policy had only failed because of 'the inadequacy of the measures applied'. The proposed measures ranged from preferential treatment in regard to the placing of government contracts, through improved capital grants and other financial inducements to set up shop amid the slagheaps, to a massive programme to rehabilitate the entire environment bequeathed by the first industrial revolution. But the most drastic proposal – in fact, on the recommendation of the Ministry of Town and Country Planning – was for a total ban on further industrial development in the London area and the Home Counties and even possibly greater Birmingham; that is to say, an attempt by administrative fiat directly to block and reverse the evolutionary processes of extinction and survival.

The Board of Trade memorandum did however acknowledge that there were other national economic interests apart from 'the need to help the neglected areas requiring industrial development'.[69] In fact, in a single short paragraph among fifty-five, mostly long, it went so far as to state:

> Vital though it is to find a solution for the problems indicated above, *our first consideration must be to raise the efficiency of industry as a whole, and particularly to stimulate the export industries.* In other words, if there should be a sharp conflict between industrial efficiency and export considerations on the one hand and location policy on the other, the decision must go in favour of the former. In general, however, a successful location policy will help to increase industrial efficiency.[70]

Here indeed lay the whole crux of the question. How could it be argued that Britain's industrial efficiency and export competitiveness would be best promoted by blocking industrial development where it was naturally happening and instead trying artificially and expensively to induce it where it was not?

In a paragraph fascinatingly entitled 'Peaches on North Walls' the Board of Trade memorandum tentatively approached this question, then quickly backed away. Firms banned from developing where they wished would then have to decide, according to the memorandum, whether to go to some other area or 'abandon their project'. The Board of Trade hoped that 'some at least' would choose to go to 'Development Areas' (the new euphemism in place of 'Special Areas'). It accepted however that the suggested policy of banning was already being criticised on the ground that 'it may kill some industrial expansion. This criticism has recently been put in this form "you can order that peaches shall not be grown on South Walls but that will not make them ripen on North Walls."' Nonetheless the Board of Trade memorandum failed to answer this criticism, taking refuge in a vague belief that companies did not mind where they installed new plants, and thus entirely begging the question of the fundamental unattractiveness of the Development Areas in comparison with the South-east – an unattractiveness which extended beyond the environment and the nature of the available workforce to inferiority of education and training provision.

Moreover, despite its length and thoroughgoing detail the Board of Trade's analysis is conspicuous for a certain important omission – that of any estimated costing of the complete package which it was recommending as able to turn the Special Areas into the equal of the Home Counties in allure to new technology and in competitive efficiency. It therefore saved itself from having to explain how these resources could be found by an impoverished country on top of the proposed welfare state and a great housing programme; or how this would prove a cost-effective national investment compared with other possible ways of spending money on technological development.

However, along with the Barlow Report this Board of Trade memorandum supplied the classic 'enlightened' Establishment case for a heavy national commitment to resuscitating the Special Areas. As such it was quickly attacked by those in Whitehall who gave absolute priority to industrial efficiency and Britain's postwar ability to survive and prosper. In particular the critics applied the toes of their boots to the fudging reference in the Board of Trade memorandum to the effect that while efficiency must come first, it would be actually *promoted* by directed location of industry. Only two days after the Board of Trade paper had been circulated, the Economic Section of the Cabinet Office cogently pointed out with regard to the suggested policy of banning or licensing development that 'care must be taken not to make too great a sacrifice of efficiency':[71]

> Although the Board of Trade Review specifically assumes that the attainment of maximum efficiency coincides with the policy of encouraging industrial development in the depressed areas . . . the Ministry of Works points to the possible serious drawbacks. It is vitally necessary to be clear on this point. At best, the case for regarding the depressed areas as the most efficient areas for production is not proven; at worst there may be a big margin on the wrong side. There is, indeed, much evidence which leads us to suggest caution here.[72]

The Economic Section therefore wanted assistance to the depressed areas to be limited to nursing care only – removing certain special disadvantages such as insufficient access to capital or poor amenities, and continuing some financial help as in the 1930s. This could be 'accepted as the price of the removal of the social evils of localised unemployment. It may be that the cost will not be very great. . . .' The Economic Section also wanted clear channels of assistance so that an accounting test could be applied to the policy as a whole. It feared that under the Board of Trade's recommendations 'the measures of intervention proposed to assist depressed areas are so many and their effects incapable of measurement that, when all was done, we would not know which measures were responsible for the success of the policy, nor at what aggregate cost it had been achieved.'[73] And so it was to prove true of all regional aid measures down to the mid-1980s.

On 4 November 1943 a memorandum by the Minister of Aircraft Production, Stafford Cripps, that oddly realist Christian Socialist who in 1945 would urge the Labour Party not to promise some easy Utopia, cunningly lent support to the Board of Trade's single reference to the primacy of industrial efficiency over regional policy. Noting that Lancashire was no longer a depressed area thanks to new engineering industries, Cripps urged that help should be given to develop particular industries, not to towns or areas as such, nor to 'inevitably dying' industries.[74] Two days later the Minister of Supply, Sir Andrew Duncan, an industrialist, wrote that he was 'sceptical' about many of the Board of Trade's proposals, especially what he termed its 'artificial methods' for helping the depressed areas. He reckoned that the Board of Trade's stated first aim of raising industrial efficiency, especially with regard to exports, was indeed 'of overwhelming importance and the artificial direction of industry to Development Areas is unlikely on the whole to be compatible with it.' Pre-war experience showed that even when contracts were placed in Special Areas, much of the work had to be sub-contracted outside them: 'there were many examples of delays in deliveries on orders placed in Depressed Areas due to technical weaknesses and to the time taken to train labour.' In his view, 'In general a policy of banning would penalise the efficient and enterprising and, if effective, would involve a great loss of business in precisely those sections of industry which can make the greatest contributions to the general economic well-being.'[75]

This fundamental disagreement over regional policy still remained unresolved when the topic was discussed – along with full employment and housing – in a major report in January 1944 on economic and industrial strategy by yet another Whitehall body, the Steering Committee on Post-War Employment. The report pronounced itself in favour of inducements rather than compulsion as the means of attracting new industries into what were now formally renamed the 'Development Areas'. It also went to the heart of the whole problem of Britain's Victorian industrial legacy in a way that the Board of Trade report of 1943 had shirked:

> We must know whether the areas are handicapped, for example, by such matters as comparative inefficiency in their basic plants, or by unsatisfactory local communications both for workpeople and goods, for these are curable, and in a short time, or whether deeper causes are at work such as a long-term shift of demand or market, or an outworn but obstinate industrial tradition, or instability of labour.[76]

The committee failed, however, to ask itself whether an 'outworn but obstinate industrial tradition' in these areas might render 'inefficiency in their basic plants' not quite so curable in a short time. But it did make absolutely plain that regional policy ought not to be a kind of extension of the welfare state:

> The policy of preference and technical nursing which we have in mind can, of course, only be temporary and conditional. Nothing could be more dangerous than to give firms in the Development Areas the impression that they will be permanently carried by Government orders irrespective of their competitive position. . . .[77]

When this report came before the Cabinet Committee on Reconstruction, the split opened wider still between the corporate strategists and the New Jerusalemers. Dalton again argued: 'There was a danger of heavy local unemployment in certain areas early after the end of the war with Germany; and this called for a policy of guiding industries into those areas. . . .'[78] He wanted the government to issue a statement that while there would be no compulsion, it was in the national interest that firms wanting to open new factories should give priority to South Wales, the north-east coast, industrial Scotland and West Cumberland. The Minister of Production, however, Oliver Lyttelton, a worldly Old Etonian and formerly an officer in the Grenadier Guards, 'thought there was too great a tendency to consider the matter from the geographical point of view, namely how to induce firms to establish themselves in the Special Areas.' He wanted to put efficiency first and foremost as the criterion for locating industry:

> Thus, some of the Welsh Valleys could not be effectively used for industrial purposes, and, hard though it may be, it was better to remove the workers from these valleys and employ them elsewhere than to offer uneconomical inducements to firms to set up in these places. The Special Areas only represented a small proportion of the labour and industry of this country.[79]

Despite this unfashionable plea, the committee decided to authorise the President of the Board of Trade to tell industrialists that the government wished them to open factories in Special Areas. It agreed that the Minister for Reconstruction should draft a government statement on policy with regard to the location of industry.

Woolton's draft, 'The Balanced Distribution of Industry',[80] followed in March 1944. It broadly echoed the Barlow Report and the 1943 Board of Trade memorandum, placing social considerations well before economic: more a policy for a grant-making charity than an investment plan for an industrial conglomerate. For it urged that industry in the old industrial areas should be diversified in order to relieve the reliance on single or few industries and export markets. To achieve this, all proposed new factory developments should be notified to the Board of Trade, so that the board could 'exercise a substantial influence' over their location, even by means of actual prohibition in some areas (presumably those where firms would most wish to go). There should be special financial inducements to firms to set up amid Victorian dereliction – like easily available short-term and long-term capital. But this was not all: the government was also to stimulate 'a progressive programme of developing and modernising the capital equipment of these areas', such as communications, docks, harbours, housing, amenities, public services.

However, Woolton did not – any more than the Board of Trade in 1943 – put a cost on all this, or suggest how that cost might be found out of Britain's likely postwar resources along with competing projects of New Jerusalem; or show how this enormous investment could ever pay an adequate return on the capital. Nonetheless, his draft paid early dividends in the form of further statements on regional policy by the Minister of Aircraft Production, Sir Stafford Cripps, and the Minister of Town and Country Planning, W. S. Morrison. Cripps now reckoned that persuasion and inducements would not prove enough to bring new industries into depressed areas; this policy had failed before the war and had even proved difficult with wartime government powers. In any case he thought that unless new industries fitted naturally into the long-term economy of such areas, 'their prolonged survival would be extremely doubtful. An apparently successful "inducement" policy followed by a crop of bankruptcies or claims for State subsidies would be no contribution to the successful development of any area.'[81] Here was shrewd and farsighted counsel. But Cripps's own solution was to opt for even grander interventions – regional development authorities on the model of the Tennessee Valley Authority vested with vast powers and capital resources, all amounting in Cripps's words to a 'new approach in keeping with the great public enterprises of this war'.[82]

Morrison, though a Conservative, spoke for his new ministry in the purest tones of New Jerusalem:

> If untrammelled freedom of choice to the industrialist gives rise, as it has done in the past, first to workpeople being left high and dry, and then to whole social communities being left high and dry, with all that is thereby entailed in wastage of human and social capital [government has] a responsibility for seeing whether positive remedies cannot be applied. . . .[83]

In his opinion, therefore,

> The combined objectives should be efficient industry, balanced employment, balanced communities – all set within an expansionist economy of development. After the war the first step will be to correct a grave lack of balance, and this calls for short-term industrial incentives of a special kind. . . .[84]

And in the end it was this kind of cloudy but sun-suffused optimism which carried the day over the scepticism of the realists. For this was 1944: New Jerusalem had by now succeeded in converting government as well as people; and realism was out of fashion. Woolton's draft government statement on 'The Balanced Distribution of Industry' was duly approved by the Cabinet Reconstruction Committee and finally by Cabinet. It formed the basis of the Distribution of Industry Act, which was enacted in the last months of the wartime coalition in 1945. Under it in 1945–7 the postwar Labour government was faithfully to fulfil the intentions of the Barlow Commission and the 1943 Board of Trade report by using building licences and continuing wartime controls to force over 50 per cent of new industrial building into the Development Areas even though these only contained 20 per cent of the national population.[85] It was also to spend nearly £13 million in loans and grants in one year alone – a lavishness abruptly curtailed by the balance-of-payments crisis of 1947.[86]

Yet this marked only the first phase of persistent attempts by both Labour and Conservative governments to preserve and revive Britain's Victorian industrial regions. These attempts were invariably to be made in the face of technological realities, just as the wartime governmental critics had forewarned; and led to such futilities as bribing or compelling firms to set up new factories on industrial estates in depressed areas in the 1950s and 1960s, only for them to close in the 1970s and 1980s because of appalling productivity records – Courtaulds and Dunlop at Speke, Liverpool; or the Rootes car factory at Linwood near Glasgow.[87] There were also to be such major individual errors of corporate strategy as the decision in 1958 on political or sentimental grounds by the then Prime Minister, Harold Macmillan, not to allow the steel industry to build one huge strip mill of Japanese size in the Midlands near its principal customers, but to split the project into two smaller mills sited out in the Celtic fringes at Llanwern and Ravenscraig, neither of them big enough to enjoy the economies of scale of rival foreign plants.[88]

In the twenty years after 1962 alone aid to 'the Regions' was to mount up to a total of £20 billion (at 1982 prices), none of it adding to British productive capacity, but at best merely switching some of the growth from where it would have happened in any case to somewhere else.[89] Moreover, even after forty years of using the life-support machine of regional aid, Whitehall still did not know what good effect, if any, had been achieved, for the recommendation of the Economic Section of the Cabinet Office in 1943 that there should be a reliable accounting test had never been fulfilled. As a Department of Industry paper laid before the Public Accounts Committee in June 1981 admitted: 'The limitations of current analytical techniques and the quality of data prevented any precise indication of the positive benefits.'[90] Even less calculable were the possible *harmful* effects of regional policy in the forty years from 1945 because new industrial development took place in towns suffering from universally acknowledged basic disadvantages, not least the kind of workforce bequeathed by the conditioning process of the first industrial revolution. It may be asked how much more productive and profitable such development would have been if it had occurred in areas where the industrial mentality of management and workforce as well as the physical environment was a 'green-field' site. No certain answer is possible, although examples of the fastest growing postwar technologies and economic regions – Japan, South Korea, the West and South-west of the United States – suggest, as common sense might suppose, that new species emerge and thrive better in new habitats.

What *is* certain is that forty years of regional policy wholly failed to fulfil the wartime hopes of the New Jerusalemers that it would achieve an equal balance of employment throughout the country. The rate of unemployment in the Victorian industrial areas remained in 1985 half as much again as that of the South-east of England – as it had been even during the postwar boom and 'full employment'.[91]

It was in fact with regard to employment policy as a whole (a topic always closely interlinked with the problem of the depressed areas) that the New Jerusalemers in the wartime coalition won yet another victory over the corporate strategists, with even more far-reaching consequences for Britain's ability to adapt and prosper in the postwar era.

That mass unemployment must never be allowed to return had been from the start a fundamental tenet of New Jerusalemism, written by Harold Nicolson into the paper on 'why are we fighting?' laid before the War Cabinet as early as July 1940, and by Toynbee and Halifax into their joint draft statement on war aims in December that year. It supplied the theme for a glib article explaining how to secure 'Work for All' in *Picture Post*'s influential special issue 'A Plan for Britain' in January 1941, and for the speeches and writings of such New Jerusalem pressure groups in 1941 and 1942 as Archbishop Temple, the '1941 Committee' and Common Wealth. 'Idleness' constituted one of the five 'giant evils' from which, Beveridge announced at the end of 1942, 'New Britain' should be free. And at this same period a MOI survey of public opinion confirmed that the top postwar priority in people's minds was 'guaranteed jobs for all'.[92] Following the *succès fou* of the Beveridge Report on social security and the February 1943 run of anti-Conservative by-election victories, the War Premier himself in his broadcast on 21 March on postwar reconstruction committed the government to abolishing unemployment by Keynesian demand management. Thus in another field of public policy had the New Jerusalem movement succeeded in determining the limits of the politically possible; indeed of the politically inevitable.

When that same month Beveridge announced that he proposed to embark on another 'Beveridge Report', this time on full employment, Whitehall was stung into its own ponderous studies of the question. In May 1943 papers by the Economic Section of the War Cabinet Secretariat (in the person of Professor Lionel Robbins, a noted academic economist) and the President of the Board of Trade were circulated to the Reconstruction Priorities Committee.[93] In July this committee decided to set up the Steering Committee on Post-War Employment composed of the senior officials of the Ministry of Labour, Reconstruction Secretariat, Board of Trade, Treasury and Economic Section of the War Cabinet Secretariat. Its remit covered not only the maintenance of the general level of employment, but also other matters bearing on the question such as the location of industry, restrictive practices and investment.[94] Nonetheless, the discussions were to turn on one central issue: whether Keynes was right or not – whether full employment *could* be maintained by means of the government feeding money into the economy in order to keep general consumer demand at a level that would require virtually the entire available labour-force to satisfy it.

Dalton, for a start, had already argued in his May 1943 paper that so boosting aggregate demand would not cure the structural unemployment in the old industrial regions. In October 1943 the Permanent Secretary to the Treasury, Sir Richard Hopkins, submitted a memorandum to his colleagues on the new steering committee that distinguished between unemployment caused by low overall consumer demand and investment, and specific causes like loss of an export market or the obsolescence of an industry in the face of new technology.[95] The Treasury did not believe that structural employment would fade away in a climate of strong aggregate demand; it argued rather that 'the factor of structural adjustment deserves to be regarded as equally important and equally fundamental.'[96] Moreover, the Treasury expressed itself deeply unhappy about the prospect of inflating demand by pumping in public money at a time when Britain was going to be financially straitened and yet faced with heavy competing calls for state expenditure. It was strongly against adopting a policy of 'indefinite continuance of unbalanced budgets' with the implied burdensome increases in public debt and interest. Deficit financing was in its view *not* the right answer to structural unemployment:

> If the principles of deficit financing were to be applied in an attempt to solve a problem of unemployment which was basically one of structural readjustment, and were in fact to prove largely ineffective for this purpose, it must not be supposed that no harm would have been done. Our financial solvency might be seriously jeopardised with repercussions on our whole economic stability, on the standard of life and ultimately on employment itself.[97]

The Keynesian Economic Section of the War Cabinet Secretariat fiercely disagreed however: 'we believe that the evils which may follow from deficit financing are capable of being overcome and are in the last resort less serious than those of unemployment.'[98] It accused the Treasury of wanting an 'essentially passive' role for the state in respect of cyclical unemployment, and of rejecting all proposed measures for managing demand and investment, a posture which the Economic Section stigmatised as 'unduly pessimistic'.[99] In a memorandum two days later the Board of Trade took a middle position: it agreed with the Treasury that 'chronic structural, or rather local, unemployment' was likely to prove a major postwar problem; that was why it wanted special measures to help the depressed areas, measures which it saw as complementary to, not competitive with, policies aimed at maintaining high aggregate demand.[100]

Thus were the battle lines drawn between the Keynesians and the sceptics. Yet underlying the argument of the Keynesians, especially popularising Keynesians like Beveridge in his report on full employment in 1944, lay certain crucial fallacies.

For a start, except during the hurricane of the world slump, unemployment had never constituted a *general* problem in Britain, but a local and structural one, just as the Board of Trade and the Treasury argued in 1943. Demand and investment in 1938 had been sufficient to maintain unemployment in South-east England at 8 per cent without government boosting – Keynes's and Beveridge's own definition of *full* employment. It was the rates of unemployment in the black patches on the map representing Victorian heavy industry and Victorian industrial areas at around 18 per cent overall and even higher in some towns that had pulled up the national average in 1938 to an apparently unacceptable level of 13 per cent. Half a century later the pattern would remain broadly unchanged – a rate of 9–10 per cent in the South-east, about equal to West Germany's, but an average of 16 per cent elsewhere.[101] As all the detailed evidence makes abundantly plain, the problem of the areas of high unemployment in the 1930s stemmed from their own obsoleteness as an industrial system, a problem not to be cured, only temporarily masked, by turning up the Keynesian burner under the economy as a whole. Such indiscriminate stimulation of purchasing power could not in the long term induce the customer to buy old-fashioned, ill-designed, ill-made and over-priced products in preference to foreign goods which were none of these things. Indeed, because of the wide superiority of imported goods, Keynesian boosting of purchasing power would simply benefit foreign industry, so endangering the balance of payments – as had large-scale purchases of equipment abroad during pre-war rearmament.

Then again, New Jerusalemers like Beveridge fallaciously looked at the British wartime experience as proof that, in his words, 'unemployment disappears and all men have worth when the State sets up unlimited demand for a common purpose. By the spectacular achievement of its planned economy war shows how great is the waste of unemployment.'[102] Yet wartime 'full employment' was in truth entirely bogus and therefore quite misleading as a guide to future policy. In the first place, the British war economy as a whole was artificial, kept going by American aid and Commonwealth credit instead of paying its own way by successful exports, and so nothing about it bore any relevance to peacetime conditions, as was indeed pointed out in 1944 by the Committee on Post-War Employment.[103] Secondly, wartime 'full employment' had in no sense been secured by an across-the-board boosting of demand and investment of a Keynesian kind. On the contrary, while some parts of the economy massively grew, other parts massively shrank. Manpower in coal mining, a pre-war unemployment black spot, actually dwindled during the war.[104] And while the special wartime need for warships and merchant ships certainly solved the grievous structural unemployment of the shipyard towns of the North-east, raising the total employed in the whole shipbuilding industry from 134,000 in 1939 to 260,000 in 1943,[105] how could Keynesian demand management serve to secure enough foreign orders in peacetime against ferocious competition to continue this happy situation?

The total manpower (not including women) employed in British manufacturing industry rose by 705,000 between June 1939 and the wartime peak in June 1943 – by no means enough to swallow up the 1,013,000 national total of unemployed males in 1939.[106] By far the biggest share of this increase of 705,000, plus the colossal rise in the number of women employed in manufacturing industry from half a million in 1939 to nearly 2 million in 1943, was gulped by the new technologies, not by the old – machine tools, light engineering and, above all, the aircraft industry and its sub-contractors (up from 35,000 in 1935 to 1,700,000 in 1943).[107] In any case, to make possible the industrial war effort as a whole and supply manpower for the armed services, employment in other sectors of the economy not essential in wartime but highly important to peacetime prosperity – food, drink, clothing, building, civil engineering, commerce and banking – had had to be cut back by no fewer than 3½ million.[108]

In point of fact, total employment in all sectors of the British productive economy (that is, other than the armed and public services, education, health, etc.) did *not* rise during the Second World War, but actually *fell* by some 1,600,000[109] – hardly the magic cure for general unemployment, let alone structural unemployment, imagined by pundits like Beveridge.

The magic wartime cure was actually provided by the manpower demands of the armed forces of the Crown, of civil defence and of the swollen wartime bureaucracy; overwhelmingly the armed forces, which rose from half a million men and women in 1939 to just over 5 million in 1943;[110] a figure more than equal to the 1939 total of unemployed plus the manpower shed by non-essential economic sectors in wartime.

The 'full employment' of the Second World War could delude in other ways still, for it included the brazier-watchers in ship repairing and the clock jumpers in shipbuilding; the strikers; the card-players and cigarette-lighter makers in the aircraft and motor-vehicle industries; – the whole gamut of low British productivity tolerated by management during the war and revealed by the documentary evidence (see above Chapters Four to Nine). On the basis of German productivity, let alone American, British industry was carrying surplus fat to an average extent of possibly a quarter of the workforce;[111] personnel essentially 'unemployed' even though attending a place of work and being paid there. As the Economic Section of the War Cabinet Secretariat drily pointed out in October 1943, 'any connection between productive efficiency and full employment is indirect and, indeed, ambiguous.'[112]

On 10 January 1944 the Steering Committee on Post-War Employment crowned its long debates by producing a 78-page survey of postwar home and international trade prospects, location of industry, training, Keynesian demand management, control of investment and much else. On the central question of demand management as a cure for unemployment and a tonic for prosperity, the report, though hedging its bets, broadly manifested a victory of the Keynesians of the Economic Section over the realists of the Treasury: 'The essence of the kind of policy here contemplated is this: so to plan the controllable items in total national expenditure that the whole is maintained at such a rate as to keep employment as constant as possible at a relatively high level.'[113] To secure this the committee pronounced itself as being not against a small creeping inflation. On the other hand it acknowledged that maintenance of aggregate demand was not 'a universal panacea' – especially with regard to backward industries and their export markets:

> An expansion of home demand will not do much in the short run to alleviate the unemployment so created in the export trades. In certain cases this development will give rise to an adverse balance of payments which would justify an adaptation of the foreign exchange rate. . . .[114]

Thus did the committee anticipate the devaluations of sterling in the postwar era by which successive governments sought in vain to countervail the effects of poor British product design, late delivery and inefficient service by manipulating a temporary price advantage.

However, the committee, while in general committing itself to a Keynesian strategy, was careful to say that 'aggregate demand is not simply a tap which can be turned on or off, according to the state of trade, and which will provide an infallible remedy for all forms of unemployment.'[115]

It therefore looked to other strategies as well – greater mobility of labour, better training, the modernisation of old industrial areas by means of regional policy, the general raising of British industry's efficiency.[116] The committee failed, however, to address itself to the crucial question of whether its central policy of maintaining 'full employment' would help or hinder these other strategies, although the behaviour of British industry and its personnel under conditions of wartime 'full employment' was hardly encouraging. To cite again the judgement of the Economic Section of the War Cabinet Secretariat, the connection between full employment and productive efficiency was 'indirect and, indeed, ambiguous'.

When the War Cabinet Reconstruction Committee began its own discussion of this report on 21 January 1944, it was quick to agree that the government should issue a public statement on employment policy without delay. Moreover, consensus extended to the basic strategy proposed by the report:

> There were general agreements as to the importance of the recognition given in the Report to the principle of maintaining aggregate demand at a high level, with a view to avoiding at least the severest fluctuations in the level of unemployment; and it was felt that this principle should be placed in the fore-front of the proposed White Paper.
>
> At the same time it was recognised that structural unemployment arising in particular industries or particular areas could not be dealt with by this method alone.[117]

Nevertheless, some unidentified realists on the committee are recorded as thinking that the report 'paid insufficient attention to international relations and the problem of the foreign balance'.[118] In a later meeting of the Reconstruction Committee about this report in May 1944, there was also argument as to the advisability of running budget deficits in order to maintain demand, and the view prevailed that for the sake of the international stability of sterling 'it was necessary not only to be, but appear, prudent in our financial policies.'[119]

The White Paper on employment policy[120] that finally emerged that month from the Reconstruction Committee's editing of the original report therefore committed itself to achieving full employment by means of Keynesian policy while at the same time hedging this promise about with cautious references to this not being a universal cure. But Beveridge's own report on the subject contained of course no such boringly unfashionable quibbles. He was quite certain not only that pumping money in appropriate quantities into the economy would ensure that 'the whole man-power of the country' was used – no complications here about structural unemployment, a problem his book simply skated over – but also that there would be no nasty side-effects such as enhanced trade-union power leading to wage inflation, overmanning or preservation of demarcations. On the contrary, in Beveridge's opinion, full employment would render such defensive measures as restrictive practices unnecessary, while he averred that British unions and workpeople had sufficiently demonstrated their sense of responsibility and citizenship to justify the expectation that there would be no slackness at work or excessive wage demands.[121] And it was this sort of glib confidence rather than cavils and caution that the nation wanted to hear in 1944, with the end of the war in sight, and New Jerusalem shimmering ever more brightly beyond.

In this way future postwar governments became finally committed to the maintenance of 'full employment' as the overriding objective of economic policy – committed at the very minimum to the qualified Keynesianism of the White Paper, but, in the expectation of public opinion, to all that Beveridge promised. Nevertheless, maintaining 'full employment' in peacetime was to prove easy enough to begin with: according to a Whitehall committee in August 1945 at the end of the war with Japan, the pre-war figure of 1,300,000 unemployed was 'more than offset' by the expected continuing requirements of the armed services, while falling productivity in industry meant that more labour rather than less would now be needed to achieve 1939 levels of production[122] – a statement which serves as apt enough comment on full employment past and full employment yet to come, and all the debate thereon.

The influence of New Jerusalem as the spirit of the age on government postwar planning went deeper than these specific victories in regard to the welfare state, regional policy and full employment; it tipped the whole balance of Whitehall's collective attention towards desirable social goals rather than industrial performance. Between 1941 and 1945 some 400 memoranda were submitted to the principal War Cabinet committees on reconstruction which were responsible for co-ordinating into an overall strategy all the studies by the complicated and often overlapping machinery of sub-committees. Yet of these 400 memoranda only 64 dealt with Britain's problems and future as an industrial exporting nation, as against 170 devoted to various aspects of New Jerusalem.[123] Out of over ninety agenda items discussed by the War Cabinet Reconstruction Committee between December 1943 and July 1944, for instance, only five were directly concerned with industrial efficiency as such, and fifty-three with New Jerusalem topics.[124] It is therefore hardly astonishing that the cumulative balance of future commitments made strange corporate strategy for carrying Britain from her current straits to future competitive success. There was, for example, the January 1945 memorandum on new construction, ultimately to form the basis of government policy, which envisaged £56 million for new domestic housing in the first year of peace; only £14 million on new buildings for industry and trade. This modest sum, a mere fourteenth of what the state had spent on new building for the aircraft industry alone since 1939, came in fact to £4.5 million less than the 1944 expenditure on free milk and vitamins for children.[125]

The earlier 1943 Treasury survey of capital expenditure after the war had assumed that capital investment in all industry other than transport and public utilities would be a third higher in real terms in 1948 than in 1938, an assumption which it considered 'appropriate to a policy of increasing efficiency by modernisation of equipment'.[126] Nevertheless this capital investment, at a total of £173 million (of which only £62 million would be net added investment rather than repairs, maintenance and depreciation), was a poor enough sum to devote to the making good of what was by then well recognised to be the ramshackle condition of British industry – amounting to no more than 2½ per cent of what the Treasury estimated as the national income for 1948.[127] In the event capital investment in industry was to rise to 5 per cent of gross national product (GNP) by 1951 – which compares with West Germany's 15 per cent by that time.[128] Thus Britain's low postwar level of industrial investment, seen by commentators as a major factor in her relative decline, was actually anticipated and complacently allowed for in wartime government planning. Moreover, it must be recalled that this estimate of £62 million a year on new industrial capital development amounts to only about a fifth of the extra annual cost of the government's proposed new social security scheme and national health service, as estimated in 1944.[129]

In any case, the 1943 forecast of industrial investment in 1948 did not represent a recommended commitment of *state* funding; it was merely a hopeful guesstimate of what might be forthcoming from the normal sources of commercial investment. In all the planning documents for the postwar era there is no equivalent at all of the vast national programmes of industrial development and modernisation under government sponsorship represented by pre-war and wartime rearmament – £900 million invested by the state between 1939 and 1945; £350 million invested in new factories and tools for the aircraft industry alone between 1935 and 1943.[130] Nor were there radical plans afoot for bringing Britain's infrastructure and transport system up to date, even though the railways – worn out by war and poor maintenance – were largely Victorian in fixed equipment; even though the docks and canals were likewise Victorian or even Georgian in layout, and their equipment such as cranage or haulage ancient; and even though British roads were recognised in wartime Whitehall as the legacy of the pre-motor era and entirely unsuitable for a modern industrial country. At the beginning of 1945 capital expenditure over the entire field of transport in the first year of peace was projected at £750,000 – a third of that allocated in the same memorandum to building new health facilities.[131] The Treasury guesstimate of national capital expenditure in 1948 had allotted £22 million to net added investment in the railways, including some electrification, and £18.5 million to new work on roads and bridges; investments no larger in real terms than those in 1938.[132]

Thus British wartime forecasts of capital investment did not even begin to conceive of the root-and-branch rebuilding of the national transport system or the massive modernisation and development of industry that would take place in European countries in the late 1940s and early 1950s, but never took place in Britain. For the big government money was already being earmarked elsewhere – into housing, into the welfare state, into as yet unquantified deficit spending in order to puff up employment.

How then, given these severe limitations because of the triumph of New Jerusalemism, did Whitehall propose to remedy what its own studies demonstrated to be the pervasive shortcomings of British industry?

Chapter Thirteen

Tinkering as Industrial Strategy

In the first place, the elaborate wartime bureaucratic apparatus by which the government controlled the economy was to be continued after the end of the war with Germany; partly because there would still be dragging on a half-cock war with Japan, partly because the acutely vulnerable state of the ruined British economy in a war-torn world appeared to require a comprehensive government grip on it in order to prevent a collapse. Early in 1943 the Board of Trade and the Treasury therefore advocated the complete battery of postwar state controls later inherited and employed by the Labour government – controls over prices of industrial and consumer goods, over traders' margins; the continuation of rationing; the state bulk-purchase and allocation of raw materials; subsidies on food; high taxation in order to hold down purchasing power; possibly even some kind of long-term prices-and-incomes policy in order to prevent what was already perceived as the inflationary pull on wages and prices likely to be exerted by full employment.[1]

However, in so recommending this continuation of wartime state control over the economy the Treasury and the Board of Trade were not intending that it should serve as the means of forcing on fast industrial growth, but instead, in the Treasury's words, as the means of 'Continuance of Policy of Stabilisation'.[2] There is here, then, an entirely opposite set of values, an entirely opposite diagnosis of national need, from those which were to motivate the West German Minister for Economics, Ludwig Erhard, in 1949, when for the sake of economic dynamism he deliberately demolished with a single explosive charge the safe but stultifying stability of pervasive government controls. Nor can the prolongation of wartime controls into peacetime in Britain be in any sense compared with the *dirigisme* of the postwar French state in sponsoring national economic development, or with the decisive role of the postwar Japanese state in collaborating with industry and the banks through the Ministry of International Trade and Industry. For the role of the British apparatus was perceived by its own advocates as the negative one of avoiding calamity; its essential inspiration lay in a fearful desire to preserve 'stability'. At best it could only serve broadly, in the words of the President of the Board of Trade, 'to secure a proper allocation of production as between the home market, relief needs and commercial exports'.[3]

In seeking to cure Britain's industrial malaise, wartime Whitehall looked to other expedients. But what is, however, so striking about Whitehall's whole approach to the problem is the underlying acceptance that in Britain the mainspring of a market economy – the vigour and enterprise of business itself – had long been broken, or at least completely run down; as indeed all the evidence went to prove. Since British industrialists and exporters simply had not got the root of the matter in them, it was taken for granted that government would have to encourage or cajole or bully them into doing what they would not do if left to themselves. The contrast with the contemporary United States or with 1950s' Germany and Japan, countries which in their different fashions relied on their industries to perform well, is stark. Indeed the British wartime analyses and proposed remedies are dismally reminiscent in tone and content of an international development agency devising means of getting a reluctant Third World economy to the point of economic take-off. As one Board of Trade report on the recovery of export markets put it in June 1943:

> It is, no doubt, partly due to uncertainty about future policy that industry tends to plan on very conservative lines: some industries recognise the need of bold and constructive plans, but still lack the drive, cohesion or powers to put them into effect. The automobile industry, for example, whilst ready to concede the necessity of some closer but as yet undefined co-operation for export, rules out the idea of a radical alteration in the structure of the industry as a step to meeting US competition.[4]

The same report noted that only 4 per cent of British goods exported to America in 1937 were dependent on modern invention or design, amounting to a mere eleventh of the quantity of such products exported by the US to Britain.[5] It was a comparison which neatly sums up the overall backwardness of British industry so bleakly revealed by rearmament and war.

But the Board of Trade also took rueful cognisance of the fact that British backwardness stemmed from inferior research and development as well as from inferior industrial operations as such. The US government had spent $108 million on research in 1938; American industry $300 million; the twenty leading American universities devoted a quarter of their expenditure to research; and then there were large specialised research institutes as well. In Britain the Department of Scientific and Industrial Research had a budget of £740,000 in 1939–40 to cover twenty-two industries. Though no complete figures were available for British industry, it was believed that its total expenditure on research did not exceed £2 million a year.[6] Britain had also fallen behind in industrial design, now a key selling factor. According to the President of the Board of Trade in June 1944:

> Something like an industrial revolution has taken place in the United States in the last 15 years – a revolution of industrial design. It has made many of our exports old-fashioned and less acceptable. It is not by accident, but by prevision and provision that there – and in

> Sweden, Czechoslovakia and Germany before the war – the design of machine-made goods has achieved a wholly new importance. On design alone we were threatened pre-war. . . . And after the war things may well be worse, because of the large progress made in other countries. . . .[7]

To tackle such a profound and many-faceted problem as the present condition of the British industrial system really required a compact and highly talented planning staff under a director of outstanding calibre – similar to that which evolved Operation Overlord, but in this case rich in the best available industrial, commercial and engineering talent. Instead, and in the British way, the task fell to a ragbag of politicians and civil servants, almost all of them Oxbridge humanists, and operating out of several Whitehall departments through the medium of membership of overlapping committees that dealt with, as it might be, 'post-war employment' or 'industrial problems (export questions)' or 'the location of industry'. The amount of paper in the form of minutes and memoranda thus generated between 1943 and 1945 would have amazed Field Marshal Montgomery or, for that matter, Albert Speer; not so much operational studies as wordy prize essays offering every intellectual distinction except clear strategic choice or decision; and the whole more redolent of the stateliness of the striped trouser than the dynamism of the rolled-up sleeve.[8]

The entire exercise was launched by the Board of Trade in June 1943 with a 45-page report on 'the Recovery of Export Markets' based on discussions with fifty-eight industries. The report was long on gloomy analysis – how in fields like motor cars and domestic electrical appliances Britain had shown 'little competitive capacity' against the United States; how the domination of Germany over European markets, if not destroyed, would 'render her a dangerous post-war competitor'; how wage costs were rising in Britain, falling in the US: how the average life of a machine tool in Britain was twenty years and in the USA three or four years.[9] But it was short on creative ideas, going no further than recommending controls over allocation of resources, government finance to guarantee exporters against risk, and action against price rings. The report had nothing to say about trade unions and the crippling effects on productivity and costs exerted by union restrictive practices. Otherwise it fell back on sententious platitudes:

> H.M. Government must be prepared to regard the furtherance of export trade as a post-war need ranking second to none other, and to give all such Governmental assistance as may be required to ensure its furtherance and, by suitable publicity, to encourage a widespread appreciation of this need. UK industrialists must widen the scope and capacity of their production, substituting new products for traditional lines of manufacture for which the export demand is likely to continue to decline.[10]

And in the teeth of its own evidence the report expressed a vague hope that Britain *could* develop new markets in American-style products such as home and office equipment, consumer durables, typewriters, calculating machines and cash registers.

As it happened, the Treasury, in consultation with the Economic Section of the War Cabinet Secretariat and the Central Statistical Office (the very names are indicative of ponderous overlap), put in a paper only ten days later on 'Influences Affecting the Level of the National Income' which, in the course of balancing up such influences, noted the 'general agreement that there was in 1938 great scope for the introduction into this country of methods and machinery which had been already adopted elsewhere, particularly in the United States'.[11] The paper quoted recent evidence to the effect that 'pre-war output per head in the US ranged from four times greater in iron and steel products, motor cars and radio sets, and nearly three times in machinery, down to 20 or 30 per cent greater in cotton textiles. . . .'[12] Yet this memorandum too had more to offer in platitudes than positive answers. It thought that while part of the American superiority lay in the size of the market, 'a major explanation of it must also have been the use of more modern machinery, methods and factory lay-out, which were capable, *in part at least* [author's italics], of being introduced into this country.'[13]

It was a 22-page report by the Board of Trade entitled 'General Support of Trade' in October 1943 that provided Whitehall's major constructive attempt to find means of jerking the British industrial system out of its inertia and defeatism; and the Board of Trade's proposals were to remain the basis of government debate until the end of the war. Nonetheless this report too was over-rich in generalised schoolmasterly abjurations to the effect that the country must elevate its hosiery:

> Industrialists must be encouraged to introduce the most up-to-date machinery. More attention must be paid to research, to industrial art, and to industrial management. Those engaged in industry, both individual firms and industrial organisations must be provided with statistical data, and kept informed as far as possible of foreign developments and trends. Above all, everything possible must be done to foster the development of new ideas and methods to secure their rapid recognition and adoption by industry. . . .[14]

The report was based on the prevailing assumption, in the words of its opening sentence, that 'British trade will need help from the Government after the war.'[15] Yet when it came to discuss what form this help should take, a characteristic British ambiguity or tentativeness of approach became manifest – neither the scruff-of-the-neck intervention in industrial change later practised by the French or Japanese; nor the reliance on free-market competition under a favourable financial régime in the American or postwar West German style:

> In general Government policy will, no doubt, be to support and encourage industry, to be prepared to assist and advise and actively to interfere only when national interests are jeopardised, or when called upon to do so by a material section of an industry. But *it is of the highest*

importance that the Government should have ready specific measures for the support of trade, measures that will offset any post-war malaise and will stimulate industry to overcome the inevitable post-war difficulties; measures that will not only help to achieve full employment but will also bring industry to a higher level of efficiency [original italics].[16]

Having asserted that there was 'no panacea for the difficulties of industry', the report proceeded to advocate a whole battery of them. To overcome the weakness of British industrial organisation arising from the predominance of little firms whose proprietors were too busy, too narrow-minded and too lacking in resources to match foreign expertise in research, development, new product design and export marketing, and too individualistic readily to co-operate with each other, the Board of Trade proposed that a series of industrial boards should be created:

> The object is to combine, as far as possible, the virtues of private initiative, and the flexibility and resilience resulting from numbers of independent firms, with co-operation among them in connection with various services which, if undue waste and inefficiency are to be avoided, should be pooled for particular industries. There will be little argument that it is desirable that industries should set up General Staffs to arrange concerted action on research, design, technical education, statistics and the promotion of export trade.[17]

Costs of administration and of pooled technical and design research and overseas trade promotion would be met by a levy.

In effect the Board of Trade was proposing compulsorily to set up equivalents of the highly effective trade associations that German industry had begun spontaneously creating in the 1890s. As the board acknowledged, British trade associations had largely proved ineffective because of the suicidal individualism of the British manufacturer.[18] And yet, and yet, the Board of Trade's new industrial boards were only to be established in those industries where a two-thirds majority of firms opted for one.

The hand proved similarly reluctant to close on the scruff of the neck in regard to the amalgamation of companies to form more powerful production and marketing groups, even though the Board of Trade admitted that pre-war government attempts to persuade industry to amalgamate had foundered on an individualism that even extended to the reluctance of some industrialists to sit down together in the same room.[19]

> While the Industrial Board should provide co-operative action of the firms in an industry for most of the purposes for which such action is needed, in certain industries it may be necessary to have closer linking of the firms by amalgamation of production and/or of marketing. . . . After the war there will inevitably be some industries where capacity will far exceed demand and the government will have to encourage an organised concentration of production on the more efficient units.[20]

Nevertheless, 'in the light of past experience the Board of Trade doubt whether sole reliance on the methods of persuasion is sufficient to ensure the raising of efficiency of industry to the level that will be needed after the war. . . .'[21] It therefore proposed that the sanction of compulsory purchase should be held in reserve to serve as the ultimate tool of reorganisation. But this sanction would be wielded by another body, a proposed Industrial Commission over and above the industrial boards, and covering the whole field of British industry:

> This commission would be responsible for a range of closely inter-related projects . . . all concerned with various aspects of industrial efficiency in the widest sense – re-equipment, reorganisation, development of new ideas. . . . The best hopes of raising the standard of industrial efficiency in this country lie in the establishment of an Industrial Commission high powered and practical in its membership and therefore enjoying both industrial and public confidence, to frame measures and carry out functions subject to the general control of the Board of Trade and of Parliament. . . .[22]

Working alongside the Industrial Commission would be a new Finance Corporation to handle the state funding necessary for schemes of amalgamation or compulsory purchase. But no direct large-scale state investment in industrial modernisation *à la* rearmament was contemplated; only the provision of 25 per cent subsidies of the purchase price of new machines in order to promote re-equipment of 'urgent national importance'. Wrote the Board of Trade: 'The need is here to dissipate a national tendency to dislike scrapping and replacing; it is a question of psychology. . . .'[23]

With regard to the grievous British weaknesses in research and development, in design and in the quality of management, the Board of Trade's proposals were limp indeed – co-operative research was to be promoted by the industrial boards and the Industrial Commission with the help of as yet unquantified government funding; another fund at the disposal of the Industrial Commission was to finance the initial development and testing of new inventions, and the setting up of pilot plants; an Advisory Bureau of Industrial Management was to promote better management through books, pamphlets and conferences, and to conduct research into the subject. A Central Council of Design complete with a 'permanent pavilion' was to be created to carry out a similarly educational and propagandist role, with the aim 'to get industry to recognise the need for improved design'.[24]

So far as they went, all of these Board of Trade panaceas for Britain's industrial ills were admirable enough – indeed, the proposals with regard to promoting industrial reorganisation formed the basis of the Industrial Organisation and Development Act of 1947, complete with Development Councils for individual industries, while the Central Council of Design duly came to life as the Council for Industrial Design, with the Design Centre in the Haymarket, London, as its 'pavilion'. But measured against the gigantic scale and depth of the problem the Board of Trade's schemes must be regarded as mere tinkering – small carrots and smaller sticks, and with the organism to be stirred into motion not so much a reluctant donkey as a decrepit elephant. In particular no attempt whatsoever was made to address the question of the unions and their restrictive practices; no compulsory amalgamations for *them*.

Nonetheless the Board of Trade's proposals turned out to be too daring for some wartime denizens of Whitehall. Professor Robbins, the noted economist, was against a single body like the Industrial Commission; better, he believed, *ad hoc* enquiries into industrial questions directly initiated by the Board of Trade.[25] The Committee on Post-War Employment agreed that government funds ought to be provided for research and development, and that the quality of management must be improved, but it anxiously recorded its view that the best means 'was a matter which required most careful consideration'.[26] It timidly accepted 'some modest provision' of government funds to promote good industrial design, but on the other hand it feared that too rapid and drastic a standardisation of products and parts (another of the Board of Trade's proposals) could have an adverse effect on employment.[27] The Economic Section of the War Cabinet Secretariat criticised the recommendations for compulsory trade associations and amalgamations, which it reckoned would lead to domination by 'restrictionist ideas'.[28] Instead it saw the solution in greater competition. It did not believe that large firms were always the most efficient. To cap its Cobdenite views, the Economic Section expressed fears that the Industrial Commission would be 'over-zealous' in recommending the scrapping of old plant: 'In principle no plant should be eliminated so long as it can cover its prime costs.'[29] It might have been a Victorian ironmaster talking.

And in truth, as the documents illustrate, wartime Whitehall in its common underlying assumptions and habits of mind *was* Victorian, as would follow from the timing and nature of its education and upbringing. For all its apparent acceptance that 'H.M. Government must be prepared to regard the furtherance of export trade as a post-war need ranking second to none other,' it was really quite unwilling to adopt this as the governing principle of all public policy. The Inland Revenue, for example, would not countenance special tax incentives or privileges to encourage capital investment at certain periods in order to counter an economic depression. This would:

> violate the fundamental principle that direct taxation constitutes the fair sharing out of the bill of national expenditure. The Income Tax is essentially a tax which purports to look at the taxable capacity of every taxpayer and measure by relation thereto how much he ought to contribute as his fair share of the national expenditure.[30]

Thus, in pursuit of Gladstonian rectitude of fiscal principle, a variety of possible inducements to growth and exports was ruled out of court.

A particularly fascinating case in point relates to the future world-market prospects of the motor-vehicle industry. The cluster of general policies best devised to promote these prospects might have consisted of motor taxation and Ministry of Transport vehicle regulations framed in order to favour the type of car or truck wanted by overseas customers rather than the lightweight models hitherto built in Britain – coupled with the construction of a motorway network to take the bigger vehicles and also provide a convenient low-running-cost transport system for industry and exports in place of the present horse-era main roads. But instead by 1945 British politicians and civil servants had succeeded in achieving an exactly opposite kind of package. For in the first place existing British motor taxation favoured low-powered cars unsuitable for world markets, while the Ministry of Transport had refused for its part in March 1945 to alter the commercial-vehicle regulations to permit trucks and coaches on British roads of 8-foot width instead of 7 foot 6 inches, so continuing to constrict British manufacturers to a lighter, smaller type of vehicle not wanted abroad. The ministry had made this refusal on the grounds that 'conditions in this country do not permit the general use of vehicles more than 7′ 6″ in width,' and after 'full consideration of its effects upon exports to the many countries where vehicles of 8′ width are allowed and desired. . .'.[31] In April 1945 the Paymaster-General argued in a paper to the Ministerial Committee on Industrial Problems that exports should come before such considerations as taxation or the optimum width of truck for British roads. He wrote of the Ministry of Transport's decision to continue to limit trucks to a width of 7 foot 6 inches: 'This argument from convenience scarcely does full justice to our desperate need for foreign exchange. . . .'[32] He pointed out that British motor tax had conduced to a result whereby Britain, with one-tenth of the US output, made 120 types of engine as against 30–40 in the US.

But in committee the Chancellor of the Exchequer immediately stated that no change of motor taxation involving loss of revenue could be considered; and that no shift of taxation from vehicles to their fuel was possible because of the difficulties of collection and the potential for evasion.[33] Nor was there any budging of the Ministry of War Transport's insistence on restricting the dimension of commercial vehicles. Yet it was this very same ministry which had itself ensured that there would be an indefinite prolongation of what it called 'conditions in this country [which] do not permit the general use of vehicles more than 7′ 6″ in width,' and even though it acknowledged at the same time that 'a large proportion of our roads remain in width and alignment as they were prior to the advent of motor traffic. When the trunk roads were surveyed in 1937, it was found that on 85 per cent of their length the overall width was not more than 60 feet.'[34] For in 1943 the Minister of War Transport had pronounced against the building of a national motorway network, despite a consultant engineer's report which calculated that over a given length it cost no more to build a motorway than to improve an existing arterial road, and that trucks could travel faster and at lower running costs on a motorway. The Minister of War Transport told his ministerial colleagues:

> while I do not propose to embark upon the construction of a widespread system of motorways, I am in favour of the construction of substantial lengths of road of this type where engineering and traffic considerations make them preferable to extensive adaptations of existing routes. . . .[35]

In his opinion, the engineer's report (itself a cautious document in favour of isolated stretches of motorway, but not of nationwide continuous through-routes) struck 'the right balance between providing progressively for our reasonable needs and launching out on the scale advocated by some enthusiasts, who are perhaps unduly influenced by continental analogies. . .'.[36] Here is caught the authentic flavour of wartime Britain preparing to leap boldly into the technological future.

The December 1943 Treasury estimate of national capital expenditure after the war confirmed the minister's 'cow-path' road policy by allotting less to highways and bridges in 1948 than in 1938;[37] and in the event the first stretch of motorway in Britain – 8½ miles long! – was not opened until 1955. A change to flat-rate motor taxation that would not discriminate against more powerful cars had to wait until 1948, when British manufacturers were already committed to a new generation of runabouts, and the regulations on the dimensions of commercial vehicles were not relaxed until 1955, when the permissible width was at last increased to 8 feet.

It was in January 1944 that the report by the Committee on Post-War Employment finally blessed the Board of Trade's proposals of development boards for different industries, but only if the majority of firms in an industry wanted one. The report made a washy reference to government being ready 'to arrange for schemes both of amalgamation and concentration'; and even went so far as to say that 'it may be necessary to contemplate, in some cases, subject to proper safeguards, compulsory purchase. . . .' But, unlike the Board of Trade, the Committee on Post-War Employment did not want the proposed Industrial Commission to enjoy executive powers: 'We should make it clear that . . . we do not contemplate that the work of the Industrial Commission should be anything but advisory. . . .'[38] Ministerial discussion of the industrial palliatives put forward in this report[39] turned on such questions as to whether the palliatives should be co-ordinated by a single ministry or by joint committees of several or even by the Cabinet itself. Otherwise it left intact the Board of Trade's proposals, as qualified by the Committee on Post-War Employment.

In October 1944 the Cabinet Reconstruction Committee approved another of the Board of Trade's original suggestions for helping industry – that two new finance corporations should be set up, the one to supply investment capital to small businesses, the other to supply the finance for industrial reorganisation.[40] In the first case the capital was to be put up by the Bank of England and the clearing banks, and in the second by City investment and insurance companies. The combined capital of the new corporations would come to £30–45 million, but borrowing powers would raise their total initial resources to £110–165 million[41] – a tiny sum measured against the deficiencies of British industry and against the grand scale of national commitments to New Jerusalem; a sum, moreover, to which, unlike those commitments, the state was to contribute nothing.

Thus was finally evolved the broad industrial 'strategy' with which Britain was to go to peace. It can hardly be said that it was equal to the task of overcoming the massive inertial resistance to change manifested by the British industrial system – not least because it still failed altogether to address the problem of the trade unions, possibly the strongest single factor militating against technical innovation and high productivity. This omission was the more serious because the experience of the war had already indicated to the percipient that under conditions of full employment the unions were likely to prove far more effective than before the war in their obstructionism and in demands for wage increases not earned by raised output. But 'politics is the art of the possible'; and the possible in a coalition government containing Labour ministers did not include close critical examination of these matters; and so the term 'restrictive practices' in wartime Whitehall discussion simply meant villainous capitalist price-rings, despite the occasional bleat from Conservative ministers that the unions too were guilty parties. Nor can it be said that this patchwork of partial and largely passive expedients, derived from the Board of Trade's original proposals, in any sense amounted to a unified strategy of action, backed by powerful executive authority, that would be capable of bringing about the fundamental restructuring of the industrial system, and of swinging the whole balance in favour of new technologies and fast-growing markets. There were not the glimmerings of the postwar Japanese concept whereby the state, through a single ministry, positively led industry and the banks in collaborative long-term development of particular sectors of the economy. Indeed, Britain's chosen expedients ignored as a model for the future her own experience of rearmament and war production, whereby companies had been compulsorily grouped round a 'lead' firm in order to develop and manufacture a new product.

The inadequacy of the proposed industrial 'grand strategy' only compounded the feebleness of specific operational strategies for attacking the problems of particular industries like steel (see above pp. 103–5), shipbuilding (see above p. 123) or motor vehicles. This was particularly serious in the case of the motor industry, for it was in this world market that Britain was to fight and lose its biggest postwar export battle, with devastating consequences for the more modern sectors of the British economy. In March 1945 a special committee submitted a report on the postwar motor industry[42] which identified virtually the same weaknesses as the 1975 report on 'the Future of the British Car Industry' by the Central Policy Review Staff:[43] too many companies; too many models, not enough standardisation of production and parts to ensure low costs; failure to design vehicles that could defeat the competition in overseas markets; limp export marketing and poor service and spares organisation – in sum, a picture of an industry that could thrive only so long as its main potential competitors remained knocked out by war and car-starved customers were willing to buy anything with four wheels and an engine.

But when it came to solutions neither this Whitehall committee nor ministers contemplated direct action by way of compelling amalgamation into a few strong manufacturing groups, let alone the kind of twenty-year development plan masterminded by the Japanese Ministry of International Trade and Industry in the 1950s, which transformed the Japanese motor industry from a workshop operation into the largest and commercially most successful in the world. Instead, British manufacturers were to be 'urged to collaborate more closely' with regard to overseas marketing and servicing; government financial assistance might be offered to induce manufacturers 'to embark on projects [i.e. larger cars for export] which they now regard as too risky'.[44] Otherwise, the only decision taken before the war's end was to set up a working party to investigate the industry, and for the Minister of Reconstruction to seek early meetings with the leaders of the big motor firms.[45] In the event there was to be no state intervention in the motor industry until the 1970s. Instead it was left to go to perdition in its own way, achieving entirely unexpected and certainly undeserved short-term export success in the happy time without rivals in the late 1940s and early 1950s, and thereafter, with its basic faults unremedied, succumbing at ever increasing speed first to renewed European competition and then to the Japanese. A prolonged Darwinian process of bankruptcy and takeover was painfully to solve the 1945 problem of too many companies and too many models, at the eventual cost of the destruction of the major part of the indigenous British motor-vehicle industry.

The truth is that the wartime British Establishment's whole approach to the question of industrial strategy was rooted in a Victorian mercantile conception of a myriad firms competing in a market place – industry was still often referred to as 'trade': 'the coal trade'; 'the steel trade'. The Establishment – politicians, civil servants, hired economists – had not yet grasped the twentieth-century concept, pioneered by the great American and German corporations, of the massive technology-led operation that conquers its own market almost on the analogy of a great military offensive.* This is what really accounts for the piecemeal and tentative nature of British industrial 'strategy' for the postwar era despite the perfectly well-recognised gravity and depth of the problem to be solved. The strategy's ineffectualness was the more potentially calamitous because the broad victory of New Jerusalem over economic realism in the struggle for priorities in national expenditure had in any case left such scant resources for capital investment in industry and infrastructure. In regard to the manifold failings of the British industrial system, therefore, the wartime coalition and its civil servants came, they saw, and they shirked it.

* This was true of Labour ministers like Hugh Dalton too, even though they were more interventionist than the Conservatives. The Labour Party's commitment to 'nationalisation' in no sense represented a real-world operational blueprint for radical industrial change, but, as is now notorious, was merely an empty, if long-revered, New Jerusalem slogan.

Chapter Fourteen

The Lost Victory

The failure to produce a bold strategy for transforming the British industrial system over a period of five to ten years rendered it the more vital that the long-term problem of creating a future technological nation of high effective intelligence and adaptability should be solved. This meant at last remedying the defects in the national education and training system which had been repeatedly identified but only partially tackled since the 1860s, and which were indeed the subject of fresh Whitehall analysis during the Second World War inspired by the urgent shortages of skilled manpower.[1] But in fact the wartime evolution of postwar educational reform was not to be founded on any such perceptions. It was to be in little sense related to a manpower policy or to the future industrial and export prospects so depressingly debated in other corners of Whitehall. It was instead to be founded in New Jerusalem aspirations; seen from the start as an important component of 'postwar reconstruction' – the creation of that better, more equal Britain to be built when there were blue birds over / the white cliffs of Dover. And such aspirations continued to determine the tenor of discussion about education in Whitehall, Westminster and in the press right up to the passing of the 1944 Education Act.[2]

As early as November 1940 (the period of the first tentative ventures in official New Jerusalemism by Nicolson, Halifax, Toynbee *et al.*) the Deputy Secretary of the Board of Education, R. S. Wood (son of a Baptist minister, City of London School and a First in classics at Jesus College, Cambridge), suggested that the board ought to be taking note of the ideas for postwar reconstruction in education already being bandied about in public, and therefore urged that senior officials of the board (now evacuated to a Bournemouth funk-hole) should undertake a 'co-operative and continuous study of educational problems'.[3]

The Permanent Secretary, Sir Maurice Holmes (Wellington College and Balliol; First in jurisprudence; author of *Some Bibliographical Notes on the Novels of George Bernard Shaw*), agreed; an informal committee of principal assistant secretaries and chief inspectors was therefore set up.[4] The first step had thus been taken along the yellow-brick road that led to the 1944 Education Act. In the meantime, outside bodies like the Workers' Educational Association had begun to press the government to announce its plans for postwar education, and when in late January 1941 the Minister without Portfolio, Arthur Greenwood, met a deputation from the WEA it spurred Wood and Holmes to get on with drafting concrete proposals that would pre-empt such external pressure groups.[5] Thus in education, as with other aspects of New Jerusalem, Whitehall found itself frogmarched by progressive public opinion faster and further than it might have wished. The new committee of principal assistant secretaries was therefore pressed by their chiefs to formulate some ideas quickly. By the end of January 1941 the committee had got far enough ahead in composing a draft memorandum to enable the President of the Board of Education in the following month to tell representatives of the Workers' Educational Association, the Trades Union Congress and the Co-operative Union that the board was planning a 'New Testament' (*sic*) on education.[6]

When in June 1941 this testament, now entitled 'Education After the War', was printed for confidential circulation (dubbed the 'Green Book' from the colour of its cover), the foreword by Holmes made it perfectly plain that its inspiration indeed lay in the spirit of New Jerusalemism. It noted that despite past educational advances 'we are still far from attaining in the field of education the social ideal the Prime Minister has set before us of establishing a state of society where the advantages and privileges, which hitherto have been enjoyed only by the few, shall be more widely shared. . . .'[7] Holmes's foreword went on to assert that the proposals outlined in the Green Book have been 'informed by this ideal'; and expressed the belief that 'the nation will expect the planning of education for the postwar world to be conceived on bold and generous lines. . . .' Holmes defined the purpose of full-time schooling as, firstly, 'to provide a school environment of adult training that will enable every child to develop his capacities to the best advantage as an individual'; secondly, 'to prepare him to take his place in the life of the community as a useful citizen. In this connection the importance of equipping him to earn a livelihood *must always be kept in mind* [author's italics]'; and thirdly, 'generally so as to assist the development of body, mind, and spirit as to enable him to lead a healthy and happy life. . .'.[8]

Here was a definition of the aims of education which most individual parents would applaud with regard to their own children. But Holmes and his colleagues were not writing as parents, but as members of a government machine currently wrestling with the problem of how to ensure that Britain in the postwar era remained a great power, recovered her former place in the first rank of industrial nations, and supported the costs of the soaring fabric of New Jerusalem. Judged against these needs, the foreword to the Green Book laid insufficient emphasis on the *national* interest. In fact, it demonstrated less of an awareness of the national interest than had Victorian blue-books like the Schools Enquiry Report, which had adopted the European view that the purpose of state-funded education was not so much to fulfil the individual as to promote national capability and success.

Nevertheless, the un-utilitarian bias of Holmes's foreword accorded only too well with the prevailing sentiments of the 'enlightened' Establishment at large about education. In a debate on the topic in the House of Lords in July 1942, for example (ironically, just a month before Lord Justice Du Parcq submitted his top-secret report on the deficiencies of British radio and radar technology), Lord Samuel, Lord Wedgwood and others held forth on the dangers of laying emphasis on technical education rather than morality. Wedgwood, a descendant of the great Georgian industrialist, pronounced: 'There is too much of what they call vocational training. We do not want to produce a set of robots who will be perfect in producing goods for other people; we want to produce people who will think. . . .'[9]

Given the climate of opinion within and without Whitehall, it is hardly surprising that when the Green Book – duly amended and edited after much discussion with various educational bodies – was published in July 1943 as the government White Paper on educational reconstruction, the introduction explicitly consigned the future creation of national wealth to a poor second place in the White Paper's priorities.

> The Government's purpose in putting forward the reforms described in this Paper is to secure for children a happier childhood and a better start in life; to ensure a fuller measure of education and opportunity for young people and to provide means for all of developing the various talents with which they are endowed and so enriching the inheritance of the country whose citizens they are. . . . It is just as important to achieve diversity as it is to ensure quality of educational opportunity. . . . In the youth of the nation we have our greatest national asset. Even on the basis of *mere expediency* [author's italics], we cannot afford not to develop this asset to the greatest advantage.[10]

It is true that the White Paper did advocate compulsory part-time education to the age of eighteen on the European model because of the need for a more intelligent workforce:

> The initial and natural advantages that gave this country, almost for the asking, its place of pre-eminence in world manufacture and world markets have long been fading. More and more in the future will it be necessary to rely on the capacity, adaptability and the quality of our industrial and commercial personnel. Had fuller attention been paid earlier to the all-important question of the training of young workers, some of the difficulties experienced by the Services and by industry during the present war would have been markedly less acute.[11]

However, it is noteworthy that such sentiments did *not* inspire the White Paper's fundamental approach to the whole question of national education, but only its approach to specific questions like further and technical education. That the White Paper showed an overriding humanist bias in favour of bringing 'liberal education' to the British masses is demonstrated by the amount of space it chooses to devote to different topics. Out of over thirty-two pages of text, only one and a half are allotted to technical, commercial and art education – just half a page more than that to religious instruction.

And religion – or, to be more precise, Christianity – played a dominating role in all that went finally to produce the 1944 Education Act. It did not merely do so indirectly, as the original Victorian inspiration of New Jerusalemism, but directly in its own right as an ideology – and, more important, an ideology espoused by extremely powerful pressure-groups in education. Thus the ever more secular Britain of the 1940s, where practising religion had dwindled into a minority cult, saw the churches and their leaders process forth in power and glory as if this were still the height of the early-Victorian religious revival, presuming again to dictate the future course of national culture. As early as December 1940 a letter to *The Times* headed 'The Foundations of Peace' from the Archbishop of Canterbury, the Cardinal Archbishop of Westminster, the Moderator of the Free Church Council and the Archbishop of York proclaimed that 'no permanent peace is possible in Europe unless the principles of the Christian religion are made the foundation of national policy and of all social life.'[12] The original Green Book, in devoting two pages to religious instruction (the same ration as to technical and commercial education), had acknowledged:

> There is a growing volume of opinion that the time has come when the place of religion as an essential element in education should be specifically recognised. It is accordingly suggested that there should be religious observance and instruction enjoined by statute in all provided Primary and Secondary Schools.[13]

But this was not enough for Canon Woodard, President of the National Society (for Promoting Religious Education), the body which ran Church of England schools. In a meeting with R. A. Butler, the President of the Board of Education, in November 1941, Woodard regretted the omission in the Green Book of any reference to Christianity 'as the necessary basis of education. . .'.[14] Shortly afterwards, and also arising out of the Green Book, the Headmasters' Conference put in a memorandum on the general aim of education which, while making no comment at all on the Green Book's proposals for technical and commercial education, stated that the conference 'wish to express their strong sense . . . that the Christian faith should be the basis and inspiration of all educational work. . .'.[15] In November 1942 a leading article in *The Times* expressed the hope that a forthcoming meeting of the Church Assembly on children and schools would recognise that 'the real issue before it was not the future of Church Schools, but the future of Christianity as the religion of the English people.'[16] A year later, when the White Paper had been massaged into a parliamentary Bill, the Bishop of Wakefield supported it in a letter to *The Times* on the ground that under it he hoped for further progress in bringing up children as practising members of the Christian Church.[17]

Nonetheless, important though the role of Christianity as an ideology was in determining the bias of wartime educational reform, the role of the churches as deeply entrenched vested educational interests of enormous power was far more crucial. Indeed, the whole process that led to the 1944

Act turned on negotiating a deal between government and churches over the future of church schools within a reformed structure of state-funded education. This was what mainly swallowed up the Board of Education's time and effort between 1941 and 1944 – not detailed operational studies and costings of a future educational system from primary school to technical university that would meet the needs of an industrial nation competing in world markets; not the completion of a fully worked-out executive blueprint. The diaries of the President of the Board of Education and his Parliamentary Secretary, Chuter Ede, in 1941–4 were stuffed not with meetings with industrialists and trade unionists and their representative organisations or with the different engineering and scientific institutions, but with skull-emptying sessions with gentlemen of the cloth (of various persuasions) on the topic of how they could continue to run a large proportion of the nation's schooling thanks to the taxpayer's subsidy. As R. A. Butler put it in characteristically elliptical fashion after he had steered his Education Bill through Parliament, 'the most interesting part of the whole thing for him had always been the religious issue. . . . it was the religious issue that took the time.'[18]

It began taking the time from the moment Butler became President of the Board of Education in July 1941, when he and Ede were optimistically hoping to settle it by autumn that year or early 1942.[19] At the beginning of August 1941 a preliminary meeting between Butler, Ede and Greenwood was almost wholly taken up with the question of the churches and religious instruction. On 15 August a deputation of thirty-three godly notables led by the Archbishop of Canterbury and three bishops called to make their case for church schools and compulsory religious indoctrination. A week later the question of such indoctrination inspired a debate for and against in the correspondence columns of *The Times*.[20] On 16 September 1941 the War Premier, who well remembered how uproar over the religious issue had bedevilled the passing of the 1902 Education Act, warned his colleagues against raising it anew in wartime.[21] On 15 October 1941 Ede met another committee of worthies who wished to advocate a Christian education, this time laymen. Meantime the Archbishop of Canterbury proceeded to publish 'Five Points' about religion, the churches and education, and these points, together with the wider aspects of the religious issue, took up six meetings at the Board of Education between 27 October and 7 November 1941 alone.[22] On 22 November 1941 a deputation arrived from the National Society, led by Canon Woodard and including the Bishop of Wakefield and Sir Walter Moberly (also chairman of the University Grants Committee, a post of key influence over higher education).[23] Sir Walter was the son of a canon of Christ Church, Oxford, and of a daughter of the Bishop of Salisbury; he had been educated at Winchester and New College, Oxford, where he took a First Class Honours Degree in classics; and later became a fellow of Merton College, Oxford, and later still a professor of philosophy. Three days after the National Society's visit came a deputation from the Catholic Education Council.[24]

Come 1942, and on 12 January the Archbishop of Canterbury gave notice to Butler and Lord Hankey (government spokesman on education in the House of Lords) that he was going to raise the educational issue in the Lords in February. Hankey bluntly told his colleagues that he was only interested in education in so far as it helped radar.[25] He did not however say this when replying to the debate. On 3 March 1942 A. L. Rowse, a romantic Oxford historian, started up a fresh correspondence in *The Times* on religion and intelligence. On 23 March 1942, after Ede had had a tiresome meeting with the Bishop of Derby, Butler remarked that he 'despaired of the Bishops. He said too many of them came from Oxford. He said it would be a good thing to abolish Oxford.'[26] More prolonged discussions and negotiations about religious indoctrination dragged on through April and May. On 13 May a suitable comment on the whole question of the churches' claims over education was supplied by a return made to Ede to the effect that, out of 8967 church schools, only 150 had been built since 1905.[27] On 9 July Ede closed the current volume of his diary with a summary of the then state of play over modernising the British education system:

> Educational development still hung on removal of denominational barriers. Opinion varies as to prospects of success but it might well be that here too many weary months would have to be spent in attempting to undo the damage caused by prejudices of past generations.[28]

On 22 July 1942 Butler was moved to say to Ede that the Church of England was 'completely fossilised'. Unfortunately he had as a politician to recognise its importance to the Conservatives. As he frankly confessed to a meeting of political and official colleagues in the previous March: 'the abolition of the Church School in the single school area would mean the death blow to the Tory Party in the villages. The Tory Party depended on the historic connection between the Church and the squire. . . .'[29]

On 3 September 1942 there took place yet another interminable meeting with a deputation of the usual clerics and devout laiety – Canterbury and York, Lords Sankey and Grey, Sir Walter Moberly, the Dean of St Paul's, Canon Woodard – on the future role of Christian indoctrination in schools and other topics galaxies away from the technological weaknesses with which Britain was then struggling. It is fascinating in this regard to learn from Ede's diary for 9 October 1942 that discussion of the school 'syllabus' with outside bodies really meant discussion of the Religious Instruction syllabus.[30]

These cited instances of wearisomely repetitive encounters represent merely the fruitiest plums from an enormous pudding of negotiation that swelled week by week, month by month, and year by year; the ingredients of every suety discussion being fully recorded by Ede in his diary. The pudding was still swelling in late 1943, when the education White Paper was in course of transformation into a politically acceptable parliamentary Bill, with this time the Roman Catholic Church as the most constipating defender of a vested interest.[31] Not that the Anglican Church had abated its own concern for the nation's schooling: on 14 December 1943, for example, the occasion of hammering out the seventeenth draft of the Bill in the Department of Education was unwittingly marked by the publication in *The Times* of letters from three bishops on the favourite topic of religious indoctrination, in which connection the Bishop of Wakefield wished to know whether or not nonconformists 'abhor teaching of the Apostles' Creed'.[32]

It is of course true that to inculcate responsible social behaviour in the young must constitute a basic element in an all-round education, although it is less obvious that this inculcation can rest only on religious dogma. But in the evolution of educational reform in 1941–4 a proper balance between a concern with moral teaching and the furtherance of capability in life and work was destroyed by that overriding preoccupation with religious instruction and the future of church schools so successfully brought about by the ecclesiastical vested interests. As a consequence the crucial question of providing the nation with an education for capability from primary school up to technical university equal to that of her competitors was squeezed away to the sidelines. Certainly Butler and his colleagues did meet representatives of industry, commerce and technology as well as the devout; certainly they conferred also with the Ministry of Labour about training. But the time and trouble spent on such contacts amounted to a mere fraction of that engrossed by the men of religion. Nor did any industrial or commercial body – any secular body at all – bring pressure on the Board of Education of that relentless and effective kind exerted by the churches. Thus in the middle of the twentieth century England was paying heavily yet again for the original decision of the 1830s to subsidise church schools rather than create *de novo* a system of purely secular state schools.

As it was, the one paramount concern for Butler lay in winning church acceptance of his proposed reforms in the administrative structure and funding of public education. As he himself acknowledged, 'we could never have carried a purely secular solution of the schools question. . . .'[33] But his proposed structural reform, merging primary, secondary and further education into one continuous ladder of opportunity instead of being largely separate compartments, also brought him up against another set of politically influential vested interests – the smaller local authorities who would lose their existing control over education. Here again Britain was still paying the price for a Victorian policy decision, in this case with regard to state schools themselves when at last set up after 1870. For instead of creating a nationwide system directly under a Ministry of Education, control had been balkanised, first to local elected school boards and then, after the Local Government Act of 1888, to eventually over 400 local authorities. Even by January 1944, when the Education Bill had begun its passage through Parliament, Butler and Ede were still negotiating on and on in detail with the so-called 'Part III' authorities who were to lose their control over schooling.[34]

In view of Butler's overwhelming political preoccupation with fixing the church bodies and the 'Part III' authorities, it can hardly occasion surprise that he and his colleagues were little concerned with the purpose and content of national education, let alone with presenting a complete 'Overlord Plan' for every sector of the system. Indeed, when the Lord

President's Committee discussed the draft White Paper in July 1943, it agreed to Sir John Anderson's suggestion that the wording should be altered 'to make it plain that we are dealing with the structure and not the content of education'.[35] Even more to the point, Butler – in order to present a politically acceptable package – deliberately avoided tackling in any detail such vital but potentially contentious topics as technical education, the adequacy of the universities as national assets, the role of the public schools, the training of teachers and, above all, the secondary-school curriculum. Instead he adopted the time-proven device of hiving them off for study and report by committees of pundits.[36] In particular, technical education, perhaps the most grievous of all Britain's educational weaknesses, was relegated in March 1944 to a committee under Lord Eustace Percy, which safely did not report until 1945.

In fact, despite all its apparent recognition of Britain's lamentable failings in technical education, the Department of Education (and the government) accorded the remedying of these failings only a fitful interest and a comparatively minor place in the whole package of educational reform which was evolved from the Green Book to the Education Act. A letter from Butler to the War Premier on 12 September 1941 demonstrates how completely his own initial priorities were to alter, to the detriment of technical education, for he therein states that the *first* question is 'the need for industrial and technical training and the linking up of schools closely with employment' and the *second* question that of church schools and religious instruction.[37]

*

> There is urgent need, in the interests of the industrial and commercial prosperity of the country, to secure an improved system of technical and commercial training. Four questions are of outstanding importance – the training of apprentices and other young workers; relations with industry and commerce; the provision of buildings and equipment; and the development of regional organisation.[38]

So pronounced the Green Book of 1941 promisingly enough. In its judgement existing evening classes and the 41,000 youngsters on day-release by employers in 1938 only touched 'the fringe of the problem of an ordered system of industrial and commercial training'; and it called for compulsory part-time day-continuation schools to age eighteen, with a curriculum so balanced as to be neither academic nor narrowly vocational.[39] It asked whether a national training policy could be worked out in consultation with industry, and whether such a policy should be voluntary or statutory.[40] The Green Book wanted much closer relations between education and industry and commerce; possibly even joint advisory committees for major industries and branches of business. It suggested that a small council of distinguished leaders from both sides of industry should be set up to collaborate with the Board of Education over broad educational policy.[41] The Book noted that the prevailing standard of technical-college buildings in Britain was 'deplorably low' and that 'only few compare with the institutions found in Germany and elsewhere', while their equipment too 'must be brought and kept up to date'.[42] It wondered whether higher technical education in the future 'can properly continue to be left to depend on local initiative', and what fresh arrangements should be made for its organisation – matters which 'will need careful consideration in the light of industrial conditions and requirements after the war'.[43] In this connection it remarked that the distribution of industry did not correlate with local government boundaries, so that a local authority's technical college might not easily provide for the needs of a larger industrial grouping. On the topic of the public grants which carried poorer students to university, the Green Book commented on the 'haphazard nature' of existing scholarships and asked whether the government should take national control of selecting and supporting the holders of grants.

Here was the preliminary, if very tentative, sketch of a programme of reform of further education that might have placed Britain on a par with the Germany or Switzerland of the 1880s, perhaps even, in some respects, of the 1930s; a remarkable step forward.

In the autumn of 1941 and the spring of 1942 the Board of Education discussed this whole field with the Ministry of Labour, which was the Whitehall department responsible for industrial training – another example of the British genius for fragmenting command and control. Ernest Bevin himself, the Minister of Labour, wanted all school-leavers at fourteen to be sent away to state boarding schools in redundant service camps until age sixteen, with vocational guidance from age thirteen onwards; the curriculum for the fourteen to sixteen year olds was to be a blend of the academic and practical crafts, although from age fifteen it was to be more akin to trade-school training. According to Bevin's ideas youngsters should pass into industry at the age of sixteen, but remain under the joint supervision of the Board of Education and Ministry of Labour with regard to their training, further education and physical welfare until they were twenty. Bevin wanted the period of apprenticeship dropped to three years instead of five years because of the training that was to be formally given in school.[44] In advocating such thoroughgoing proposals, he was of course spurred by his desperate problem in finding the skilled manpower demanded by war production. Butler, for his part, while agreeing on the importance of organising the entire training and care of youth aged fourteen to eighteen under 'some nodal organisation', came in general to regard Bevin's ideas as 'semi-Fascist' in their emphasis on compulsory training.[45] Moreover, as Ede pointed out, Bevin's plan, only affecting those who left school at age fourteen, would 'reproduce the present deplorable gulf between the black-coated and the manual worker'.[46]

Despite such reservations, Butler was clear that the two ministries must co-operate over reform, and that in particular it was necessary 'to get a concordat with the Ministry of Labour about what is industrial supervision and what is educational supervision . . .' in order to avoid 'a major overlap'.[47] Here again was the pernicious and obfuscating distinction, successfully established by the liberal-arts lobby in the great Victorian educational debate, between 'education' and 'training'; between cultivation of the mind and mere nuts and bolts; a distinction now institutionalised in the divided responsibilities of the two ministries. In April 1942 a joint meeting is therefore found pondering this tricky question: at what stage should responsibility for a further education blending the academic with the practical pass from Education to Labour?[48]

In July 1942, when the impetus over further technical education had somewhat languished, Butler took time off from interviewing bishops to prod his Deputy Under-Secretary, Sir Robert Wood, on the subject. 'We do not', he wrote, 'seem to have progressed in the matter of contacts with Industry, and recently the Engineering employers called off their own request for training. How do I set about making Industry play?'[49] Butler said he also wished to discuss the question of day-continuation classes with industrialists – eliciting the discouraging reply from Wood that this would be useless, as industrialists were against such classes; a comment unflattering to the enlightenment of the 'practical man' of British industry.

With regard to adult education, Butler remarked in his note that the Green Book failed to weigh up the pros and cons and suggest a positive policy. 'It seems to me that we need to define what are the objects of Adult Education and what are the powers we must seek from Parliament if we are to achieve these objects.'[50] Although he was, he wrote, now getting to grips with the religious question, he wanted advice on technical, day-continuation and adult education, and how these should be fitted in with other proposed reforms of the system: 'Politics is said to be "l'art du possible." The question is – what is possible; and what is our order of priority?'[51]

Wood in his reply agreed on the necessity for more and better state-funded technical education, since industry itself would not do it, and since technical training at present was almost all part-time and the pupils were individual volunteers: 'I think . . . that a major objective to which we should set ourselves is to secure the development of a more organised system of training, involving day release, wherever technical education can properly be said to be required.'[52] This would, he added, fit in with Bevin's ideas of supervising youth to the age of eighteen. It was therefore Wood's hope that in conjunction with the Ministry of Labour and with the agreement of industry there could be a formal requirement that vocational education should be given to all those who needed it. Nonetheless, Wood recommended no further action at that moment beyond sending out a questionnaire to industry. Otherwise he limited himself to suggesting that the 1939 programme for building technical colleges should be completed;[53] a proposal hardly equal to the scale of Britain's comparative shortfall in such institutions.

In the meantime Butler and his colleagues had met the Joint Consultative Committee of the Trades Union Congress and the British Employers' Federation to discuss British inferiority of technical training in terms of postwar world competition, and successfully sold them the idea that a committee should be set up to look into the problem. This met for the first time in October 1942 and completed its work by June 1943; its report, concentrating on compulsory part-time further education, was circulated at the beginning of September 1943.[54] Much of this report was taken up with yet another detailed analysis of pre-war deficiencies and of the predominantly untrained make-up of the British workforce in various industries. It opined that the failure to implement the 1918 Education Act's provision for compulsory day-continuation classes had been largely due to 'the only half-awakened educational consciousness of the country as a whole and to the lack of appreciation of the value of Further Education on the part of industry and commerce'.[55] However, the committee encouragingly believed that industry and commerce were now waking up to a sense of responsibility to young workers as 'potential capital'.[56]

In therefore advocating that such part-time day-continuation classes should at last be inaugurated after the war, the committee – like the Green Book – proposed a curriculum nicely balanced between the vocational and the cultural. Yet its report allots twice the space to outlining the cultural part of the curriculum as it does to the vocational, so belying its apparent balance; so belying as well its assertion that experience 'both in this country and abroad has shown that no aspect of education gives more vitality to the content than that which links the content to the job'.[57] Moreover, while the report's appendix on vocational courses is merely a summary of specialist replies to a questionnaire about time-tabling, the appendix on non-vocational courses is rich with broad philosophic statements about the humanising role of liberal studies, so that pupils will 'learn to be honourable, tolerant and kindly in dealing with their fellows; . . . learn to acquire an independent and balanced outlook on life'; qualities, however, that do not all necessarily make for the amassment of material riches, either in the individual or in the nation. Thus even in a specialist report about remedying the professional ignorance of the British workforce the tradition of Newman and the Arnolds, the ideal of knightly Christian conduct, imposed their domination.

In any event, the government had by now already made public its general views on further and technical education in the White Paper on educational reconstruction in July 1943, arguing in favour of compulsory part-time schooling to age eighteen on the ground that its introduction before the war might have spared the country its present acute shortage of skilled manpower.[58] The White Paper virtually repeated verbatim the Green Book's comments about the poor buildings and equipment prevailing in British technical colleges in comparison with 'what can be seen in many other countries which have been our competitors in world markets. . .'. It saw as the principal reason for the failure of technical education in Britain to make 'that advance which the needs of a highly industrialised community demand' the fact that the 'provision of further education is at present a power and not a *duty* of Local Education Authorities,' and, by implication, that too many such authorities had neglected adequately to exercise the power. Therefore it proposed that the provision of such education should become a duty, with the requirement to submit schemes to the Board of Education.

The White Paper chided industry and commerce for having made little demand on the vocational education already available in technical colleges, and called for 'a much closer collaboration between industry and commerce and the education service . . . if the country is to develop a national system and to secure a personnel with a training and knowledge adequate to the needs of the future.'[59] The war, it declared, had shown that technical colleges could help in training:

> to a degree, and in a way, the possibilities of which industry has not hitherto generally appreciated. What is wanted . . . is that industry and commerce should review their arrangements for training, and should co-operate in associating the technical colleges and the art schools more fully with the industrial and commercial life of the country. . . .[60]

The White Paper went on to refer optimistically to the joint consultations already begun with industry by the Board of Education and the Ministry of Labour:

> with a view to working out more ordered systems of training and apprenticeship adapted to the conditions of today. . . . In this way it is hoped to build up in each industry a system which will be accepted and applied, not to individual firms here and there, but on a national basis throughout the industry.[61]

These ideas and hopes about better co-operation between industry and technical education in the postwar era must be accounted all too cloudy; they offer a dismaying contrast to the hard-minded and entirely successful wartime training programmes in technical colleges and universities mentioned in passing by the White Paper. For during the war when the country had needed technical personnel of varying levels of skill, it had swiftly instituted specific schemes with specific output targets. The results were impressive – 6000 state bursaries awarded for two-year university technical degree courses; over 4000 Higher National Certificate holders trained in technical colleges on six-month courses for industry and the armed services; nearly 4000 Engineering Cadetships awarded for courses recognised by the professional engineering institutions as equal to a National Diploma.[62] It is the absence of a comparable planning for defined objectives that renders the White Paper's scant coverage of technical and further education so constructively feeble.

Yet even its vague aspirations in this field were belied by the actual sums of money it provisionally allotted to developing different sectors of education in the first seven years of the postwar era and beyond. In those first seven years technical and adult education was to receive (over and above current levels of expenditure) a cumulative total of £2.7 million, and young people's colleges £5.3 million – together only half as much as school medical care and nursery schools, at £6.3 million and £10.8 million.[63] Even more to the point, a much slower start was to be made in developing technical and adult education than other sectors. In the first year of postwar reform, not an extra penny was to be spent in this field – as against £500,000 on nursery schools. In the second and third years of development, technical education was to receive the ridiculous additional sums of £30,000 and £60,000, as against £1 million on school medical care and £1.5 million on nursery schools.[64] As the White Paper lamely explained: 'Although the development of technical and adult education is not included among the matters to be dealt with in the first four year plan, some allowance has been made for preliminary expenditure in respect of technical education.'[65] Even after the first seven years, when expenditures were supposed to reach their planned maxima, technical and adult education's share amounted only to £1.2 million per annum above current levels, while nursery schooling was to receive £5 million per annum extra.[66]

Nonetheless, the quality newspapers greeted the White Paper, in the words of *The Times* headline, as 'A Landmark in Education'; they had little to say about the proposals for further and technical education, and less by way of criticism. As the *Manchester Guardian* reported: 'Measures, *not specified with precision* [author's italics], are indicated for the development of technical and adult education. . . .'[67] The *Guardian* believed that 'industry is probably in a readier mood to help to make it work than it was after the last war.' The *Daily Telegraph* did remind its readers that 'So long as the mass of the children leave school at 14 and thereafter receive no systematic training, we cannot hope for a nation of the efficiency required by modern demands.'[68] But the *Sunday Times* contentedly noted: 'Nor, arrived at sixteen [the proposed new school-leaving age] is [the child] to be turned loose upon the world. Mr Butler's plans for continued education up to 18 are *cautious and modest* [author's italics].'[69]

However, in the following month the Board of Education's own consultative committee on engineering harshly criticised the White Paper,[70] pointing out 'the relatively poor provision for technical and adult education' in the financial figures in the appendix, and arguing that this was inconsistent with the assertions in the White Paper itself about the urgency of the problem and the need for action. The engineers' committee then came back to the central issue, raised as long ago as the 1860s, of the British need to beat the competition in terms of technical excellence:

> Switzerland and Sweden, two countries greatly handicapped by nature and position, have clearly indicated what must be done by way of technical education to achieve and maintain pre-eminence in engineering. A highly trained scientific and technical personnel is of course a prerequisite; and although the universities provide the initial training of a small minority, our existing technical colleges, on which the bulk of training for industry falls, are neither equipped nor staffed to deal adequately with modern demands. . . .[71]

The committee also doubted whether the White Paper's stratagem of imposing a *duty* on local education authorities to provide technical education would really prove enough to ensure that the desired development take place; in other words, it feared that the governmental hand was still not going to close tightly enough on the scruff of the neck of the unwilling.[72]

Further criticism followed. At the end of September 1943 the principal of Bradford Technical College wrote in a letter to *The Times* on the need to develop some technical colleges into higher technical institutions (on the model of the German *Technische Hochschulen*, although he did not say so). Furthermore, he also regarded the proposed expenditure of £100,000 on technical and adult education in the fourth year of the plan of educational reform as inadequate.[73] Since similar discontent was mounting widely in industry and in the educational profession, the officials of the Department of Education began to urge their chiefs that more must be done, or appear to be done. R. S. Wood wrote to Butler on 5 October 1943 that he agreed that the projected expenditures were 'far from satisfactory' and that the poor impression created by them had been made worse by the omission of any mention of technical education in the White Paper's opening general section about the educational 'four-year plan'. He further agreed that replies given by government spokesmen to criticisms in the House of Commons during the debate on the White Paper were 'not really satisfactory'.[74] He therefore suggested that the Chancellor of the Exchequer be asked to agree to a public promise of further development in technical education, even if it were not possible in the first two to four years to build large new institutions. Accordingly, Butler wrote to Anderson and won his consent to Butler's draft of a statement to the House of Commons:

> the estimates in the White Paper had regard to the inevitable time-lag before the scheme procedure [for the general administrative reform of the education system] could make its effect felt: the development of technical provision which could be put in hand immediately following upon the cessation of hostilities will, however, be pressed forward to meet the requirements of industry and commerce and to assist them in the tasks of readjustment and recovery.[75]

This classic exercise in the emission of governmental smoke did not however befog the critics. In February 1944, Attlee, the Lord President of the Council and Deputy Prime Minister, was writing anxiously to Anderson (copy to Butler) with regard to a forthcoming Commons resolution calling for much larger support to universities and technical institutions, and to co-operative research and development between industry and state research bodies, in order to make sure that Britain could meet postwar competition. Attlee suggested, and Anderson agreed, that there should be either a government statement or a promise of a White Paper on the topic.[76] R. S. Wood's own solution was that the appointment of a proposed departmental committee on technical education (the Percy Committee) should be announced either before or during this debate.[77] Wood's own enthusiasm for the whole question of technical education is well revealed by the remark with which he follows this suggestion:

> Apart from that, *I suppose we shall have to talk in some general terms* [author's italics] about the future development of technical education and perhaps make some sort of reference to the contribution which has certainly been made to the war effort, and could equally be made in the postwar years, by way of increasing the number of folk coming forward into industry with various degrees of scientific equipment. . . .[78]

And so on 5 April 1944, in order to still the critics at this time when the Education Bill was on its way through Parliament, the appointment of the Percy Committee on Higher Technological Education was duly announced. Nevertheless, the critics had already achieved a notable if only partial success: to the applause of *The Times*,[79] the government had now raised the original White Paper provision of £2.7 million for technical and adult education over seven years to £35 million – a figure that may be compared with the £10 million spent in 1944 alone on free milk and vitamins for children.

However, fresh criticism of the government's relative neglect of technical education continued to erupt. Even though the House of Commons was throughout the passage of the Bill overwhelmingly concerned with the religious, moral and administrative aspects, including the question of church schools,[80] some members did try to point out that the nation's future might depend on its capability as well as on its moral tone. Sir Harold Webbe, the member for the Westminster Abbey constituency, surveyed the longstanding British inferiority in technical education and asked: 'What does the Bill do about it? In precise terms, I believe, precisely nothing.'[81] Even though, he went on, the government had raised their estimate for technical and adult education by fourteen times, where, he wanted to know, were the great technical institutions like those of Germany and the USA?[82] Where indeed? In answer, Ede could only offer the usual government spokesman's vague assurances.[83] On 23 March Ede was confiding to his diary that the 'opening clauses had gone slowly owing to a desire on the part of many [*sic*] members to talk on technical and adult education. I came in later on Young People's Colleges and had rather a sticky time.'[84] On 12 April a letter appeared in *The Times* signed by ten leading industrialists and trade unionists which roundly stated: 'In our public provision for training craftsmen, England is now definitely a backward country. . . .' The signatories thought that the newly announced Percy Committee's terms of reference 'did not touch' the real problem of providing enough good technical schools, equipment and teachers, coupled with a new regional organisation for such education that made industrial sense.

Nevertheless, the further passage of the Bill through the Commons evoked relatively little debate on such questions – not least because the Bill itself contained little matter on them. Of 104 clauses taken in Committee of the Whole House over several weeks, three related to young people's colleges and one to technical and further education; all the rest related to administrative changes, religious instruction, the role of church schools, and proposed reforms in general full-time schooling.[85] In the Third Reading Debate, which was largely a feast of collective self-congratulation from all sides of the House about how brilliantly the problem of church schools and religious instruction had been solved, and how the Bill ushered in a new era of greater educational opportunity, only the member for The Wrekin, Arthur Colegate, a businessman and former director of Brunner Mond, chose to make a speech on the topic of technical training.[86] Even Butler when winding up the debate made no reference to this topic or to adult education, preferring to trumpet forth the theme of the broad educational advance accomplished by the Bill: 'This Bill is a national achievement, a national achievement which shows to our own people, to our Empire and to foreign countries the intensity and vitality of the greatness of our people.'[87]

And indeed the Bill (to be enacted in August 1944) contains no specific reference at all to vocational education, but merely lays a general duty on local education authorities to submit to the Ministry of Education development schemes for 'further education', and also to establish and maintain county colleges for compulsory day-continuation attendance by young people. The date for commencing the establishment of such colleges was to be determined by the government, but to be 'not later than three years after the date of commencement of this part of the Act'.[88] Moreover, while there is a schedule attached to the Act laying down specific procedures for preparing and bringing into operation a syllabus on religious instruction, no such schedule exists for technical and vocational education.[89]

It is fair to say that with regard to the whole field of education for competitive efficiency as an industrial nation the vaunted 1944 Education Act offered not so much an executive operational framework as an opened gate to an empty construction site on which local authorities might or might not (depending on their zeal and the effectiveness of the ministry's nagging) build the technical and further education system that Britain so desperately needed. Yet even the most zealous local education authority would have to work within government limits on expenditure. What therefore followed in the next forty years was yet another halting, spasmodic, spotty advance like those following the Technical Instruction Act of 1889 and the Education Act of 1902; this time with extra grit in the wheels contributed by government expenditure cuts in the wake of sterling crises or because of the competing costs of the welfare state and of maintaining Britain's world and Commonwealth strategic roles. In 1947, for example, capital expenditure for new construction over the whole field of further education was fixed at some £2 million, out of a total figure for all educational building of £24 million – a sum just enough to pay for one new technical college to be built in Birmingham.[90]

True to the traditional British pattern with regard to measures of reform and their actual results, it was left to the next major enquiry into technical education to document how little had been achieved by the 1944 Act. For the 1956 White Paper on technical education, after remarking that more schools and technical colleges had been built since 1944 and much more interest in such training displayed by employers and parents, was to play yet again an old favourite:

> But this is nothing like enough. From the USA, Russia and Western Europe comes the challenge to look at our system of technical education to see whether it bears comparison with what is being done abroad. Such comparisons cannot be made accurately because standards and systems of education vary so much, but it is clear enough that all these countries are making an immense effort to train more scientific and technical manpower and that we are in danger of being left behind.[91]

The 1956 White Paper was therefore to advocate a five-year expansion plan at the cost of £100 million. It was also to advocate the establishment – a century after Germany – of *Technische Hochschulen*, or, in its phraseology, 'Colleges of Advanced Technology', as vainly called for by Sir Harold Webbe in the Commons debates on the 1944 Education Bill, as vainly recommended in the eventual report of the Percy Committee in 1945, and as entirely neglected by Butler and his officials in evolving their reforms between 1941 and 1944. In 1963 the Robbins Report on higher education was to go even further and call for five 'Special Institutions for Scientific and Technological Education and Research, comparable in size and standing and in advanced research to the great technological institutions of the United States of America and the Continent',[92] and for the colleges of advanced technology (at last created in 1960) to be promoted to full university status – some seventy years after their German equivalents.

Unfortunately, by the time these two fresh reports appeared Britain's most formidable industrial competitors, Germany and Japan, had fully recovered from defeat and occupation, and were already motoring past the trundling British economy. Owing therefore to the original petty scope of wartime plans for technical and higher education, Britain had missed a unique and irrecoverable opportunity to catch up in this field before it was too late.

But wholly left out of consideration by Butler and his colleagues, and thus not figuring at all in the 1944 Education Act, was the question of Britain's poor provision of traditional universities compared with other countries, her much smaller student numbers in proportion to population. The question was left out for the very good reason that the Department of Education had no responsibility for universities or the education which they provided. Thanks to the instinctive British urge to disintegrate functions rather than integrate them, the responsibility for dispensing public funds to universities and for influencing the course of their academic development had been vested since 1922 in the University Grants Committee. Apart therefore from a temporary scheme to boost the throughput of students through existing universities by subsidising ex-servicemen to take the course of their choice in the *alma mater* of their choice, the wartime coalition proposed to do nothing to reform the universities or create new ones. Not until 1945 was the Barlow Committee on Scientific Manpower to be appointed, and not until 1946 was it to report, recommending that the output of science graduates should be doubled; a target not hit until the end of the 1950s.[93] A single new university college was to be founded before the 1960s, that of North Staffordshire in 1949. It was left to the Robbins Report of 1963 to recommend the first major wave of new university foundations in Britain since before the Great War; another disastrous loss of time and opportunity.

In its wartime planning for the postwar era Whitehall no less neglected other crucial aspects of Britain's inferiority in professional training for industrial success. At the time of the Second World War Britain possessed not a single business or management school like those of America and Germany, able to prepare persons of high ability to run complex modern large-scale commercial operations, and to turn out needed specialists like cost-accountants and systems-analysts.[94] The London School of Economics and the Oxbridge economics departments had already become another mandarin preserve for academic theorising unsullied by anything so sordid as business, while Bachelor of Commerce courses in British universities at large could not compare with the German and American business schools either in rigour and scope, or in sheer scale of output.[95] In particular, accounting in Britain hardly meant more than lowly book-keeping or the drawing up of balance sheets by chartered accountants. Cost-accounting, the means by which a well-run business in the US or Germany was continually monitored and controlled (including analysis of the costs of parts and production of individual products), remained limited to a few, and often multinational, concerns.[96]

The consequent professional callowness of the British 'practical man' as manager, so widely manifested by the experience of rearmament and war production, was well recognised by the Board of Trade in its major 1943 report on 'General Support of Trade':[97]

> The development of the art of industrial management in industry has been slow in this country and has been left, in the main, to the large organisations able to employ specialists in particular branches of management; e.g. personnel management, production control, office systems, distribution methods and costing. . . .

However, the Board of Trade's preferred remedy proved to be the usual limp dab at a problem: no question here of creating at an early date several American-type business schools. For the board merely suggested that an 'Advisory Bureau of Industrial Management' backed by government funding be set up, with the functions, firstly, of promoting 'the adoption of improved methods of management by arranging for the publication of books and pamphlets, by organising conferences, etc. . . .'; secondly, of promoting 'research into managerial problems and to allocate funds to other non-profit-making bodies to extend their advisory services'; thirdly, of allocating funds 'to enable existing non-profit-making bodies to extend their advisory services'; and finally, of forming 'a register of firms qualified to provide advice on various aspects of efficiency in management'.[98]

These cautious ideas eventually led to the founding of the British Institute of Management in 1947, a valuable instrument of propaganda, but hardly an answer to the array of first-class business schools to be deployed by Britain's competitors after the war. And so here again it was left to a renewed analysis of a problem many years later to pillory an earlier failure to tackle it promptly and ruthlessly – the analyst in this case being Lord Franks, a member of the newly created National Economic Development Council, who in 1963 in his book *British Business Schools* was to call for two such schools to be set up; one in London, associated with Imperial College and the London School of Economics, and the other associated with Manchester University.[99] But by this period, of course, relative British industrial decline had already entered its acute phase. Therefore the neglect in wartime to plan for the immediate postwar creation of business schools marks yet another failure to exploit a unique and irrecoverable breathing-space in which a major defect in the British industrial system could have been put right.

A hardly less serious opportunity was missed in the field of industrial design. In 1943–4 two specialist committees reported on this topic. The first, appointed by the Department of Overseas Trade and chaired by Lord Weir, remarked on the rapid development of industrial design as a profession in the United States over the previous twenty years, and on how American manufacturers were already scrapping old machines simply for the sake of 'new, better and cheaper style goods'.[100] The Weir Committee drew attention to such arcane considerations as the need for British manufacturers to study foreign consumer tastes, and to hire good designers from outside consultancies. It identified a 'serious defect' in existing British design education: 'At present functional design is not usually studied in technical colleges and art schools are not well placed to give training in modern technique.' The reason for this shortcoming of the art schools lay, in the committee's judgement, in that:

> there has been too much emphasis on the words 'Art' and 'Artist'. Manufacturers, particularly in the more technical industries, are suspicious of the artist and the art school, and it is a cardinal point in our recommendations that a status and prestige should be built up around the words 'design' and 'designer'.[101]

The second report on design, rendered to the Presidents of the Boards of Trade and Education by officials of both departments, glumly noted that while there were 'facilities in the art schools for glass, pottery and furniture, hardly any means exist for training the designer for light engineering production (including plastics) in this country, whereas in the USA several institutions provide special courses for this purpose.'[102] The officials recalled that since 1932 there had been five major British reports on design and training for design.[103] 'The first four', they wrote drily, 'are mainly in the mood of culture. The last is commercial – and not commercial-at-large but written with a wide-open sense of the immediate post-war problems of the export trade.'[104]

The sour irony in all this is that as long ago as 1837 the British state had taken its very first faltering step in the sphere of education by setting up a school of design under the Board of Trade, to be followed in the wake of the Great Exhibition of 1851 by a Department of Science and Art, also under the Board of Trade. Nothing could better illustrate how progress in Britain, however keenly perceived as overdue, moves at the pace of a man immersed in treacle.

The diagnoses made by the two committees of 1943–4 on design also throw fresh light on the perpetual tendency of British education and training to move 'up-market' away from the practical and the industrial towards the highminded pursuit of pure 'culture': or, to paraphrase the Weir Committee, too much emphasis on 'Art' and 'Artist', not enough on 'design' and 'designer'. They throw fresh light too on a parallel British art-school predilection for handicraft over industrial modes of production, especially in such fields as pottery; and on the reciprocal attitude of the 'practical man' of British industry in scorning art-school-trained designers, with the consequence that talented British students emigrated, later to emerge as successful designers in the USA.[105] All in all, here was a neat enough summation of the longstanding mutual antipathy between British education and British industry. Equally familiar is the reason adduced by the Weir Committee as to why shortcomings in the teaching of design to schoolchildren had not been remedied thus far: the Board of Education and the Scottish Education Department had been 'hampered by their policy not to impose a curriculum on the schools'.[106]

Regrettably, this reluctance to impose anything on anybody, which pervaded the whole of Whitehall's approach to the problem of British industrial incompetence and the associated weaknesses of British education and training, no less applied to the future of British industrial design. Apart from the eventually implemented proposal for a council of industrial design (the director 1947–60 being Gordon Russell, a furniture designer in the 'arts and crafts' cottagey tradition), with a design centre in London, the Boards of Trade and Education and their advisory committees could only recommend that art and handicraft should become compulsory in the junior classes of all secondary schools; that there should be compulsory courses in design 'discrimination' in teachers' training colleges; and that the Royal College of Art should be reorganised as a centre for industrial design rather than merely fine arts.[107] It is enough to say that this package of measures was to prove quite insufficient between 1945 and 1960 to swing the balance in art schools far enough from art and handicraft to industrial and commercial design, or to awaken the British manufacturer to the importance of first-class designers to his survival in home and foreign markets. In the event, poor design – old-fashioned, dowdy, crudely amateurish – was to play a major role in the rout from 1960 onwards of British industries from machine tools to textiles and motor vehicles, while disconsolate British designers of high talent either went abroad, or, staying at home, designed for foreign companies.[108] There was to be no course in interior design or industrial design related to engineering until 1966–7. Once again, fresh reports and fresh recommendations, this time dating from 1970 to 1983, were to signpost the inadequacies of earlier measures.[109]

It might be argued that the financial and material constraints of a war-ruined Britain would have rendered it impossible anyway to embark on those large-scale developments in technical and managerial education that were neglected by wartime Whitehall, and only recommended by major reports after the war, in particular from 1956 onwards. But in point of fact the scant share of resources allotted to developing further and technical education – indeed the scant share of national resources allotted to developing education in general – stemmed from the coalition government's overriding priority to New Jerusalem, politics being the art of the possible, and the possible having been successfully defined by the New Jerusalem evangelists. This was why Butler and his colleagues in the original 1943 education White Paper placed spending on schools for toddlers well above schools for technicians and technocrats (see above p. 287). This was why the whole of education received such a mean share of predicted total postwar public current expenditure compared with New Jerusalem projects – £67 million a year extra after seven years compared with an initial extra outlay of £293 million a year on social security and a national health service.[110] It was also why in January 1945 the government allotted only £5 million to new buildings and equipment for education in the first year of peace, as against £2.5 million to capital expenditure on health and £56 million on new housing.[111]

Even a major provision of the 1944 Education Act was to fall victim in the event to the *Zeitgeist*'s sloganising aspiration for broad social advance. For compulsory part-time day-continuation education in 'young people's colleges' to age eighteen, blending the academic with the practical on the model of the German *Fachschulen* and other long-established European equivalents, was to remain a dead letter, just as it had after 1918, because the postwar Labour government, faced with a shortage of teachers and school places, chose to give priority instead to raising the general school-leaving age to fifteen – greater opportunity for all; a principle dear to the party's heart. It was for similar reasons that the wartime coalition had originally committed itself to raising the school-leaving age, even though the Department of Education well knew at the time that resources could not suffice both for that and for part-time further education, nor indeed even for the raising of the school-leaving age to sixteen (as then intended) alone.[112] An unpublished official study said of the Labour government's decision: 'Clearly, now that the school-leaving age was to be raised in April 1947, there was little prospect of any rapid extension of the education service in the field of Further Education.'[113] Yet had governments opted instead for compulsory part-time education for one day a week between ages fourteen and eighteen, it would have meant that each school 'place' would have served five students instead of one.[114] It would have provided an education related to a working life, whereas raising the school-leaving age meant an extra year (or years) of scholastic study that would be irrelevant and boring to many youngsters, and lead to no useful paper qualification. As Ede had acknowledged at the very time when the raising of the school-leaving age to sixteen was being written into the wartime reforms, the teachers themselves lacked the faintest idea how they were going to pad out the extra years, especially for the 'non-bookish'.[115]

And so, in the familiar pattern, it was left to the 1959 report by the Crowther Committee (of the Central Advisory Council for Education) to recommend afresh that compulsory part-time education to age eighteen, together with county colleges, should now be inaugurated.[116] But even forty years after the ending of the Second World War the question was still to be a matter for preliminary discussion; yet another colossal wasted opportunity.

Nevertheless, it has always to be remembered that between 1941 and 1944 Butler and his colleagues were overwhelmingly preoccupied with reshaping the structure of full-time education, primary and secondary, so that both became stages in a continuing process under the same education authorities. It was therefore the more vital that this one *Schwerpunkt* of the 1944 Education Act should succeed in overturning the dominance of Victorian academic ideals over British state-funded schooling, its curricula and its pecking order of intellectual snobbery.

In 1938, the Spens Report had proposed radical measures for breaking that dominance, exerted as it was through the medium of the grammar school and its high prestige. It wanted there to be three parallel types of state-funded secondary school, the modern, the technical and the grammar, each to enjoy parity of esteem, resources and quality of teaching, so that pupils of a practical, problem-solving bent should be equally well served and well valued as the bookish – and equally well value themselves, rather than feel academic rejects.[117] According to the Spens Report, the curriculum at grammar schools was 'still largely planned in the interests of the pupils who intended to go to a University', even though 85 per cent of all pupils did not remain at school beyond the age of sixteen. And although the report did not bother to say so, the current requirements of university entrance were, like the grammar schools themselves, the legacy of traditional Oxbridge's victory in the nineteenth-century educational debate; they therefore constituted the other claw in academicism's grip on British education.

The Spens Report's analysis of the problem and suggested remedy provided the starting-point for the Department of Education's wartime ponderings about secondary education;[118] and the remedy itself was embodied in the Green Book's call for a tripartite system of technical, modern and grammar schools. But the Green Book had little to say about what should be taught in these schools, an omission which prompted the Permanent Under-Secretary, Sir Maurice Holmes, to urge that the curriculum needed to be reviewed 'and related to the civilisation we live in'.[119]

The 1943 White Paper followed Spens and the Green Book in lamenting that the grammar school 'enjoys a prestige in the eyes of parents and the general public which completely overshadows all other types of school for children over 11'.[120] It even displayed enlightenment on the topic of the curriculum:

> An academic training is ill-suited for many of the pupils who find themselves moving along a narrow educational path bounded by the School Certificate. . . . Further, too many of the nation's abler children are attracted into a type of education which prepares primarily for the University and for the administration and clerical professions; too few find their way into schools from which the design and craftsmanship sides of industry are recruited.[121]

Regrettably, however, the White Paper failed to delve any deeper into the curriculum; and even more regrettably failed to come up with concrete proposals for remedying its existing bias. Instead it announced that this would be the subject of a forthcoming report by a special committee of the Secondary Schools Examination Council on 'Curriculum and Examinations'. Although this committee had been appointed early in 1941, before Butler became President of the Board of Education, Butler used it as a device for side-tracking away from his White Paper the potentially awkward question of the purpose and content of education.[122] But in the event the committee's report was to prove a decisively influential statement of educational philosophy, like Newman's in 1852 or Morant's and Mackail's in 1904–5 (see above p. 213–14 and p. 225).

The choice of chairman of this committee, though obvious enough in terms of eminent membership of the 'enlightened' Establishment, proved calamitous. Dr Cyril Norwood, classicist, president of St John's College, Oxford, former headmaster of Harrow (where the boys called him 'Boots' because these were what he wore instead of shoes), had written *The English Tradition in Education*, the book which in 1929 had praised the recapture in modern British schools of the old ideals 'which inspired the knighthood of medieval days', and celebrated the fact that 'the tradition of English education which holds the field today' was 'based upon religion'.[123] In his influential treatise Dr Norwood devoted much of the space to religion, but did manage to spare ten pages to note the ignorance of young Englishmen about commerce, and deplore the empire's shortage of biologists, botanists and other useful practitioners, although without drawing any connection between these phenomena and the kind of education advocated by his book.

Norwood's committee consisted of twelve other members of the 'enlightened' Establishment who also dwelt protected from the icy winds of competitive life in an environment of secure posts and handsome stipends, and who would like him swiftly perish if the glass were ever broken and the heating switched off – headmistresses and headmasters (of grammar schools, of course), secretaries of various educational bodies, a chief education officer. The committee did not include an industrialist, a trade unionist or an engineer.[124] Of fifty-eight bodies asked to give evidence, only ten were connected with the productive economy.[125] It opened its proceedings in October 1941 in the Beit Room at Rhodes House, in Oxford; a suitably nostalgic location.

Norwood and Butler had already agreed that the committee should review 'the whole field of secondary education after the War'.[126] Norwood therefore briefed his committee that they must consider 'post-primary education as a whole, including the Technical School, Grammar School and Modern School – in urban and rural areas, the training of future airmen, farmers and sailors'.[127] This admirably broad view represented in reality an exercise in hypocrisy, if not actual deception, for Norwood was to tell Butler the following month that he would not be going into great detail in considering the future of education in the technical and modern schools.[128] In the words of a member of his committee at the time, Norwood 'regarded himself as entrusted with the task of charting the scope of the Grammar Schools in the wider field of Secondary Education. . .'.[129] It was only too true. Norwood steered his willing committee towards his own cherished objective with no less pertinacity than Beveridge; and that objective was to preserve the domination of the grammar school and its academic values at the cost of other kinds of secondary school and of any type of education inspired by purposes related to life and work in the modern world.

The main topics proposed by him for discussion in future meetings were therefore entirely concerned with the grammar school, its curriculum and the requirements of the university entrance. But it is in a paper which he circulated to his committee that he plainly states his Christian and platonic prejudices. In the first place, he suggests as a basic principle that 'the purpose of education is to help each individual to realise the full potential of his personality – body, mind and spirit. . .': no recognition therefore at all of the balancing necessity for the individual (or the nation) to make a way in the world. He asks: Is his committee to accept, reject or criticise the 'orthodox' view that the purpose of education (in his definition) cannot be realised 'unless the spiritual values of truth, goodness and beauty are considered to be absolute values? that this must be based on a religious interpretation of the world which for us must be the Christian religion?'[130] Or, Norwood proceeds rhetorically, are we to accept, reject or criticise the alternative modern theory that all values (including truth, beauty and goodness) are relative? that:

> hitherto, education had been backward-looking, designed to confirm and entrench established names; and the new world requires a forward-looking education, based on science, using scientific method to adapt conduct to changing needs, and knowledge to changing circumstances?[131]

With regard to the tripartite system of secondary schools suggested by Spens and the Green Book, Norwood asks if 'parity or esteem' can be achieved by material, administrative and financial parity or a single code. 'Can a school with a leaving age of 16 ever have parity of esteem with one with a leaving age of 18? Is it all a game of "Let's pretend"?'

His like-minded committee duly responded as he wished.[132] The Norwood Report, published in July 1943,[133] was adorned on the title page with a quotation from Plato's *Laws* in the original Greek, together with a translation for the benefit of any passing businessman or electronics engineer. The introduction opened by repeating *verbatim* Dr Norwood's earlier definition for the benefit of his committee of the purpose of education. It then proceeded to answer all the rhetorical questions put by him to his colleagues, and in so doing restated – at this time of critical British dependence on American technology and of accumulating Whitehall reports on British industry's dismal postwar export prospects – the pseudo-aristocratic frivolities of Dr Arnold and Cardinal Newman:

> We believe that education cannot stop short of recognising the ideals of truth and beauty and goodness as final and binding for all times and in all places, as ultimate values; we do not believe that these ideas are of temporary convenience only, as devices for holding together society till they can be dispensed with as knowledge grows and organisation becomes more scientific. Further, we hold that the recognition of such values implies, for most people at least, a religious interpretation of life, which for us must mean the Christian interpretation of life. We have no sympathy, therefore, with a theory of education which pre-supposes that its aim can be dictated by the provisional findings of special Sciences, whether biological, psychological or sociological, that the function of education is to fit pupils to determine their outlook and conduct according to the changing standards of the day.[134]

The Norwood Report did not reject science altogether; indeed it agreed 'wholeheartedly' that scientific method and planning 'can do much to help in the realisation of the "good life"':

> But our belief is that education from its own nature must be ultimately concerned with values which are independent of time or a particular environment, though realisable under changing forms of both, and therefore no programmes of education which concern themselves only with relative ends and the immediate adaptation of the individual to existing surroundings can be acceptable.[135]

Given such fundamentalism, it is hardly surprising that the Norwood Committee absolutely rejected contemporary demands for 'Education for Life', with studies in international relations, economic and social structure, local and central government, the history and economic resources of other countries; let alone outright career preparation.[136] Nor does it surprise that the committee could not view the question of modern languages 'solely as one of practical utility in terms of employment or career'. The committee had, however, a particular reason for saying this: 'The majority of Grammar school pupils will not take up work in which a knowledge of modern languages will be the first or even a major requisite.' And therefore:

> If pupils who go on to read Modern Languages at a University are disregarded, the great majority of the remainder can use a modern

> language learnt at school either as a tool in their further study of other subjects, or for the odd occasions on which it is of value to them for pleasure or not at all.[137]

The committee proclaimed, moreover, that the role and importance of classics remained undiminished, especially for the study of divinity.[138] As for art education, this provided 'a powerful means of raising public taste' and could 'exert a powerful influence towards the replacement of ugliness by what is beautiful in all spheres of national life',[139] a view that owed more to Ruskin than to the *Bauhaus* – of which it is highly probable the Norwood Committee had never heard. The committee's report devoted three pages to the needs of commerce, as against seven on religion. It complacently argued that 'the history of the last three years' had disproved criticism of traditional academic education, which in its opinion constituted not only the best kind of education and suited for the best kind of pupil, but also offered the best possible preparation for a business career.[140]

The importance of this amazing document in terms of the future of secondary education at a critical juncture in British history resides in that it publicly affirmed in uncompromising language the prevailing outlook and beliefs of the British educational establishment, and in particular of those who controlled, and would control, the levers of the educational system. After all, the signatories of the Norwood Report included the headmistress of Manchester Grammar School for Girls, the headmaster of Leeds Grammar School, the secretary and president respectively of the Associations of Assistant Masters and Mistresses in Secondary Schools, the secretary of the Association of Education Committees, the secretary to the Matriculation and Schools Examination Council of the University of London, the chairman of the Northern Universities Joint Matriculation Board, the chief education officer for Birmingham, and the secretary to the Syndicate of Local Examiners, University of Cambridge. And since the 1944 Education Act was, by its authors' deliberate design, merely an 'enabling' measure, the realisation of its intentions depended entirely on those it so 'enabled' – the educational establishment as represented by the Norwood Committee, as well as the local authorities, with their traditional intellectual snobberies. In this way the Act delivered the future of a tripartite secondary education, in which modern and technical schools would enjoy parity of provision and status with grammar schools, into the hands of those who (in a self-fulfilling judgement) believed that modern and technical education constituted second-class studies for rude mechanicals.[141] As a consequence, the hopeful intentions of the 1944 Act (as spelt out more fully in the preceding White Paper) were never to be realised; in fact the very reverse.

For in the first twenty years of the postwar era (before the introduction of comprehensive education gathered momentum in the mid-1960s) the number of grammar-school places was actually to increase faster than the rise in the secondary-school population, while technical schools, far from witnessing a major expansion in numbers and an enhancement of their status, were never to cater for more than 2 per cent of that school population – and even that percentage was eventually to halve.[142] Thus the third leg of Butler's tripod, the one with the most relevance to British industrial success and also the one which might have fostered a technological national culture in place of a literary one, was simply never to be built. And the secondary modern school, though greatly expanded in numbers in the postwar era, was to remain in the eyes of parents and children alike a mere educational settling-tank for academic failures, never to achieve the excellence and reputation of the German *Realschule*. How could it with staff of inferior quality to that in the grammar school, with larger classes than the grammar school, with resources per child barely a third of those enjoyed by the grammar school, and with no examination specifically designed for its pupils but instead only the highly academic General Certificate of Education formulated by university examining boards for the benefit of the bookish?[143]

So the grammar school and its Victorian academicism and its anti-industrial ethos continued to command the heartland of the British state-funded education. The breakdown, virtually on the start-line, of the single *Schwerpunkt* of wartime plans for educational reform therefore consummated the coalition government's failure to exploit a unique opportunity for radical change across the whole front of Britain's crippling weaknesses in education and training; a failure the more calamitous because other nations, with other educational priorities, would again set out to win in the class-room and on campus the commercial triumphs of the morrow.

And so in the 1960s, when Britain's easy ride in the booming postwar world was over and she was undergoing steady defeat at the hands of the revived Europeans and the Japanese, she was still to lack the superlatively well-trained, intelligent and adaptable workforce, from boardroom to shopfloor, that she now even more badly needed. For the institutions which, had they been set on foot in 1945, would by now have been producing that workforce, were instead either just being started or still being talked about.

Not until 1965 was there launched a fresh attempt to break the dominance of the grammar school over secondary education, this time by means of merging the 1944 Act's three types of school into a single 'comprehensive' establishment; and even then grammar-school values, as manifested by an obsession with results in academic examinations set by university boards, were still to triumph. Not until 1982 was the central government to intervene directly in the schools in order to promote a technical and vocational emphasis in the curriculum, by means of the Technical and Vocational Education Initiative, significantly placed in the control of the Manpower Services Commission rather than the Ministry of Education and Science, that repository of tradition and caution. In the field of industrial training it was not until 1963 that the British state was at last to intervene in order to ensure common standards and policies.[144] Not until the early 1980s, and then partly as a palliative for youth unemployment, was the British state to begin emulating German provisions for teenage vocational preparation by introducing the Youth Opportunities Scheme.[145]

But even as late as 1985 the compulsory day-continuation classes written into the 1944 Education Act were still to remain a matter of discussion.

With regard to higher technical education, it was not until 1960 that Britain was to create her first colleges of advanced technology, some 120 years after Germany; and not until after 1963 that these were to become full technical universities, some 70 years after their German equivalents.[146] It was not to be until the mid-1960s, in the wake of the Robbins Report on higher education, that Britain embarked on the large-scale creation of new universities, and even then the liberal-arts tradition proved so strong that it came to dominate them too; in 1969, for instance, more than 1500 places, mostly in science and engineering, were to remain unfilled.[147] And not until 1965 were the first two British business schools to be set up – sixty-six years later than the Harvard Business School.[148]

Thus at no time before or since the 1944 Education Act did Britain's educational reforms achieve the 'critical mass', the concentration of offensive weight along a chosen thrustline, necessary for decisive consequences – any more than did her parallel attempts to modernise her industrial system.

This prolonged delay before the immense omissions of the wartime coalition's educational planning began to be repaired, together with the piecemeal nature of developments even thereafter, was to mean that as late as the 1980s Britain was still to lag far behind her competitors in education for capability as an industrial society. Of the broad mass of school-leavers at age sixteen, fewer than five out of ten British youngsters would be leaving with a piece of paper that an employer would regard as having any worth, as against nine out of ten German youngsters.[149] Whereas in France and Germany 80–90 per cent of school-leavers and in Japan no fewer than 94 per cent would enjoy systematic job preparation or further education before entering the labour market, only 30 per cent of British school-leavers were to be so fortunate:[150] the remaining 70 per cent being only equipped to be coolies, like their fathers and grandfathers, but in a technological world that had little need of coolies. It is no wonder, then, that at the beginning of the 1980s less than half as many British workers in manufacturing industry would be qualifying as craftsmen per year as German, although the national populations would be broadly comparable;[151] or that Britain would be turning out only about a third as many graduate engineers as France (with a slightly smaller national population), and only a quarter as many as Japan (with twice the British population).[152] It is no wonder either that across the spectrum of manufacturing industry from boardroom to workbench, as many as 68 per cent of British employees were to lack any formal qualification (even including degrees) whatever, as against only 36 per cent in Germany.[153]

In the words of Geoffrey Holland, director of the Manpower Services Commission, in August 1984, when launching *yet another* study of Britain's backwardness in education for industrial capability compared with her rivals: 'We're not only not in the same league, we're not in the same game.'[154]

*

The wartime coalition government therefore failed across the whole field of industrial and educational policy to evolve coherent medium- or long-term strategies capable of transforming Britain's obsolete industrial culture, and thereby working a British economic miracle. Instead all the boldness of vision, all the radical planning, all the lavishing of resources, had gone towards working the *social* miracle of New Jerusalem.

Yet New Jerusalem was not the only wartime fantasy to beguile the British from a cold, clear vision of their true postwar priorities. Their political leaders and the governing Establishment, conditioned as they had been from their Edwardian childhoods to take it for granted that Britain stood in the first rank of nation states, simply could not accept that British power had vanished amid the stupendous events of the Second World War, and that the era of imperial greatness that had begun with Marlborough's victories had now ineluctably closed. Instead they thought that Britain was suffering from mere short-term weaknesses in the wake of her wartime sacrifices; and they were resolved to restore and perpetuate Britain's traditional world role. The pursuit of this hallucination in the next quarter of a century was to cost Britain in defence expenditure up to double the proportion of GNP spent by European industrial competitors who limited themselves to contributing to the non-nuclear defence of the North Atlantic Treaty area.[155] It was to impose a heavy dead weight on Britain's sluggish economy and on her fragile balance of payments, suck away from exports scarce manufacturing resources in advanced technology, and continue the wartime concentration of much of Britain's even scarcer R and D resources on defence projects.[156]

And so it was that, by the time they took the bunting down from the streets after VE-Day and turned from the war to the future, the British in their dreams and illusions and in their flinching from reality had already written the broad scenario for Britain's postwar descent to the place of fifth in the free world as an industrial power, with manufacturing output only two-fifths of West Germany's, and the place of fourteenth in the whole non-communist world in terms of annual GNP per head.[157]

As that descent took its course the illusions and the dreams of 1945 would fade one by one – the imperial and Commonwealth role, the world-power role,[158] British industrial genius, and, at the last, New Jerusalem itself,[159] a dream turned to a dank reality of a segregated, subliterate, unskilled, unhealthy and institutionalised proletariat hanging on the nipple of state maternalism.

References

Prologue

1. Issue of 9 May 1945.
2. White Paper on *Statistics Relating to the War Effort of the United Kingdom*, Cmd 6564 (November 1944).
3. Quoted in the *Daily Telegraph*, 14 May 1945.
4. Issue of 24 May 1945.
5. Speech of 1 February 1944, quoted in CAB 117/202, File 53/13/92.
6. *Daily Telegraph*, 4 June 1945.
7. *Daily Telegraph*, 5 June 1945.
8. *Daily Telegraph*, 21 June 1945.
9. *Tyneside Story* (MOI 1943); *Clydebuilt* (MOI 1944).
10. Cmd 6564.
11. See CAB 78/23, GEN 42, for minutes of the meetings of the Official Committee on Publication of Statistics with regard to the War Effort, 31 August and 15 September 1944.
12. INF/292, Home Intelligence Report No. 218, week 28 November–5 December 1944.
13. As quoted in *Current Affairs*, No. 45, 5 June 1943.
14. Quoted in R. B. McCallum and Alison Readman, *The British General Election of 1945* (Oxford, Oxford University Press, 1947), p. 159.
15. 1983 figures: *World Bank Development Report 1985* (London and New York, Oxford University Press, 1985), table 1, p. 175.
16. Central Statistical Office, *United Kingdom Balance of Payments* (London, HMSO, 1985), table 2.3, p. 16.
17. 1983 figures: *World Bank Development Report 1985* (London and New York, Oxford University Press, 1985), tables 1 and 3, pp. 175 and 179.
18. Department of Employment press release, 30 August 1985. See National Economic Development Council, *Third Annual Report: British Industrial Performance* (London, National Economic Development Council, 1985), *passim* for a survey of Britain's inferior economic performance to the leading industrial nations over the previous twenty years in terms of growth, investment, profits, productivity, falling share in world manufacturing output and increasing import penetration into the British domestic market – all before the advent of North Sea oil in quantity at the beginning of the 1980s began to distort the British economy. Cf. *Bank of England Quarterly Bulletin*, 19, 1 (1979), 6–9 and 13–19.
19. Sidney Pollard, *The Wasting of the British Economy* (London, Croom Helm, 1982); Robert Bacon and Walter Eltis, *Britain's Economic Problem: Too Few Producers*, 2nd edn (London, Macmillan, 1978).
20. Britain received over one-third more Marshall Aid than West Germany:

$2.7 billion as against $1.7 billion. Between 1945 and 1950 Britain received a total in grants and loans from the United States, Canada and the International Monetary Fund of some $8 billion. British figures supplied to the author by the Treasury; West German figures by the German Embassy in London.

Chapter One: The Dream of New Jerusalem

1. See Correlli Barnett, *The Collapse of British Power* (London, Eyre Methuen, 1972; paperback edn, Gloucester, Alan Sutton, 1984), part V, for an analysis of public opinion and grand strategy 1918–39.
2. See ibid., part I, for a full analysis of the impact of the romantic movement on the British national character. Also Martin Wiener, *English Culture and the Decline of the Industrial Spirit, 1850–1980* (Cambridge, Cambridge University Press, 1981), *passim*, but especially chs 4 and 7; Clive Aslet, *The Last Country Houses* (New Haven and London, Yale University Press, 1982), *passim*, but especially ch. 7.
3. Quoted in Mark Girouard, *The Return to Camelot: Chivalry and the English Gentleman* (New Haven and London, Yale University Press, 1981), p. 61.
4. Ibid., p. 260.
5. Ibid., pp. 260–1.
6. Letter of 9 May 1836, quoted in T. W. Bamford, *Thomas Arnold* (London, The Cresset Press, 1960), p. 120.
7. Quoted in G. A. N. Lowndes, *The Silent Social Revolution* (London, Oxford University Press, 1937), p. 108; for an analysis of the effects of the Victorian public school and Oxbridge, see Barnett, *The Collapse of British Power*, part I; also Michael Sanderson, *The Universities in the Nineteenth Century* (London, Routledge & Kegan Paul, 1975), *passim*.
8. Herbert Butterfield, *Christianity in European History* (London, Oxford University Press, 1951), pp. 40–1.
9. T. Bell, quoted in Brian Simon, *Education and the Labour Movement, 1870–1920* (London, Lawrence & Wishart, 1965), p. 12.
10. Quoted in ibid., p. 50.
11. Clement R. Attlee, *The Will and the Way to Socialism* (London, Methuen, 1935), p. 6.
12. See William Harrington and Peter Young, *The 1945 Revolution* (London, Davis-Poynter, 1978), ch. 8.
13. Ibid., p. 95.
14. Sir Richard Acland, *How It Can Be Done: A careful examination of the ways in which we can, and cannot, advance to the kind of Britain for which many hope they are fighting* (London, Macdonald, 1943), Preface.
15. Quoted in Harrington and Young, *The 1945 Revolution*, p. 100.
16. Quoted in F. A. Iremonger, *William Temple Archbishop of Canterbury: His Life and Letters* (Oxford, Oxford University Press, 1948), p. 5.
17. Quoted in ibid., p. 82.
18. Ibid., p. 84.
19. Ibid., p. 147.
20. Ibid., p. 97.
21. Ibid., p. 333.
22. Ibid.
23. Ibid., p. 498.
24. Ibid., p. 429.
25. Ibid.
26. Ibid., p. 580.

27. Kingsley Martin, *Harold Laski (1893–1950): A Biographical Memoir* (London, Victor Gollancz, 1953), pp. 33 and 164.
28. Quoted in ibid., p. 126.
29. Quoted in ibid., p. 128.
30. Quoted in Richard M. Titmuss, *Problems of Social Policy* (London, HMSO and Longmans, Green, 1951), p. 508.
31. Cf. *The Journey Home: A report prepared by Mass-Observation for the Advertising Service Guild; fifth in a series of 'Change' Wartime Surveys* (London, John Murray, 1944), especially pp. 7, 11, 13, 39 and 70–1.
32. Ian McLaine, *Ministry of Morale: Home Front Morale and the Ministry of Information in World War II* (London, George Allen & Unwin, 1979), p. 10.
33. Ibid.
34. Nigel Nicolson, *Portrait of a Marriage* (London, Futura Publications, 1974), p. 198.
35. McLaine, *Ministry of Morale*, p. 103.
36. Halifax to Duff Cooper, 9 August 1940, in INF/862.
37. CAB 87/1, Memorandum RP(41)1.
38. Cf. paper by Lord Davidson, 31 October 1940, in INF 1/849.
39. INF 1/863.
40. PREM 4/100/4, WEA(40)14, 13 December 1940.
41. Ibid.
42. Obituary, *The Times*, 16 August 1984.
43. INF 1/177.
44. G. N. Clarke, in E. T. Williams and C. S. Nicholls (eds.), *The Dictionary of National Biography 1961–1970* (Oxford, Oxford University Press, 1981), p. 1063.
45. A. P. Ryan of the BBC to H. Nicolson of the MOI, 20 March 1941, in INF 1/177.
46. INF 1/177.
47. Ibid.
48. Letter of 9 October 1941 to Brendan Bracken, Minister of Information, in INF 1/864, Post-War Aims and Reconstruction Problems.
49. Cf. memorandum by Michael Balfour of the MOI of 15 October 1941, note by A. P. Ryan of the BBC of 17 October, in INF 1/864.
50. INF 1/177.
51. Paul Addison, *The Road to 1945: British Politics and the Second World War* (London, Jonathan Cape, 1975), pp. 158–9.
52. Ibid., pp. 188–9.
53. *Current Affairs*, 26 September 1942.
54. *Current Affairs*, No. 28.
55. CAB 117/209, File No. 53/14/5.
56. Ibid.
57. Ibid.
58. Nicholas Davenport in *The Dictionary of National Biography 1961–1970*, p. 266.
59. CAB 117/209, File No. 53/14/5, letter of 6 December 1942.
60. Ibid.
61. CAB 87/76, SIC(41)1, first meeting on 8 July 1941.
62. Janet Beveridge, *Beveridge and His Plan* (London, Hodder & Stoughton, 1954), pp. 49–50.
63. Quoted in José Harris, *The Dictionary of National Biography 1961–1970*, p. 106.
64. CAB 87/76, SIC(41)1.
65. Cf. CAB 87/79, SIC(42)33, and CAB 87/80, SIC(42)76: see below pp. 238–41 for an analysis of the argument over costings.
66. CAB 87/81, SIC(42)100 (Revise), 10 July 1942.
67. Ibid.

68. PREM 4 89/2, Part II.
69. CAB 65/28, WM(42)153, 16 November 1942.
70. PREM 4 89/2, Part II.
71. Cherwell to the Prime Minister, 25 November 1942, in PREM 4 89/2, Part II.
72. Cmd 6404.
73. PREM 4 89/2, Part II.
74. Cmd 6404.
75. Sir William H. Beveridge, *The Pillars of Security and Other War-Time Essays and Addresses* (London, George Allen & Unwin, 1943).
76. INF 1/864, Home Intelligence Report No. 114, 1–8 December 1942.
77. Cited in CAB 65/35.
78. Quoted in Janet Beveridge, *Beveridge and His Plan*, p. 135.
79. Quoted in Henry Pelling, *Britain and the Second World War* (London, Fontana, 1970), p. 170.
80. CAB 65/28, 159(42), 26 November 1942.
81. WM(43)8, cited in CAB 87/13.
82. CAB 87/13, PR(43)2, 20 January 1942.
83. CAB 87/13, PR(43)13, 11 February 1943.
84. Addison, *The Road to 1945*, pp. 224–5.
85. INF 1/864, Home Intelligence Report No. 124, 9–16 February 1943.
86. Ibid., Home Intelligence Report No. 125, 16–23 February 1943.
87. Ibid., Appendix to Home Intelligence Report No. 130, 23–30 March 1943.
88. Addison, *The Road to 1945*, pp. 225–6.
89. INF 1/864, letter of 6 March 1943 from Sir John Anderson to Brendan Bracken.
90. Full text in *Current Affairs*. No. 45, 5 June 1943.
91. CAB 66/38, WP(43)255.
92. CAB 66/39, WP(43)308, 1 July 1943.
93. CAB 66/42, WP(43)467, 19 October 1943.
94. Cmd 6458.
95. Cmd 6502 and 6527.
96. Cmd 6550.
97. CAB 87/7, R(44)18, memorandum by the Minister of Reconstruction on Post-War Housing, 22 January 1944.
98. Cmd 6609.
99. Attlee Papers 2/2, Churchill Archives Centre. Cambridge.
100. Beveridge, *The Pillars of Security*, p. 137.
101. Ibid., p. 13.
102. Addison, *The Road to 1945*, pp. 242–3.
103. *Full Employment in a Free Society: A Report by William H. Beveridge* (London, George Allen & Unwin, 1944).
104. Ibid., p. 18.
105. Ibid., p. 29.
106. Ibid.
107. Ibid., p. 174
108. Ibid., p. 200.
109. Addison, *The Road to 1945*, p. 249.
110. W. E. Williams, 'When the Lights Go On', *Current Affairs*, No. 48, 31 July 1943.
111. Ibid.
112. No. 56, 20 November 1943.
113. No. 71, 17 June 1944.
114. *Current Affairs*, No. 75, 12 August 1944.
115. Nos. 76 and 81, 26 August and 4 November 1944.

116. Lt-Colonel J. T. Burgess AEC, in *Current Affairs*, No. 92, 7 April 1945.
117. *The Journey Home*, p. 44: see also J. L. Hodson, *The Sea and the Land* (London, Victor Gollancz, 1945), pp. 238 and 349.
118. INF 1/864, Home Intelligence Report No. 214, 1–7 November 1944.
119. See McCallum and Readman, *The British General Election of 1945* (London, Oxford University Press, 1947), *passim*; also Charles Madge (ed.), *Pilot Guide to the General Election* (London, Pilot Press, May 1945).
120. McCallum and Readman, *The British General Election of 1945*, pp. 45–6.
121. Quoted in ibid., p. 48.
122. Ibid., pp. 94–9 and 242.
123. Ibid.
124. Ibid.
125. Cf. *News Chronicle* Gallup Polls, cited in ibid., pp. 203–4, 237 and 244.

Chapter Two: The Illusion of Limitless Possibility

1. *Current Affairs*, 28 March 1942.
2. Quoted in *Current Affairs*, No. 45, 5 June 1943.
3. No. 48, 31 July 1943.
4. No. 82, 18 November 1944.
5. Quoted in *Current Affairs*, No. 98, 30 June 1945.
6. Ibid.
7. CAB 87/2, RP(42)2.
8. CAB 87/12, PR(43)1 and PR(43)13; cf. also CAB 87/63, EC(43)6, Treasury memorandum on the Maintenance of Employment, 16 October 1943.
9. CAB 87/14, R(I)(44)5, 23 June 1944.
10. W. K. Hancock and M. M. Gowing, *British War Economy* (London, HMSO and Longmans, Green, 1949), p. 523.
11. Quoted in ibid., p. 542.
12. Letter to Laski, quoted in Paul Addison, *The Road to 1945: British Politics and the Second World War* (London, Jonathan Cape, 1975), p. 272.
13. R. B. McCallum and Alison Readman, *The British General Election of 1945* (Oxford, Oxford University Press, 1947), pp. 48–60.
14. Quoted in Kingsley Martin, *Harold Laski (1893–1950): A Biographical Memoir* (London, Victor Gollancz, 1953), p. 159.
15. Quoted in McCallum and Readman: *The British General Election of 1945*, p. 111.
16. See above p. 55.
17. CAB 87/13, PR(43)2, 20 January 1943.
18. CAB 87/16, R(44)60, 11 September 1944.
19. *Observer*, 18 February 1943, quoted in Sir William H. Beveridge, *The Pillars of Security and Other War-Time Essays and Addresses* (London, George Allen & Unwin, 1943), p. 124.
20. Sir William H. Beveridge, *Full Employment in a Free Society, A Report by William H. Beveridge* (London, George Allen & Unwin, 1944). p. 146.
21. Ibid., p. 157.
22. CAB 87/12, PR(43)13.
23. Ibid.
24. Cf. CAB 87/12, PR(43)14.
25. CAB 87/12, PR(43)1 and PR(43)2.
26. CAB 87/8, R(44)128, 23 June 1944; see also memorandum by the Minister of Production on the draft housing White Paper, in CAB 87/6, R(44)54, 31 July 1944.
27. Cf., for example, CAB 87/7, Committee on Reconstruction, with eighty-

four memoranda in the volume, of which nineteen touch on industry or the location of industry, and thirty on welfare, town and country planning and housing. Or CAB 87/6, covering twenty-nine meetings of the committee in 1944, with sixteen agenda items on industry, finance for industry, wages and restrictive practices, and eighteen on town and country planning, welfare and building.

28. *Current Affairs*, No. 28, 10 October 1942.
29. Ibid.
30. *Current Affairs*, No. 45, 5 June 1943, 'Social Security' by Mrs W. E. Williams; No. 81, 4 November 1944, 'A Weapon Against Want' by Major Richard Bennett RA.
31. *Current Affairs*, No. 56, 20 November 1943, 'Building the Post-War Home' by R. S. Townroe, member of the Central Housing Advisory Committee of the Ministry of Health.
32. No. 82, 18 November 1944, 'What Has Happened at Home?' by Macdonald Hastings, and No. 98, 30 June 1945, 'The "Cost" of the War' by Gertrude Williams.
33. *Current Affairs*, No. 98, 30 June 1945.
34. Cf. *Current Affairs*, 28 February 1942, 'America in Total War' by Geoffrey Crowther.
35. *Current Affairs*, No. 62, 12 February 1944, 'What We'll Find in Germany' by Major R. A. Birch RA.
36. *Current Affairs*, No. 67, 22 April 1944, 'How About Japan?' by John Morris.
37. See CAB 87/76–82.
38. CAB 87/79, SIC(42)33, Memorandum by the Government Actuary on Finance of the Chairman's Draft Proposals, 22 April 1942; CAB 87/80, SIC(42)76. Memorandum by the Economic Section of the War Cabinet Secretariat on The Economic Aspects of the Proposed Reforms of Social Insurance and Allied Services, 16 June 1942; CAB 87/82, SIC(42)137, Memorandum by Government Actuary, 19 August 1942.
39. CAB 87/76, SIC(41)2, 3 and 4.
40. CAB 87/76, SIC(41)20, 11 December 1941.
41. CAB 87/76, SIC(41)22, 19 December 1941.
42. CAB 87/77, SIC(42)2, 21 January 1942.
43. CAB 87/81, SIC(42)100 (Revise), 10 July 1942.
44. CAB 87/81, SIC(42)100.
45. CAB 87/82, SIC(42)161, 30 September 1942, Appendix E.
46. CAB 87/79, SIC(42)33.
47. CAB 87/80, SIC(42)76, 16 June 1942.
48. CAB 87/82, SIC(42)166, 10 October 1942.
49. PREM 4 89/2.
50. PREM 4 89/1.
51. See above pp. 27–32.
52. Beveridge, *The Pillars of Security*, p. 76.
53. Ibid., p. 57.
54. Beveridge, *Full Employment*, p. 23.
55. Ibid., p. 31.
56. Ibid., pp. 157 and 159.
57. Ibid., p. 188.
58. Ibid., p. 214.
59. Ibid., p. 235.
60. Ibid., p. 118.
61. Janet Beveridge, *Beveridge and His Plan* (London, Hodder & Stoughton, 1954), pp. 123–4.

62. INF 1/862, letter to Duff Cooper, 30 July 1940, about a meeting of non-Cabinet ministers.
63. Quoted in J. L. Hodson, *The Sea and the Land* (London, Victor Gollancz, 1945), p. 238.
64. Issue for 12 June 1945 (by-line 'B.B.B').
65. Quoted in Charles Madge (ed.), *Pilot Guide to the General Election* (London, Pilot Press, May 1945).
66. Quoted in McCallum and Readman, *The British General Election of 1945*, p. 138.
67. Quoted in W. K. Hancock and M. M. Gowing, *British War Economy* (London, HMSO and Longmans, Green, 1949), p. 546.

Chapter Three: 'The Prospect is Bleak': 1943–45

1. CAB 87/14, R(I)(44)5, The Long Term Prospects of British Industry, 23 June 1944.
2. CAB 87/6, R(44)53 and R(44)92, memoranda by the First Lord of the Admiralty and the Minister of War Transport: R(44)52, meeting of the Reconstruction Committee, 10 July 1944.
3. CAB 87/9, R(44)152, 2 September 1944.
4. CAB 87/15, R(IE)(45)3.
5. Ibid.
6. CAB 87/18, R(IO)(45)12.
7. CAB 87/18, R(IO)(45)16, 22 May 1945.
8. Sir Archibald McKinstry, Appendix I to CAB 87/18 R(IO)(45)16.
9. CAB 87/15, R(I)(45)9, 21 March 1945.
10. Ibid.
11. Calculated from C. H. Feinstein, *National Income, Expenditure and Output of the United Kingdom, 1855–1965* (Cambridge, Cambridge University Press, 1972), table 51.
12. *The United States Strategic Bombing Survey*, with an introduction by David MacIsaac, 10 vols. (New York and London, Garland Publishing, 1976), vol. I, *The Effects of Strategic Bombing on the German War Economy (European Report no. 3)*, table 5, p. 27.
13. Feinstein, *National Income*, table 51; *USSBS*, vol. I, *Effects*, table 5, p. 27.
14. CAB 102/81, First Draft of *British War Economy* (see below note 20).
15. M. M. Postan, *British War Production* (London, HMSO and Longmans, Green, 1952), table 29, p. 207; *USSBS*, vol. I, *Effects*, appendix, table 26, p. 224.
16. British figure calculated from Postan, *British War Production*, table 29, p. 207, and William Hornby. *Factories and Plant* (London, HMSO and Longmans, Green, 1958), p. 338. German figures calculated from USSBS, vol. I, *Effects*, appendix, tables 26 and 29, pp. 224 and 227.
17. *USSBS*, vol. I, *Effects*, appendix, table 7, p. 208.
18. German figure for 1943 from *USSBS*, vol. II, Aircraft Division Industry Report, *Strategic Bombing of the German Aircraft Industry (European Report no. 4)*, p. 84. British figure from CAB 87/13, (PR)98, and Postan, *British War Production*, table 41, p. 310: total aircraft industry workforce (excluding sub-contractors) 510,000; total output in structure weight in 1944 was 221,985,000 lb; therefore output per worker per day 1.19 lb.
19. German figures from *USSBS*, vol. I, *Effects*, appendix, tables 9, 104 and 105, pp. 211 and 279; British figures from *Statistical Digest of the War* (London, HMSO and Longmans, Green, 1951), table 126, and CAB 102/409, Labour Requirements and Supply for the Ministries of Supply and Production, draft

by Mrs Inman for use in official history *Labour in the Munitions Industries* (see below note 93 to Chapter Eight).

20. Britain: 1938 – 226,993,000 tons; 1944 – 184,098,400 tons; from Ministry of Fuel and Power, *Statistical Digest for 1944*, Cmd 6639 (1944), quoted in W. K. Hancock and M. M. Gowing, *British War Economy* (London, HMSO and Longmans, Green, 1949), p. 479. Germany: 1938 – 232,300,000; 1944 – 249,100,000; from *USSBS*, vol. I, *Effects*, table 55, p. 92.
21. See above note 20.
22. *USSBS*, vol. I, *Overall Report (European War) (European Report no. 2)*, chart no. 25, p. 62; Hornby, *Factories and Plant*, p. 193; *USSBS*, vol. I, *Effects*, appendix, table 106, p. 281.
23. CAB 66/36, WP(43)159, 21 April 1943.
24. Cf. R. J. Overy, *The Air War*, 1939–45 (London, Europa Publications, 1980), ch. 7, *passim*; Postan, *British War Production*.
25. See for example Max Hastings, *Overlord: D-Day and the Battle for Normandy, 1944* (London, Michael Joseph, 1984); Carlo D'Este, *Decision in Normandy* (London, William Collins, 1983); Richard Lamb, *Montgomery in Europe, 1943–5: Success or Failure?* (London, Buchan & Enright, 1983).

Chapter Four: An Industrial Worst Case: Coal

1. Quoted in David Fraser, *Alanbrooke* (London, William Collins, 1982), p. 137.
2. *Coal Mining: Report of the Technical Advisory Committee* (the Reid Report), Cmd 6610 (1945).
3. CAB 123/21, WP(44)565, 10 October 1944.
4. WM(44)136, 12 October 1944, cited in CAB 123/21.
5. W. H. B. Court, *Coal* (London, HMSO and Longmans, Green, 1951), p. 109.
6. Ibid., p. 110.
7. CAB 66/23, WP(42)148, 6 April 1942.
8. CAB 65/26, WM46(42)1, 10 April 1942.
9. CAB 87/92, CM(42)16, 1941 figure: Memorandum by the Board of Trade on the Wartime Organisation of the Coal Industry, 24 May 1942.
10. CAB 87/92, CM(42)2, Report by T. E. B. Young.
11. Ibid.
12. Ibid.
13. Ibid.
14. Ibid.
15. CAB 87/92, CM(42)7th, 14 May 1942.
16. CAB 87/92, CM(42)2nd, 23 April 1942.
17. CAB 87/92, CM(42)10th, 29 May 1942.
18. CAB 87/92, CM(42)5, Summary by the Mines Department of Reports of the Coal Production Technical Advisers, 28 April 1942; CM(42)17, Draft Report to the War Cabinet, 26 May 1942.
19. H. Wilson, *New Deal for Coal* (London, Contact Books, 1945), p. 3, quoting from *Ministry of Fuel and Power: Statistical Digest for 1938*, Cmd 6538 (1941).
20. Ibid, quoting from Tory Reform Committee pamphlet, *A National Policy for Coal* (1945).
21. Ibid., quoting from Cmd 6538.
22. Ibid., p. 8.
23. 1943 figures, ibid., pp. 8–9.
24. Ibid., table III, p. 9.
25. Ibid., table X, pp. 30–1.
26. Ibid., table IV, p. 11.

27. The Emmott Committee, *Report of an enquiry into the relationship of technical education to other forms of education and to industry and commerce* (1927).
28. Cmd 6610.
29. CAB 87/92, CM(42)16, 24 May 1942.
30. Wilson, *New Deal for Coal*, table XVIII, p. 121, quoting from Cmd 6538 and *Board of Trade Journal*, October 1944.
31. *The Times*, 11 April 1942.
32. See below pp. 79–80.
33. Wilson, *New Deal for Coal*, p. 34.
34. Ibid., p. 38.
35. Cf. J. U. Nef, *The Rise of the British Coal Industry*, 2 vols. (London, George Routledge, 1932), especially part IV, chs 1 and 2; S. G. Checkland, *The Rise of Industrial Society in England* (London, Longmans, 1964), especially part II, ch. 4; Peter Mathias, *The First Industrial Nation* (London, Methuen, 1969), especially Prologue and chs 2 and 5.
36. Cmd 6610, p. 3.
37. Ibid.
38. Ibid., p. 4.
39. Ibid.
40. A. J. Taylor, 'Labour Productivity and Technical Innovation in the British Coal Industry 1850–1914', *English Historical Review*, Second Series, XIV, 1 (1961), p. 48.
41. Michael P. Jackson, *The Price of Coal* (London, Croom Helm, 1974), p. 5.
42. Ibid.
43. Ibid.
44. M. Bulmer (ed.), *Mining and Social Change: Durham County in the Twentieth Century* (London, Croom Helm, 1978), p. 26, quoting from M. Benney, *Charity Main: A Coalfield Chronicle* (London, George Allen & Unwin, 1946).
45. Benney, quoted in ibid., p. 27.
46. Sid Chaplin, transcript of a talk to Durham University, 1971, quoted in ibid., p. 81.
47. Jackson, *The Price of Coal*, p. 7.
48. Ibid., p. 21.
49. Wilson, *New Deal for Coal*, table IX, p. 28.
50. CAB 87/92, CM(42)5, 28 April 1942; and Cmd 6610.
51. CAB 87/92, CM(42)5, 28 April 1942; and Cmd 6610.
52. Cmd 6610.
53. Wilson, *New Deal for Coal*, p. 29.
54. Ibid., p. 26 and footnote 4, table IX, p. 28.
55. *Report of the Royal Commission on the Coal Industry*, Cmd 2600 (1925), p. 112.
56. Cmd 6610, pp. 34–5.
57. Ibid., p. 35.
58. Ibid., p. 36.
59. Ibid.
60. Ibid.
61. Coal Industry Commission, *Final Report*, Cmd 361 (1919), p. 35.
62. Ibid., pp. 49–50.
63. Cmd 2600, p. 237.
64. Jackson, *The Price of Coal*, p. 27.
65. Wilson, *New Deal for Coal*, p. 26.
66. Ibid., p. 23.
67. Ibid., p. 35.
68. Ibid., pp. 31–4.
69. Jackson, *The Price of Coal*, p. 44.
70. Court, *Coal*, p. 110.

71. Ibid., pp. 120–2.
72. T. E. B. Young, CAB 87/92, CM(42)5th, 11 May 1942: see also Dr H. S. Houldsworth in CM(42)7th, 14 May 1942.
73. T. E. B. Young, CAB 87/92. CM(42)5th, 11 May 1942.
74. Memorandum WP(42)224 in CAB 66/25.
75. Ibid.
76. *Coal*, Cmd 6364.
77. Ibid.
78. Ibid.
79. See above pp. 74–5.
80. Court, *Coal*, p. 198.
81. Wilson, *New Deal for Coal*, p. 115.
82. Ibid., p. 116.
83. Court, *Coal*, pp. 219–26; Jackson, *The Price of Coal*, pp. 48–9.
84. Court, *Coal*, pp. 226–8.
85. Jackson, *The Price of Coal*, p. 52.
86. Court, *Coal*, pp. 253–4.
87. Jackson, *The Price of Coal*, p. 53.
88. Ibid., p. 55.
89. Court, *Coal*, pp. 261–7.
90. Wilson, *New Deal for Coal*, table XVIII, p. 121.
91. Court, *Coal*, pp. 266–7.
92. Jackson, *The Price of Coal*, p. 54.
93. Wilson, *New Deal for Coal*, p. 117.
94. CAB 71/11, LP(43)8, 29 January 1943.
95. CAB 71/14, LP(43)219, 4 October 1943.
96. CAB 87/93, CI(43)1, Memorandum by the Minister of Fuel and Power on 'Causes and Remedies of Decline in the Output of Coal', 8 November 1943.
97. Ibid.
98. Ibid.
99. Ibid.
100. CAB 66/41, WP(43)446, Examination of the Present System of Control in the Coalmining Industry and Future Policy.
101. CAB 87/93, CI(43)1, Appendix II.
102. Ibid.
103. Ibid.
104. Ibid.
105. CAB 65/36, WM 137(43)8, Cabinet decision to create Committee on the Organisation of the Coal Industry, 8 October 1943: CAB 87/93, Committee on the Organisation of the Coal Industry: WP(44)115, Report by the Committee, 16 February 1944.
106. Court, *Coal*, pp. 286–7.
107. Wilson, *New Deal for Coal*, p. 107.
108. Court, *Coal*, p. 283.
109. Wilson, *New Deal for Coal*, p. 127 and footnote 1.
110. Court, *Coal*, p. 279.
111. Ibid., pp. 280–1.
112. Ibid., p. 280.
113. Wilson, *New Deal for Coal*, p. 76.
114. Ibid., p. 80.
115. Quoted in Cmd 6610.
116. Wilson, *New Deal for Coal*, p. 133.
117. Ibid., p. 132.
118. Cf. the Minister of Fuel and Power in the debate of 13 July 1944, Hansard,

Parliamentary Debates (House of Commons), Fifth Series, vol. 401, col. 1917; Wilson, *New Deal for Coal*, p. 132; Cmd 6610.

119. Cmd 6610.
120. Wilson, *New Deal for Coal*, p. 76.
121. G. D. H. Cole, *National Coal Board* (London, Fabian Society, revised edn 1949), pp. 10–11.
122. Cmd 6610.
123. Wilson, *New Deal for Coal*, p. 131.
124. Ibid.

Chapter Five: 'In Great Need of Modernisation': Steel

1. *Daily Telegraph*, 4 June 1945. See above p. 1.
2. CAB 87/10, R(45)17, 30 April 1945: discussions on a joint memorandum by Minister of Supply and President of the Board of Trade on iron and steel, 6 April 1945, R(45)36, covering a report by their officials on the industry and the measures necessary to ensure its efficiency after the war.
3. CAB 87/10, R(45)36.
4. Ibid.
5. Ibid.
6. T. H. Burnham and G. O. Hoskins, *Iron and Steel in Britain, 1870–1930* (London, George Allen & Unwin, 1943), table 39, p. 145. In 1945 the Krupp-AG at Essen-Borbeck had furnaces of 180,000 tons annual capacity: Combined Intelligence Objectives Sub-Committee, Item Nos. 2, 3, 4, 11, 18 and 21, File No. XXXII–67, *Krupp A.G., Bochumer Verein* (London, HMSO, 1945).
7. CAB 87/10, R(45)6.
8. Ibid. According to British Intelligence Objectives Sub-Committee, Final Report No. 1287, Item Nos. 21 and 31, *Rolling Mills at the Reichswerke (Hermann Göring), Braunschweig* (London, HMSO, 1947), the integrated works at Braunschweig had an annual ingot make of I million tons.
9. W. K. Hancock and M. M. Gowing, *British War Economy* (London, HMSO and Longmans, Green, 1949), p. 381, footnote 2.
10. 63,198,000 tons: Cmd 6564.
11. H. Duncan Hall, *North American Supply* (London, HMSO and Longmans, Green, 1955), p. 94, footnote 1.
12. Memorandum from the Minister of Production to the Prime Minister, 14 October 1942, in ibid., p. 391.
13. CAB 16/141, DPR 152, 7th Progress Report.
14. CAB 16/141, DPR 193, 12th Report by the Air Ministry, for April 1937.
15. CAB 16/141, DPR 198, 13th Report by the Air Ministry, for May 1937.
16. CAB 16/141, DPR 199, 13th Report by the Admiralty.
17. CAB 16/142, DPR 202, 13th Report by the Ministry of Labour, at May 1937.
18. CAB 16/142, DPR 209, 14th Report by the Ministry of Labour, at June 1937.
19. CAB 16/142, DPR 245, 19th Report by the Ministry of Labour, at December 1937.
20. CAB 27/648, CP 247(38), Report of the Committee on Defence Programmes and their Acceleration.
21. CAB 16/142, DPR 211, Report by a Sub-Committee on Essential Raw Materials.
22. Ibid.
23. Cmd 5507.

24. Ibid., appendix V.
25. J. C. Carr and W. Taplin, assisted by A. E. G. Wright, *History of the British Steel Industry* (Cambridge, Mass., Harvard University Press, 1962), p. 557; Burnham and Hoskins, *Iron and Steel in Britain*, table 39, p. 145.
26. Cmd 5507, appendix IX.
27. Ibid., pp. 39–40.
28. Ibid., p. 40.
29. Report by the Dock Facilities Sub-Committee of the Iron and Steel Federation, quoted in Carr and Taplin, *British Steel Industry*, p. 582, footnote 2.
30. Burnham and Hoskins, *Iron and Steel in Britain*, table 79, p. 201; Cmd 5507.
31. Cmd 5507, p. 32.
32. Ibid., p.29.
33. Ibid., pp. 52–3.
34. Ibid., table 41, p. 149.
35. Ibid., table 72, p. 193.
36. Ibid., p. 153.
37. Ibid., p. 49.
38. Carr and Taplin, *British Steel Industry*, p. 365.
39. K. Middlemass and J. Barnes, *Baldwin: A Biography* (London, Weidenfeld & Nicolson, 1969), pp. 311–13.
40. Ibid., p. 314, footnote.
41. Cf. *Final Report of the Committee on Industry and Trade* (1928–9), Cmd 3282, especially p. 185; also the committee's *Survey Metal Industries* (see below note 95).
42. Cf. Burnham and Hoskins, *Iron and Steel in Britain*, pp. 47–8; Carr and Taplin, *British Steel Industry*, p. 359.
43. Burnham and Hoskins, *Iron and Steel in Britain*, p. 210.
44. Carr and Taplin, *British Steel Industry*, p. 410.
45. Ibid.; Burnham and Hoskins, *Iron and Steel in Britain*, pp. 209–10.
46. Carr and Taplin, *British Steel Industry*, p. 410.
47. Burnham and Hoskins, *Iron and Steel in Britain*, table 5, p. 30.
48. Ibid., tables 1 and 3, pp. 26–7.
49. Ibid., p. 29.
50. Ibid., pp. 52–3.
51. Ibid., p. 31.
52. Quoted in Carr and Taplin, *British Steel Industry*, pp. 151–2.
53. Cf. Robert R. Locke, *The End of the Practical Man: Entrepreneurship and Higher Education in Germany, France and Great Britain 1880–1940* (Greenwich, Conn., and London, Jai Press, 1984), pp. 70–2.
54. Michael Sanderson, *The Universities and British Industry 1850–1970* (London, Routledge & Kegan Paul, 1972), p. 17.
55. Ibid., pp. 21–5.
56. Cd 9071.
57. See Locke, *The End of the Practical Man*, Introduction.
58. Cf. Carr and Taplin, *British Steel Industry*, pp. 158–63; Burnham and Hoskins, *Iron and Steel in Britain*, pp. 37–43.
59. Carr and Taplin, *British Steel Industry*, p. 214.
60. Ibid., p. 222.
61. Quoted in ibid.
62. Quoted in ibid., p. 214.
63. Report of meeting, as quoted in ibid., p. 208.
64. *History of the Ministry of Munitions* (London, HMSO, 1922), vol. VIII, part II, pp. 1–2.
65. Ibid., p. 2.

66. Ibid., vol. II, p. 58.
67. But see the amusingly ingenious attempts by self-dubbed 'cliometricians' to prove by numbers that British steel entrepreneurs made profit-wise decisions in sticking in the mud instead of investing in new plant and processes; cf. Donald N. McCloskey, *Economic Maturity and Entrepreneurial Decline: British Iron and Steel, 1870–1913* (Cambridge, Mass., Harvard University Press, 1973).
68. *Iron and Coal Trades Review*, 24 December 1909.
69. Issue of 31 January 1908.
70. Burnham and Hoskins, *Iron and Steel in Britain*, p. 37.
71. Cmd 5507, pp. 63–5.
72. Burnham and Hoskins, *Iron and Steel in Britain*, p. 43.
73. Carr and Taplin, *British Steel Industry*, pp. 15–16.
74. Quoted in ibid., p. 19.
75. Ibid., pp. 22–3.
76. Ibid.
77. Ibid., p. 218.
78. Sanderson, *Universities and British Industry*, pp. 16–18 and 88–9.
79. Carr and Taplin, *British Steel Industry*, p. 36.
80. Ibid., p. 37.
81. Burnham and Hoskins, *Iron and Steel in Britain*, pp. 28 and 30.
82. Ibid.
83. Paul Benoist, 'Itinéraire de mon Voyage en Angleterre', September 1842 (France: Archives Nationales). I am grateful to Professor Robert Locke for furnishing me with copies of this unpublished correspondence, and pointing out their interest.
84. Ibid.
85. House of Commons, *Report from the Select Committee on Scientific Instruction; with the Proceedings of the Committee, Minutes of Evidence and Appendix, 1867–8*, 15 July 1869, vol. XV.
86. Command paper 4139.
87. Quoted in Carr and Taplin, *British Steel Industry*, p. 48.
88. Quoted in ibid.
89. Quoted in ibid., p. 49.
90. Ibid., pp. 200–1.
91. Quoted in ibid., pp. 207–8.
92. Cd 9071.
93. Cd 9035.
94. Quoted in Burnham and Hoskins, *Iron and Steel in Britain*, pp. 235–6.
95. Board of Trade, *Survey of Metal Industries* (London, HMSO, 1928).
96. Burnham and Hoskins, *Iron and Steel in Britain*, p. 247.
97. Cmd 5507.
98. Ibid., p. 13.
99. Ibid.
100. Ibid., p. 64.
101. Ibid., p. 65.
102. Carr and Taplin, *British Steel Industry*, pp. 538–48; BIOS, Final Report No. 1287, *Rolling Mills at the Reichswerke*.
103. Report included in CAB 87/10, R(45)36.
104. Ibid.
105. Ibid.
106. Ibid.
107. *Productivity Report on Simplification in British Industry (1950)*.
108. CAB 87/10, R(45)36.
109. Ibid.

110. CAB 87/10, R(45)17.
111. Ibid.
112. Ibid.

Chapter Six: 'The Fossilisation of Inefficiency': Shipbuilding

1. S. Pollard and P. Robertson, *The British Shipbuilding Industry, 1870–1914* (Cambridge, Mass., and London, Harvard University Press, 1979), p. 73.
2. BT 28/319, Report to the Machine Tool Controller on the Equipment of Shipyards and Marine Engineering Shops by Mr Cecil Bentham, 30 September 1942 (the Bentham Report).
3. Pollard and Robertson, *The British Shipbuilding Industry*, pp. 29 and 128–9.
4. Ibid., p. 159.
5. Ibid., p. 167.
6. Ibid., p. 73.
7. Ibid., p. 74.
8. Ibid., pp. 136–7.
9. Ibid., p. 138.
10. Ibid., p. 140.
11. Ibid., pp. 145–6.
12. Ibid., p. 148.
13. S. Pollard, 'British and World Shipbuilding, 1890–1914: A Study in Comparative Costs', *Journal of Economic History*, XVII (1957), p. 426.
14. Leslie Jones, *Shipbuilding in Britain Mainly Between the Two World Wars* (Cardiff, University of Wales Press, 1957), table XX, p. 64.
15. Ibid.
16. J. M. Reid, *James Lithgow: Master of Work* (London, Hutchinson, 1963), p. 106.
17. Board of Trade, *Report on Shipping and Shipbuilding after the War*, Cd 2154 (1918), p. 53.
18. CAB 27/476, CDC (31)2. Report by Admiral of the Fleet Sir Frederick Field to the Committee of Imperial Defence Sub-Committee on the League of Nations Disarmament Conference. For an account of British partial disarmament 1922–32, owing to a desire for economy and to the pressure of moralising internationalism, see Correlli Barnett, *The Collapse of British Power* (London, Eyre Methuen, 1972; paperback edn, Gloucester, Alan Sutton, 1984), pp. 268–98 and 337–44.
19. CAB 16/137, DPR/44, Meeting of the Defence Policy and Requirements Committee, 21 October 1937.
20. CAB 16/140, DPR 96, Second Report by the Ministry of Labour, June 1936.
21. CAB 16/140, DPR 112, Special Enquiry into the supply of skilled labour in the shipbuilding industry by the Ministry of Labour, July 1936.
22. Cf. CAB 16/141, DPR 127, DPR 142 and DPR 154.
23. William Hornby, *Factories and Plant* (London, HMSO and Longmans, Green, 1958), p. 37.
24. Ibid.
25. Ibid., p. 39.
26. CAB 16/140–1, documents cited.
27. CAB 16/141, DPR 140, 6th Report by the Admiralty, for November 1936.
28. CAB 16/141, DPR 184, 11th Report by the Admiralty, for April 1937.
29. Hornby, *Factories and Plant*, p. 40.
30. Ibid., p. 43.
31. S. W. Roskill, *The War at Sea* (London, HMSO, 1954), vol. I, appendix R, p. 615; vol. II, appendix O, p. 485.

32. Ibid., vol. II, p. 92.
33. ADM 1/11892, Labour in Naval and Mercantile Shipyards (the Barlow Report).
34. Ibid.
35. Quoted in CAB 102/407, unpublished official history study by Mrs P. Inman, Labour Requirements and Supply for the Ministries of Supply and Production: Shipbuilding and Marine Engineering 1935–45 (see below note 93 to Chapter Eight).
36. ADM 1/11892.
37. Ibid.
38. Ibid.
39. CAB 102/407, quoting letter of 30 April 1942.
40. Ibid.
41. CAB 102/407.
42. ADM 1/11892.
43. BT 28/319.
44. Ibid.
45. Ibid.
46. Ibid.
47. Ibid.
48. Ibid.; British Intelligence Objectives Sub-Committee, Final Report No. 822, Item Nos. 12 and 29, *Shipbuilding: Notes on Visit to Blohm und Voss, Deutsche Werft, Germania Werft and Deschimag* (London, HMSO, 1946).
49. BT 28/319; BIOS, Final Report No. 822, *Shipbuilding*.
50. BT 28/319.
51. Ibid.
52. Ibid.
53. Ibid.
54. Ibid.
55. BT 28/319, Continuation of Report after Additional Visits.
56. Letter to Earl of Elgin, chairman of the Fairfield Shipbuilding and Engineering Co. Ltd, 1942, quoted in Reid, *James Lithgow*, p. 201.
57. ADM 1/12506 Report of the Shipyard Development Committee, 3 August 1943.
58. ADM 1/12506 Shipyard Development Committee, Sub-Committee on Machine Tools, meeting of 6 January 1943.
59. ADM 1/12506, Machine-Tool Sub-Committee meeting, 23 February 1943.
60. ADM 1/12506, Report of the Shipyard Development Committee, 3 August 1943.
61. Ibid.
62. Roskill, *War at Sea*, vol. II, appendix O, p. 485: vol. III, part I, appendix K, p. 388.
63. M. M. Postan, *British War Production* (London, HMSO and Longmans, Green, 1952), table 29, p. 295, and pp. 300–3.
64. CAB 102/407.
65. CAB 102/86, *British War Economy* (see above note 20 to Chapter Three): Comments and Criticisms: letter to Hancock signed 'Betty' (Dr C. B. A. Behrens, fellow of Newnham College, Cambridge), 16 August 1947.
66. Quoted in CAB 102/407.
67. Ibid.
68. Quoted in J. L. Hodson, *The Sea and the Land* (London, Victor Gollancz, 1945), p. 65.
69. CAB 87/63, EC(43)2, 13 October 1943.
70. CAB 87/63, EC(43)2, Memorandum by the Minister of Labour, 13 October 1943.

71. CAB 102/407.
72. LAB 10/132, Trade Stoppages, Weekly Return to the Minister, November 1940 to December 1944.
73. CAB 102/407.
74. Ibid.
75. To Clyde Control Committee, 21 May 1943, quoted in ibid.
76. Ibid.
77. Ibid.
78. Mass-Observation, *Report on behalf of the Advertising Service Guild,* No. 2: Home Propaganda (London, John Murray, 1941): this report noted the total ineffectiveness of a 1941 poster showing a heroic riveter, with the slogan 'Every Rivet a Bullet – Speed the Ships'.
79. CAB 102/407.
80. CAB 87/7, R(44)53, Memorandum by the First Lord on the Shipbuilding Industry, 16 March 1944.
81. Ibid.
82. CAB 87/6, R(44)52, 10 July 1944.
83. Andrew Shonfield. *British Economic Policy Since the War* (Harmondsworth, Penguin Books, 1958), p. 42.
84. Ibid.

Chapter Seven: A Mass Industry Improvised: Aircraft 1936–39

1. Cf. CAB 53/4, Chiefs of Staff Committee meetings, especially COS 130; CAB 53/24, Chiefs of Staff Committee Memoranda, especially COS 341, 372, 373, 374: CAB 53/30, COS 551; CAB 16/110, CP 193(34), Interim Report by the Ministerial Committee on Disarmament dealing with Air Defence; CAB 16/138, DPR 13, Memorandum by CAS, July 1935; Correlli Barnett, *The Collapse of British Power* (London, Eyre Methuen, 1972: paperback edn, Gloucester, Alan Sutton, 1984), pp. 410–16, 436–8, 494–510, 526 and 528; Brian Bond, *British Military Policy Between the Two World Wars* (Oxford, Clarendon Press, 1980), ch. 7; Uri Bialer, *The Shadow of the Bomber: The Fear of Air Attack and British Politics, 1932–1939* (London, Royal Historical Society, 1980), *passim;* G. C. Peden, *British Rearmament and the Treasury, 1932–1939* (Edinburgh, Scottish Academic Press, 1979), chs 4 and 5; Robert Paul Shay Jr, *British Rearmament in the Thirties: Politics and Profits* (Princeton, Princeton University Press, 1977), *passim,* but especially pp. 30–46, 51–6, 73–5, 136–42, 170–3 and 203–17.
2. Max Hastings, *Bomber Command* (London, Michael Joseph, 1979), p. 116.
3. M. M. Postan, *British War Production* (London, HMSO and Longmans, Green, 1952), p. 124.
4. Ibid., p. 125.
5. CAB 102/41, Aircraft Production Quantities.
6. R. J. Overy, *The Air War,* 1939–45 (London, Europa Publications, 1980), table 12, p. 150.
7. *History of the Ministry of Munitions* (London, HMSO, 1922), vol. VII, part I, p. 61.
8. Ibid., p. 103.
9. Ibid., p. 14.
10. Ibid., vol. VIII, part I, p. 35.
11. Air Ministry, Directorate of Civil Aviation, *Report on the Progress of Civil Aviation 1930* (London, HMSO, 1931).
12. CAB 32/127, IC(36)10.
13. Ibid., pp. 2–3.

14. CAB 32/129, E(37)16, Policy for the Production of Civil Aircraft Within the Commonwealth.
15. P. Fearon, 'Aircraft Manufacturing', in Neil K. Buxton and Derek H. Aldcroft (eds.), *British Industry Between the Wars: Instability and Industrial Development, 1919–1939* (London, Scolar Press, 1979), pp. 232–3.
16. Derek Wood and Derek Dempster, *The Narrow Margin: The Battle of Britain and the Rise of Air Power*, 1930–40 (London, Hutchinson, 1961), pp. 36–7.
17. Fearon, 'Aircraft Manufacturing', p. 233.
18. Wood and Dempster, *The Narrow Margin*,, pp. 433–42.
19. Fearon, 'Aircraft Manufacturing', pp. 216–19.
20. Weir Papers 19/1, Churchill College, Cambridge, Memorandum by the Secretary of the Air Ministry on the Aircraft Industry, 19 November 1935.
21. Weir Papers 19/1.
22. Weir Papers 19/2, Paper dated 7 January 1938.
23. M. M. Postan, D. Hay and J. D. Scott, *Design and Development of Weapons: Studies in Government and Industrial Organisation* (London, HMSO and Longmans, Green, 1964), pp. 36–7.
24. Weir Papers 19/10–11, Aircraft Factories on Air Ministry Work, April 1935.
25. Postan, Hay and Scott, *Design and Development of Weapons*, pp. 29–31.
26. See Robert R. Locke, *The End of the Practical Man: Entrepreneurship and Higher Education in Germany, France and Great Britain, 1880–1940* (Greenwich, Conn., and London, Jai Press, 1984), *passim*, but especially chs 2, 3, 5 and 6.
27. Postan, Hay and Scott, *Design and Development of Weapons*, pp. 33–4.
28. Wood and Dempster, *The Narrow Margin*, p. 87.
29. Ibid.; Weir Papers 19/12–13, Paper by the Air Member for Research and Development, Air Marshal Sir Hugh Dowding, 7 August 1935.
30. Weir Papers 19/12–13.
31. Postan, Hay and Scott, *Design and Development of Weapons*, pp. 38–9.
32. Fearon, 'Aircraft Manufacturing', p. 235.
33. For the evolution of the 'shadow' factory scheme, see Weir Papers 17/7, 8 19/1, 2; also CAB 16/109, DRC 14; CAB 16/123, papers DPR 3, 4, 8, 9, DRC 37; W. Hornby, *Factories and Plant* (London, HMSO and Longmans, Green, 1958), pp. 199–203.
34. CAB 16/112, DPR(DR)9, 12 February 1936.
35. CAB 16/123, DPR(DR)1.
36. CAB 16/136, DPR 20, meeting of Defence Policy and Requirements Committee, 7 May 1936.
37. CAB 16/140, DPR 96.
38. Ibid.
39. CAB 16/141, DPR 154, 7th Report by the Ministry of Labour.
40. CAB 16/141, DPR 180, 10th Report by the Ministry of Labour, at February 1937.
41. CAB 16/142, DPR 209, 14th Report by the Ministry of Labour, at June 1937.
42. CAB 16/142, DPR 231, 17th Report of the Ministry of Labour, at October 1937.
43. CAB 16/142, DPR 240 and 245, 18th and 19th Reports by the Ministry of Labour, at November and December 1937.
44. CAB 16/142, DPR 86, Financial Settlement with Aircraft 'Shadow' Firms, Memorandum by the Secretary of State for Air, 18 May 1936.
45. Hornby, *Factories and Plant*, pp. 324–5.
46. Ibid., p. 326; see also pp. 321–31 for a general discussion of the weakness of the British machine-tool industry.
47. CAB 16/136, DPR 28.
48. Weir Papers 19/7, EPM 155(36), Notes on Wellington and Wellesley

production furnished by Vickers to Secretary of State's progress meeting, 14 December 1936.

49. CAB 16/136, DPR 33, 21 January 1937.
50. CAB 16/140, DPR 82.
51. Ibid.
52. CAB 16/140, DPR 93.
53. CAB 16/141, DPR 193, 12th Report by the Air Ministry, for April 1937.
54. Ibid.
55. CAB 16/142, DPR 246, 20th Report by the Air Ministry, for January 1938.
56. CAB 16/143, DPR 297, 26th Report by the Air Ministry, for February 1939.
57. CAB 16/140, DPR 115, 4th Report by the Air Ministry, for July and August 1936.
58. CAB 16/142, DPR 213, 15th Report by the Air Ministry, for July and August 1937.
59. Cf. CAB 16/141, DPR 169, 9th Report by the War Office, up to 1 February 1937.
60. CAB 16/141, DPR 126, 5th Report by the War Office, up to 1 October 1936.
61. CAB 16/141, DPR 138, 6th Report by the War Office, up to 1 November 1936.
62. CAB 16/137, DPR 33, Meeting of the DPRC, 21 January 1937.
63. CAB 16/137, DPR 38, Meeting of the DPRC, 22 April 1937.
64. CAB 16/137, Meetings of the DPRC: DPR 36, 18 March 1937; DPR 38, 22 April 1937; DPR 39, 29 April 1937.
65. CAB 16/143, DPR 290, 25th Report by the War Office, 15 December 1938.
66. CAB 16/141, DPR 151, 7th Report by the War Office, 14 December 1936.
67. CAB 16/141, DPR 157, 8th Report by the War Office, up to 1 January 1937.
68. CAB 16/141, DPR 200, 13th Report by the War Office, up to 1 June 1937.
69. CAB 16/142, DPR 247, 20th Report by the War Office, up to 1 February 1938.
70. CAB 16/141, DPR 194, 12th Report by the Admiralty, for April 1937.
71. CAB 16/142, DPR 249, 20th Report by the Admiralty, 18 February 1938.
72. CAB 16/140, DPR 85, first War Office Report on Munitions Supply, May 1936.
73. CAB 16/140, DPR 116, 4th Report by the War Office, up to 1 September 1936; cf. also CAB 16/141, DPR 138, Report by the War Office, up to 1 November 1936.
74. CAB 16/141, DPR 169, 9th Report by the War Office, up to 1 February 1937; CAB 16/141, DPR 183, 11th Report by the War Office, up to 1 April 1937; CAB 16/143, DPR 276, 23rd Report by the War Office, July 1938.
75. CAB 16/141, DPR 200, 13th Report by the War Office, up to 1 June 1937; CAB 16/142, DPR 247, 20th Report by the War Office, up to 1 February 1938.
76. CAB 16/142, DPR 232, 17th Report by the Admiralty, for October 1937.
77. CAB 18/141, DPR 129, 5th Report by the Admiralty, 20 October 1936.
78. CAB 16/142, DPR 224, 16th Report by the Admiralty, for October 1937.
79. Ibid.
80. CAB 27/648, Committee on Defence Programmes and Their Acceleration, appointed by the Cabinet on 26 October 1938; CP 234(38), Memorandum by the Minister for the Co-ordination of Defence, 21 October 1938.
81. CAB 36/4, 54, Meeting of the Joint Defence Committee, 30 May 1938; this seems to belie the account in Postan, *British War Production*, pp. 360–1, of the satisfactory nature of valve production in 1936–41.
82. CAB 27/627, FP(36)57, COS 698, 'The Military Implications of German Aggression against Czechoslovakia', 21 March 1938; for an analysis of this document and its role in Chamberlain's handling of the Czech crisis and of

his own Cabinet dissidents, see Barnett, *Collapse of British Power*, pp. 474–6 and 505–47.

83. CAB 27/627, FP(36)57, COS 698.
84. Weir Papers 19/10–11; Postan, Hay and Scott, *Design and Development of Weapons*, appendices II, V and VI; see also Barnett, *Collapse of British Power*, pp. 479–82.
85. CAB 16/140, DPR 115, 4th Report by the Air Ministry, for July and August 1936.
86. CAB 16/142, DPR 246, 20th Report by the Air Ministry, for January 1938.
87. CAB 16/140, DPR 115, 4th Report by the Air Ministry, for July and August 1936.
88. CAB 16/140, DPR 125, 5th Report by the Air Ministry, for September 1936.
89. CAB 16/141, DPR 137, 6th Report by the Air Ministry, for October 1936.
90. CAB 16/141, DPR 148, 7th Report by the Air Ministry, for November 1936.
91. CAB 16/141, DPR 193, 12th Report by the Air Ministry, for April 1937.
92. CAB 16/141, DPR 198, 13th Report by the Air Ministry, for May 1937.
93. CAB 16/142, DPR 228, 17th Report by the Air Ministry, for October 1937.
94. CAB 16/142, DPR 236, 18th Report by the Air Ministry, for November 1937.
95. CAB 16/142, DPR 241 and 246, 19th and 20th Reports by the Air Ministry, for December 1937 and January 1938.
96. CAB 16/141, DPR 181, 11th Report by the Air Ministry, for February 1937.
97. CAB 16/142, DPR 228, 17th Report by the Air Ministry, for October 1937.
98. CAB 16/142, DPR 241, 19th Report by the Air Ministry, for December 1937.
99. Weir Papers 19/9, 11th meeting of Secretary of State for Air's Progress Meetings on RAF expansion, 3 February 1938.
100. Ibid., EPM 42(38), 21 February 1938.
101. CAB 16/143, DPR 269, 22nd Report by the Air Ministry, for March and April 1938.
102. CAB 16/137, DPR 35, 19 February 1937.
103. CAB 16/137, DPR 43, 30 September 1937.
104. CAB 16/137, DPR 40, meeting of 24 June 1937.
105. CAB 16/142, DPR 205, 14th Report by the Air Ministry, for June 1937.
106. CAB 16/141, DPR 137, 6th Report by the Air Ministry, for October 1936; CAB 16/142, DPR 228, 17th Report by the Air Ministry, for October 1937.
107. Postan, Hay and Scott, *Design and Development of Weapons*, p. 124, footnote 1.
108. CAB 16/141, DPR 156, 8th Report by the Air Ministry, for December 1936.
109. CAB 16/142, DPR 241, 19th Report by the Air Ministry, for January 1938.
110. CAB 16/142, DPR 241, 19th Report by the Air Ministry, for December 1937.
111. CAB 16/140, DPR 125, 5th Report by the Air Ministry, for September 1936.
112. CAB 16/141, DPR 193, 12th Report by the Air Ministry, for April 1937.
113. CAB 16/137, DPR 40, Meeting of the DPRC, 24 June 1937.
114. CAB 16/141, DPR 193, 12th Report by the Air Ministry, for April 1937.
115. CAB 16/142, DPR 246, 20th Report by the Air Ministry, for January 1938; CAB 27/627, COS 698; see above p. 139.
116. Postan, Hay and Scott, *Design and Development of Weapons*, p. 123.
117. Overy, *The Air War*, table 12, p. 150; Postan, Hay and Scott, *Design and Development of Weapons*, appendix I.

Chapter Eight: New Technology and Old Failings: Aircraft 1939–44

1. G. C. Peden, *British Rearmament and the Treasury 1932–1939* (Edinburgh, Scottish Academic Press, 1979), appendix, table D, p. 208.
2. Robert Paul Shay Jr, *British Rearmament in the Thirties: Politics and Profits* (Princeton, Princeton University Press, 1977), p. 165.
3. CAB 24/274, CP 24(38), Defence Expenditure in Future Years, Further Report by the Minister for the Co-ordination of Defence, February 1938.
4. Ibid.
5. CAB 27/648, Appendix to CP 247(38), October 1938.
6. Peden, *British Rearmament and the Treasury*, appendix, table D, p. 208.
7. CAB 27/648, CP 247(38).
8. CAB 29/159, AFC 1, Strategic Memorandum by the Chiefs of Staff, 20 March 1939; CAB 16/209, SAC 4, Memorandum to the Strategical Appreciation Committee by Sir Alan Barlow, Under-Secretary to the Treasury, 6 April 1939.
9. W. K. Hancock and M. M. Gowing, *British War Economy* (London, HMSO and Longmans, Green, 1949), p. 116.
10. M. M. Postan, *British War Production* (London, HMSO and Longmans, Green, 1952), pp. 124 and 128.
11. CAB 66/11, WP 40(40)324.
12. H. Duncan Hall, *North American Supply* (London, HMSO and Longmans, Green, 1955), pp. 208, 215–16 and 247–78.
13. Ibid., table 29, p. 432.
14. Hancock and Gowing, *British War Economy*, pp. 366 and 370.
15. CAB 87/13, PR(43)98, 10 November 1943.
16. Ibid.
17. Ibid.
18. Ibid.
19. Ibid.
20. Postan, *British War Production*, appendix 4, p. 484.
21. CAB 102/274, Aircraft Production and Factories: papers prepared for official history, *Factories and Plant* (see below note 98).
22. R. J. Overy, *The Air War, 1939–45* (London, Europa Publications, 1980), table 15, p. 168.
23. According to CAB 87/13, PR(43)98, the number of workers directly employed by the airframe and engine factories (excluding sub-contractors) came to 510,000; according to Postan, *British War Production*, table 41, p. 310, total British production in structure weight in 1944 was 221,985,000 lb; 221,985,000 ÷ 365 ÷ 510,000 = 1.19 lb.
24. Overy, *The Air War*, table 15, p. 168; *The United States Strategic Bombing Survey*, with an introduction by David MacIsaac, 10 vols. (New York and London, Garland Publishing, 1976), vol. II, Aircraft Division Industry Report, *Strategic Bombing of the German Aircraft Industry* (*European Report no.* 4), p. 84; corroborative evidence is supplied by a secret Whitehall calculation in February 1944 which concluded that it could take 17,000 man-hours under the best British production to make a Heinkel 111, as against the published German figure of 12,000; 4300 man-hours to make an ME 109G against the German figure of 3900: see AVIA 10/269, Labour Statistics, 20 October 1942–16 August 1944, Memo by AD Stats 3 to Professor Postan, 16 February 1944.
25. CAB 102/41, Aircraft Production Programmes and Quantities, Air Ministry Directorate of Statistics and Plans, 15 January 1940.
26. Cf. AVIA 10/83, Sir Roy Fedden's Mission to Germany 1945: also Combined Intelligence Objectives Sub-Committee, Report Item 25, File No. XXV–42,

Survey of Production Techniques used in the German Aircraft Industry, July 1945.

27. M. M. Postan, D. Hay and J. D. Scott, *Design and Development of Weapons: Studies in Government and Industrial Organisation* (London, HMSO and Longmans, Green, 1964), p. 129.
28. Ibid.
29. A 'miserable failure', according to D. A. Parry, Reciprocating Aero-Engines and Engine Accessories Production and Programmes 1935–45, in CAB 102/51.
30. AVIA 10/106, Précis on the Work of the Fedden Mission, circulated on 22 April 1943.
31. CAB 70/6, DC(S)(43)2, Defence Committee (Supply).
32. See Postan, Hay and Scott, *Design and Development of Weapons*, ch. 9, for a full account of the development of the jet engine and its airframe in Britain.
33. Ibid.; Air Ministry, *The Rise and Fall of the German Air Force* (Air Ministry Pamphlet No. 248, 1948), pp. 310–14 and 369.
34. Postan, Hay and Scott, *Design and Development of Weapons*, pp. 146–7 and 150–3.
35. Ibid., pp. 42–4.
36. Ibid., pp. 15–24.
37. Ibid., pp. 37–40.
38. Spitfire figure in AVIA 10/269, Labour Statistics, 20 October 1942 to 16 August 1944; Messerschmitt 109G figure in AVIA 10/269, Memorandum by AD Stats 3 to Professor Postan, 16 February 1944; Tempest or Typhoon comparison with ME 109F calculated by managing director of Rolls-Royce, in Ian Lloyd, *Rolls-Royce: The Merlin at War* (London, Macmillan, 1978), p. 70.
39. CIOS, Item No. 25, File No. XXV–42.
40. AVIA 10/104, Report of British Mission to United States of America to Study Production Methods.
41. Ibid.
42. AVIA 10/106, Précis on the Work of the Fedden Mission, circulated on 22 April 1943.
43. Ibid.
44. Ibid.
45. Ibid.
46. AVIA 10/83, Sir Roy Fedden's Mission to Germany 1945. Purpose: to investigate current research and projects. Conclusions and Recommendations.
47. Ibid.
48. AVIA 10/85, Farren Mission to Germany: A Survey of a Cross Section of German Aircraft, Aircraft Engine and Armament Industries.
49. Ibid.
50. AVIA 10/113, Visit to Messerschmitt Plant at Oberammergau-Bavaria, June 18–25, 1945, Report by Mr R. M. Clarkson, de Havilland Aircraft Company.
51. AVIA 10/269.
52. AVIA 10/104.
53. AVIA 10/106.
54. AVIA 10/104.
55. Ibid.
56. AVIA 10/110, Report on his visit to America, June 18-August 18, 1943, by Cdr (E) M. Luby RN.
57. AVIA 10/108, Report on Visit to the United Kingdom, by Mr Ed Walton (Aircraft Report – Harriman Mission, July 1943).
58. AVIA 10/104.

59. Ibid.
60. AVIA 10/99, Fedden Mission Report, June 1943.
61. BT 28/377, Report on Vickers-Armstrong (Aircraft) Ltd, Weybridge, by five expert Inspectors of Labour Supply.
62. Ibid.
63. Ibid.
64. Ibid.
65. Ibid.
66. Ibid.
67. CAB 102/393, Development of Jet Propulsion and Gas Turbine Engines in the United Kingdom – revised draft by Miss C. Keppel.
68. Ibid.
69. CAB 102/51, Reciprocating Aero-Engines and Engine Accessories Production and Programmes 1935–45, by D. A. Parry.
70. Ibid.
71. Ibid.
72. AVIA 10/269, Memorandum by DDG Stats P, 25 May 1943.
73. Ibid.
74. Ibid.
75. AVIA 15/2548, Trade disputes in the aircraft and munitions industries, memorandum from ADAP 8, 30 September 1943.
76. Ibid.
77. CAB 102/406, Labour Welfare and Utilisation in the Aircraft Industry, by J. B. Jeffreys: draft used by Inman in writing *Labour in the Munitions Industries* (see note 93 below).
78. Ibid.
79. Ibid.
80. Ibid.
81. Ibid.
82. CAB 102/406.
83. British combined and averaged figure for men and women working up to fifty-two hours a week, for May 1943: 20.85 per cent; June–November 1943: 10.8 per cent – H. M. D. Parker, *Manpower: A Study of War-Time Policy and Administration* (London, HMSO and Longmans, Green, 1957), p. 445; CAB 102/406. American figure for autumn 1942: 6–7 per cent; Dunbar Report, AVIA 10/104.
84. CAB 102/406.
85. Ibid.
86. Ibid.
87. Ibid.
88. AVIA 15/2536, Training of Labour for the Aircraft Industry.
89. Ibid.
90. Ibid.
91. Overy, *The Air War*, pp. 173–4.
92. CAB 16/140, DPR 118.
93. P. Inman, *Labour in the Munitions Industries* (London, HMSO and Longmans, Green, 1957), p. 29.
94. Ibid.
95. CAB 102/405, Labour Requirements and Supply 1940–44, by D. Mack Smith.
96. Inman, *Labour in the Munitions Industries*, p. 61.
97. CAB 87/63, EC(43)2, 13 October 1943.
98. William Hornby, *Factories and Plant* (London, HMSO and Longmans, Green, 1958), p. 303; Postan, *British War Production*, p. 304.

99. CAB 70/6, DC(S)(43)1, Defence Committee (Supply), meeting of 7 January 1943.
100. CAB 102/406.
101. BT 28/543, Five-Man Board – Labour Efficiency, meeting of fourteen civil servants on 3 November 1942; CAB 102/406.
102. CAB 102/406, by Miss A. G. Shaw.
103. Inman, *Labour in the Munitions Industries*, pp. 430–1; CAB 102/406.
104. AVIA 10/269, 29 April 1944.
105. Hornby, *Factories and Plant*, pp. 258 and 262; AVIA 10/83.
106. British figure for total structure weight produced in March 1944 of 20,300,000 lb in AVIA 10/311, Ministry of Aircraft Production Statistical Review, 1946; total workforce in parent and shadow airframe and engine factories 510,000 according to CAB 87/13, PR(43)98; 20,300,000 ÷ 31 ÷ 510,000 = 1.28 lb. German figure of 96,215,900 lb for the best quarter of 1944 from USSBS, vol. I, *The Effects of Strategic Bombing on the German War Economy* (*European Report no. 3*), appendix, table 101, p. 277; total manpower German airframe and engine factories 545,600; 96,215,900 ÷ 91 ÷ 545,600 = 1.93 lb. American figure from Overy, *The Air War*, p. 173.
107. CAB 102/406, Paper before the Munitions Management and Labour Efficiency Committee of the Production Efficiency Board, 17 November 1944.
108. I have read the criticisms of this chapter and the preceding one by Dr David Edgerton in *Twentieth Century British History*, vol. 2, No.3, 1991, pp. 360–79, 'The Prophet Militant and Industrial: The Peculiarities of Correlli Barnett', and also conducted a lengthy correspondence with him about his more general criticisms of my account of British industry and education since the mid-nineteenth century. I have also read his book *England and the Aeroplane: An Essay on a Militant and Technological Nation* (Macmillan, in association with the Centre for the History of Science, Technology and Medicine, University of Manchester), published in 1991, five years after the first edition of *The Audit of War*. Nonetheless, I have seen no reason to amend my narrative and footnotes, or the calculations therein.

Chapter Nine: The Dependence on America: Radar and Much Else

1. William Hornby, *Factories and Plant* (London, HMSO and Longmans, Green, 1958), p. 331.
2. CAB 102/510; see also CAB 102/508, Machine Tools and Production Problems 1940–44, by W. C. Hornby and Miss J. Embery, and CAB 102/509, Directorate of Machine Tools, by W. C. Hornby.
3. *Hornby, Factories and Plant*, p. 331.
4. Ibid., p. 332.
5. Ibid., pp. 299–320.
6. BT 28/435, Paper by Garro Jones, Chairman of the Production Planning and Personnel Committee of the Radio Board, 7 May 1943.
7. Hornby, *Factories and Plant*, p. 335.
8. Ibid., pp. 334–6.
9. CAB 102/510.
10. Ibid.
11. Ibid.
12. Hornby, *Factories and Plant*, p. 338; *The United States Strategic Bombing Survey*, with an introduction by David MacIsaac, 10 vols. (New York and London, Garland Publishing, 1976), vol. 1, *The Effects of Strategic Bombing on the German War Economy* (*European Report no. 3*), appendix, table 30, p. 227; see

also H. M. D. Parker, *Manpower: A Study of War-Time Policy and Administration* (London, HMSO and Longmans, Green, 1957), pp. 69–81 and 126.

13. Calculated from figures in Hornby, *Factories and Plant*, pp. 331, 335 and 338.
14. *USSBS*, vol. I, *Over-all Report* (*European War*) (*European Report no. 2*), p. 86; vol. I, Effects, appendix, table 29, p. 227.
15. *USSBS*, vol. I, *Effects*, p. 49; see also Combined Intelligence Objectives Sub-Committee, Item No. 31, File No. XXVIII–10, Machine Tool Targets Leipzig.
16. Cf. CAB 16/143, DPR 296, Annex B, 25th Report by the War Office, January 1939; M. M. Postan, D. Hay and J. D. Scott, *Design and Development of Weapons: Studies in Government and Industrial Organisation* (London, HMSO and Longmans, Green, 1964), pp. 308–57; G. MacLeod Ross, *The Business of Tanks 1933 to 1945* (Ilfracombe, Arthur H. Stockwell, 1976), *passim*.
17. Ross, *The Business of Tanks*, p. 149.
18. Postan, Hay and Scott, *Design and Development of Weapons*, p. 312.
19. Correlli Barnett, *The Desert Generals*, 2nd edn (London, George Allen & Unwin, 1983), p. 91.
20. Major-General I. S. O. Playfair, *The Mediterranean and Middle East* (London, HMSO, 1960), vol. III, appendix 8, p. 437.
21. Postan, Hay and Scott, *Design and Development of Weapons*, pp. 312–13; Ross, *The Business of Tanks*, p. 153.
22. Postan, Hay and Scott, *Design and Development of Weapons*, p. 313.
23. Ibid.
24. Ibid., pp. 341–51.
25. Ibid., p. 339.
26. Ibid., p. 334.
27. Ian Lloyd, *Rolls-Royce: The Merlin at War* (London, Macmillan, 1978), pp. 113–15.
28. Postan, Hay and Scott, *Design and Development of Weapons*, p. 319.
29. Ibid., appendix VII, pp. 543–5.
30. British figures calculated from *Statistical Digest of the War*, table 126, Armoured Fighting Vehicles: peak production of tanks and self-propelled guns in 1942, 8111, equalling 204,000 tons; British workforce 243,000 as at September 1941, according to CAB 102/409. German figures calculated from *USSBS*, vol. I, *Effects*, appendix, tables 9 and 105, pp. 210–11 and 280: peak production of tanks, self-propelled guns and assault guns in 1944, 19,002, including 8334 tanks, equalling 548,575 metric tons; German workforce at peak in January 1944, 428,000 *including* those on truck manufacture.
31. Ibid.; *USSBS*, vol. I, *Effects*, appendix, tables 9 and 105, pp. 210–11 and 280.
32. See Playfair, *The Mediterranean and Middle East*, vol. III, appendix 8; vol. IV, appendix 9; for technical comparison of British and German tanks, see Christopher F. Foss, *The Illustrated Encyclopedia of the World's Tanks and Fighting Vehicles* (London, Salamander Books, 1977), pp. 28–30, 34–5, 40–3, 111–15, 122–4 and 126–7.
33. Postan, Hay and Scott, *Design and Development of Weapons*, p. 362.
34. Playfair, *The Mediterranean and Middle East*, vol. III, p. 220.
35. Quoted in ibid., pp. 214–15.
36. Ibid., vol. IV, pp. 8–9.
37. L. F. Ellis, *Victory in the West*, vol. I: *The Battle of Normandy* (London, HMSO, 1962), appendix IV, p. 546.
38. M. M. Postan, *British War Production* (London, HMSO and Longmans, Green, 1952), table 36, p. 247.
39. Hornby, *Factories and Plant*, p. 193.
40. Ibid.
41. *USSBS*, vol. I, *Effects*, appendix, table 106, p. 281.

42. Hornby, *Factories and Plant*, p. 193.
43. H. Duncan Hall, *North American Supply* (London, HMSO and Longmans, Green, 1955), p. 417.
44. Ibid.
45. Author's own experience as a National Serviceman after the war.
46. See above pp. 58–9; CAB 87/15, R(I)(45)9, 21 March 1945; see also M. Miller and R. A. Church. 'Motor Manufacturing', in Neil K. Buxton and Derek H. Aldcroft (eds.), *British Industry Between the Wars: Instability and Industrial Development, 1919–1939* (London, Scolar Press, 1979), p. 208.
47. A. E. Kahn, *Britain in the World Economy* (London, Pitman, 1946), pp. 112–13.
48. Postan, *British War Production*, p. 356.
49. This short account of state-sponsored research is based on Postan, Hay and Scott, *Design and Development of Weapons*, chs 16 and 17.
50. Michael Sanderson, *The Universities and British Industry, 1850–1970* (London, Routledge & Kegan Paul, 1972), p. 240.
51. AVIA 10/348, Comments on the History of Radio and Rádar, by A. P. Rowe, 2 October 1947.
52. AVIA 10/342, RADIO (42)21, 7 December 1942, Radio Board: Organisation of Board; incorporation of technical committees; note by Professor G. P. Thompson.
53. AVIA 10/342, RADIO (44)18, 13 April 1944, The Radio Program (sic); Production of Radio Valves; Memorandum by Chairman of Production Planning Committee; Annex, memorandum by Watson Watt on the operational importance of radar.
54. AVIA 10/338, SBM 335/41, Air Supply Board, 14 May 1941.
55. ADM 1/15218, letter to Secretary of OPTEC from the RDF Board, 13 January 1943; Annex to OPTEC (43)3.
56. AVIA 7/1674, correspondence and meetings between TRE, Ministry of Aircraft Production and The Gramophone Company.
57. AVIA 7/1675, letter of 14 October 1943.
58. Ibid.
59. CAB 66/27, WP(42)352, 11 August 1942 (the Du Parcq Report).
60. BT 28/435, Panel Investigation: Radio Personnel: Memorandum by Sir Robert Watson Watt received in the Ministry of Production on 27 April 1944.
61. AVIA 10/342, RADIO (42), 4th Meeting of Radio Board, 10 December 1942; verbal outline by G. Garro Jones MP, Chairman of OPTEC.
62. AVIA 10/342, RADIO (43)43 and PRODUCTION (43)30, 15 April 1943; Report by Paymaster-General on Service Radio Requirements in 1943.
63. Ibid.
64. AVIA 10/342, RADIO (43)46, Our Radio Program (reference RADIO (43), 8th meeting, Minute 8), Memorandum by G. Garro Jones MP, in response to Radio Board's request to PPPC to consider the Paymaster-General's memorandum (RADIO (43)43 and PRODUCTION (43)30, 15 April 1943), 28 April 1943.
65. CAB 102/88, First draft of *British War Production* (see above note 38), p. 554.
66. Quoted by Lord Justice Du Parcq in his report, CAB 66/27, WP(42)352, 11 August 1942.
67. AVIA 10/342, RADIO (43)46, Memorandum by G. Garro Jones MP, 28 April 1943.
68. Cf. R. E. Catterall, 'Electrical Engineering', in Buxton and Aldcroft, *British Industry Between the Wars*, pp. 92–3; Sanderson, *The Universities and British Industry*, pp. 92–3 and 108–10.
69. Catterall, 'Electrical Engineering', p. 249.

70. Ibid., pp. 247–9.
71. Ibid.
72. Ibid., pp. 249–51; *History of the Ministry of Munitions* (London, HMSO, 1922), vol. VIII, part III, passim.
73. Catterall, 'Electrical Engineering', p. 256.
74. Ibid., p. 271.
75. AVIA 10/338 War Cabinet – Radio Production Committee and General Questions on the Radio Industry. Report to the Minister of Production of the Committee set up to enquire into the utilization of Labour in THE RADIO INDUSTRY, 31 March 1943.
76. AVIA 10/342, RADIO (43)46, Radio Board, 28 April 1943.
77. Ibid.
78. CAB 102/279, Admiralty Equipment Production – Papers used by Mr Hornby when writing *Factories and Plant* (see note I above) interview with Commander G. Naish, 8 January 1946.
79. AVIA 10/342, RADIO (43)46.
80. Bowen Papers, EGBN 4/1, Churchill Archives Centre, Cambridge.
81. Ibid.
82. AVIA 10/342, RADIO (43)46, 28 April 1943.
83. CAB 66/27, WP(42)352.
84. AVIA 10/338, PRODUCTION (44)23, 29 June 1944, WAR CABINET: Production Planning Radio Committee; the Radio Production Executive; First Annual Report of the Executive.
85. AVIA 10/338, Report to the Minister of Production on the Utilisation of Labour in the Radio Industry, 31 March 1943; AVIA 10/342, RADIO (43), 14th meeting, 19 August 1943.
86. AVIA 10/338, 31 March 1943.
87. Ibid.
88. CAB 66/27, WP(42)352.
89. AVIA 10/342, RADIO (43)46, Memorandum by G. Garro Jones MP, 28 April 1943.
90. Ibid.
91. CAB 66/27, WP(42)352.
92. AVIA 10/338, ASC 12/42, 5 May 1942.
93. AVIA 7/1674, meeting on 2 April 1943 between The Gramophone Company and the Ministry of Aircraft Production.
94. AVIA 10/338, Aircraft Supply Council, minutes of 49th meeting, 7 May 1942.
95. ADM 1/15218, Operations and Technical Radio Committee, Papers 1–67, OPTEC (43)9, Note by the Chairman on numbers of research workers in radio, 8 February 1943.
96. AVIA 10/338, 31 March 1943.
97. Ibid.
98. AVIA 10/348, Comments on the History of Radio and Radar, by A. P. Rowe, 2 October 1947.
99. Cf. AVIA 7/1674, H_2S Electrical Units, Production: letter from The Gramophone Company to the MAP, 26 June 1942; letter from the Superintendent of TRE to MAP, 28 June 1942; letter from Chief Engineer TRE to MAP, 14 October 1942.
100. CAB 66/27, WP(42)352.
101. Bowen Papers, EGBN 4/1.
102. CAB 66/27, WP(42)352.
103. WM(42)128, cited in CAB 21/1100, Radio Board, Establishment of.
104. WP(42)415 (Revise), cited in CAB 21/1100.
105. AVIA 10/342, War Cabinet: Radio Board Papers, Minutes of Meetings,

Conclusions, and Reports, October 1942–November 1944; RADIO (42)14, 23 October 1942.

106. AVIA 10/342, RADIO (42), 2nd meeting, 9 October 1942.
107. ADM 1/15218, OPTEC (43)1.
108. AVIA 10/338, 31 March 1943.
109. AVIA 10/338, PRODUCTION (44)23, 29 June 1944, WAR CABINET: Production Planning Radio Committee; the Radio Production Executive; First Annual Report of the Executive.
110. AVIA 10/338, 31 March 1943.
111. AVIA 10/338, PRODUCTION (44)23.
112. Ibid.
113. Ibid.
114. AVIA 10/338, Air Supply Board, 16 March 1943.
115. Ibid., AVIA 10/338, SBM 431/43, Air Supply Board, 19 October 1943.
116. AVIA 10/342, RADIO (43)46, Memorandum by G. Garro Jones MP, 28 April 1943.
117. AVIA 10/342, RADIO (43)64, 13 August 1943.
118. CAB 102/644, Development and Production of Radio and Radar, Section III, First Draft.
119. Ibid.
120. AVIA 10/342, RADIO (43), 14th Meeting, 19 August 1943.
121. ADM 1/15218, OPTEC (43)8, meeting of 3 February 1943: Note dated 26 January.
122. AVIA 10/338, SBM 401/43, Air Supply Board, 28 September 1943.
123. AVIA 10/338, SBM 83/44, Air Supply Board, Note by DCCP on Plant for Production of Miniature Valves, 7 March 1944.
124. AVIA 10/342, RADIO (44)28, Memorandum, 9 June 1944.
125. Ibid.
126. AVIA 10/342, RADIO (44)25, 1 May 1944: see also BT 28/1172, Radio Valve Production; Note to Garro Jones on new War Office designs, 19 April 1944.
127. ADM 1/15218, RADIO (43)53, 22 May 1943, United States Special Mission on Radar – Report by the Chairman of the Working Party, Professor G. P. Thompson, on discussions with the US mission.
128. Bowen Papers, EGBN 4/6, interview with Dr Bowen, 29 April 1943.
129. ADM 1/15218, OPTEC (43)45, Note by the Chairman on Basic Radar Research in the United Kingdom, 5 October 1943.
130. Margaret Gowing, *Britain and Atomic Energy, 1939–1945* (London and New York, Macmillan, 1964), ch. 4, especially pp. 162–77.
131. Cf. AVIA 10/108, letter to the Pentagon from Mr Ed Walton, 31 July 1943, reporting that Rolls-Royce had 60 per cent more R and D personnel on jet engines than reciprocating, and expressing the hope that the US would increase its own efforts.
132. R. V. Jones, *Most Secret War: British Scientific Intelligence, 1939–1945* (London, Hamish Hamilton, 1978), p. 464.
133. British Intelligence Objectives Sub-Committee, Overall Report No. 12, *German Gas Turbine Development during the Period 1939–1945* (London, HMSO, 1949), by J. W. Adderley MBE BA AFRAeS, member of the staff of Power Jets (R & D) Ltd.
134. CAB 102/393, Development of Jet Propulsion and Gas Turbine Engines in the United Kingdom – revised draft by Miss Keppel; CAB 102/394, Comments on above draft by Air Commodore F. Whittle, 13 August 1947. According to Whittle, American Hastelloy B turbine blades had to be obtained in order to tide over between the REX 78 and Nimonic 80, while

the American GE impeller was obtained as an interim measure to cure vane vibration.

135. Jones, *Most Secret War*, p. 230.
136. On pre-war rearmament developments, see CAB 16/140, DPR 90 and DPR 116; CAB 16/141, DPR 131; CAB 16/142, DPR 242 and DPR 247; on ICI in this period and in the war, see W. J. Reader, *Imperial Chemical Industries: A History*, vol. II: *The First Quarter-Century*, 1925–1952 (London, Oxford University Press, 1975), part III.
137. W. J. Reader, 'The Chemical Industry', in Buxton and Aldcroft, *British Industry Between the Wars*, p. 176.
138. Ibid., pp. 176–7.

Chapter Ten: The Legacy of the Industrial Revolution

1. Joseph Conrad, *The Nigger of the 'Narcissus': A Tale of the Sea* (London, The Gresham Publishing Company, 1925), pp. 162–3.
2. Richard Hoggart, The *Uses of Literacy: Aspects of Working-class Life, With Special References to Publications and Entertainments* (London, Chatto & Windus, 1971), p. 16.
3. Llewellyn Woodward, *The Age of Reform* (Oxford, Clarendon Press, 1962), p. 2.
4. J. Steven Watson, *The Reign of George III*, 1760–1815 (Oxford, Clarendon Press, 1960), p. 511; Ruth Glass (ed.), *The Social Background of a Plan: A Study of Middlesbrough* (London, Routledge & Kegan Paul, 1948), pp. 45 and 255.
5. E. P. Thompson, *The Making of the English Working Class* (London, Pelican Books, 1974), p. 486.
6. Ibid., p. 599.
7. Ibid., p. 597.
8. Ibid., p. 464.
9. Hoggart, *The Uses of Literacy*, p. 73.
10. Ibid., p. 20.
11. Glass, *The Social Background of a Plan*, p. 21.
12. Ibid., p. 31.
13. Ibid.
14. Hoggart, *The Uses of Literacy*, p. 116.
15. Ibid., p. 73.
16. See ibid., pp. 32–41.
17. Ibid., p. 32.
18. Ibid., p. 66.
19. See Carlo Cipolla (ed.), *The Fontana Economic History of Europe* (London, William Collins/Fontana Books, 1975), vol. III: *The Industrial Revolution*, p. 436; vol. IV: *The Emergence of Industrial Societies*, part I, pp. 102–3 and 155–7; part II, pp. 635–6.
20. Quoted in Hoggart, *The Uses of Literacy*, p. 234.
21. Ibid., pp. 233–4.
22. *Report of the Royal Commission on the Distribution of the Industrial Population* (the Barlow Report), Cmd 6153 (1940), p. 24 and table 3. Commission set up July 1937, report completed August 1939.
23. Ibid., p. 39.
24. *22nd Abstract of Labour Statistics of the United Kingdom*, Cmd 5556 (1939); *Ministry of Labour Gazette*, quoted in Gavin McCrone, *Regional Policy in Britain* (London, George Allen & Unwin, 1969), table II, p. 100.

25. John Boyd Orr, *Food, Health and Income: Report on a Survey of Adequacy of Diet in Relation to Income* (London, Macmillan, 1936), p. 39.
26. *The Registrar General's Statistical Review of England and Wales for the Six Years 1940–45*, vol I: *Medical* (London, HMSO, 1949), table XIV, p. 34.
27. Ibid., table XXVII, p. 60.
28. Ibid., pp. 25–6.
29. Ibid., table, p. 115.
30. Ibid., table CV, p. 220.
31. Ibid., p. 45.
32. *Summary Report of the Ministry of Health for the year ended 31 March 1943*, Cmd 6468 (1943), two surveys by Dr Meiklejohn, p. 9.
33. Orr, *Food, Health and Income*, p. 50.
34. See ibid., table II (appendix VI), p. 66; and Richard M. Titmuss, *Problems of Social Policy* (London, HMSO and Longmans, Green, 1951), p. 523, footnote 1.
35. Hoggart, *The Uses of Literacy*, p. 50.
36. Glass, *The Social Background of a Plan*, p. 68.
37. Trustees of the Carnegie United Kingdom Trust, *Disinherited Youth: A Report on the 18-plus Age Group. Enquiry Prepared for the Trustees of the Carnegie United Kingdom Trust.* Enquiry officers: C. Cameron (Glasgow), A. Lush (Cardiff), G. Meara (Liverpool). Research 1937–9; report completed 1941 (Edinburgh, 1943), table 34, p. 57.
38. Ibid., pp. 57–8.
39. Ibid., p. 58.
40. Glass, *The Social Background of a Plan*, p. 50.
41. Professor Robert Cowan, quoted in Cmd 6153, pp. 53–4. It is not necessary here to summarise all the well-known literature on the state of industrial towns and the condition of the working class, beginning with the Health of Towns Commission of 1844, but only to recapitulate the main issues.
42. Witness to the 1844 Health of Towns Commission, quoted in J. L. and Barbara Hammond, *The Bleak Age* (Harmondsworth, Pelican Books, 1947), p. 54.
43. Cf. ibid., pp. 52–7.
44. Professor W. M. Frazer, quoted in Cmd 6153, p. 54.
45. Hammonds, *The Bleak Age*, p. 59.
46. See Correlli Barnett, *The Collapse of British Power* (London, Eyre Methuen, 1972; paperback edn, Gloucester, Alan Sutton, 1984), pp. 430–2.
47. Frederic Manning, *Her Privates We* (London, Peter Davies, 1930), p. 418.
48. Ibid., p. 23.
49. B. Seebohm Rowntree, *Poverty: A Study of Town Life* (London, Macmillan, 1910), p. 156.
50. Ibid., p. 155.
51. Edmund Blunden, *Undertones of War* (London, Richard Cobden-Sanderson, 1928), p. 34.
52. Siegfried Sassoon, *Memoirs of an Infantry Officer* (London, Faber & Faber, 1930), p. 103.
53. Ibid., p. 153.
54. R. H. Sherrard, *The Child Slaves of Britain* (London, Hurst & Blackett, 1905), p. 85.
55. Glass, *The Social Background of a Plan*, p. 51.
56. Cmd 6153, pp. 84–5.
57. Ibid., appendix IV, A Memorandum on Planning in Some Other Countries, by Mr G. C. Pepler, pp. 289, 299–306 and 311.
58. Infant mortality per 1000 live births: Liverpool 76, Rotterdam 31; crude

death rates per 1000 living: Liverpool 13.2, Rotterdam 7.6 – Cmd 6153, p. 62.

59. Ibid., p. 80.
60. Titmuss, *Problems of Social Policy*, p. 132, quoting the League of Nations Annual Epidemiological Report for 1937.
61. Carnegie Trust, *Disinherited Youth*, pp. 3–5 and 19–23.
62. Ibid., p. 28.
63. T. Ferguson and J. Cunnison, *In Their Early Twenties: A Study of Glasgow Youth* (London, Oxford University Press for the Nuffield Foundation, 1956), pp. 100–1 (sequel to T. Ferguson and J. Cunnison, *The Young Wage-Earner: A Study of Glasgow Boys* (London, Oxford University Press for the Nuffield Foundation, 1951)).
64. Hoggart, *The Uses of Literacy*, p. 110.
65. Ibid., pp. 110–12.
66. CAB 87/63, EC(43)1, 15 October 1943.
67. CAB 87/63, EC(43)18, meeting of the Committee on Post-War Employment, 9 November 1943.
68. Titmuss, *Problems of Social Policy*, p. 115.
69. Ibid.
70. Ibid., p. 125.
71. CAB 102/244, Report by Dr K. Mellanby circulated in March 1941 by the Board of Education to local authorities, in History of Education: The Medical Services of Education and the Special Schools; revision by Mrs S. M. Ferguson of E. K. Ferguson's draft.
72. Titmuss, *Problems of Social Policy*, p. 126.

Chapter Eleven: Education for Industrial Decline

1. Trustees of the Carnegie United Kingdom Trust, *Disinherited Youth: A Report on the 18-plus Age Group, Enquiry Prepared for the Trustee of the Carnegie United Kingdom Trust*. Enquiry officers: C. Cameron (Glasgow), A. Lush (Cardiff), G. Meara (Liverpool). Research 1937–9; report completed 1941 (Edinburgh, 1943), tables 10, 11 and 12, p. 20.
2. Ibid., p. 21.
3. Ibid., tables 9 and 10, pp. 19–20.
4. Ibid., p. 23.
5. CAB 102/240, Education History: The Education Act 1944, unpublished history by Dr S. Weitzman; Central Statistical Office, *Statistical Abstract for the United Kingdom for each of the fifteen years 1924–1938* (London, HMSO, 1940), tables 41, 56 and 66.
6. A. E. Morgan, *The Needs of Youth: A Report Made to King George's Jubilee Trust Fund* (London, Oxford University Press, 1939), pp. 13–19. Total age group fourteen to eighteen: 2,531,000; number on part-time courses at technical, commercial and art colleges: 108,526; number at day-continuation schools: 20,550. Note that the *Statistical Abstract* gives slightly different figures for 1938 – cf. table 45; ED 136/96 gives thirty-two schools with 19,500 pupils; CAB 117/109 gives 41,000 day-release pupils.
7. *Wegweiser durch das gewerbliche Berufs- und Fachschulwesen des Deutschen Reiches. Schuljahr 1938* (Langensalza-Berlin-Leipzig, Verlag von Julius Beltz, 1941), Zahlenmässige Nachweisungen über das Berufs-, Berufsfach- und Fachschulwesen des Deutschen Reiches, Stand von Mai 1938: Ubersicht A: Berufsschulen, pp. 362–3.
8. Ibid.

9. ED 136/296, Memorandum by R. S. Wood, initialled R.A.B., 5 May 1942 on The Education and Training of the Adolescent.
10. *Education in 1937, being the Report of the Board of Education and the Statistics of public education for England and Wales,* Cmd 5776 (1938), figure for England and Wales, table 7.
11. Ibid., table 39.
12. Ibid., table 49. The author himself took the examination; and saw what happened to his school fellows who then left school at sixteen.
13. Cmd 5776, p. 26.
14. Ibid.
15. CAB 102/240.
16. Ibid.
17. Ruth Glass (ed.), *The Social Background of a Plan: A Study of Middlesbrough* (London, Routledge & Kegan Paul, 1948), p. 129; see also pp. 118–29, and Carnegie Trust, *Disinherited Youth, passim,* on the relation of home background to examination entrance, passing and ultimate scholastic achievement.
18. Cited in Michael Sanderson, *The Universities and British Industry, 1850–1970* (London, Routledge & Kegan Paul, 1972), p. 276.
19. Ibid., p. 278.
20. CAB 102/240.
21. Total obtaining the *Zeugnis der mittleren Reife* in *Volkschulen* and public *Mittelschulen* in school year 1937 was 32,409 as against 54,795 in England and Wales obtaining School Certificate: *Statistisches Jahrbuch für das Deutsche Reich,* 57. Jahrgang 1938 (Berlin, Statistisches Reichsamt, 1938), pp. 599–600; Cmd 5776, p. 26.
22. One in 1000 of the population still in secondary education at age seventeen as against one in 2000 in Britain, state-funded schools only. German figure: 64,738 out of national population of 69 million, *Wegweiser durch das Höhere Schulwesen des Deutschen Reiches, Schuljahr 1937* (Berlin, Weidmannsche Verlagsbuchhandlung, 1938), Tabelle 1 1c, p. 184; Tabelle 4, p. 114. British figure (England and Wales): 18,968 out of a population of 41 million, Cmd 5776, table 39.
23. German figure, state-funded schools only: 41,143, or one in 1677 of the population, *Statistisches-Jahrbuch,* Jahrgang 1938, p. 603; England and Wales figure, state-funded schools only: 8034 or one in 4589, Cmd 5776, p. 26.
24. Glass, *The Social Background of a Plan,* pp. 94–5.
25. Tom Brennan, *Midland City: Wolverhampton: Social and Industrial Survey* (London, Dennis Dobson, 1948), p. 173.
26. CAB 117/111, Committee on Reconstruction Problems, Part III Education Authorities – correspondence and statistics in connection with the Minister without Portfolio's Report to the President of the Board of Education, 1942.
27. Cf. *Statistical Abstract for the United Kingdom, 1924–1938,* tables 45 and 59; Cmd 5776, tables 53, 61 and 62, and p. 28; ED 136/296.
28. ED 136/296, Education after the War; Technical Education: Memorandum by H. B. Wallis, 5 September 1941, summarising existing provision for further education.
29. *Wegweiser durch das gewerbliche Berufs- und Fachschulwesen des Deutschen Reiches, 1938,* p. 374.
30. ED 136/296.
31. *Wegweiser durch das gewerbliche Berufs- und Fachschulwesen des Deutschen Reiches, 1938,* Ubersicht C, p. 376.
32. One in 420 to one in 1000.
33. Robert R. Locke, *The End of the Practical Man: Entrepreneurship and Higher*

Education in Germany, France and Great Britain, 1880–1940 (Greenwich, Conn., and London, Jai Press, 1984), pp. 33–41 and 51–3.
34. Sanderson, *The Universities and British Industry*, table 19, p. 261.
35. Ibid., table 20, p. 263.
36. *Percy Committee on Higher Technological Education: Report of a Special Committee appointed in April 1944* (London, HMSO, 1945); Veröffentlichung aus dem Jahre 1943 unter dem Titel *Zehnjahresstatistik des Hochschulbesuchs – Band III: Abschlussprüfungen*, reprinted in Veröffentlichung des Statistischen Bundesamtes, Fachserie II, Reihe 42, *Prüfungen an Hochschulen 1981* (Bonn, Statistisches Bundesamt, 1981), table 'Der Verlauf der Bestandenen Abschlussprufüngen nach Fachgruppen unter Prüfungsfachern im Altreich und in Grossdeutschland, 1937'.
37. *Prüfungen an Hochschulen 1981*, table 'Der Verlauf der Bestandenen Abschlussprüfungen, 1937'; Sanderson, *The Universities and British Industry*, table 28, p. 297.
38. See Cmd 5776, table 73.
39. Cf. CAB 87/14, Ministerial Sub-Committee on Industrial Problems, Memorandum by President of the Board of Trade on Industrial Design, comparing Britain, America, Germany, Sweden and Czechoslovakia in this field, 20 June 1944.
40. See S. J. Prais, *Vocational Qualifications of the Labour Force in Britain and Germany*, and S. J. Prais and Karin Wagner, *Schooling Standards in Britain and Germany: Some Summary Comparisons Bearing on Economic Efficiency* (London, National Institute of Economic and Social Research, 1981 and 1983), with regard to the 1970s.
41. *Report of the Endowed Schools (Schools Inquiry) Royal Commission*, Command paper 3966 (1867–8), vol. I, part I, p. 72.
42. Quoted in R. H. Heindel, *The American Impact on Great Britain, 1898–1914* (New York, Octagon Books, 1968), p. 153.
43. Lyon Playfair, *Industrial Instruction on the Continent* (London, Royal School of Mines, 1852).
44. *Report of the Royal Commission on the State of Popular Education in England* (the Newcastle Commission), Command paper 2794–1 (1861), vol. I: *Report*.
45. *Report of the Royal Commission on the Revenues and Management of certain Colleges and Schools, and the studies pursued and instruction given therein* (the Clarendon Commission), Command paper 3288 (1864), vol. I: *Report*, pp. 28–33.
46. House of Commons, *Report from the Select Committee on Scientific Instruction: with the Proceedings of the Committee, Minutes of Evidence and Appendix, 1867–8*, 15 July 1869, vol. XV.
47. Ibid., p. vi.
48. Ibid.
49. Ibid.
50. *Report of the Royal Commission on Scientific Instruction and the Advancement of Science, 6th Report* C. 1279 (1875), p. 10.
51. *Second Report of the Royal Commissioners on Technical Instruction*, C. 3981 (1884), vol. I: *Report*, p. 20.
52. Ibid., p. 337.
53. Ibid., p. 48.
54. Ibid., p. 84.
55. Ibid., pp. 213–14.
56. Ibid., p. 369.
57. Ibid., pp. 505–8.
58. All cited in Heindel, *American Impact on Great Britain*, p. 215.

59. *Report of the Consultative Committee on Attendance, Compulsory or Otherwise, at Continuation Schools*, Cd 4757 (1909), vol. I.
60. *Report of the Departmental Committee on Juvenile Education in Relation to Employment after the War* (the Lewis Report) (London, HMSO, 1917), Final Report, p. 5.
61. The Emmott Committee, *Report of an enquiry into the relationship of technical education to other forms of education and to industry and commerce* (1927).
62. *Final Report of the Committee on Industry and Trade*, Cmd 3282 (1928–9), p. 218.
63. *Report of the Consultative Committee of the Board of Education on Secondary Education with Special Reference to Grammar Schools and Technical High Schools* (the Spens Report) (London, HMSO, 1939), pp. 71–2.
64. Correlli Barnett, *The Collapse of British Power* (London, Eyre Methuen, 1972; paperback edn, Gloucester, Alan Sutton, 1984), p. 94.
65. CAB 102/240, p. 134.
66. Ibid., p. 136, footnote 1.
67. Ibid.
68. Ibid.
69. *Second Report, Minutes of Evidence*, Cd 4715, pp. 20–1.
70. Ibid.
71. AVIA 15/2536, Training of Labour for the Aircraft Industry: General Policy, Memorandum of 28 January 1942; see also correspondence in the same file of February 1943 on the failure to use government training centres.
72. Ibid., 'General Appreciation', by E. J. B. Tagg, on training of labour in the aircraft industry, 6 February 1942.
73. Ibid., Labour Circular No. 32, 15 September 1941.
74. Ibid., 'General Appreciation', by E. J. B. Tagg, 6 February 1942.
75. Ibid., Report of 18 February 1943.
76. Ibid., Training Report, after official's visit to North-West Regional Headquarters, 20–21 October 1943.
77. Sanderson, *The Universities and British Industry*, pp. 79–80; see his ch. 3 for the founding of civic colleges and universities 1850–1914.
78. Ibid., p. 95, and table 9, p. 101.
79. *Report of the Board of Education 1908–9*, Cd 5130 (1910).
80. Cmd 3282, p. 213,
81. Ibid.
82. Ibid.
83. Ibid.
84. *Committee on Education and Industry (England and Wales), Second Report* (London, HMSO, 1929), p. 20.
85. Quoted in Sanderson, *The Universities in the Nineteenth Century* (London, Routledge & Kegan Paul, 1975), pp. 123–4.
86. Letter of 9 May 1836, quoted in T. W. Bamford, *Thomas Arnold* (London, The Cresset Press, 1960), p. 120.
87. Ibid.
88. Ibid., p. 498.
89. Quoted in ibid., p. 104.
90. See Sanderson, *The Universities in the Nineteenth Century*, pp. 82–3.
91. Quoted in ibid., p. 35.
92. Herbert Spencer, *Education: Intellectual, Moral and Physical* (London, Williams & Norgate, 1861), p. 25.
93. Ibid., p. 38.
94. Ibid., p. 39.
95. Quoted in Sanderson, *The Universities in the Nineteenth Century*, p. 127.
96. Ibid.

97. Ibid.
98. Ibid., pp. 140–1.
99. W. E. Bowen, *Edward Bowen: A Memoir* (London, Longmans, Green, 1902), p. 110.
100. Cf. *Civil Service Commission Open Competition Reports and Examination Papers for August* (London, HMSO, 1900, 1905 and 1910); *Civil Service Commission Regulations, Examination Papers and Table of Marks for Class One Clerkships* (London, HMSO, 1885 and 1891); *Civil Service Commission Reports* (London, HMSO, 1895, 1896 and 1900).
101. Rupert Wilkinson, *The Prefects: British Leadership and the Public School Tradition* (London, Oxford University Press, 1964), pp. 101–2.
102. Dr Cyril Norwood, *The English Tradition in Education* (London, John Murray, 1929), p. 19.
103. Cited in Sanderson, *The Universities and British Industry*, pp. 34–5.
104. Ibid.
105. Ibid., p. 45.
106. Ibid., p. 38.
107. Ibid., p. 44.
108. Sanderson, *The Universities in the Nineteenth Century*, p. 234.
109. Ibid., p. 236.
110. T. J. N. Hilken, *Engineering at Cambridge University*, 1783–1965 (Cambridge, Cambridge University Press, 1967), pp. 223–5 and 246.
111. Royal Society Yearbook for 1903 (London, Royal Society, 1903), pp. 180–95.
112. See Barnett, *The Collapse of British Power*, pp. 33–43 and 59–63; Martin Wiener, *English Culture and the Decline of the Industrial Spirit, 1850–1980* (Cambridge, Cambridge University Press, 1981), chs 2 and 7; Mark Girouard, *The Return to Camelot: Chivalry and the English Gentleman* (New Haven and London, Yale University Press, 1981), chs 11 and 14; Jonathan Gathorne-Hardy, *The Public School Phenomenon, 1597–1977* (London, Hodder & Stoughton, 1977), *passim*, but especially chs 8 and 9.
113. Sir Ralph Furse, quoted in Robert Heussler, *Yesterday's Rulers* (New York, Syracuse University Press, 1963), pp. 82–3.
114. Barnett, *The Collapse of British Power*, pp. 63–8.
115. Sanderson, *The Universities and British Industry*, p. 62.
116. Ibid., pp. 64–5.
117. Ibid., p. 104
118. Ibid., pp. 84–94.
119. Robert R. Locke. *The End of the Practical Man: Entrepreneurship and Higher Education in Germany, France and Great Britain, 1880–1940* (Greenwich, Conn., and London, Jai Press, 1984). table II.1, p. 34; Sanderson, *The Universities in the Nineteenth Century*, p. 243.
120. Sanderson, *The Universities in the Nineteenth Century*, pp. 243–4.
121. Sanderson, *The Universities and British Industry*, table 20, p. 263.
122. *Report of the Royal Commission on the Elementary Education Acts* (*England and Wales*), C. 5485 (1886–8). Final Report: Summary of Recommendations, p. 213.
123. Ibid.
124. Quoted in CAB 102/240, p. 105, footnote 1.
125. *Second Report on Higher Education*, Cd 1738 (1903).
126. CAB 102/240, p. 106.
127. Ibid., p. 101.
128. Quoted in ibid., section 4, p. 4.
129. *Report of the Consultative Committee of the Board of Education on Secondary Education*, pp. 71–2.

130. Ibid., p. 72
131. Ibid.
132. Ibid.
133. History 82 per cent; Geography 69 per cent; Religious Knowledge 17.7 per cent; Latin 38 per cent; Maths 92 per cent; Chemistry 35.3 per cent; Physics 26.9 per cent; General Science 6.2 per cent; Heat, Light and Sound 3.6 per cent; Electricity and Magnetism 3.5 per cent; Mechanics 2.1 per cent; Commercial Subjects 1.9 per cent; Technical Drawing 0.6 per cent; Economics 0.5 per cent. Cmd 5776, table 49.
134. Matthew Arnold, *Culture and Anarchy* (New York, Macmillan, 1894, 1st edn 1869), pp. 43–4.
135. Quoted in J. Stuart Maclure, *Educational Documents: England and Wales, 1816 to the Present Day* (London, Methuen, 1965), p. 40.
136. Command paper 2794–I.
137. See Command paper 3966, *passim*.
138. G. A. N. Lowndes, *The Silent Social Revolution* (London, Oxford University Press, 1937), p. 89.
139. *Report of the Royal Commission on Secondary Education*, C. 7862 (1895), vol. I: *Report*.
140. Ibid.
141. According to Cd 5130, the figure was 2768.
142. Quoted in Maclure, *Educational Documents*, p. 173.
143. CAB 102/240, pp. 133–4.
144. C. L. Mowat, *Britain Between the Wars, 1918–1940* (London, London University Paperbacks, 1968), p. 207.
145. Report of the Consultative Committee of the Board of Education on the Education of the Adolescent (London, HMSO, 1926).
146. CAB 102/240, Section 4, p. 26.
147. See above note 63.
148. CAB 102/240, Section 4, p. 44, footnote 4; p. 45, footnote 1.
149. Ibid., p. 58.
150. CAB 117/109, Committee on Reconstruction Problems – Policy with regard to Education (1941–3): Education After the War (the Green Book) (June 1941), p. 23.
151. Having read Dr David Edgerton's criticisms in his article 'The Prophet Militant and Industrial: The Peculiarities of Correlli Barnett' (*Twentieth Century British History*, vol. 2 and no. 3) of my treatment of the history of British vocational and technical education, I have again to record my profound disagreement with his perverse interpretation of the evidence. My own text and footnotes therefore stand without amendment.

Chapter Twelve: New Jerusalem or Economic Miracle?

1. W. K. Hancock and M. M. Gowing, *British War Economy* (London, HMSO and Longmans, Green, 1953), p. 523.
2. CAB 87/2, RP(42)2.
3. CAB 87/13, PR(43)2, 20 January 1943.
4. Ibid.
5. PREM 4 89/ 1, note from Chancellor of the Exchequer to Prime Minister, 11 January 1943, enclosing RP(43)5, Treasury memorandum on The Social Security Plan.
6. Ibid.
7. Ibid.
8. Ibid.

9. PREM 4 89/2, Part II.
10. CAB 87/81, SIC(42)166, 10 October 1942.
11. PREM 4 89/1, RP(43)5.
12. CAB 87/13, PR(43)12, 13 February 1943.
13. Ibid.
14. Ibid.
15. Ibid.
16. CAB 87/13, PR(43)35, 'Influences Affecting the Level of the National Income', 25 June 1943.
17. Ibid.
18. Ibid.
19. C. H. Feinstein, *Statistical Tables of National Income, Expenditure and Output of the United Kingdom, 1855–1965* (Cambridge, Cambridge University Press, 1972), tables 2, 3 and 5.
20. Kenneth O. Morgan, *Labour in Power, 1945–1951* (London, Oxford University Press, 1984), p. 161.
21. Ibid., p. 381.
22. Cf. A. W. Dilnot, J. A. Kay and C. N. Morris, *The Reform of Social Security* (Oxford, Oxford University Press for Institute for Fiscal Studies, 1984); Professor Sir Douglas Hague, chairman of Social Science Research Council, 'Spending, the Nightmare Ticket': article in *The Times*, 18 October 1943; Digby Anderson (ed.), *The Ignorance of Social Intervention* (London, Croom Helm, 1980).
23. *New Towns for Old* and *When We Build Again* (1942); *A City Reborn, New Builders* and *Proud City* (1945).
24. The Official Committee on Post-War Internal Economic Problems.
25. CAB 87/3, RP(43)24. Also IEP(43)12.
26. CAB 87/3, RP(43)24, appendix I, The Economic Background of the Post-War Building and Construction Programme.
27. Ibid., appendix IV.
28. CAB 87/12, PR(43)2, 28 January 1943.
29. Ibid.
30. Ibid., White Paper on *Training in the Building Industry*, Cmd 6428 (February 1943).
31. CAB 87/12, PR(43)15, 30 July 1943.
32. CAB 87/12, PR(43)29, discussion on postwar building based on papers submitted by the Minister of Works (PR(43)54), the Minister of Health (PR(43)56) and the Minister of Agriculture and Fisheries (PR(43)63), 20 September 1943.
33. Ibid.
34. The Steering Committee on Post-War Employment.
35. CAB 87/7, R(44)6, Report of the Steering Committee on Post-War Employment, 11 January 1944.
36. CAB 87/7, R(44)9, Report of the Sub-Committee on Post-War Building, 15 March 1944.
37. CAB 87/8, R(44)128, 23 June 1944.
38. Ibid.
39. CAB 87/13, PR(43)44.
40. CAB 87/8, R(44)128.
41. Ibid.
42. CAB 87/7, R(44)12 and CAB 87/8, R(44)122.
43. Ibid.
44. CAB 87/6, R(44)59.
45. CAB 87/10, R(45)8, Requirements and Priorities for Post-War Building Work Other Than Housing, 16 January 1945.

46. CAB 87/10, R(45)6.
47. Cmd 6609.
48. Morgan, *Labour in Power*, p. 163; Andrew Shonfield, *British Economic Policy Since the War* (Harmondsworth, Penguin Books, 1958), pp. 34–7.
49. Cf. the area-by-area analysis by the Board of Trade in 1943 in CAB 87/63, EC(43)5, 18 October 1943.
50. *Report of the Industrial Transference Board for 1928*, Cmd 3156 (1928), p. 54.
51. CAB 87/56, IEP(42)36, 26 August 1942, Nuffield College Social Reconstruction Survey on Methods of Influencing the Location of Industry.
52. Ibid.
53. Ibid.
54. Gavin McCrone, *Regional Policy in Britain* (London, George Allen & Unwin, 1969), p. 101.
55. CAB 87/63, EC(43)5, 18 October 1943; cf. also *Report of the First Commissioner for the Special Areas in England and Wales* (1936), quoted in CAB 87/63, EC(43)4.
56. Cmd 6153.
57. Ibid., pp. 193–4.
58. CAB 87/91, IL(41) series, 52/4, Memorandum by the Minister without Portfolio after reading memoranda by the departments of Transport, Agriculture, Education, Health, Scotland, Board of Trade, Works and the Electricity Commission, 13 March 1941.
59. Ibid.
60. CAB 87/91, IL(41)2, 25 June 1941.
61. CAB 87/55, IEP(43)13, meeting on the Location of Industry, 25 June 1943.
62. CAB 87/13, PR(43)29, Maintenance of Unemployment and Depressed Areas, 27 May 1943.
63. Ibid
64. See McCrone, *Regional Policy in Britain, passim*, especially pp. 197–202.
65. Ibid.
66. CAB 87/63, EC(43)5, 18 October 1943.
67. Ibid.
68. Ibid.
69. Ibid.
70. Ibid.
71. CAB 87/63, EC(43)13, 20 October 1943.
72. Ibid.
73. Ibid.
74. CAB 87/63, EC(43)19, 4 November 1943.
75. Ibid.; see also CAB 87/63, EC(43)18, for similar comments by the Permanent Secretaries of the Ministries of Supply and Aircraft Production and even the Board of Trade in a meeting of the Post-War Employment Committee on 9 November 1943.
76. CAB 87/7, R(44)6, Report of the Steering Committee on Post-War Employment, 11 January 1944; Committee set up as a result of decision of Committee on Reconstruction Priorities, 13 July 1943 (PR(43)15,1).
77. CAB 87/7, R(44)6.
78. CAB 87/5, R(44)11, 28 January 1944.
79. Ibid.
80. CAB 87/7, R(44)58, 22 March 1944.
81. CAB 87/7, R(44)66, Post-War Employment: Location of Industry, Memorandum by the Minister of Aircraft Production, 30 March 1944.
82. Ibid.
83. CAB 87/8, R(44)72, The Balanced Distribution of Industry, 7 April 1944.
84. Ibid.

85. McCrone, *Regional Policy in Britain*, pp. 109–12.
86. Ibid., p. 114.
87. Ivon Fallon, *Sunday Telegraph*, 21 January 1979, 'Why Dunlop Closed at Speke'; Peter Hetherington, *Guardian*, 22 July 1981, 'It Was Always Worse in Glasgow. Nothing Has Changed'; Julian Dresser, *Sunday Times*, 9 September 1984, 'Is There New Life in Old Trafford?' (answer: no); McCrone, *Regional Policy in Britain*, *passim*, but especially pp. 118–80.
88. McCrone, *Regional Policy in Britain*, p. 118.
89. *Regional Industrial Development*, Cmnd 9111 (1983).
90. Quoted by Graham Searjeant, *Sunday Times*, 7 June 1981.
91. In 1938, the North-east, North-west, Scotland and Wales had 18 per cent unemployment overall; London and the South-east, less than 3 per cent; in 1960–6, the northern areas, Scotland and Wales, 3 per cent; London and the South-east, 1 per cent; in 1985, the North, North-west, Scotland and Wales, 16.3 per cent; London and the South-east 9.8 per cent. McCrone, *Regional Policy in Britain*, table I, p. 20 and table II, p. 100; Department of Employment press notice, 30 August 1985.
92. See Chapter One above for a full account and references.
93. CAB 87/13, PR(43)26, appendix A; PR(43)29.
94. CAB 87/13, PR(43)37, and PR(43)39.
95. CAB 87/64, EC(43)6, Memorandum by Treasury on maintenance of Employment, timing and planning of public investment, and control and timing of private investment (including suggested Public Finance Corporation), etc., 16 October 1943.
96. Ibid.
97. CAB 87/63, EC(43)6, covering Note by the Treasury.
98. CAB 87/63, EC(43)9, 18 October 1943.
99. Ibid.
100. CAB 87/63, EC(43)12, 20 October 1943.
101. McCrone, *Regional Policy in Britain*, table II, p. 100; Department of Employment press notice, 30 August 1985.
102. Sir William H. Beveridge, *Full Employment in a Free Society: A Report by William H. Beveridge* (London, George Allen & Unwin, 1944), p. 29.
103. CAB 87/7, R(44)6.
104. Michael P. Jackson, *The Price of Coal* (London, Croom Helm, 1974), p. 52.
105. CAB 102/407.
106. H. M. D. Parker, *Manpower: A Study of Wartime Policy and Administration* (London, HMSO and Longmans, Green, 1957), table 26, p. 211; Industrial Group I comprising metal manufacture, engineering, motor vehicle and aircraft manufacture, shipbuilding and ship repair, metal goods, chemicals, explosive, paint, etc.
107. CAB 102/41.
108. Hancock and Gowing, *British War Economy*, p. 351.
109. Ibid.
110. Ibid.
111. See Chapter Three above.
112. CAB 87/63, EC(43)15, Note by Economic Section on the Board of Trade Memorandum on General Support of Trade (EC(43)4), 20 October 1943.
113. CAB 87/63, R(44)6; also CAB 87/7, R(44)6.
114. CAB 87/63, R(44)6.
115. Ibid.
116. See below pp. 266–74.
117. CAB 87/5, R(44)8, 21 January 1944.
118. Ibid.
119. CAB 87/5, R(44)37, 9 May 1944.

120. Cmd 6527.
121. Beveridge, *Full Employment in a Free Society*, p. 200; see above pp. 34 and 48–9.
122. CAB 87/89, EC(45)8, 15 August 1945.
123. CAB 87/1–13.
124. CAB 87/5.
125. CAB 87/10, R(45)8.
126. CAB 87/7, R(43)4, Central Statistical Office of the Treasury, 2 December 1943.
127. CAB 87/12, PR(43)13.
128. Shonfield, *British Economic Policy*, p. 35.
129. CAB 87/7, R(44)2; Cmd 6502, appendix E.
130. Hancock and Gowing, *British War Economy*, p. 352; CAB 87/13, PR(43)98.
131. CAB 87/10, R(45)8.
132. CAB 87/7, R(43)4.

Chapter Thirteen: Tinkering as Industrial Strategy

1. CAB 87/12, IEP(43)11, Official Committee on Post-War Internal Economic Problems: Treasury memorandum on 'Continuance of Policy of Stabilisation'; Memorandum by the Board of Trade on 'The Control of Industrial Prices', 5 March 1943.
2. Ibid.
3. CAB 87/3, RP(43)25, 15 June 1943.
4. Ibid., Report on the Recovery of Export Markets and the Promotion of the Export Trade, prepared by the Post-War Export Trade Committee, 15 June 1943.
5. Ibid.
6. Ibid.
7. CAB 87/14, Ministerial Sub-Committee on Industrial Problems: memorandum by the President of the Board of Trade on Industrial Design, 20 June 1944.
8. Cf. CAB 87/15, Ministerial Sub-Committee on Industrial Problems (Export Questions); CAB 87/17, Official Sub-Committee on Industrial Problems; CAB 87/55–6, Official Committee on Internal Economic Problems; CAB 87/63, Committee on Post-War Employment; CAB 87/91, Sub-Committee on Location of Industry; to say nothing of the main War Cabinet reconstruction committees in CAB 87/1–13. But cf. especially the 45-page Report on the Recovery of Export Markets and the Promotion of Export Trade, prepared by the Secretary for Overseas Trade, Harcourt Johnstone, in CAB 87/3, RP(43)25, 15 June 1943; and Memorandum by the Board of Trade on General Support of Trade, CAB 87/63, EC(43)4, 15 October 1943.
9. CAB 87/3, RP(43)25, 15 June 1943.
10. Ibid.
11. CAB 87/13, PR(43)35, 25 June 1943.
12. Ibid.
13. Ibid.
14. CAB 87/63, EC(43)4, 15 October 1943.
15. Ibid.
16. Ibid.
17. Ibid.
18. Cf. ibid.
19. Ibid.
20. Ibid

21. Ibid.
22. Ibid. In an article, 'Enterprise and Welfare States: A Comparative Perspective' in *Transactions of the Royal Historical Society*, 40 (1990), pp. 175–95, Dr Jose Harris attacked my account in the present chapter of the founding and potentially limitless cost of the postwar Welfare State. Nevertheless, her criticisms were largely misdirected in that they principally related to the postwar era, whereas the narrative of *The Audit of War* ends in May 1945, with only a brief glance forward into the future.

    However, my new book, *The Lost Victory: British Dreams, British Realities, 1945–1950* (Macmillan, 1995; Pan Books, 1996), does deal in detail with the soaring costs of 'New Jerusalem' after its foundation in the immediate postwar era. I can therefore say that Dr Harris's main point in her article that by 1950 Great Britain was spending a lower percentage of GNP on welfare than West Germany, Austria and Belgium is invalid when placed in wider context. For none of these countries was also spending nearly 8 per cent of GNP on defence like Britain. Indeed, West Germany and Austria were not spending a penny. Moreover, none of these countries stood in such urgent need of modernising industry and infrastructure as Britain.

    For that matter, no country anywhere chose like Britain to set up a more lavish and expensive welfare state in the immediate aftermath of a ruinous war, and when bankrupt, living off foreign tick, carrying a heavy burden of defence costs, and with an industrial system needing radical reconstruction. In the case of West Germany, she did not embark on her first major postwar improvement on the welfare system inherited from the Weimar Republic and Bismarck until 1957, when her 'economic miracle' was complete.
23. Ibid.
24. Ibid.
25. CAB 87/63, EC(43)7, 27 October 1943.
26. CAB 87/63, EC(43)10, 30 October 1943.
27. Ibid.
28. CAB 87/63, EC(43)15, 20 October 1943.
29. Ibid.
30. CAB 87/63, EC(43)6, 16 October 1943.
31. CAB 87/15, R(I)(45)9, Report by Official Sub-Committee on Post-War Resettlement of the Motor Industry, 21 March 1945.
32. CAB 87/15, R(I)(45)11, 3 April 1945.
33. CAB 87/15, R(I)(45)6, 5 April 1945.
34. CAB 87/3, RP(43)27, 20 July 1943.
35. Ibid.
36. Ibid.
37. CAB 87/7, R(43)4.
38. CAB 87/7, R(44)6, 11 January 1944.
39. Cf. CAB 87/5–9.
40. CAB 87/9, R(44)174, 19 October 1944.
41. Ibid.
42. CAB 87/15, R(I)(45)9, Report by Official Sub-Committee on Post-War Resettlement of the Motor Industry, 21 March 1945.
43. London, HMSO, 1975, *passim*.
44. CAB 87/15, R(I)(45)9.
45. CAB 87/15, R(I)(45)6, meeting of the Ministerial Sub-Committee on Industrial Problems, 5 April 1945.

Chapter Fourteen: The Lost Victory

1. ED 136/296, Education After the War: Technical Education, Memorandum by H. B. Wallis, 5 September 1941, summarising existing provision for further education.
2. Cf. CAB 102/240.
3. CAB 102/240, quoting M/Ed File, Secretary's Clerk's Papers 2152(A)I.
4. CAB 102/240.
5. Ibid.
6. Ibid.
7. CAB 117/109, Committee on Reconstruction Problems – Policy with regard to Education (1941–3): Education After the War (the Green Book) (June 1941).
8. Ibid.
9. Quoted in ibid.
10. Cmd 6458.
11. Ibid.
12. Quoted in CAB 102/240.
13. CAB 117/109.
14. ED 136/218, 24 November 1941.
15. Ibid.
16. CAB 102/252, Chuter Ede Diary (copies by Dr S. Weitzman), vol. IV, entry for 13 November 1942.
17. CAB 102/256, quoted in Chuter Ede Diary for 4 September 1943–11 January 1944, entry for 14 December 1943.
18. ED 138/20, Note of an interview of R. A. Butler by Dr S. Weitzman, 25 May 1945.
19. CAB 102/249, Chuter Ede Diary, vol. I, 15 July–3 October 1941, entry for 30 July 1941.
20. Ibid.
21. Ibid.
22. CAB 102/250, Chuter Ede Diary, vol. II, 4 October–12 December 1941.
23. Ibid., entry for 22 November 1941.
24. Ibid., entry for 25 November 1941.
25. CAB 102/251, Chuter Ede Diary, vol. III, 13 December 1941–18 February 1942, entry for 12 January 1942.
26. CAB 102/252, Chuter Ede Diary, vol. IV, 19 February–23 April 1942, entry for 23 March 1942.
27. CAB 102/253, Chuter Ede Diary, vol. V, 27 April–19 July 1942, entry for 13 May 1942.
28. Ibid., entry for 9 July 1942.
29. As recorded in CAB 102/252, Chuter Ede Diary, vol. IV, entry for 19 March 1942.
30. CAB 102/254, Chuter Ede Diary, vol. VI, entry for 9 October 1942.
31. CAB 102/256, Chuter Ede Diary, vol. VIII, 4 September 1943–11 January 1944; cf. especially entry for 13 September 1943.
32. Ibid.
33. ED 138/20, interview by Dr S. Weitzman, 25 May 1945.
34. CAB 102/257, Chuter Ede Diary, vol. IX, 12 January–20 June 1944, entry for 20 January 1944.
35. CAB 102/244, Chuter Ede Diary, vol. VII, 22 January–3 September 1943, entry for 6 July 1943.
36. ED 138/20, Note by Mrs Goodfellow on progress from the Green Book to the 1944 Act .
37. ED 136/215.

38. CAB 117/109; Green Book, p. 21.
39. Ibid.
40. Ibid., p. 22.
41. Ibid., p. 23.
42. Ibid.
43. Ibid.
44. ED 136/292, Education After the War: Discussion and Correspondence with the Ministry of Labour: minutes by R. S. Wood to Butler, 4 and 9 September 1941, reporting on meetings with Sir Frank Tribe, Permanent Under-Secretary at the Ministry of Labour: note by Butler on meeting with Bevin, 4 September 1941; letter from Bevin to Butler enclosing memorandum setting out his views, 11 October 1941.
45. Ibid., Note by Butler to Deputy Secretary, 21 October 1941: CAB 102/254, Chuter Ede Diary, vol. VI, 10 July 1942–21 January 1943, entry for 4 November 1942.
46. Ibid., Note to Deputy Secretary, 21 October 1941.
47. Ibid., Note by Butler to Deputy Secretary, 21 October 1941.
48. CAB 102/252, Chuter Ede Diary, vol. IV, entry for 1 April 1942.
49. ED 136/683, Day Continuation Schools 1936–44, Note by Butler to R. S. Wood on Technical, Day Continuation and Adult Education, 30 July 1942.
50. Ibid.
51. Ibid.
52. ED 136/683, memorandum by R. S. Wood, 20 August 1942.
53. Ibid.
54. Ibid., Board of Education: Day Continuation School Committee, Report on a System of Compulsory Part-Time Day Education, circulated 6 September 1943.
55. Ibid.
56. Ibid.
57. Ibid.
58. Cmd 6458.
59. Ibid.
60. Ibid.
61. Ibid.
62. H. M. D. Parker, *Manpower: A Study of Wartime Policy and Administration* (London, HMSO and Longmans, Green, 1957), pp. 326–30; CAB 102/239; CAB 87/54, IEP(41)20, Memorandum by the Minister of Labour on Experience of Large Scale Training Schemes under the Ministry of Labour and National Service, 7 November 1941.
63. Cmd 6458, appendix, table 1.
64. Ibid.
65. Ibid.
66. Ibid.
67. Issue of 17 July 1943.
68. Ibid.
69. Issue of 18 July 1943.
70. ED 136/427, file of correspondence about engineering aspects of the White Paper: 'Memorandum on the White Paper proposals in so far as they affect Technical Education for Engineering'.
71. Ibid.
72. Ibid.
73. Letter in issue of 30 September 1943.
74. ED 136/427.
75. ED 136/427, letter from Butler to Chancellor of the Exchequer, 19 October 1943; reply from Chancellor of the Exchequer, 23 October 1943.

76. ED 136/350, letter from Attlee to Anderson, 25 February 1944; reply from Anderson, 4 March 1944.
77. ED 136/350, minute of 6 March 1944.
78. Ibid.
79. Leading article, 17 December 1943.
80. Second Reading debate: see Hansard, *Parliamentary Debates* (House of Commons), Fifth Series, vol. 396, cols 207–319, 406–90, 1647–727 and 1679–99. Committee of Whole House: see ibid., vol. 397, cols 44–143, 197–302, 998–1036, 1067–88, 1119–217, 2221–343 and 2356–460; vol. 398, cols 685–815, 1071–214, 1264–396, 1578–697, 1828–976 and 2027–142; vol. 399, cols 1744–2112. Report and Third Reading: see ibid., vol. 399, cols 2113–267.
81. Ibid., vol. 396, cols 1679–83.
82. Ibid., col. 1687.
83. Ibid., col. 1699.
84. CAB 102/257, Chuter Ede Diary, vol. IX, entry for 23 March 1944; see Hansard, *Parliamentary Debates* (House of Commons), Fifth Series, vol. 398, cols 1071–214.
85. Hansard, *Parliamentary Debates* (House of Commons), Fifth Series, vol. 397, cols 44–143, 197–302, 998–1036, 1067–88, 1119–217, 2221–343 and 2356–460; vol. 398, cols 685–815, 1071–214, 1264–396, 1578–697, 1828–976 and 2027–142; vol. 399, cols 1744–2267.
86. Ibid., vol. 399, cols 2113–93
87. Ibid., cols 2256–67.
88. 7 & 8 Geo. 6, c. 31.
89. Ibid.
90. CAB 102/239, the 1944 Act and its implementation (unpublished narrative); see also *Explanatory Memorandum by the President of the Board of Education on the Education Bill*, Cmd 6492 (1943).
91. Cmd 9703.
92. *Report of the Committee on Higher Education*, Cmnd 2154 (1963).
93. *Report of the Committee on Scientific Manpower*, Cmd 6824 (1946).
94. Cf. Robert R. Locke, *The End of the Practical Man: Entrepreneurship and Higher Education in Germany, France and Great Britain, 1880–1940* (Greenwich, Conn., and London, Jai Press, 1984), chs 3 and 5.
95. Ibid., pp. 138–9.
96. Ibid., pp. 91–7, 123–39 and 168–78.
97. CAB 87/63, EC(43)4, 25 October 1943.
98. Ibid.
99. Michael Sanderson, *The Universities and British Industry* (London, Routledge & Kegan Paul, 1972), p. 377.
100. CAB 87/14, R(I)(44)4, Ministerial Sub-Committee (of Reconstruction Committee) on Reconstruction Problems: Memorandum by President of the Board of Trade on Industrial Design, 20 June 1944; Annex I, Weir Committee Report.
101. Ibid., Annex I.
102. Ibid., Annex II.
103. Gorell Report (1932); Council for Art and Industry, *Education for the Consumer* (1935); Hambledon Report on the Royal College of Art (1935); Council for Art and Industry's *Design and the Designer in Industry* (1937); and the Weir Committee (1943).
104. CAB 87/14, R(I)(44)4, Annex II.
105. Ibid.
106. Ibid., Annex I.

107. Ibid., Memorandum by the President of the Board of Trade, and Annexes I and II.
108. Design Council, *Industrial Design in the United Kingdom* (London, Design Council, 1977). Cf. Peter Gorb, 'How to Manage by Design', *Management Today*, May 1976; Lord (Wilfred) Brown, 'Product Design', unpublished paper prepared for NEDO (January 1977).
109. Cf. *The Structure of Art and Design Education in the Further Education Sector*, report to the Design Council on the Design of British Consumer Goods (London, Design Council, 1983). It was chaired by David Mellor, Des. RCA.
110. Cmd 6458, appendix, table I; Cmd 6550, table V; Cmd 6502, appendix E.
111. CAB 87/10, R(45)8.
112. Cf. ED 136/292, 8 September 1941, Memorandum by M. G. Holmes to Butler on Raising Age to 16; also CAB 102/255, Chuter Ede Diary, vol. VII, entries for 8 February and 5 March 1943.
113. CAB 102/239, the 1944 Act and its implementation.
114. Ibid.
115. CAB 102/255, Chuter Ede Diary, vol. VII, entry for 5 March 1943.
116. *15 to 18*, Report of the Central Advisory Council for Education – England, 2 vols. (London, HMSO, 1959).
117. *Report of the Consultative Committee of the Board of Education on Secondary Education with Special Reference to Grammar Schools and Technical High Schools* (the Spens Report) (London, HMSO, 1938), pp. 376–81.
118. CAB 117/109, *passim*; CAB 102/240, memorandum by R. S. Wood, 17 January 1941, and *passim*; see also ED 136/212, 'Green Book' drafting, Preliminary Papers; also ED 136/215 and ED 136/218.
119. CAB 117/109.
120. Cmd 6458.
121. Ibid.
122. CAB 117/109, memorandum by Holmes, 5 November 1941, suggesting that the committee should take on content as well as curriculum.
123. Dr Cyril Norwood, *The English Tradition in Education* (London, John Murray, 1929), pp. 19 and 121.
124. ED 136/681, Committee on Curriculum and Examinations 1941–4; General file of correspondence. The members of the committee were:
Dr C. Norwood (Chairman)
Miss M. G. Clarke, Headmistress of Manchester High School for Girls
Miss O. M. Hastings, President, Association of Assistant Mistresses in Secondary Schools
Mr A. W. S. Hutchings. Secretary, Association of Assistant Masters in Secondary Schools
Dr P. D. Innes CBE, Chief Education Officer for Birmingham
Professor Joseph Jones JP, Chairman of the Brecon Education Committee
Dr J. E. Myers, Chairman, Northern Universities Joint Matriculation Board
Mr E. W. Nesbitt, Assistant Master, Ryhope Secondary School, and member of the executive committee of the National Union of Teachers
Sir Reginald Sharp, Secretary of the Association of Education Committees
Mr S. H. Shurrock, Secretary to the Matriculation and Schools Examination Council, University of London
Dr Terry Thomas, Headmaster, Leeds Grammar School
Mr W. Nalder Williams, Secretary to the Syndicate of Local Examiners, University of Cambridge
Secretary: R. H. Barrow, HM Inspector
125. ED 136/681, COM 4.
126. ED 136/681, Minutes of first meeting, 18 October 1941.
127. Ibid.

128. ED 138/16, Committee on Curriculum and Examinations: Action leading to the setting up of the Committee; meeting between Butler and Norwood, 27 November 1941.
129. Ibid., W. N. Williams, Secretary to the Syndicate of Local Examiners, University of Cambridge, to President of the Board of Education, December 1941.
130. ED 136/681.
131. Ibid.
132. For its proceedings, see ED 136/681.
133. London, HMSO.
134. Ibid.
135. Ibid., p. viii.
136. Ibid., pp. 56–8.
137. Ibid.
138. Ibid., pp. 119–22.
139. Ibid., p. 69.
140. Ibid., pp. 56–8 and 131.
141. Cf. ibid., pp. 1–15.
142. Anthony Heath, 'Class and Meritocracy in British Education', in Alex Finch and Peter Scrimshaw (eds.), *Standards, Schooling and Education* (Milton Keynes, The Open University, 1980), p. 288; *Education and Industry* (London, National Economic Development Council, 1983), p. 5; P. J. A. Landymore, 'Education and Industry Since the War', in Derek Morris (ed.), *The Economic System in the UK* (Oxford, Oxford University Press, 1985), *passim*.
143. Anthony Crosland, 'Comprehensive Education', in Finch and Scrimshaw, *Standards, Schooling and Education*, p. 29; *Education and Industry*, p. 5.
144. J. Stuart Maclure, *Educational Documents: England and Wales, 1816 to the Present Day* (London, Methuen, 1965), pp. 274–7, citing the White Paper on Industrial Training (1962), and the Act of 1963.
145. Cf. *Education and Training for Young People*, Cmnd 9482 (1985).
146. Maclure, *Educational Documents*, p. 288.
147. Sanderson, *The Universities and British Industry*, p. 375: see his ch. 13, *passim*.
148. Ibid., p. 377: Locke, *The End of the Practical Man*, p. 135.
149. S. J. Prais and Karin Wagner, *Schooling Standards in Britain and Germany: Some Summary Comparisons Bearing on Economic Efficiency* (London, National Institute of Economic and Social Research, 1983), p. 7; Central Policy Review Staff, *Education, Training and Performance* (London, HMSO, 1980), p. 13.
150. Prais and Wagner, *Schooling Standards in Britain and Germany*, p. 7; National Economic Development Office and Manpower Services Commission, *Competence and Competition: Training and Education in the Federal Republic of Germany, the United States and Japan*, a report prepared by the Institute of Manpower Studies (London, NEDO Books, 1984), p. 50 and table 5.6, p. 75.
151. S. J. Prais, *Vocational Qualifications of the Labour Force in Britain and Germany* (London, National Institute of Economic and Social Research, 1981), table 4, p. 18a: figures for 1977.
152. *The Times*, 2 October 1982; NEDO and MSC, *Competence and Competition*. pp. 2, 3 and 69; table 6.4, p. 83.
153. Prais, *Vocational Qualifications*, table 1, p. 2a.
154. Reported in the *Daily Telegraph*, 30 August 1984; the study in question was NEDO and MSC, *Competence and Competition*.
155. In 1953 Britain spent 11.3 per cent of GNP; West Germany 4.9 per cent; Italy 4.6 per cent; France, with her own imperial illusions, 11 per cent. In 1965 Britain spent 7.1 per cent; West Germany 5.1 per cent; Italy 4.0 per

cent; France 6.6 per cent. Figures from International Institute of Strategic Studies, *The Military Balance, 1966–67* (London, IISS, 1966), table 3, p. 45. In 1970 Britain spent 4.9 per cent of GNP on defence; West Germany 3.3 per cent; Italy 2.8 per cent; France 4.0 per cent: *The Military Balance, 1971–72* (London, IISS, 1971), table 3, p. 60.

156. Cf. Mary Kaldor, 'Technical Change in the Defence Industry', and C. Freeman, 'Government Policy' (especially pp. 322–4), both in Keith Pavitt (ed.), *Technical Innovation and British Economic Performance*, Social Policy Research Unit, Sussex University (London, Macmillan, 1980).

157. 1983 figures: *World Bank Development Report 1985* (New York, Oxford University Press for the World Bank, 1985), tables 1 and 3, pp. 175 and 179.

158. For the end of empire and the world role, see Keith Robbins, *The Eclipse of a Great Power: Modern Britain, 1870–1975* (London, Longmans, 1983); L. W. Martin, *British Defence Policy: The Long Recessional* (London, IISS, 1969); Paul M. Kennedy, *The Rise and Fall of British Naval Mastery* (London, Allen Lane, 1976), ch. 12; Desmond Wettern, *The Decline of British Seapower* (London, Jane's Publishing, 1982); Correlli Barnett, *Britain and Her Army* (London, Allen Lane, 1970), ch. 20; Margaret Gowing. *Independence and Deterrence: Britain and Atomic Energy, 1945–1952*, vol. I: *Policy Making* (London, Macmillan, 1982). See also press reports on a review of British economic decline and its effects on foreign policy submitted to the then Foreign Secretary, Dr David Owen, in 1979 by Sir Nicholas Henderson, then ambassador in Washington (cf. *Daily Telegraph*, 1 June 1979).

159. For the failure of New Jerusalem, even at unimagined cost, to realise wartime hopes that inequalities of life, opportunity and attainment could be largely eliminated, and poverty abolished, see (apart from EDUCATION, already discussed) HOUSING: Patrick Dunleavy, *The Politics of Mass Housing in Britain, 1945–1975: A Study of Corporate Power and Professional Influence in the Welfare State* (Oxford, Clarendon Press, 1981); Department of the Environment Report, *Tenants and Town Hall* (London, HMSO, 1979); National Consumer Council, *Soonest Mended* (London, NCC, 1979); David Donnison with Paul Soto, *The Good City* (London, William Heinemann, 1980); Paul Harrison, *The Inner City* (Harmondsworth, Penguin Books, 1983). THE CLASS DIVIDE: Arthur Marwick, *Class: Image and Reality, In Britain, France and the USA since 1930* (London, William Collins, 1980); A. M. Halsey, A. F. Heath and J. M. Ridge, *Origins and Destinations: Family, Class and Education in Modern Britain* (Oxford, Clarendon Press, 1979); John H. Goldthorpe, *Social Mobility and Class Structure in Modern Britain* (Oxford, Clarendon Press, 1979). POVERTY AND HEALTH: MORI Survey for London Weekend Television, reported in the *Sunday Times*, 21 August 1983. GENERAL SOCIAL POLICY: Eileen Younghusband, *Social Work in Britain, 1950–75*, 2 vols. (London, George Allen & Unwin, 1978); David Donnison, *Social Policy Revisited* (London, George Allen & Unwin, 1975), and *The Politics of Poverty* (London, Martin Robertson, 1981); Digby Anderson (ed.), *The Ignorance of Social Intervention* (London, Croom Helm, 1980); Peter Wedge and Juliet Essen, *Children in Adversity* (London, Pan Books, 1982).

Bibliography

UNPUBLISHED SOURCES

Public Record Office

Admiralty (ADM series)

ADM 1/11892 Labour in Naval and Mercantile Shipyards.
ADM 1/12506 Shipyard Development Committee 1943.
ADM 1/15218 Operations and Technical Radio Committee: Papers 1–67, 1942–43 [includes papers on the Radio Board].

Air Ministry (AIR series)

AIR 2/6976 Radio and Radio Board, and OPTEC Committee: Briefs for Meetings, Information for.
AIR 19/355 Radio Board.

Ministry of Aircraft Production (AVIA series)

AVIA 7/1674 H_2S Electrical Units. Production [1942–3].
AVIA 7/1675 H_2S Electrical Units. Production [1943–4].
AVIA 9/37 Minister's Papers: Appointment of Sir Charles Bruce-Gardner's Committee to report on productivity in the aircraft industry, December 1942.
AVIA 10/83 Sir Roy Fedden's Mission to Germany 1945: Purpose to investigate current research and projects.
AVIA 10/85 Farren Mission to Germany: A Survey of a Cross Section of German Aircraft, Aircraft Engine and Armament Industries, July 1945.
AVIA 10/99 Fedden Mission [to United States] Report, dated June 1943.
AVIA 10/104 Report of British Mission to United States of America to Study Production Methods, Sept.–Oct. 1942.
AVIA 10/106 Sir Roy Fedden's visit to USA: Terms of Reference; Report – Programme of Meetings (including Précis on the Work of the Fedden Mission, or Preliminary Report, circulated on 22 April 1943).
AVIA 10/108 Report on Visit to United Kingdom, by Mr Ed Walton (Aircraft Report – Harriman Mission, July 1943).
AVIA 10/110 Report on his visit to America, June 18–August 18, 1943, by Cdr (E) M. Luby RN.
AVIA 10/113 Visit to Messerschmitt Plant at Oberammergau-Bavaria, June 18–25, 1945, Report by Mr R. M. Clarkson, de Havilland Aircraft Company.
AVIA 10/269 Labour Statistics 20/10/42–16/8/44.
AVIA 10/311 MAP Statistical Review 1939–45 (l946).
AVIA 10/338 War Cabinet – Radio Production Committee and General Questions on the Radio Industry, 1941–1944 [includes papers of the Radio Production Executive].
AVIA 10/340 Radio Components Production 1942–1943.

AVIA 10/348 Comments on the History of Radio and Radar, by A. P. Rowe, 2 October 1947.
AVIA 10/342 War Cabinet – Radio Board Papers: Minutes of Meetings, Conclusions and Reports (Oct. 1942–Nov. 1944).
AVIA 10/344 Radio 1943–1945.
AVIA 15/2536 Training of Labour for the Aircraft Industry: General Policy.
AVIA 15/2548 Trade disputes in aircraft and munitions industries, 1 Jan.–31 Dec. 1944.

Ministry of Production (BT series)
BT 28/319 Report to the Machine Tool Controller on the Equipment of Shipyards and Marine Engineering Shops, by Mr Cecil Bentham, 30 September 1942. Continuation of Report after Additional Visits.
BT 28/360 Industrial Capacity Committee.
BT 28/377 Report on Vickers-Armstrong (Aircraft) Ltd, Weybridge, by five expert Inspectors of Labour Supply.
BT 28/435 Production Planning and Personnel Committee of the Radio Board.
BT 28/543 Five-Man Board – Labour Efficiency.
BT 28/1172 Radio Valve Production.

Cabinet and Cabinet Committees: Minutes and Memoranda (CAB series)
CAB 16/109–12 Report, Proceedings and Memoranda of the Defence Requirements Sub-Committee of the Committee of Imperial Defence 1933–5.
CAB 16/123 Defence Policy and Requirements: Defence Requirements Enquiry Sub-Committee 1936.
CAB 16/136–43 Minutes of Meetings of the Defence Policy and Requirements Committee 1936–9.
CAB 21/1100 Cabinet Registered Files: Radio Board, Establishment of.
CAB 24/274 Cabinet Memoranda to 1939.
CAB 27/476 Minutes and Memoranda of the Committee on Preparations for the League of Nations Disarmament Conference 1931–2.
CAB 27/627 Minutes and Memoranda of the Cabinet Committee on Foreign Policy 1936–9.
CAB 27/648 Defence Programmes and their Acceleration Committee.
CAB 29/159 Anglo-French Staff Conversations, London, 1939.
CAB 32/127 Imperial Conference, London, 1937 – Cabinet Committee 1936–7.
CAB 32/129 Imperial Conference, London, 1937 – Memoranda.
CAB 36/1–13 Minutes and Memoranda of the Joint Overseas and Home Defence Committee 1920–39, vol. 4.
CAB 53/1–11 Committee of Imperial Defence: Meetings of the Chiefs of Staff Committee, vol. 4.
CAB 53/12–54 Committee of Imperial Defence: Memoranda of the Chiefs of Staff Committee, vol. 30.
CAB 65 series War Cabinet Minutes: vols. 25, 26, 28, 35, 36, 40.
CAB 66 series War Cabinet Memoranda (WP) and (CP) series, vols. 11, 23, 27, 38, 39, 42.
CAB 70 series Defence Committee (Supply), vols. 5, 6.
CAB 71/1–22 Lord President's Committee 1940–45, vols. 12, 13, 14, 16, 17.
CAB 78/4 Committees: Miscellaneous and General Series – MISC 33: Naval Construction. MISC 35: the Aircraft Programme.
CAB 78/23 Publication of Statistics, Aug.–Sept. 1944.

CAB 87 series (Committees on Reconstruction)
CAB 87/1–3 Reconstruction Problems, March 1941–Oct. 1943.
CAB 87/5–10 Reconstruction, Dec. 1943–May 1945.

CAB 87/12–13 Reconstruction Priorities, Jan.–Nov. 1943.
CAB 87/14–15 Reconstruction (Industrial Problems) May 1944–June 1945.
CAB 87/17–18 Reconstruction: (Official) Industrial Problems, March 1944–May 1945.
CAB 87/55–7 Post-war Internal Economic Problems, Nov. 1941–Oct. 1943.
CAB 87/60 Official History of Post-war Economic Problems and Anglo-American Co-operation.
CAB 87/63 Post-war Employment, July 1943–Jan. 1944.
CAB 87/64 Economic Aspects of Reconstruction Problems, Oct. 1941–Feb. 1942.
CAB 87/76–82 Social Insurance and Allied Services, July 1941–Oct. 1942.
CAB 87/89 Working Party on Controls, 1945.
CAB 87/91 Location of Industry, Jan.–July 1941.
CAB 87/92 Coal Mining Industry, Apr.–May 1942.
CAB 87/93 Organisation of the Coal Industry, Oct. 1943–Feb. 1944.
CAB 87/94 Distribution of Industry, Oct. 1944–Mar. 1945.
CAB 87/95 External Economic Policy, Feb. 1944.

CAB 102 series (Cabinet Office Historical Section; Official War Histories (1939–1945), Civil) [Note: Consists of draft narratives, some never published; studies for the use of official historians; and correspondence]
CAB 102/41 Aircraft Production Programmes and Quantities.
CAB 102/47 Development and Production of Propellers, by D. McKenna.
CAB 102/48 Undercarriages – Development and Production, by E. Bridge.
CAB 102/51 Reciprocating Aero-Engines and Engine Accessories Production and Programmes 1935–45, by D. A. Parry.
CAB 102/52 Aircraft – the Spares Problem, by D. A. Parry.
CAB 102/86–7 *British War Economy*: Comments and correspondence thereon.
CAB 102/88–9 First draft of *British War Production*, by M. M. Postan.
CAB 102/90–3 *British War Production*: Comments and criticism thereon.
CAB 102/238–9 History of Education [Unpublished history by Dr S. Weitzman].
CAB 102/240 Education History: The Education Act 1944 [unpublished history by Dr S. Weitzman].
CAB 102/244 History of Education: The Medical Services of Education and the Special Schools; revision by Mrs S. M. Ferguson of E. K. Ferguson's draft.
CAB 102/249–57 Chuter Ede Diary [copies of the original in the British Library by Dr S. Weitzman], 1941–44.
CAB 102/274 Aircraft Production and Factories: papers used by Mr Hornby when writing official history, *Factories and Plant*, chs VI–VIII.
CAB 102/279 Admiralty Production – Fire Control Apparatus.
CAB 102/393 Development of Jet Propulsion and Gas Turbine Engines in the United Kingdom – revised draft by Miss C. Keppel.
CAB 102/394 Comments thereon by Air Commodore F. Whittle.
CAB 102/399 Labour in the Coal Mining Industry.
CAB 102/402 Labour Efficiency in the British Airframe Industry.
CAB 102/405 Labour Requirements and Supply 1940–44, by D. Mack Smith.
CAB 102/406 Labour Welfare and Utilisation in the Aircraft Industry, by J. B. Jeffreys; draft used by Mrs Inman in writing *Labour in the Munitions Industries*.
CAB 102/407 Labour requirements and Supply for the Ministries of Supply and Production: Shipbuilding and Marine Engineering 1935–45; unpublished study by Mrs P. Inman.
CAB 102/409 Labour Requirements and Supply for the Ministries of Supply and Production; draft by Mrs Inman for use in official history, *Labour in the Munitions Industries*.

CAB 102/508 Machine Tools and Production Problems 1940–44, by W. C. Hornby.
CAB 102/509 Directorate of Machine Tools, by W. C. Hornby.
CAB 102/510 Machine-Tools 1940–44, by D. Mack Smith.
CAB 102/524 Execution of the Naval New Production Programmes 1939–45.
CAB 102/527 Naval New Construction Programmes and Their Execution: Final Draft by Mrs D. McKenna.
CAB 102/532 Electrical Items, including Fire Control Gear.
CAB 102/540 Production of Naval Machinery and Naval Engines, 1939–45; Engineer-in-Chief's Department, Admiralty.
CAB 102/643–4 *History of Development and Production of Radio and Radar*; first draft of Section Three, by K. E. B. Jay and T. N. Scott.

CAB 117 series (Reconstruction Secretariat Files)
CAB 117/109 Committee on Reconstruction Problems – Policy with regard to Education (1941–3).
CAB 117/111 Committee on Reconstruction Problems: Part III Education Authorities – correspondence and statistics in connection with the Minister without Portfolio's Report to the President of the Board of Education, 1942.
CAB 117/112–13 Committee on Reconstruction Problems; Education: Resolutions, Statements and Meetings with Various Local Government Authorities in connection with Part III Education Authorities.
CAB 117/165 Committee on Reconstruction Problems – Nuffield College Survey: Memorandum on Wartime Survey.
CAB 117/202 Post-war prospects: the Chemical Industry.
CAB 117/209 Committee on Reconstruction Problems – Government Policy and Public Opinion.

CAB 123 series (Lord President of the Council: Secretariat Files)
CAB 123/21 Report by US Mission of Technical Experts after Visits to British Coalfields.

Board of Education (ED series)
ED 136/212 'Green Book' drafting, Preliminary Papers.
ED 136/215 Untitled file, containing correspondence with regard to the 'Green Book'.
ED 136/218 Meetings with outside bodies with regard to the 'Green Book'.
ED 136/277 Education After the War – 'Green Book' discussions, meetings and correspondence with regard to the 'Green Book' with the Association of Teachers in Technical Institutions.
ED 136/292 Education After the War: Discussions and Correspondence with the Ministry of Labour.
ED 136/296 Education After the War: Technical Education.
ED 136/350 Correspondence with regard to Scientific Research and Technical Education, 1944.
ED 136/427 Untitled file, containing correspondence over the engineering aspects of the 1943 White Paper on educational reconstruction.
ED 136/681 Committee on Curriculum and Examinations, 1941–1944: General file of correspondence.
ED 136/683 Day Continuation Schools 1936–44.
ED 138/16 Committee on Curriculum and Examinations [Norwood]: Action leading to the setting up of the Committee.
ED 138/20 Notes of Interviews of R. A. Butler by Dr S. Weitzman.

Ministry of Information (INF series)
INF 1/177 Reconstruction and Radio.
INF 1/292 Home Intelligence Weekly Reports.

INF 1/849 Policy Committee, Ministry of Information; Minutes and Papers.
INF 1/862 Post War Aims.
INF 1/863 Post War Aims.
INF 1/864 Post War Aims and Reconstruction Problems.

Ministry of Labour and National Service (LAB series)

LAB 10/128 Committee of Investigation: Dilution through female labour in the Sheet Metal Industry.
LAB 10/132 Trade Stoppages – Weekly Return to the Minister November 1940 to December 1944. [Note at head of file states that the Return was called the 'Weekly Strike Chart' within the Ministry of Labour.]
LAB 10/248 Review of Industrial Relations Policy: Post War Measures on Compulsory Arbitration.

War Premier's Personal Papers: Civil (PREM 4)

PREM 4 89/1 Parts I and II.
PREM 4 89/2.
PREM 4 100/4 and 5.

Churchill Archives Centre

Attlee Papers.
Bevin Papers.
Bowen Papers.
Colquhoun Papers.
Crawford Papers.
Goodeve Papers.
Swinton Papers.
Weir Papers.

France: Archives Nationales

Fonds Benoist d'Azy.

COMMAND PAPERS AND OFFICIAL PUBLICATIONS

Command Papers

2794–1 *Report of the Commissioners appointed to inquire into the State of Popular Education in England.* Vol. I. *Report* (1861).
3288 *Report of Her Majesty s Commissioners appointed to inquire into the Revenues and Management of certain Colleges and Schools and the Studies pursued and Instruction given therein.* Vol. I. *Report* (1864).
3966 *Report of the Endowed Schools (Schools Inquiry) Royal Commission.* Vol. I. (1867–8).
4139 *Report of the Committee of Council of Education* (1868–9).
C. 1279 *Report of the Royal Commission on Scientific Instruction and the Advancement of Science. 6th Report* (1875).
C. 3981 *Second Report of the Royal Commissioners on Technical Instruction.* Vol. I. *Report* (1884).
C. 5485 *Report of the Royal Commission on the Elementary Education Acts (England and Wales), (1886–8). Final Report* (1888).
C. 7862 *Report of the Royal Commission on Secondary Education.* Vol. I. *Report* (1895).
Cd 1738 *Second Report on Higher Education* (1903).
Cd 4715 *Second Report Minutes of Evidence* (1903).
Cd 4757 *Report of the Consultative Committee on Attendance Compulsory or Otherwise at Continuation Schools.* Vol. I (1909).
Cd 5130 *Report of the Board of Education 1908–9* (1910).

Cd 9035 *Report of the Board of Trade Committee on the Iron and Steel Trades after the War* (1917).
Cd 9071 *Final Report of the Committee on Commercial and Industrial Policy after the War* (1918).
Cmd 361 *Coal Industry Commission. Final Report* (1919).
Cmd 2154 Board of Trade, *Report on Shipping and Shipbuilding after the War* (1918).
Cmd 2600 *Report of the Royal Commission on the Coal Industry* (1925).
Cmd 3156 *Report of the Industrial Transference Board for 1928* (1928).
Cmd 3282 *Final Report of the Committee on Industry and Trade* (1928–9).
Cmd 5507 *Report by the Import Duties Advisory Committee: The Present Position and Future Development of the Iron and Steel Industry* (1937).
Cmd 5556 *22nd Abstract of Labour Statistics of the United Kingdom* (1939).
Cmd 5776 *Education in 1937 being the Report of the Board of Education and the Statistics of public education for England and Wales* (1938).
Cmd 6153 *Royal Commission on the Distribution of the Industrial Population* (1940).
Cmd 6364 *Coal* (1942).
Cmd 6404 *Social Insurance and Allied Services* (1942).
Cmd 6428 *Training in the Building Industry* (1943).
Cmd 6458 *Educational Reconstruction* (1943).
Cmd 6468 *Summary Report on the Ministry of Health for the year ended 31 March 1943* (1943).
Cmd 6492 *Education Bill: Explanatory Memorandum by the President of the Board of Education* (1943).
Cmd 6502 *A National Health Service* (1944).
Cmd 6523 *Principles of Government in Maintained Secondary Schools* (1944).
Cmd 6527 *Employment Policy* (1944).
Cmd 6538 Ministry of Fuel and Power, *Statistical Digest for 1938* (1941).
Cmd 6550–1 *Social Insurance*. Parts I and II (1944).
Cmd 6564 *Statistics Relating to the War Effort of the United Kingdom* (1944).
Cmd 6609 *Housing Policy* (1945).
Cmd 6610 *Coal Mining: Report of the Technical Advisory Committee* (1945).
Cmd 6639 Ministry of Fuel and Power, *Statistical Digest for 1944* (1944).
Cmd 6824 *Report of the Committee on Scientific Manpower* (1946).
Cmd 9703 *Technical Education* (1956).
Cmnd 2154 *Report of the Committee on Higher Education* (1963).
Cmnd 9111 *Regional Industrial Development* (1983).
Cmnd 9482 *Education and Training for Young People* (1985).

Official Publications

Parliamentary Debates (Hansard)
House of Commons, Fifth Series, 1943–4, vols. 396–9, 401.

British Intelligence Objectives Sub-Committee
BIOS Final Report No. 35, Item No. 26, *Report on Visit to Daimler-Benz AG at Stuttgart-Untertürkheim* (London, HMSO, 1946).
BIOS Miscellaneous Report No. 77, *European Electron Induction Accelerators* (London, HMSO, 1948).
BIOS Final Report No. 184, Item No. 9, *German Camera Industry* (London, HMSO, 1946).
BIOS Final Report No. 252, Item No. 9, *I.G. Photopaper Fabrik (AGFA) Leverkusen, near Cologne* (London, HMSO, 1946).
BIOS Final Report No. 822, Item Nos. 12 and 29, *Shipbuilding: Notes on Visits to Blohm und Voss, Deutsche Werft, Germania Werft, and Deschimag* (London, HMSO, 1946).

BIOS Final Report No. 1287, Item Nos. 21 and 31, *Rolling Mills at the Reichswerke (Hermann Göring Works), Braunschweig* (London, HMSO, 1947).
BIOS Final Report No. 1544, Item No. 31, *The German Crane Industry* (London, HMSO, 1946).
BIOS Final Report No. 1648, Item No. 31, *Manufacture of Air Compressors and Pneumatic Tools and Appliances in Germany* (London, HMSO, 1948).
BIOS Final Report No. 1735, Item No. 31, *German Optical Machine Tools* (London, HMSO, 1948).
BIOS Overall Report No. 12, *German Gas Turbine Development during the period 1939–45* (London, HMSO, 1949), by J. W. Adderley MBE BA AFRAeS, member of staff of Power Jets (R & D) Ltd.

Combined Intelligence Objectives Sub-Committee

CIOS Item Nos. 1, 7, 9, File No. XXI–I, *Organization of Telefunken* (London, HMSO, 1945).
CIOS Item No. 5, File No. XXXI–66, *Notes on Aircraft Gas Turbine Engine Developments at Junkers, Dessau, and Associated Factories* (London, HMSO, 1946).
CIOS Item Nos. 2, 3, 4, 11, 18 and 21, File No. XXXII–67, *Krupp A.G., Bochumer Verein* (London, HMSO, 1945).
CIOS Item Nos. 5, 25 and 27, File No. XXVIII–25, *German Airframe Tooling and Methods, Messerschmitt Works* (London, HMSO, 1945).
CIOS Item Nos. 19 and 26, File No. XXXIII–13, *Robert Bosch and Deckel Co.* (London, HMSO, 1945).
CIOS Item No. 21, File No. XXIX–29, *Developments in Tool Die and Special Steels* (London, HMSO, 1945).
CIOS Item No. 25, File No.I–II, *S.N.C.A. du Nord Factory, Meulan-les-Mureaux* (London, HMSO, 1944)
CIOS Item No. 25, File No. XXV–42, *Survey of Production Techniques Used in the German Aircraft Industry* (London, HMSO, 1945).
CIOS Item No. 25, File No. XXVI–6, *Focke Wulf Designing Offices and General Management, Bad Eilsen* (London, HMSO, 1945).
CIOS Item No. 27, File No.XXV–51, *The Schacht Marie Salt Mine, Beendorf (Dispersal of Siemens, Berlin)* (London, HMSO, 1945).
CIOS Item No. 31, File No. XXV–36, *German Mechanical Engineering Industry* (London, HMSO, 1945).
CIOS Item No. 31, File No. XXVIII–10, *Machine Tool Targets Leipzig* (London, HMSO, 1945).

Other Official Publications

Air Ministry, Directorate of Civil Aviation, *Report on the Progress of Civil Aviation 1930* (London, HMSO, 1931).
The Rise and Fall of the German Air Force (London, Air Ministry Pamphlet No. 248, 1948)
Board of Education, *Committee on Education and Industry (England and Wales), Second Report* (London, HMSO, 1929).
15–18, Report of the Central Advisory Council for Education – England, 2 vols. (London, HMSO, 1959).
Report of the Committee on Higher Technological Education (London, HMSO, 1945).
Report of the Consultative Committee of the Board of Education on Secondary Education with Special Reference to Grammar Schools and Technical High Schools (London, HMSO, 1939).
Report of the Departmental Committee on Juvenile Education in Relation to Employment after the War (London, HMSO, 1917).
Board of Trade, *Survey of Metal Industries* (London, HMSO, 1928).

Central Policy Review Staff, *The Future of the British Car Industry* (London, HMSO, 1975).

Central Statistical Office, *Statistical Abstract for the United Kingdom for each of the fifteen years 1924–1938* (London, HMSO, 1940).

Civil Service, *Civil Service Commission Open Competition Reports and Examination Papers for August* (London, HMSO, 1900, 1905 and 1910).

Civil Service Commission Regulations, Examination Papers and Table of Marks for Class One Clerkships (London, HMSO, 1885 and 1891).

Civil Service Commission Reports (London, HMSO, 1895, 1896 and 1900).

Department of Education and Science, *The School Curriculum* (London, HMSO, 1981).

Department of Employment, Press release, 30 August 1985: employment figures for August 1985.

Department of the Environment, *Tenants and Town Hall* (London, HMSO, 1979).

History of the Ministry of Munitions, 12 vols. (London, HMSO, 1922).

House of Commons, *Report from the Select Committee on Scientific Instruction: with the Proceedings of the Committee, Minutes of Evidence and Appendix, 1867–8*, 15 July 1869, vol. XV.

Registrar General, *The Registrar General's Statistical Review of England and Wales for the Six Years 1940–45*, vol. I: *Medical* (London, HMSO, 1949).

American

United States Strategic Bombing Survey, with an introduction by David MacIsaac, 10 vols. (New York and London, Garland Publishing, 1976), vol. I.

German

Prüfungen an Hochschulen 1981 (Bonn, Statistisches Bundesamt, 1981).

Statistisches Jahrbuch für das Deutsche Reich, 57. Jahrgang 1938 (Berlin, Statistisches Reichsamt, 1938).

Wegweiser durch das gewerbliche Berufs- und Fachschulwesen des Deutschen Reiches, Schuljahr 1938 (Langensalza-Berlin-Leipzig, Verlag von Julius Beltz, 1941).

Wegweiser durch das Höhere Schulwesen des Deutschen Reiches, Schuljahr 1937 (Berlin, Weidmannsche Verlagsbuchhandlung, 1938).

SECONDARY SOURCES

Acland, Sir R., *How It Can Be Done: A careful examination of the ways in which we can, and cannot, advance to the kind of Britain for which many hope they are fighting* (London, Macdonald, 1943).

Addison, P., *The Road to 1945: British Politics and the Second World War* (London, Jonathan Cape, 1975).

Anderson, D. (ed.), *The Ignorance of Social Intervention* (London, Croom Helm, 1980).

Trespassing?: Businessmen's Views on the Education System (London, The Social Affairs Unit, 1984).

Anglo-American Council on Productivity, *Productivity Report on Simplification in British Industry* (London, 1950).

Archer, R. L., *Secondary Education in the Nineteenth Century* (London, Frank Cass, 1966; 1st edn 1921).

Argles, M., *South Kensington to Robbins: An Account of English Technical Education since 1851* (London, Longmans, 1964).

Army Bureau Of Current Affairs, *Current Affairs*, Nos. 1–100 (1942–5).

Arnold, M., *Culture and Anarchy* (New York, Macmillan, 1894; 1st edn 1869).

Aslet, C., *The Last Country Houses* (New Haven and London, Yale University Press, 1982).

Attlee, C. R., *The Will and the Way to Socialism* (London, Methuen, 1935).

Bacon, R. and Eltis, W., *Britain's Economic Problem: Too Few Producers*, 2nd edn (London, Macmillan, 1978).
Bamford, T. W., *Rise of the Public Schools* (London, Thomas Nelson, 1967).
Thomas Arnold (London, The Cresset Press, 1960).
Barnett, C., *Britain and Her Army* (London, Allen Lane, 1970).
The Collapse of British Power (London, Eyre Methuen, 1972; paperback edn, Gloucester, Alan Sutton, 1984).
The Desert Generals, 2nd edn (London, George Allen & Unwin, 1983).
Beer, M., *A History of British Socialism*, 2 vols. (London, George Bell, 1919 and 1920).
Bell, Q., *Bloomsbury* (London, Weidenfeld & Nicolson, 1968).
Beveridge, J., *Beveridge and His Plan* (London, Hodder & Stoughton, 1954).
Beveridge, Sir W. H., *Full Employment in a Free Society: A Report* (London, George Allen & Unwin, 1944).
The Pillars of Security and Other War-Time Essays and Addresses (London, George Allen & Unwin, 1943).
Bialer, U., *The Shadow of the Bomber: The Fear of Air Attack and British Politics, 1932–1939* (London, Royal Historical Society, 1980).
Blunden, E., *Undertones of War* (London, Richard Cobden-Sanderson, 1928).
Bond, B., *British Military Policy Between the Two World Wars* (Oxford, Clarendon Press, 1980).
Bowen, W. E., *Edward Bowen: A Memoir* (London, Longmans, Green, 1902).
Brennan, T., *Midland City: Wolverhampton; Social and Industrial Survey* (London, Denis Dobson, 1948).
Bulmer, M. (ed.), *Mining and Social Change: Durham County in the Twentieth Century* (London, Croom Helm, 1978).
Burnham, T. H. and Hoskins, G. O., *Iron and Steel in Britain; 1870–1930* (London, George Allen & Unwin, 1943).
Butterfield, H., *Christianity in European History* (London, Oxford University Press, 1951).
Christianity and History (London, George Bell, 1950).
Buxton, N. K. and Aldcroft, D. H. (eds.), *British Industry Between the Wars: Instability and Industrial Development, 1919–1939* (London, Scolar Press, 1979).
Carr, J. C. and Taplin, W., assisted by Wright, A. E. G., *History of the British Steel Industry* (Oxford, Basil Blackwell and Cambridge, Mass., Harvard University Press, 1962).
Carr-Saunders, A. M. and Jones, D. C., *A Survey of the Social Structure of England and Wales* (London, Oxford University Press, 1927).
Checkland, S. G., *The Rise of Industrial Society in England* (London, Longmans, 1964).
Cipolla, C. (ed.) *The Fontana Economic History of Europe* (London, William Collins/Fontana Books, 1975), vol. 3: *The Industrial Revolution;* vol. 4: *The Emergence of Industrial Societies.*
Clark, K., *The Gothic Revival* (Harmondsworth, Penguin Books, 1964).
Coates, K. and Silburn, R., *Poverty, Deprivation and Morale in a Nottingham Community: St Ann's* (Nottingham, Nottingham University Department of Adult Education, 1967).
Cole, G. D. H., *National Coal Board* (London, Fabian Society, revised edn 1949).
Conrad, J., *The Nigger of the 'Narcissus': A Tale of the Sea* (London, The Gresham Publishing Co., 1925).
Court, W. H. B., *Coal* (London, HMSO and Longmans, Green, 1951).
Cox, J. G., with Kriegbaum, H., *Growth, Innovation and Employment: An Anglo-German Comparison* (London, Anglo-German Foundation for the Study of Industrial Society, 1980).

Dale, H. E., *The Higher Civil Service of Great Britain* (London, Oxford University Press, 1941).
Darwin, B., *The English Public School* (London, Longmans, 1929).
Design Council, *Industrial Design in the United Kingdom* (London, Design Council, 1977).
D'Este, C., *Decision in Normandy* (London, William Collins, 1983).
Dilnot, A. W., Kay, J. A. and Morris, C. N., *The Reform of Social Security* (Oxford, Oxford University Press for Institute for Fiscal Studies, 1984).
Donnison, D., *Social Policy Revisited* (London, George Allen & Unwin, 1975).
The Politics of Poverty (London, Martin Robertson, 1981).
with Soto, P., *The Good City* (London, William Heinemann, 1980).
Dougan, D., *The Shipwrights: The History of the Ship-Constructors and Shipwrights Association, 1882–1963* (Newcastle, Frank Graham, 1975).
Dunleavy, P., *The Politics of Mass Housing in Britain, 1945–1975: A Study of Corporate Power and Professional Influence in the Welfare State* (Oxford, Clarendon Press, 1981)
Edgerton, Dr D., *The Prophet Militant and Industrial: The Peculiarities of Correlli Barnett* (Twentieth Century British History, 1991, vol. 2, No. 3).
Ellis, L. F., *Victory in the West*, vol. I: *The Battle of Normandy* (London, HMSO, 1962).
Emmott Committee, *Report of an enquiry into the relationship of technical education to other forms of education and to industry and commerce* (1927).
Feinstein, C. H., *National Income, Expenditure and Output of the United Kingdom, 1855–1965* (Cambridge, Cambridge University Press, 1972).
Ferguson, T. and Cunnison, J., *In Their Early Twenties: A Study of Glasgow Youth* (London, Oxford University Press for the Nuffield Foundation, 1956).
The Young Wage-Earner: A Study of Glasgow Boys (London, Oxford University Press for the Nuffield Foundation, 1951).
Finch, A. and Scrimshaw. P. (eds.), *Standards, Schooling and Education* (Milton Keynes, The Open University, 1980).
Education and Industry (London, National Economic Development Council, 1983).
Finer, H., *The British Civil Service* (London, Fabian Society, 1927).
Ford, P., *Work and Health in a Modern Port* (London, George Allen & Unwin, 1934).
Foss, C. F., *The Illustrated Enycyclopedia of the World's Tanks and Fighting Vehicles* (London, Salamander Books, 1977).
Fraser, Sir D., *Alanbrooke* (London, William Collins, 1982).
Gathorne-Hardy, J., *The Public School Phenomenon, 1597–1977* (London, Hodder & Stoughton, 1977).
Gaunt, W., *The Pre-Raphaelite Dream* (London, The Reprint Society, 1943).
Victorian Olympus (London, Jonathan Cape, 1952).
Girouard, M., *The Return to Camelot: Chivalry and the English Gentleman* (New Haven and London, Yale University Press, 1981).
Glass, R. (ed.), *The Social Background of a Plan: A Study of Middlesbrough* (London, Routledge & Kegan Paul, 1948).
Golden, L., *Echoes From Arnhem* (London, William Kimber, 1984).
Goldthorpe, J. H., *Social Mobility and Class Structure in Modern Britain* (Oxford, Clarendon Press, 1979).
Gowing, M., *Britain and Atomic Energy, 1939–1945* (London and New York, Macmillan, 1964).
Independence and Deterrence: Britain and Atomic Energy, 1945–1952, vol. I: *Policy Making* (London, Macmillan, 1982).
Guttsman, W. L., *The British Political Elite* (London, MacGibbon & Kee, 1963).

Hague, Sir D. (Chairman of the Social Science Research Council), 'Spending, the Nightmare Ticket', *The Times*, 18 October 1943.
Hall, H. D., *North American Supply* (London, HMSO and Longmans, Green, 1955).
Halsey, A. M., Heath, A. F. and Ridge, J. M., *Origins and Destinations: Family, Class and Education in Modern Britain* (Oxford, Clarendon Press, 1979).
Hammond, J. L. and B., *The Bleak Age* (Harmondsworth, Pelican Books, 1947).
Hancock, K. and Gowing, M., *British War Economy* (London, HMSO and Longmans, Green, 1953).
Harrington, W. and Young, P., *The 1945 Revolution* (London, Davis-Poynter, 1978).
Harris, Dr J., *Enterprise and Welfare States: A Comparative Perspective* (Transaction of the Royal Historical Society, 40, 1990).
Harrison, P., *The Inner City* (Harmondsworth, Penguin Books, 1983).
Hastings, M., *Bomber Command* (London, Michael Joseph, 1979).
Overlord: D-Day and the Battle for Normandy (London, Michael Joseph, 1984).
Heindel, R. H., *The American Impact on Great Britain, 1898–1914* (New York, Octagon Books, 1968).
Heussler, R., *Yesterday's Rulers* (New York, Syracuse University Press, 1963).
Hilken, T. J. N., *Engineering at Cambridge University, 1783–1965* (Cambridge, Cambridge University Press, 1967).
Hobsbawm, E. J., *Industry and Empire* (Harmondsworth, Pelican Books, 1969).
Hodson, J. L., *The Sea and the Land* (London, Victor Gollancz, 1945).
Hoggart, R., *The Uses of Literacy: Aspects of Working-Class Life, With Special Reference to Publications and Entertainments* (London, Chatto & Windus, 1971).
Hollis, C., *Eton: A History* (London, Hollis & Carter, 1960).
Hornby, W., *Factories and Plant* (London, HMSO and Longmans, Green, 1958).
Inman, P., *Labour in the Munitions Industries* (London, Longmans, Green, 1957).
International Institute for Strategic Studies, *The Military Balance, 1966–67* (London, IISS, 1966).
The Military Balance, 1971–72 (London, IISS, 1971).
Institute of Manpower Studies, *Competence and Competition: Training and Education in the Federal Republic of Germany, the United States and Japan* (London, NEDO Books, 1984).
Iremonger, F. A., *William Temple Archbishop of Canterbury: His Life and Letters* (Oxford, Oxford University Press, 1948).
Jackson, M. P., *The Price of Coal* (London, Croom Helm, 1974).
Johnstone, J. K., *The Bloomsbury Group* (London, Secker & Warburg, 1954).
Jones, L., *Shipbuilding in Britain Mainly Between the Two World Wars* (Cardiff, University of Wales Press, 1957).
Jones, R. V., *Most Secret War: British Scientific Intelligence, 1939–1945* (London, Hamish Hamilton, 1978).
Kahn, A. E., *Britain in the World Economy* (London, Pitman, 1946).
Kennedy, P. M., *The Rise and Fall of British Naval Mastery* (London, Allen Lane, 1976).
Labour Party, *Let Us Face the Future* (general election manifesto) (1945).
The Old World and the New Sociey (London, 1942).
Up with the Houses! Down with the Slums! (London, 1942).
Lamb, R., *Montgomery in Europe, 1943–5: Success or Failure?* (London, Buchan & Enright, 1983).
Laski, H., *Where do we go from here?* (Harmondsworth, Penguin Books, 1940).
Lloyd, I., *Rolls-Royce: The Merlin at War* (London, Macmillan, 1978).
Locke, R. R., *The End of the Practical Man: Entrepreneurship and Higher Education*

in Germany, France and Great Britain, 1880–1940 (Greenwich, Conn., and London, Jai Press, 1984).

Lowndes, G. A. N., *The Silent Social Revolution* (London, Oxford University Press, 1937).

McCallum, R. B. and Readman, A., *The British General Election of 1945* (Oxford, Oxford University Press, 1947).

McCloskey, D. N., *Economic Maturity and Entrepreneurial Decline: British Iron and Steel, 1870–1913* (Cambridge, Mass., Harvard University Press, 1973).

McCrone, G., *Regional Policy in Britain* (London, George Allen & Unwin, 1969).

McLaine, I., *Ministry of Morale: Home Front Morale and the Ministry of Information in World War II* (London, George Allen & Unwin, 1979).

Maclure, J. S., *Educational Documents: England and Wales, 1816 to the Present Day* (London, Methuen, 1965).

Mack, E. C., *Public Schools and British Opinion Since 1860* (New York, Columbia University Press, 1941).

Macmillan, H., *Winds of Change* (London, Macmillan, 1966).

Madge, C. (ed.), *Pilot Guide to the General Election* (London, Pilot Press, 1945).

Manning, F., *Her Privates We* (London, Peter Davies, 1930).

Martin, K., *Harold Laski (1893–1950): A Biographical Memoir* (London, Victor Gollancz, 1953).

Martin, L. W., *British Defence Policy: The Long Recessional* (London, IISS, 1969).

Marwick, A., *Britain in the Century of Total War* (London, The Bodley Head, 1968).

Class: Image and Reality, in Britain, France and the United States since 1930 (London, William Collins, 1980).

Mass-Observation, *Report on behalf of the Advertising Service Guild*, No. 2: *Home Propaganda* (London, John Murray, 1944).

The Journey Home. A report prepared by Mass-Observation for the Advertising Service Guild (London, John Murray, 1944).

Mathias, P., *The First Industrial Nation* (London, Methuen, 1969).

Mess, H. A., *Industrial Tyneside: A Social Survey for the Bureau of Research for Tyneside* (London, Ernest Benn, 1928).

Middlemass, K. and Barnes, J., *Baldwin: A Biography* (London, Weidenfeld & Nicolson, 1969).

Morgan, A. E., *The Needs of Youth: A Report Made to King George's Jubilee Trust Fund* (London, Oxford University Press, 1939).

Morgan, K. O., *Labour in Power, 1945–1951* (London, Oxford University Press, 1984).

Morris, D. (ed.), *The Economic System in the UK*, 3rd edn (Oxford, Oxford University Press, 1985).

Mowatt, C. F., *Britain Between the Wars, 1918–1940* (London, London University Paperbacks, 1968).

National Consumer Council, *Soonest Mended* (London, 1979).

National Economic Development Council, *Third Annual Report: British Industrial Performance* (London, National Economic Development Council, 1985).

National Economic Development Office and Manpower Services Commission, *Competence and Competition: Training and Education in the Federal Republic of Germany, the United States and Japan* (London, NEDO Books, 1984).

Nef, J. U., *The Rise of the British Coal Industry*, 2 vols. (London, George Routledge, 1932).

Newman, J. H., *The Idea of a University* (New York, Longmans, Green, 1947).

Newsome, D., *Godliness and Good Learning* (London, John Murray, 1961).

Nicolson, N.. *Portrait of a Marriage* (London, Futura Publications, 1974).

Norwood, C., *The English Tradition in Education* (London, John Murray, 1929).

Orr, J. B., *Food, Health and Income: Report on a Survey of Adequacy of Diet in Relation to Income* (London, Macmillan, 1936).

Overy, R. J., *Goering: The 'Iron Man'* (London, Routledge & Kegan Paul, 1984).

The Air War, 1939–45 (London, Europa Publications, 1980).

'German Air Strength, 1933 to 1939: A Note', *Historical Journal*, 27(2) (1984), pp. 465–71.

'The German Pre-War Aircraft Production Plans: November 1936–April 1939', *English Historical Review*, XC, no. CCCLVII (October 1975), pp. 778–97.

Paneth, M., *Branch Street: A Sociological Study* (London, George Allen & Unwin, 1944).

Parker, H. M. D., *Manpower: A Study of War-Time Policy and Administration* (London, HMSO and Longmans, Green, 1957).

Pavitt, K. (ed.), *Technical Innovation and British Economic Performance* (Science Policy Research Unit, Sussex University; London, Macmillan, 1980).

Peden, G. C., *British Rearmament and the Treasury, 1932–1939* (Edinburgh, Scottish Academic Press, 1979).

Pelling, H., *Britain and the Second World War* (London, Fontana, 1970).

Perry, P. J. C., *The Evolution of British Manpower Policy from the Statute of Artificers 1583 to the Industrial Training Act 1964* (London, published by the Author, 1976).

Playfair, Major-General I. S. O., *The Mediterranean and Middle East* (London, HMSO, 1960), vol. III.

Playfair, Lyon, *Industrial Instruction on the Continent* (London, Royal School of Mines, 1852).

Pollard, S., *The Wasting of the British Economy* (London, Croom Helm, 1982).

'British and World Shipbuilding, 1890–1914: A Study in Comparative Costs', *Journal of Economic History*, XVII (1957), p. 426.

and Robertson, P., *The British Shipbuilding Industry, 1870–1914* (Cambridge, Mass., and London, Harvard University Press, 1979).

Postan, M. M., *British War Production* (London, HMSO and Longmans, Green, 1952).

Hay, D. and Scott. J. D., *Design and Development of Weapons: Studies in Government and Industrial Organisation* (London, HMSO and Longmans, Green, 1964).

Prais, S. J., *Vocational Qualifications of the Labour Force in Britain and Germany* (London, National Institute of Economic and Social Research, 1981).

and Wagner, K., *Schooling Standards in Bntain and Germany: Some Summary Comparisons Bearing on Economic Efficiency* (London, National Institute of Economic Research, 1983).

Ranulf, S., *Moral Indignation and Middle-Class Psychology* (Copenhagen, Levin & Munksgaard, 1938).

Reader, W. J., *Imperial Chemical Industries: A History*, vol. II: *The First Quarter Century, 1925–1952* (London, Oxford University Press, 1975).

Reid, J. M., *James Lithgow: Master of Work* (London, Hutchinson, 1963).

Robbins, K., *The Eclipse of a Great Power: Modern Britain, 1870–1975* (London, Longmans, 1983).

Roskill, S. W., *The War at Sea*, 3 vols. (London, HMSO, 1954–61).

Ross, G. MacLeod, *The Business of Tanks 1933 to 1945* (Ilfracombe, Arthur H. Stockwell, 1976).

Rowntree, B. Seebohm, *Poverty: A Study of Town Life* (London, Macmillan, 1910).

Sanderson. M., *The Universities and British Industry, 1850–1970* (London, Routledge & Kegan Paul, 1972).

The Universities in the Nineteenth Century (London, Routledge & Kegan Paul, 1975).

Sassoon, S., *Memoirs of an Infantry Officer* (London, Faber & Faber, 1930).

Shay, R. P., Jr, *British Rearmament in the Thirties: Politics and Profits* (Princeton, Princeton University Press, 1977).

Sherrard, R. H., *The Child Slaves of Britain* (London, Hurst & Blackett, 1905).

Shonfield, A., *British Economic Policy Since the War* (Harmondsworth, Penguin Books, 1958).

Simon, B., *Education and the Labour Movement, 1870–1920* (London, Lawrence & Wishart, 1965).

Smith, H. Llewelyn, *The New Survey of London Life and Labour* (London, King, 1930).

Spencer, H., *Education: Intellectual, Moral and Physical* (London, Williams & Norgate, 1861).

Taylor, A. J., 'Labour Productivity and Technical Innovation in the British Coal Industry 1850–1914', *Economic History Review*, Second Series, XIV, I (1961), p. 48.

Terraine, J., *The Right of the Line: The Royal Air Force in the European War, 1939–1945* (London, Hodder & Stoughton, 1985).

Thompson, E. P., *The Making of the English Working Class* (London, Pelican Books, 1974).

Thring, E., *Theory and Practice of Teaching* (Cambridge, Cambridge University Press, 1910).

Titmuss, R., *Problems of Social Policy* (London, HMSO and Longmans, Green, 1951).

Trustees of the Carnegie United Kingdom Trust, *Disinherited Youth: A Report on the 18-plus Age Group; Enquiry Prepared for the Trustees of the Carnegie United Kingdom Trust* (Edinburgh, 1943).

Turner, H. A. and Clack, G., *Labour Relations in the Motor Industry* (London, George Allen & Unwin, 1967).

Watson, J. Steven, *The Reign of George III, 1760–1815* (Oxford, Clarendon Press, 1960).

Wedge, P. and Essen, J., *Children in Adversity* (London, Pan Books, 1982).

Wettern, D., *The Decline of British Seapower* (London, Jane's Publishing, 1982).

Wiener, M., *English Culture and the Decline of the Industrial Spirit, 1850–1980* (Cambridge, Cambridge University Press, 1981).

Wilkinson, R., *The Prefects: British Leadership and the Public School Tradition* (London, Oxford University Press, 1964).

Williams, E. T. and Nicholls, C. S. (eds.), *The Dictionary of National Biography 1961–1970* (Oxford, Oxford University Press, 1981).

Williams, R., *The Long Revolution* (London, Chatto & Windus, 1961).

Wilson, H., *New Deal for Coal* (London, Contact Books, 1945).

Winstanley, D. A., *Later Victorian Cambridge* (Cambridge, Cambridge University Press, 1947).

Wood, D. and Dempster, D., *The Narrow Margin: The Battle of Britain and the Rise of Air Power, 1930–40* (London, Hutchinson, 1961).

Woodward, L., *The Age of Reform* (Oxford, Clarendon Press, 1962).

World Bank, *World Development Report 1985* (London and New York, Oxford University Press, 1985).

Worswick, G. D. N. and Ady, P. H., *The British Economy, 1945–50* (Oxford, Oxford University Press, 1952).

Younghusband, E., *Social Work in Britain, 1950–75*, 2 vols. (London, George Allen & Unwin, 1978).